REFERENCE GUIDE TO ENGLISH

A Handbook of English as a Second Language

Shu-I Hsiao

REFERENCE GUIDE TO ENGLISH

A Handbook of English as a Second Language

Alice Maclin
Dekalb Community College

Holt, Rinehart and Winston

**New York   Chicago   San Francisco   Dallas
Montreal   Toronto   London   Sydney**

To My Husband

Library of Congress Cataloging in Publication Data

Maclin, Alice.
   Reference guide to English.

   Includes index.
   1. English language—Text-books for foreigners.
I. Title.
PE1128.M3254   428.2′4   80–29208
ISBN 0–03–053226–4

PREFACE

The *Reference Guide to English* is intended for classroom or individual use by nonnative speakers of English who are on an intermediate or advanced level in their studies of the language. Such students still have gaps in their knowledge, gaps that become increasingly apparent as they put the language in written form. This book is a ready reference that can help students locate and correct their problems with or without the help of a teacher. The book is not a comprehensive review of all aspects of grammar and usage, but its sections cover the vast majority of language problems that arise in the writing in an academic or business setting.

Alphabetical order makes the sections easy to find. The sections represent smaller units of information than some handbooks present. Every piece of information about nouns, for example, is not presented together. Sections on countable and uncountable nouns, word formation of nouns, articles, and determiners, for example, are presented separately in alphabetical order. All the information needed by a student having difficulty with the agreement of subject and verb is found together. This organization of material makes for repetition, but the book is intended, not to be read through from beginning to end, but to be used as a reference. Students who have a moderate knowledge of English grammar will not need to thumb back and forth from one reference to another. Those with very little grammatical background will, however, be able to find cross-references to the information they need.

Although much of the information in this book is the same sort that can be found in any freshman composition or business handbook, some of the material usually found in such handbooks has been simplified and reduced to make room for sections dealing with problems of language peculiar to nonnative speakers. Extensive sections on articles, determiners, adjective forms, word order of adverbs, questions, and operators, to name a few, deal with problems encountered minimally or not at all by native speakers. Problems of rhetoric are dealt with particularly as they relate to problems with the language, as in an extensive section on comparison and contrast and in related sections on comparison of adjectives under adjectives and comparison of adverbs under adverbs. The sections on capitalization and punctuation represent what I believe to be a consensus—or in some cases a majority vote—of the views of the authors of the most widely used composition handbooks. Problems of organization and format, especially those that cause difficulties for users of other alphabets, are discussed. Although this book is by no means comprehensive in

v

its treatment of differences between British and U.S. usage, differences are mentioned in many cases, particularly in those that cause problems for students who have studied in English contexts.

Because current methods of language teaching and backgrounds of students vary so widely throughout the world, many students who speak fluently have great difficulty writing without making many mistakes. The *Reference Guide to English* mentions differences between the spoken and written forms, but it is primarily a guide to the written language, not to idiomatic American speech.

The difficulty of the material in this book varies greatly. Although some of the explanations are very simple, others are more difficult and are not always easily mastered by some native speakers. In general, each long section is arranged roughly in order of difficulty and/or in order of urgency. That is, the most basic and frequent problems are discussed first. The section on adjectives, for example, begins with a discussion of forms and word order, two problems that would not be discussed at all in a book for native speakers. The section on parallel structure, on the other hand, is not essentially different from such a section written for native speakers, and is suitable for advanced students.

Agreement of subject and verb can indeed be taught, but agreement on grammatical terminology eludes us. The basic framework of the book is traditional grammar for a number of reasons: most students coming from outside the United States have some familiarity with it because of earlier studies or, in some cases, because traditional terms are also used in their own languages; traditional terms are used in dictionaries; traditional grammar still "works" when expanded by the insights of more recent grammatical theory. Not everyone agrees, however, even on the terminology of traditional grammar. My choices are without apology eclectic, based on what my own experience has shown to be useful in the classroom. Learning the term *dependent clause*, for example, does seem to help students avoid writing such clauses as fragments, and it does not seem to hinder their understanding that a dependent clause is one method of subordination. Quirk and his colleagues would not, I am sure, agree with every one of my choices, but I have always given careful consideration to their terminology before substituting something simpler. Because students today come from such diverse backgrounds, many alternate terms are cross-referenced in the index.

Since students have been learning languages not their own for thousands of years, obviously they can learn by many different methods. A great teacher once said, "Any method in the hands of a good teacher is a good method." Good teachers like their students, like what they are teaching, and believe their students can learn. Teachers with such qualities will, I hope, find that this book helps their students learn, no matter what course books or methodology they are following. This book is intended to supplement, not replace, other texts, no matter what their pedagogical orientation is.

The book's index is extensive, including some grammatical terms that do not appear in the text cross-referenced to those that do. In addition, concepts such as "obligation," "possibility," and "prohibition" are cross-referenced to the relevant grammatical sections. Words of special difficulty that are used to illustrate points of grammar are indexed, but individual words in long lists and tables are not listed separately. The following headings contain lists and tables of words that are not completely indexed:

Abbreviations

Adjectives, word order

Adjectives, constructions that follow the verb

Capitalization

Determiners

Finite verbs

Gender

Infinitive/-*ing* choice

Interrupters

Modifiers

Objective complement

Participles, used as adjectives

Pronouns

Sentence patterns

Stative verbs

Subjunctive

Two-word verbs

Verbs, irregular

Word formation

Special thanks go to the National Endowment for the Humanities for a fellowship that enabled me to spend a summer at the University of Texas studying the history of grammar in a seminar led by the late David DeCamp, whose advice is responsible for any sound features the book may have. Thanks also go to my colleagues Zenobia Liles of DeKalb Community College and to Carol Lowthian of Georgia State University, who helped me catch many errors in the manuscript; the errors that remain are my responsibility, not theirs. Their discussions were helpful and positive. Special thanks go to my typists, Susan Box, Ellen Brown, and Pat Merola, and to Ruth Golley for assistance with the index. My thanks go above all to my husband for his patient endurance and constant encouragement throughout.

Finally, my gratitude to the reviewers, whose comments and suggestions made at various stages in the development of the manuscript were most helpful: Betty S. Azar, Saint Louis University; Barbara W. Buchanan, Utah State University; Robert Grindell, Kansas State University; Mary Heise, Creighton University; Ellen Hoekstra, Henry Ford Community College; Lyle Johnson, Santa Ana College; Kathleen Kidder, Queens College; and Kathleen List, University of Michigan.

A. M.

CONTENTS

Abbreviations

Abbreviations are used differently according to the subject matter and the purpose of your writing. Formal academic writing, scientific writing, and business writing have different usages. You can find lists of abbreviations in all dictionaries and in handbooks for secretaries.

Formal Academic Writing (Humanities)

Avoid most abbreviations in formal writing for the humanities. Write out in full the following kinds of words even if you know an abbreviation for them:

1. Proper names and titles: William, not Wm.; Mister, not Mr.
2. Street, Road, Boulevard, and other geographical terms: Street, not St.
3. Cities, states, provinces, and countries: Los Angeles, not L.A.; Ontario, not Ont.; EXCEPTION: use Washington, *D.C.* (See below under "Business Writing" for addresses and postal abbreviations.)
4. Months and days of the week: February, not Feb.; Sunday, not Sun.
5. Units of measure: ounces, not oz.; hours, not hrs.
6. References to volumes, chapters, and pages when these references are part of the composition: page for p.; volume for vol. In footnotes and bibliographies, however, follow the standard forms for accepted abbreviations. (see **Documentation**)
7. Do not use an ampersand (&) in place of *and* unless a business firm uses it in its name.

Some abbreviations are acceptable in formal academic writing, but not all authorities agree on their forms and usage.

1. Use abbreviations from Latin with care, even the ones that are now considered English words and do not need to be underlined. Use the English words that mean the same when you can, as you are less likely to make mistakes with them. (See **Documentation** for additional forms that you must use correctly in footnotes and bibliographies.)

c. or ca.: <u>circa</u>, about, to indicate a date that is not known for certain (c. 1290 or 1290?)
i.e.: <u>id est</u>, that is
inter alia: among other things
e.g.: <u>exempli gratia</u>, for example
etc.: <u>et cetera</u>, and so forth. Avoid this form; never use *and* immediately before *etc.*
v. or vs.: <u>versus</u>, against
v.z.: <u>videlicet</u>—that is or namely, to introduce examples or lists.

2. Use abbreviations with times and dates.

a.m. and p.m. for *ante meridiem* and *post meridiem* to mean before noon and afternoon only if you also also use numbers to show exact time.

INCORRECT:	The plane arrived in the a.m.
CORRECT:	The plane arrived at 11:23 a.m.

A.D.: Latin *anno domini* for *in the year of our Lord;* in formal writing put A.D. before the date, as in A.D. 1791.
B.C.: before Christ; put B.C. after the date, as in 431 B.C.
C.E. and B.C.E. are sometimes used instead of A.D. and B.C. C.E. means Common Era, as in 1791 C.E. B.C.E. means Before Common Era, as in 431 B.C.E.

3. Use all capital letters (sometimes called solid caps) for abbreviations for most government agencies, international organizations, and other well-known groups. Periods are usually not used, especially if the abbreviation stands for the first letters of the words that make the name. (An abbreviation made from the first letters of words is called an acronym.)

GOP: Grand Old Party, a political party (the Republican Party)
IRS: Internal Revenue Service (government agency)
OPEC: Organization of Petroleum Exporting Countries (international organization)
TVA: Tennessee Valley Authority (public utility company)
UAW: United Auto Workers (labor union)
WHO: World Health Organization (United Nations agency)

4. Use abbreviations for titles before and after proper names if your style sheet allows them. Periods are usually used with abbreviations of titles in the United States, although they are often left out in British usage. Put a comma before a title that follows a name.

Arlene Simpson, *Ph.D.*
Dr. James H. Wester, *Jr.*
St. Anne (Saint Anne)
Laney Sanderson, *Esq.*
Mr. and *Mrs.* Paul Jorgenson

Do not put the same title both before and after a name.

INCORRECT:	*Dr.* Agnes J. Hodges, *M.D.*
CORRECT:	Agnes J. Hodges, *M.D.*
CORRECT:	*Dr.* Agnes J. Hodges

Jr. for *Junior* and *Sr.* for *Senior* are often used to identify a father and son who have the same name. They can be used with *Mr.*:

Mr. Martin Williams, Sr. (father or, occasionally, grandfather)
Mr. Martin Williams, Jr. (son or, occasionally, grandson)

Sometimes a father, son, and grandson all have the same name. While all three are living, the grandson is identified by *III*.

Mr. Martin Williams III

Esq. for *Esquire* is a term of courtesy used after a man's name chiefly in Great Britain. Do not use any other title before the name if you use *Esq.* after it. Except for use by some lawyers, *Esq.* is almost never used in the United States.

Paul Reynolds, Esq.

NOTE: Titles are not used in signatures on letters, applications, checks, and legal documents. Do not use *Mrs.* with the first name only.

5. When the last word in a sentence is an abbreviation that is followed by a period, do not add another period; use only one period at the end of the sentence:

My doctor is Agnes J. Hodges, M.D.
Ken's lawyer is Paul Hopkins, Jr.

Scientific and Technical Writing

Since different disciplines have different accepted styles, you need to consult the style sheet of the academic field you are writing about. Ask your instructor or a librarian to help you find the style sheet you need. Botany, biology, and zoology use the same style manual, but different manuals or style sheets are published for chemistry, geology, linguistics, mathematics, physics, and psychology. In general, more abbreviations are used in scientific and technical writing than in the humanities, and footnotes and bibliographies are also different. (see **Documentation**)

The following kinds of abbreviations are usually used in scientific and technical writing:

1. Units of measure: time, linear measure, area, volume, capacity, weight, temperature, and circular measure. Periods are usually not used.

10 km, ft^2 or sq ft, in^3, cc or cm^3, qt, pt, lbs, and so forth
10°C or 10°F (Celsius or Fahrenheit)
a 90° angle (a ninety degree angle)
15,000 rpm (revolutions per minute)
55 mph (miles per hour)

When alternate abbreviations exist, such as cc and cm^3, use the same form all the time.

2. In most scientific and technical papers, abbreviate and do not underline the names of periodicals.

J. Am. Chem. Soc. for *Journal of the American Chemical Society*
Botan. Rev. for *Botanical Review*

3. Use an ampersand (&) in place of *and* in titles.

Arch. Biochem. & Biophys. for *Archives of Biochemistry and Biophysics*

Business Writing

In writing the body of a letter, follow the rules for formal academic writing (humanities) above. For addresses on letters and envelopes in very formal correspondence, follow the rules for formal academic writing. For addresses in everyday business correspondence, follow the policy of the business or institution. United States government agencies follow a guide published by the Government Printing Office (GPO).

1. You may abbreviate numbers used as street names: 1st, 2nd, 3rd, 4th, 5th, 6th, 7th, 8th, 9th, and 10th. Do not put a period after these abbreviations:

101st Street   37th Avenue

But, if local usage writes a name out in full, follow local usage:

Fifth Avenue   Tenth Street

2. Geographical locations may be abbreviated.

Ave. for Avenue	Dr. for Drive
Bldg. for Building	Pl. for Place
Blvd. for Boulevard	Rd. for Road
Ct. for Court	St. for Street

3. North, South, East, and West as adjectives may be abbreviated to the first letter. Do not abbreviate the name of a street.

1021 N. 101st St.   **but**   1021 North Ave.

4. Some cities use a location after the street.

1021 N. 101st St., *N.E.* (northeast)

5. The zip code or zone number is a geographical abbreviation. Be sure to put it in all addresses in countries that use it. In the United States the zip code uses five numbers; some countries use numbers and letters. Do not put a comma between the end of the address and the zip code.

383 Madison Avenue
New York, N.Y. 10017

200 Euston Road
London NW1 2DB

6. Abbreviations for U.S. states and possessions are either traditional or postal. Traditional abbreviations are usually followed by a period. Postal abbreviations have two capital letters with no space between them and are not followed by a period. Use traditional abbreviations for Canadian addresses.

Abbreviations of U.S. States and Possessions and Canadian Provinces

	Traditional	Postal
Alabama	Ala.	AL
Alaska	Alaska	AK
Alberta	Alta.	
Arizona	Ariz.	AZ
Arkansas	Ark.	AR
British Columbia	B.C.	
California	Calif. or Cal.	CA
Colorado	Colo.	CO
Connecticut	Conn.	CT
Delaware	Del.	DE
District of Columbia	D.C.	DC
Florida	Fla.	FL
Georgia	Ga.	GA
Guam	Guam	GU
Hawaii	Hawaii	HI
Idaho	Idaho	ID
Illinois	Ill.	IL
Indiana	Ind.	IN
Iowa	Ia.	IA
Kansas	Kans.	KS
Kentucky	Ky.	KY
Louisiana	La.	LA
Maine	Me.	ME
Manitoba	Man.	
Maryland	Md.	MD
Massachusetts	Mass.	MA
Michigan	Mich.	MI
Minnesota	Minn.	MN

	Traditional	Postal
Mississippi	Miss.	MS
Missouri	Mo.	MO
Montana	Mont.	MT
Nebraska	Nebr., Neb.	NB
Nevada	Nev.	NV
New Brunswick	N.B.	
Newfoundland	Nfld.	
New Hampshire	N.H.	NH
New Jersey	N.J.	NJ
New Mexico	N. Mex., N.M.	NM
New York	N.Y.	NY
North Carolina	N.C.	NC
North Dakota	N. Dak., N.D.	ND
Nova Scotia	N.S.	
Ohio	Ohio	OH
Oklahoma	Okla.	OK
Ontario	Ont.	
Oregon	Oreg., Ore.	OR
Pennsylvania	Penn., Penna.	PA
Prince Edward Island	P.E.I.	
Puerto Rico	P.R.	PR
Quebec	Que.	
Rhode Island	R.I.	RI
Saskatchewan	Sask.	
South Carolina	S.C.	SC
South Dakota	S. Dak., S.D.	SD
Tennessee	Tenn.	TN
Texas	Texas	TX
Utah	Utah	UT
Vermont	Vt.	VT
Virginia	Va.	VA
Virgin Islands	V.I.	VI
Washington	Wash.	WA
West Virginia	W. Va.	WV
Wisconsin	Wis., Wisc.	WI
Wyoming	Wyo.	WY

Absolutes

Absolutes (also called nominative absolutes) are phrases made of a noun or pronoun and an *-ing* or past participle. Absolutes modify the whole clause to which they are related. They do not modify one single word in the independent clause. Use a comma to separate absolutes from the independent clause. (see **Clauses**)

ABSOLUTE	INDEPENDENT CLAUSE
noun　　　　*participle* The *door having been locked* with two bolts,	we felt safe for the night.
noun　*participle* No more *money being* available,	the committee voted to keep last year's budget.
noun　　　　*participle* Her *head* almost *hidden* by a very large hat,	the old woman waited on the corner.

The absolute may follow the independent clause.

INDEPENDENT CLAUSE	ABSOLUTE
We felt safe for the night,	the *door having been locked* with two bolts.
The committee voted to keep last year's budget,	no more *money being* available.
The old woman waited on the corner,	her *head* almost *hidden* by a very large hat.

Abstract and Concrete

Abstract and *concrete* are terms used to show the difference between ideas that exist only in the mind (abstract) from things that can be touched, tasted, smelled, heard, or seen (concrete). Concrete things are *tangible;* that is, they are directly perceived by the senses. Abstractions are *intangible;* they cannot be directly perceived by the senses. Clear writing develops ideas that are abstract by suggesting concrete examples.

AN ABSTRACT IDEA	A CONCRETE EXAMPLE
friendship	what my friend Ed does to help me
beauty	Miss Universe a Ferrari a rainbow Michelangelo's sculpture *David* the Alps
education	my experience in the first grade
motherhood	how my mother helps me

If an idea is more general, it is on a *higher* level of abstraction. If it is more specific, it is on a *lower* level of abstraction.

LEVEL OF ABSTRACTION

higher		←	→	*lower*
beauty	beauty in nature	mountains	the Alps	the Matterhorn
family rela- tionships	my family	my parents	my mother	something my mother does
education	my educa- tion	my primary school	my first- grade teacher	how my first-grade teacher taught us arithmetic
health	child health	childhood diseases	measles	my case of the mea- sles

(see **Generalization** and **Outlining**)

Abstract nouns in English are usually uncountable. (see **Countable and uncountable nouns**)

Active verbs, see **Voice**

Adjective/Adverb Choice _____

Adjectives and adverbs function differently in the sentence. Adjectives modify nouns, but adverbs can modify verbs, adjectives, other adverbs, participles, and the whole clause.

Many adverbs end in *-ly*. Adjectives have a number of different endings. (see **Word formation, suffixes**) A few words have the same form for both adjective and adverb uses. (see **Adverbs, forms**)

Do not use an adverb as the complement of a linking verb (the most common linking verbs are *be, feel, taste, appear, seem,* and *become*).

SUBJECT	LINKING VERB	PREDICATE ADJECTIVE MODIFIES SUBJECT
The *food*	smelled tasted appeared	good. (not *well*)
He	felt	*happy* about his schedule.
The *horse*	seemed	*strong.*
As he practiced, *he* became		*quick* at shooting goals.

Good and *well* have different meanings after linking verbs. *Well* means "in good physical health."

The little *boy* is *well.* (not sick)
The little *boy* is *good.* (well-behaved)

If you want to modify the verb, use an adverb.

The old man could not *hear well.* (*Well* modifies *hear,* not *man.*)
The blind man *easily felt* his way with his cane. (*without difficulty,* the way he walked along, feeling with his cane)
The blind man felt *easy* about walking with his cane. (His mind was *easy, not afraid. Felt* in this sentence means *had a mental condition.*)

Adjectives

Use adjectives to make writing more specific and concrete. Words, phrases, and clauses can be used as adjectives. This section tells about single-word adjectives. (see **Clauses, Modifiers, Prepositional phrases,** and **Verbals**)

Some modifying words cannot be used with all nouns: *much/many, few/little, some,* and *several* for example. (see **Countable and uncountable nouns** and **Determiners**)

Form of Adjectives

Do not add an -*s* to words that are used as adjectives before plural nouns.

SINGULAR	PLURAL
a red car	the red cars
a warm coat	some warm coats
a six-year-old child	three six-year-old children
an informative lecture	informative lectures

Do not put an -*s* on a word that modifies a noun, whether the modifier comes before the noun or after the verb.

Miss Johnson gave informative lectures. (before the noun)
Miss Johnson's lectures were informative. (after the verb)
The children had new pencil boxes. (before the noun)
Flower pots full of red blossoms brightened the porch. (before the noun)
Some ancient ruins show primitive building methods. (before the noun)
Some ancient ruins show methods of building that are primitive. (after the verb)

NOTE: A few nouns that already end in -*s* can be used to modify other nouns. These nouns keep the -*s*. The -*s* on these words does not show plural.

Peter has opened a new savings account.
Did you hear the news broadcast?
Our club is having a tennis tournament.

NOTE: Do not be confused by the changes in pronoun forms. Possessive pronouns take their number from the word they stand for (antecedent).

	antecedent	possessive pronoun	noun	
SINGULAR:	Patricia found	her	book. books.	(*her* refers to a singular word, Patricia)
PLURAL:	The girls found	their	book. books.	(*their* refers to a plural word, girls)

This, that, these, and *those* take their number from the word they modify when they are used as adjectives.

> Patricia found this book. (singular noun)
>   that
>
> Patricia found these books. (plural noun)
>   those

Word Order of Adjectives

Adjectives come between a determiner and the noun that they modify. Predeterminers and determiners are not included in the table below. (see **Determiners**) Although a long string of modifiers is possible, you will rarely use more than four or five before one noun. You can put additional modifiers in a prepositional phrase after the noun. You can put *very* immediately before adjectives that can be compared (gradable adjectives), and you can put *enough* immediately after them.

Some speakers of English may not follow this order exactly, but you will not be wrong if you follow it.

Word Order of Adjectives before a Noun

general description, opinion	size, shape, condition, age, temperature	color	origin	noun modifier (see below)	type	noun
fine	small, round			maple	writing	table
fresh	new	white				paint
famous	old		English		country	house
expensive	new				private	school
	tall, thin, young			basketball		player
good					home	cooking
	large, juicy				McDonald's	hamburger
	ragged, worn-out	red			golf	shirt
	hot, steamy, 100°				summer	day
interesting	new		Canadian		historical	novel

Coordinate Adjectives

Two or more adjectives that come from the same group are called co-ordinate adjectives. When you put coordinate adjectives before the noun they modify, put a comma or *and* between them.

> Arthur was a *tall and thin and young* basketball player.
> Arthur was a *tall, thin, young* basketball player.
> July twenty-first was a very *hot and humid* day.
> July twenty-first was a very *hot, humid* day.
> Our friends took us to a *famous and expensive* restaurant.
> Our friends took us to a *famous, expensive* restaurant.
> A *large and juicy* McDonald's hamburger is delicious.
> A *large, juicy* McDonald's hamburger is delicious.

In the sentence above, *McDonald's* is a type, not a possessive form. The hamburger does not belong to a person named McDonald. A personal possessive form that shows who buys the hamburger is a determiner that comes before the first adjective (see **Determiners**):

> *John's* large, juicy McDonald's hamburger is delicious.

Noun Modifiers

You can use nouns to modify other nouns. A noun can change the meaning of the noun that follows it. If you use more than one noun as a modifier, put the nouns that modify in the order shown:

Word Order of Noun Modifiers

MATERIAL	OPERATION	POWER	PLACE/ PURPOSE	NOUN
steel			typing	table
	automatic	electric		blanket
		gasoline-powered	lawn	mower
plastic			sewer	pipes
	frost-free	electric		refrigerator
stainless-steel		electric	garbage	compacter

Word Order of All Premodifiers

PREDE-TERMINER	DETER-MINER	ORDINAL NUMBER	CARDINAL NUMBER	ADJEC-TIVES	NOUN MODI-FIERS	HEAD NOUN
all	the	first	five	new	steel	beams
a few of	Margaret's	last	dozen			roses
both	the	first	two	old	oak	trees

Word Order of Adjectives Used as Complements

Adjectives can be used as predicate adjectives after a linking verb or as objective complements after a direct object. After a linking verb, an adjective modifies the subject of the clause. After some transitive active verbs, an adjective can modify the direct object. An adjective that modifies the direct object is called an objective complement. (see **Complements**)

SUBJECT	LINKING VERB	PREDICATE ADJECTIVE
Ernest	is	handsome.
The carpenters	are	skillful.
The air	seems	heavy.
The runner	felt	faint.
This pillow	feels	comfortable.
The sky	is growing	dark.

TRANSITIVE VERB	DIRECT OBJECT	OBJECTIVE COMPLEMENT
Many girls *found*	Greg	handsome.
His father *thought*	him	foolish.
Our teacher *does* not *consider*	us	stupid.
The news *made*	us	happy.

A-word Modifiers

A few words that begin with *a-* are formed from a preposition that is no longer used in modern English, *a-*, + another word. The *a-* means *on, in,* or *at*. These modifiers can follow a noun or a linking verb or be used like a participle, but they cannot go before the noun they modify. Think of *a*-word modifiers as one-word prepositional phrases. Not all adjectives and adverbs that begin with *a-* are like these special *a*-words.

	ALIKE			IDENTICAL
CORRECT:	The twins look *alike*.		CORRECT:	The twins look *identical*.
INCORRECT:	The *alike* twins are here.	**but**	CORRECT:	The *identical* twins are here.

	ALIVE			LIVING
CORRECT:	The man was *alive* then.		CORRECT:	The man was *living* then.
INCORRECT:	The *alive* man was rescued.	**but**	CORRECT:	The *living* man was rescued.

A-words often show a temporary state rather than a permanent one.

> Our team was *ahead* during the first half, but we lost in the last ten minutes. *Ahead* at the beginning, we lost later.

Penny was *asleep* earlier, but she is *awake* now. Her mother found her *awake.*

Some words that mean the opposite of *a*-words also follow the words they modify.

afraid/unafraid	apart/together	away/here
ahead/behind	asleep/awake	alike/unlike

The angry parents tried to keep the lovers *apart,* but their friends brought them *together.*

Some additional *a*-words that come after the word or words they modify:

ablaze	abroad	alone	astride	ajar	atop	aware

A-words can modify as adjectives and as adverbs depending on the meaning of the sentence.

Becky's trip *abroad* was very interesting. (adjective modifying *trip*)
Becky went *abroad* last summer. (adverb modifying *went*)
A door *ajar* is an invitation to burglars. (adjective modifying *door*)
The door was left *ajar.* (adverb modifying *was left*)

A-words are compared with *more* and *most*, never with *-er* and *-est.*

NOTE: Most adjectives beginning with *a-* can go in front of the nouns they modify.

The *alert* watchdog barked at the intruder.
She is an *able* doctor.
Active children are often noisy.

Comparison of Adjectives

Adjectives that can be compared are sometimes called *gradable* adjectives. Comparative forms of adjectives show differences (contrasts) between two things or groups. Superlative forms show differences in three or more things or groups.

With one-syllable adjectives, add *-er* for the comparative and *-est* for the superlative. Most adverbs forms are made in the same way.

ADJECTIVE	COMPARATIVE	SUPERLATIVE
few	fewer	(the) fewest (of all)
young	young*er* (than)	(the) young*est* (of all)
tall	tall*er* (than)	(the) tall*est* (of all)
fast	fast*er* (than)	(the) fast*est* (of all)

Paul is a *fast* runner.
Paul is a *faster* runner than Eric.
Paul is the *fastest* runner in our class.

More AND most

Many words of two syllables and all words of more than two syllables make the comparative form with *more* and the superlative form with *most*. Two-syllable adjectives ending in *-ful* or *-re* usually take *more* and *most*. Two-syllable adjectives ending in *-er* or *-y* usually add *-er* and *-est*.

beautiful	more beautiful (than)	(the) most beautiful (of all)
doubtful	more doubtful (than)	(the) most doubtful (of all)
industrious	more industrious (than)	(the) most industrious (of all)

but

pretty	prettier	prettiest
tender	tenderer	tenderest

For the opposite meaning use *less* and *least*.

beautiful	less beautiful (than)	(the) least beautiful (of all)
industrious	less industrious	(the) least industrious (of all)

Use *more* and *most* before past participles (*-ed* verb forms).

tired	more tired (than)	(the) most tired (of all)
bent	more bent (than)	(the) most bent (of all)

Use *more* or *most* with *like*.

> Martha looks *more like* her mother than Shirley does.
>
> Louis looks *most like* his father. He is the *most like* his father of all the children in the family.

NEVER use *more* before an adjective or adverb that already has the *-er* ending or *most* before an adjective or adverb that already has the *-est* ending.

> INCORRECT: Sara ran *more faster* than Pat.
> CORRECT: Sara ran *faster* than Pat.

If you need the opposite meaning of a one-syllable word and of many longer words, use a different word instead of *less* or *least*. Use an *antonym*, a word with an opposite meaning, if you can.

> young/younger/youngest—old/older/oldest
> tall/taller/tallest—short/shorter/shortest
> beautiful/more beautiful/most beautiful—ugly/uglier/ugliest
>
> John is *shorter* than Pat.   **not**   John is *less tall than* Pat.

(For rules for spelling comparative and superlative forms, see **Spelling**.)

IRREGULAR COMPARISONS

Some very common adjectives have irregular forms.

ADJECTIVE	COMPARATIVE	SUPERLATIVE
good	better (than)	(the) best (of all)
bad	worse (than)	(the) worst (of all)
little	less (than)	(the) least (of all)
much	more (than)	(the) most (of all)
many	more (than)	(the) most (of all)
far	farther (than)	(the) farthest (of all)
	further (than)	(the) furthest (of all)

Use *the* before superlatives. (see below, p. 18, and **Articles**)

A few words add *-most* as an ending to show a superlative meaning.

innermost	outermost
foremost	uppermost
furthermost	utmost

NOTE: *Most* can be used to mean *very*: The guide was *most* helpful.

Use *little/less/least* and *much/more/many* with uncountable (mass) nouns; use *few/fewer/fewest* and *many/more/most* with countable nouns. For the difference between *few* and *a few* and between *little* and *a little* see **Confusing choices**. For differences in usage and examples of sentences with *little, much, few,* and *many,* see **Countable and uncountable nouns**.

DOUBLE COMPARISONS

One comparison may depend on another: the first clause states a cause and the second clause states an effect. Put a comma between the clauses that make a double comparison.

CAUSE	EFFECT
The *better* our social life is,	the *less* we study.
The *fatter* the cattle are,	the *happier* the farmer is.
The *more* it rains,	the *more* it floods.

ILLOGICAL COMPARISONS

Be careful to compare two things that are the same.

INCORRECT:	The *books* for chemistry cost more than *history*.
CORRECT:	The *books* for chemistry cost more than the *books* for history.
	The *books* for chemistry cost more than *those* for history.

Books must be compared to *books* or to a pronoun that stands for books, such as *those*.

| INCORRECT: | The *population* of Japan has a greater density than *Canada*. |
| CORRECT: | The *population* of Japan has a greater density than the *population* of Canada. |

You must compare *population* to *population*.

GRAMMATICAL CONSTRUCTIONS IN COMPARISONS

Use the same construction for both parts of the comparison. Use an operator if you need to repeat a verb. (see **Operators**)

| AWKWARD: | The population of Japan has a greater density than Canada's population (does or has). |
| IMPROVED: | Japan's population has a greater density than Canada's (population). |

You can leave out the noun in the second part of the comparison after a possessive if the meaning of the sentence is clear without it.

| INCORRECT: | *Boxers* train differently from *football*. |

You cannot compare *boxers* (people) to *football* (a game).

CORRECT:	*Boxers* train differently from football *players*.
	Athletes who box train differently from *athletes* who play football.
	Athletes who box train differently from *those* who play football.
	An *athlete* who boxes trains differently from *one* who plays football.

PRONOUNS IN COMPARISONS

When you use a pronoun in the second part of the comparison, use
1. *the one* to replace a singular countable noun.
2. *that* to replace a singular countable noun that does not refer to a person and is modified by a prepositional phrase.
3. *that* to replace an uncountable noun.
4. *those* or *the ones* to replace plural countable nouns.

The *book* for chemistry costs more than *the one* for history. (singular, uncountable)

The *population of Japan* has a greater density than *that of Canada*. (singular, followed by a prepositional phrase)

Some people think that the *beauty* of the mountains is greater than *that* of the desert. (uncountable)

Children who go to school every day usually learn faster than *those (the ones)* who are often absent. (countable, plural)

People who live in the arctic need warmer clothes than *those* who live in the tropics. (irregular plural)

Use a subject pronoun in the second part of the comparison if you use a personal pronoun.

David liked that movie as much as *we* (did).
Martha can find out as easily as *she* (can).
Paul is no taller than *he* (is).

COMPARISON OF ABSOLUTES

Do not compare things or ideas that are either true or not true. You cannot be *more asleep* or *more awake,* for example. A debt is either *paid* or not *paid.* People are either *present* or *absent,* or *dead* or *alive.* To show a state near an absolute state, use *nearly, barely,* or *almost.*

The dog that was hit by a car is *barely alive.*
After studying all night, Tom felt *nearly dead.*

Although you will sometimes see the rule broken, accurate writers do not compare absolutes such as *unique, possible, impossible, horizontal, perpendicular, round, square,* and *fatal.*

INCORRECT:	John's work was more impossible than mine.
CORRECT:	John's work was difficult; mine was nearly impossible.
INCORRECT:	The accident was completely fatal.
CORRECT:	The accident was fatal.
	The accident was nearly fatal.
	The accident was almost fatal.

COMPARISON OF EQUALS

Use the *as . . . as* construction to show that two things or groups are similar.

Barbara is *as* tall *as* Carol (is).

The *as . . . as* construction can mean that Barbara and Carol are the same height, or it can mean that Barbara is *at least as tall as* Carol (no shorter than Carol). Barbara could be taller than Carol. You may need to give the reader more information.

Barbara is *as tall as* Carol; in fact, they are the same height.

Martin is *as tall as* Tim; in fact, Martin is taller.

You can also use the *as . . . as* or *so . . . as* construction in the negative to show differences.

Leonard is *not so tall as* Arthur.

REPETITION OF THE VERB AFTER COMPARISONS

Follow the rules for operators in verb repetition. (see **Operators**) You do not have to repeat or use an operator substitute for a verb that does not change in tense or number. *Be, have, do,* or a modal that is used in the first part of the sentence can be repeated. Replace all other verbs with a form of *do.*

> Barbara and Carol *are* taller than Anne *is.* (You must use *is* because the number changes from plural to singular.)
> Peter *will run* as fast tomorrow as Paul *did* yesterday. (You must use *did* because the tense changes.)
> Dogwood trees *do* not grow as tall as oaks (*do*). (You may repeat *do* or leave it out.)
> Barbara *is* as tall as Carol (*is*).
> Peter *can* run as fast as Paul (*can*).
> Peter *runs* as fast as Paul (*does*).
> Martin *studies* as hard as Ben (*does*).

THE + ADJECTIVE: ADJECTIVES USED AS NOUNS

Use *the* followed by an adjective alone like a noun phrase. (Possessive pronoun forms can replace *the.*) The meaning is *people who are sick, old,* and so forth (a generalization).

the sick	the rich	the innocent	our young
the old	the poor	the foolish	their hungry
the young	the hungry	the successful	your rich
the strong	the frightened	the middle-aged	our poor

Comparative and superlative forms can be used. These forms can be modified. They take plural verbs.

> *The wise* accomplish more than *the foolish.*
> *The very young* are likely to catch contagious diseases.
> *The youngest* and *the oldest* are the most likely to be ill.

Use this construction with *the* to refer to national groups. If the word does not already end in a -*ch*, -*s*, or -*sh* sound, add an -*s* to the adjective form. Use plural verbs with these forms.

Words that end in a -*ch*, -*s*, or -*sh* sound:

> The Chine*sh* are helpful.
>> Engli*sh*
>> Fren*ch*
>> Swi*ss*

Words that do not end in a -*ch*, -*s*, or -*sh* sound:

> The American*s* are helpful.
>> Greek*s*
>> Pakistani*s*

A few adjectives can be used with *the* to show abstract ideas, *the thing that is. . . .* Use singular verbs with these forms.

> *The unknown* is often feared.
> We do *the difficult* tomorrow; *the impossible* takes longer.

Adverbs That Modify Adjectives

Put adverbs before the adjectives that they modify. (see **Adverbs**)
EXCEPTION: *enough* when it is an adverb.

	ADVERB	ADJECTIVE	ADVERB
He gave us	*remarkably*	*clear* directions.	
The movie was a	*very*	*exciting* one.	
She was	*rather*	*quiet.*	
The test was	*unusually*	*difficult.*	
The test was		*difficult*	*enough.*
The movie was		*exciting*	*enough.*

NOTE: Another adverb cannot come before an adjective if *enough* follows it. (see **Enough**)

Adjectives after the Impersonal It Is

Adjectives can be used after *it is* to introduce the true subject of a clause.

	INFINITIVE PHRASE
It is *good*	to see you.
dangerous	to speed.
impossible	to go now.
difficult	to find the answer.

	NOUN CLAUSE
It is *certain*	that he will win.
clear	that she cheated.

Avoid the *it is* construction in writing by using the idea in the infinitive phrase or in the clause as the subject of the sentence. (see **It, Impersonal Use**)

Improved Sentences With *It Is* Taken Out

Seeing [to see] you is a pleasure.
Speeding [to speed] is dangerous.
Going [to go] now is impossible.
Finding [to find] the answer is difficult.
That he will win [his winning] is certain.
That she cheated [her cheating] is known.

Phrases and Clauses that Modify Adjectives

Some adjectives following linking verbs (*be, feel, seem, appear*) can be followed by phrases or clauses that complete the meaning of the adjective. When the sentence is completed by a clause, *that* can be left out if it is not the subject of the completing clause.

ADJECTIVE ALONE:	Clarence is *certain.*
PREPOSITIONAL PHRASE:	Clarence is *certain of success.*
INFINITIVE PHRASE:	Clarence is *certain to succeed.*
CLAUSE:	Clarence is *certain (that) he will succeed.*
INVERTED WORD ORDER:	*Certain of success,* Clarence will enter the race.
	Certain to succeed, Clarence will enter the race.
	Certain (that) he will succeed, Clarence will enter the race.

It is difficult to know which preposition must follow an adjective and which construction you can use after it. Some adjectives must be followed by a prepositional phrase or a clause. Look the adjective up in a dictionary written for non-native users of English if you are not sure how to use it. Most adjectives can be used without a prepositional phrase or clause following them, however. (see also **Participles, used as adjectives**)

ADJECTIVE CONSTRUCTIONS THAT FOLLOW THE VERB

Accustomed, contrary, and *probable* almost always have complements, but all the other adjectives can be used without complements in their most common meanings.

Adjective followed by a prepositional phrase:

Charles is afraid *of thieves.* (person)
high *places.* (thing)
having an accident. (*-ing* form)

Adjective followed by an infinitive phrase—leave out the preposition (see **Infinitive -ing choice**):

Charles is afraid *to ask.*

Adjective followed by a noun clause:

Charles is afraid *that he will lose his money.* (*that* clause—leave out the preposition)
Charles is afraid *of what may happen.* (*what* or *who* clause following the preposition—*whatever* and *whoever* are also sometimes possible)

If the meaning of the adjective allows it, any adjective can be used in the construction *too* + adjective + infinitive phrase or *so* + adjective + *that* clause:

The reasons are *too obvious to mention.* . . . *so obvious (that) we will not mention them.*
The men were *too proud to ask for help.* . . . *so proud (that) they would not ask for help.*

Adjective Constructions That Follow the Verb

ADJECTIVE	PREPOSITION	FOLLOWED BY PERSON/THING	FOLLOWED BY -ing FORM	INFINITIVE PHRASE—OMIT PREPOSITION	that CLAUSE—OMIT PREPOSITION	who(ever) OR what(ever) CLAUSE—AFTER PREPOSITION
able	to			X		X
accustomed	of	X	X			X
afraid	with	X	X	X	X	X
angry	about	X	X			X
aware	of	X	X		X	X
capable	of	X	X			X
careful	of	X	X		X	X
	about	X	X		X	X
	with	X		X		X
	also with -ing form without a preposition					
certain	about, of	X	X	X	X	X
close	to, by	X	X			X
confident	of	X	X	X		X
conscious	of	X	X			X
contrary	to	X	X			X
critical	of	X		X		X
difficult				X		
disappointed	about, at	X	X		X	X
	with, in	X	X			
doubtful	about	X	X			X
easy	on, with	X	X	X		X

(continued on page 22)

Adjective Constructions That Follow the Verb (*cont.*)

ADJECTIVE	PREPOSITION	FOLLOWED BY PERSON/THING	FOLLOWED BY *-ing* FORM	INFINITIVE PHRASE—OMIT PREPOSITION	*that* CLAUSE—OMIT PREPOSITION	*who(ever)* OR *what(ever)* CLAUSE—AFTER PREPOSITION
equal	to	X	X			X
essential	to	X	X		X	X
evident	to	X		X	X	X
experienced	in	X	X			X
expert	at	X	X			X
	with	X	X			X
famous	for		X			X
full	of		X			X
glad	about	X	X	X	X	X
good (successful)	at	X	X	X		X
(kind)	to	X		X		X
(helpful)	for	X	X	X		X
harmful	to, for	X	X	X		X
honest	about	X	X	X		X
	in	X	X			X
ignorant	of	X	X			X
important	for	X	X	X	X	X
impossible		X		X	X	X
interested	in	X	X	X	X (only after *it is*)	X
likely		X		X	X (only after *it is*)	X
necessary	for	X	X		X (only after *it is*)	X
obvious	to	X	X		X (only after *it is*)	X

Adjective	Preposition					
positive	of, about	X	X	X		X
possible	for	X	X		X (only after *it is*)	X (only after *it is*)
prepared	—	X				
probable	—				X (only after *it is*)	X
proud	of	X	X	X	X	X
qualified	for	X	X			X
ready	for	X	X	X		X
right	about	X	X	X		X
sensitive	to, about	X	X	X		
separate	from	X	X	X		
serious	about	X	X	X		
shocked	at	X	X	X		X
similar	to	X	X	X		
subject	to	X	X			X
successful	in	X	X	X		
sufficient	for	X	X			X
suitable	for	X				X
sure	—	X	X	X	X	X
surprised	at	X	X	X		X
unlikely	—	X			X (only after *it is*)	X
wrong	about	X	X	X		X

Adverbs

Adverbs modify or change the meaning of other words. Words that modify a verb, an adjective, another adverb. a participle, a phrase, a clause, or even a whole sentence are called adverbs. Adverbs can be classified according to form, meaning, and function.

Only certain adverbs can be used with certain tenses. (see **Tense**)

Some adverbs cannot be used with certain verbs. (see **Stative verbs**)

Word Order of Adverbs

The *word order of adverbs* is limited. You can put an adverb in the middle of a clause or at the beginning or end of the clause. Frequency adverbs are most often put in the middle, but in a special place in the middle. You can put an adverb between the subject and main verb, but after *be* alone; *do not put an adverb between the main verb and its object.* In a verb phrase of several words, put the adverb after the auxiliary or modal and before the main verb.

ADVERB, BEGINNING POSITION	SUBJECT	MODAL OR AUXILIARY	ADVERB, MIDDLE POSITION	MAIN VERB	ADVERB, END POSITION
Sometimes	Jerry	can		run	*quickly.*
	Jerry	can	*sometimes*	run	*quickly.*
	Jerry	can		run	*quickly sometimes.*

Directly following a form of *to be* if it is the only verb:

	Jerry			is	*sometimes helpful.*

When *to be* is the only verb in the clause, middle-position adverbs follow any form of it. Adverbs are frequently used in the middle position.

Diana *is always* friendly.
Larry and Tim *are never* friendly.
The Pendletons *were often* friendly.

SUBJECT	MODAL OR AUXILIARY	ADVERB, MIDDLE POSITION	MAIN VERB	DIRECT OBJECT
Diana		*often*	found	the Pendletons helpful.
She	can	*often*	visit	them.
They	are	*frequently*	helping	her.

Do not put an adverb between the main verb and a direct object.

INCORRECT:	Diana found *often* the Pendletons helpful.
INCORRECT:	She can visit *often* them.
INCORRECT:	They are helping *frequently* her.

Put *still, just, ever, never, almost, hardly,* and *quite* in the middle position. Very rarely, *never* comes at the beginning for emphasis in an inverted clause.

> Miller has *just* missed his bus.
> He will *never* oversleep again.
> *Never* again will he trust his sister to wake him up early.

Never and *again* are sometimes separated.

> *Never* will he trust his sister to wake him up early *again.*

ADVERB, BEGINNING POSITION	SUBJECT	MODAL OR AUXILIARY	ADVERB, MIDDLE POSITION	MAIN VERB	END POSITION
	Miller	has	*just*	missed his bus.	
	He	will	*never* (again)	oversleep	*(again).*
Never again		will he		trust his sister to wake him.	

Time adverbs usually come at the end of the clause. They do not usually come in the middle. Do not confuse time and frequency adverbs. Time adverbs answer the question *when?* Frequency adverbs answer the question *how often?* Put more specific time adverbs before more general ones. Time adverbs are often prepositional phrases made with *at, by, in, for,* or *since.* (see **Prepositions, time**)

> Roberta's mother will arrive *next week.*
>   *at ten o'clock Saturday.*
>   *at ten o'clock Saturday, December 15.*

WORD ORDER FOR SEVERAL ADVERBS IN THE SAME CLAUSE
Adverbs of *frequency* answer the question *how often?* (*always, never, seldom, frequently*)
Adverbs of *manner* answer the question *how?* (*easily, with difficulty, by plane, on foot*)
Adverbs of *place* answer the question *where?* (*here, there, in China, at home*)
Adverbs of *time* answer the question *when?* (*now, then, yesterday, to-morrow, in 1906, on May 7, at 10:00 a.m.*)

(Adverbs of frequency, manner, place, and time are discussed in detail below, pp. 30–34. This section deals only with their word order in the sentence.)

Put frequency adverbs in the middle position. Put time adverbs at the beginning or end. They are more emphatic at the beginning. Put manner, place, and time adverbs in that order if they are together at the end of the sentence. If you have several adverbs, you may move the time adverb(s) to the beginning of the sentence. You may move other adverbs to the beginning of the sentence for emphasis.

ADVERB, BEGINNING POSITION	SUBJECT	MODAL OR AUXILIARY	ADVERB, MIDDLE POSITION	MAIN VERB	MANNER	ADVERB, END POSITION PLACE	TIME
(*Last week*)	Roberta			arrived	*by plane*	*in Toronto*	(*last week*).
(*In his life*)	Arthur	has	*never*	traveled	*by ship*	*to Hong Kong*	(*in his life*).
(*Tomorrow*)	Dale	will	(*easily*)	pass	(*easily*) *with difficulty.*		(*tomorrow*).

NOTE: A single-word adverb of manner can come in the middle position, especially if other words follow the verb. If the verb does not have a complement or another adverb following it, the single-word adverb of manner is likely to follow the verb because of the rhythm of the sentence. Do not put an adverb of manner that is a phrase in the middle position.

> Dale will pass *easily*.
> Dale will pass *easily* tomorrow.
> Dale will *easily* pass the test.
> Dale will pass the test *with difficulty*.
> AWKWARD: Dale will *with difficulty* pass the test.

With *place* as well as *time*, put more specific information before more general information. (The day of the week is considered more specific than the date.)

> They arrived in Montreal, Canada, on Friday, September 26, 1980.
> Joseph was born in Mercy Hospital, San Francisco, California, on June 3, 1965. (note commas: see **Punctuation, comma**)

WORD ORDER OF ADVERBS THAT MODIFY ADJECTIVES AND PARTICIPLES

Put adverbs that modify adjectives and participles directly before the words they modify.

> Joy and Lee are *very* happy. (*very* modifies *happy*)

> Why are you *so* angry when we were *only* late? (*so* modifies *angry* and *only* modifies *late*)

> The couple who were celebrating their anniversary had been *happily* married for fifty years. (*happily* modifies *married*)

Forms of Adverbs

Many single-word adverbs are formed by adding *-ly* to another word, usually an adjective: *soft* becomes *softly*, *bright* becomes *brightly*, and *honest* becomes *honestly*.

Learn the spelling rules that change other words to adverb forms.
1. If the base word ends in -*l*, add -*ly*.

carefu*l*, carefu*lly*
helpfu*l*, helpfu*lly*

2. If the base word ends in -*y*, change *y* to *i* and add -*ly*.

happ*y*, happ*ily*
da*y*, da*ily*

3. If the base word ends in -*e*, drop the *e* and add -*ly*.

tru*e*, tru*ly*	abl*e*, ab*ly*	gentl*e*, gent*ly*
du*e*, du*ly*	suitabl*e*, suitab*ly*	simpl*e*, simp*ly*

EXCEPTIONS: wis*e*, wis*ely*, sol*e*, sol*ely*

4. If the base word ends in -*ic*, add -*ally*.

economi*c*, economi*cally*   automati*c*, automati*cally*
histori*c*, histori*cally*   scientifi*c*, scientifi*cally*
specifi*c*, specifi*cally*   criti*c*, criti*cally*
publi*c*, publi*cly*

Some words have the same form whether they are used as adjectives or adverbs. Other -*ly* words cannot be used as adverbs.
1. words referring to time ending in -*ly* that can be adjectives or adverbs:

early   monthly
hourly   weekly
daily   early

2. words ending in -*ly* that are adjectives, never adverbs:

courtly (manners)	heavenly (music)	lonely (people)
deadly (weapons)	leisurely (pace)	lovely (friendship)
earthly (comfort)	lively (party)	worldly (wisdom)

and others formed from words referring to people:

brotherly, sisterly, motherly
kingly, queenly, princely
friendly, scholarly, saintly

3. other irregular forms that can be adjectives or adverbs:

high	adjective:	She has a *high* position.
	adverb:	She threw the ball *high* in the air.
	highly means *greatly*:	She was *highly* regarded.
fast	adjective:	You had a *fast* trip.
	adverb:	You must have been driving *fast*.

hard	adjective:	He had to make a *hard* choice.
	adverb:	He worked *hard*.
	hardly means *scarcely:*	He was *hardly* able to choose.
late	adjective:	She has a *late* appointment.
	adverb:	She arrived *late*.
	lately means *recently:*	She has not seen the doctor *lately*.
likely	adjective:	Paula is a *likely* candidate for the job.
	adverb:	The bus will *very likely* leave on time. (Most writers modify *likely* by a word such as *very, more,* or *most* when using it as an adverb.)
	like is a preposition that means *similar to:*	Paula looks *like* her sister.
low	adjective:	The roof is *low*.
	adverb:	The branch of the tree hung *low* over the porch.
	lowly means *not a high position:*	He disliked his *lowly* job.
straight	adjective:	The *straight* road led to the farmhouse.
	adverb:	The road led *straight* to the farmhouse.
deep	adjective:	Keep away from *deep* water.
	adverb:	The treasure was buried *deep* in the earth.
	deeply refers to emotions:	I am *deeply* sorry about your accident.
near	adjective:	The end of the job is *near*.
	adverb:	The dog was afraid to come *near*.
	nearly means *almost:*	We *nearly* had an accident.

(see also **Adjectives, a-word modifiers**)

Comparison of Adverbs

The adverbs that can be compared are called *gradable*. They can be modified by *very, so,* and *too* and can be compared by adding *-er* or *-est* suffixes or by putting *more* or *most* before them. (see **Adjectives, comparison of**)

Adverbs that can be compared include those that answer the questions

how often?—àdverbs of frequency (*seldom, often, rarely, frequently*)
when?—adverbs of relative time (*early, soon, late, recently*)
where?—adverbs of place (*near, far, close, distant*)
how?—adverbs of manner (*badly, cleanly, carelessly, poorly, skillfully, slowly, well*)

Absolutes cannot be compared in their common uses. You obviously cannot say *more always, most never,* or *more ten o'clock.* (see below for more about these classes of adverbs)

Put *-er* or *-est* at the end of words of one syllable, following spelling rules for suffixes. (see **Spelling**)

fast, fast*er*, fast*est*
slow, slow*er*, slow*est*
late, lat*er*, lat*est*
early, earl*ier*, earl*iest* (Some two-syllable adverbs have the *er/est* ending.)

Irregular adverb forms are closely related to irregular adjective forms.

	COMPARATIVE	SUPERLATIVE
well	better	best
badly	worse	worst
far	farther	farthest
	further	furthest

COMPARISON IN THE CLAUSE

1. To show differences, use the comparative and superlative forms: *-er, -est, more,* or *most*

carefully.
Jane prepares her work *carelessly.*
well.

more carelessly
Jane prepares her work *more carefully than* Winifred (does hers).
better than

Jane prepares her work *the best* (of all).

or

Use *not* + $\frac{so}{as}$ + base adverb + *as:*

well
Winifred does *not* prepare her work $\frac{so}{as}$ *carefully as* Jane (does hers).
carelessly

NOTE: Some people prefer *so* in negative sentences.

2. To show likeness, use *as* + base adverb + *as:*

carefully
Winifred prepares her work *as carelessly as* Jane (does hers).
well

NOTE: Only a form of *be, have,* and *do* can be repeated after *so* or *as.* You must replace other verbs with a form of *do.* (See **Operators**; also see **Adjectives, comparison of,** for a more detailed discussion of the meaning of the *so/as . . . as* construction.)

Some adverbs can modify adjectives and other adverbs in the comparative and superlative degree.

MODIFIER	ADJECTIVE	ADVERB
much	more careful	more carefully
very much	better	better
far	worse	worse
no (*any* in questions)	easier	more easily
a little	happier	more happily

COMPARATIVES:

Winifred is (*very*) *much more careful* now. (adjective)

Winifred does her work (*very*) *much more carefully.* (adverb)

There is *no more careful a* worker than Winifred. (adjective)

Is there *any* worker *more careful* than Winifred? (adjective)

Jane works *no more carefully* than Winifred (does). (adverb)

Winifred is *a little more careful* now. (adjective)

Winifred works *a little more carefully* now. (adverb)

SUPERLATIVES WITH **very:**
Winifred works the *very best.*
Winifred is the *very best* worker.

	earliest
	best
	worst
very +	first
	last
	farthest
	closest

Do not use *very* before *most* except when *most* is a pronoun:

This is the *very most* we can do. (meaning *this is the very best offer we can make*)

ADVERBS OF FREQUENCY

Adverbs of frequency answer the question *how often?* (See also above, "Word Order," for more about their position in the sentence.) Usually put single-word adverbs of frequency in the middle position and put phrases of frequency in the end position. Put *scarcely ever* in the middle position. Some common adverbs of frequency are:

AFFIRMATIVE	NEGATIVE
always	never
usually	rarely
frequently	seldom
often	scarcely ever
sometimes	occasionally
generally	
many times	
every day/week/month	
twice/three times a day/week/month	

>   *often*
> Priscilla must *always* work on Fridays.
>   *never*
>
> Priscilla must *scarcely ever* work on Fridays.
>
>   *every week.*
> Priscilla must work on Fridays *many times.*
>   *twice a month.*

Do not use *no, not,* or *never* in the same clause with a negative adverb of frequency. (see **Negation**)

ADVERBS OF RELATIVE TIME

Adverbs of relative time can be used with all tenses as meaning permits, but they are used especially with the continuous/progressive tenses. Put them in the middle position in the clause. The most common adverbs of relative time are *just, still, already* (*yet* in negative), *lately, recently,* and *soon.*

tense	
PRESENT CONTINUOUS/ PROGRESSIVE:	Russell was *recently* looking for that book.
PAST:	He *recently* found it.
PRESENT PERFECT:	He has *just* found it.
FUTURE CONTINUOUS/ PROGRESSIVE:	He will *soon* be using it in his computer class.
PAST PERFECT:	When he bought the house, it had *recently* been remodeled.
PAST:	He *soon* decided to make it larger, however.

ADVERBS OF MANNER

Adverbs of manner answer the question *how?* or *how well?* Usually put them at the end of the clause or in the middle position in the perfect tenses. Putting them at the beginning of the sentence gives them strong emphasis. Do not put these adverbs between the main verb and the direct object.

CORRECT:	Don cleaned the room *carefully*. (*very carefully*)
CORRECT:	He *carefully* cleaned the room.
CORRECT, EMPHATIC:	*Carefully* he cleaned the room.
INCORRECT:	He cleaned *carefully* the room.

Do not confuse the adverb construction with the adjective after *be* or after another linking verb. (see **Adjective constructions that follow the verb,** and **Predicate complements**)

    predicate
    adjective
He is *careful* to clean the room.

Many adverbs of manner are closely related to adjective and noun forms of the same base word. The endings (suffixes) show whether the word is an adverb, an adjective, or a noun. (see **Word formation, suffixes**)

How did he do the work?
             explain the problem?
He did it . . .

SINGLE-WORD ADVERB	PREPOSITIONAL PHRASE *with* + NOUN	PREPOSITIONAL PHRASE: IN A(N) (ADJECTIVE) *way* OR *manner*
badly	—	in a bad manner
carefully	with care	in a careful manner
carelessly	with carelessness	in a careless manner
clearly	with clarity	in a clear manner
—	with difficulty	in a difficult manner
foolishly	with foolishness	in a foolish manner
gradually	—	in a gradual manner
hesitantly	with hesitance	in a hesitant manner
quickly	—	—
wisely	with wisdom	in a wise manner
well	—	

Using *in a manner that was* + adjective is also possible, but avoid this construction because it is wordy. Avoid using two or three words if one will do. The single-word adverb is usually the best choice.

Put adverbs of manner that are closely connected in meaning with the subject of the clause directly after the subject instead of after the verb. These adverbs correspond to predicate adjectives.

adverb of
subject   manner
Mary   *kindly*   helped the old woman.

MEANING: It   was   *kind*   of Mary to help the old woman.

predicate adjective

adverb of manner

Mary helped the old woman *kindly*.

MEANING: Mary helped the old woman *in a kind manner*.

Some additional adverbs that correspond to predicate adjectives are *angrily, bravely, cruelly, faithfully* (and others in *-fully*), *foolishly, pleasantly*.

ADVERBS OF PLACE

Adverbs of place answer the question *where?* Like adverbs of time (below), they can be a single word or a phrase. Put them before or after the main clause. Put more specific information before more general information.

> We have just moved *to a new house in the city.*
> My brothers were born in *Montreal, Canada.*
> You will find the book *in the upper right-hand corner of the bookcase in my bedroom.*

Learn the correct preposition to show different kinds of place. (see **Prepositions, space and movement**)

ADVERBS OF TIME

Adverbs of time answer the question *when?* They can be a single word, a phrase, or a dependent clause. Put them before or after the main clause. Put more specific information before more general information.

> My youngest sister was born at 3:15 a.m., March 23, 1970.

Use *at* before clock time, *on* before a day or date, and *in* before a month used alone, a year, or a century. Use commas to separate several items if you do not use prepositions.

> My youngest sister was born *at* 3:15 a.m.
>   *on* March 23.
>   *in* 1970.

> My youngest sister was born at 3:15 a.m., March 23, 1970.

> Many surprising events took place *in* the 1960s.

> Industrialization in England began *in* the eighteenth century.

(see **Prepositions, time**)

Dependent clauses of time (see **Clauses, adverb**)

Put a comma after a dependent clause at the beginning of the sentence, but do not put a comma between an independent clause and a dependent clause that comes at the end of the sentence. (see **Punctuation, comma**)

> AT THE BEGINNING: *When the industrial revolution in England began,* it brought many changes.
>
> AT THE END: The industrial revolution in England brought many changes *when it began.*

ADVERBS THAT EMPHASIZE

Adverbs that emphasize are *only* and *even.* In writing, put *only* and *even* directly before the word they modify. Where you put them makes a great change in the meaning of the clause.

> *Only* I (no one else) told Fred to come last week.
> I *only* told Fred to come last week. (told, not commanded)
> I told *only* Fred (no one but Fred) to come last week.
> I told Fred *only* to come last week. (to come, not to do anything else.)
> I told Fred to come *only* last week. (Before an adverb of time, *only* means either *as recently as* or *at no other time.*)

ADVERBS THAT MODIFY THE WHOLE CLAUSE

Adverbs that modify the whole clause usually come at the beginning or at the end of the clause or directly after the subject.

1. Adverbs that express the writer's attitude:

briefly	certainly	in fairness
of course	perhaps	objectively

> The solution, *certainly,* cannot be found in new laws.
> Let us *briefly* consider the next piece of evidence.

2. Adverbs (conjunctive) that join ideas within the sentence or with ideas in other sentences or paragraphs (see **Clauses, connectors** and **Interrupters** for their arrangement according to meaning):

also	therefore	however	too
as well	furthermore	consequently	subsequently
besides	in addition to	nevertheless	as a result

Do not confuse conjunctive adverbs with coordinating conjunctions. (see **Comma Splice**)

> *Therefore,* we must conclude that the result is correct.
> We, *therefore,* must conclude that the result is correct.
> We must, *therefore,* conclude that the result is correct.
> We must conclude, *therefore,* that the result is correct.
> We must conclude that the result is correct, *therefore.*

(Although authorities do not agree about comma rules, you will not be wrong if you separate interrupters from the rest of the clause by commas.)

ADVERBS THAT INTRODUCE DEPENDENT CLAUSES

Adverbs that introduce dependent clauses but that also refer to a noun or pronoun earlier in the sentence (the time *when,* the place *where*) are sometimes called relative adverbs. In this book these words are discussed as subordinating conjunctions. (see **Conjunctions**)

Agreement of pronoun and antecedent, see **Reference of the pronoun**

 # Agreement of Subject and Verb _____

The subject and main verb of a clause must agree in number. Use a singular verb with a singular noun or pronoun or with an uncountable (mass) noun. Use a plural verb with a plural noun or pronoun. Countable nouns that indicate more than one person or thing are plural in English. Even though many people do not follow some of these rules in speaking, you must follow them in formal writing.

Most English nouns add an -*s* to show a change from singular to plural. (see **Number**)

	SINGULAR	PLURAL	SINGULAR	PLURAL
REGULAR:	star	stars	dog	dogs
	girl	girls	basket	baskets
IRREGULAR:	man	men	child	children

In the present tense forms, most verbs add an -*s* to the simple (infinitive) form in the third person singular only. The only verb that shows a difference between singular and plural in the past tense is *be* (*was* and *were*).

SINGULAR (-*s* on verb in present tense; no -*s* on noun)	PLURAL (-*s* on noun; no -*s* on verb)
That star shines brightly tonight.	Those stars shine brightly every night.
That star *is* shining brightly tonight. (irregular)	Those stars are shining brightly tonight. (irregular)

Modals have the same form for singular and plural. (see **Modal**)

SINGULAR	PLURAL
He can go.	They can go.
He should come now.	They should come now.

In writing you will use the simple present tense more than you use it in speaking. Do not forget the -*s* on the singular verb form in the present tense.

1. Find the true subject of the clause and be sure the verb agrees with it.

a. Prepositional phrases that come between the subject and verb do not usually affect the subject-verb agreement. The noun closest to the verb is not always the subject of the clause (see item 5 below, p. 39)

	plural subject	*prepositional phrase*	*plural verb*

CORRECT: Several *sections* of this music *are* difficult to learn.

	singular subject	*prepositional phrase*	*singular verb*

CORRECT: The *print* in these books *is* easy to read.

	singular subject	*prepositional phrase*	*singular verb*

CORRECT: This *man* along with his sons always *catches* the largest fish.

NOTE: *along with* means something added to *man;* the meaning is similar to *this man and his sons.* But only *this man and his sons* takes a plural verb. *Along with* is a preposition.

	plural compound subject	*plural verb*

This *man and his sons* always *catch* the largest fish.

More prepositions like *along with* are

together with	except
as well as	but (meaning *except*)
in addition to	no less than

subject	*prepositional phrase*	*verb*
All the boys	except John but John	*are* going.
Martha	as well as her sisters together with her sisters in addition to her sisters	*is* going.
The *construction*	of these buildings of this building	*is* sound.
The *reasons*	for his change in plans	*are clear.*
The *reason*	for his change in plans	*is* clear.

b. Dependent clauses do not affect subject-verb agreement

subject	*dependent clause*	*verb*

A *person* who has good friends *enjoys* life more.
A *child* who has many pets *learns* about animals.

c. Predicate nouns or pronouns do not affect subject-verb agreement. The noun or pronoun that comes before a linking verb is its subject. (see **Linking verbs**) *subject*   *verb*

The most difficult *part* of biology courses *is* the labs.

    subject verb

The   *labs*   *are* the most difficult part of biology courses.

d. Choose between *there is* and *there are* and similar expressions by finding the true subject after the verb. (*It is* never changes to *it are*.)

   verb   *subject*

There *are*   several *bananas* on the table.

There *is*   no *reason* for you to do that.

Here *are*   the *books* you asked me to get.

Here *are*   three maple *trees*.

A prepositional phrase in the place of *there* or *here* does not affect the verb form.

   prepositional
     phrase   *verb*   *subject*

On the table   *are* several   *bananas*.

In front of   the building *are* three maple trees.

Avoid too much use of phrases such as *it is, there is,* and *there are* in formal writing. Use the true subject at the beginning of the sentence.

   CORRECT: There are several bananas on the table.

   IMPROVED: Several bananas are on the table.

EXCEPTION: Use *it* in statements about the weather and time.

   It is too hot to work today.

   It rained yesterday, but it isn't raining today.

   It is ten o'clock already.

2. After *or* or *nor* the verb agrees with the subject closest to it.

   Not John *nor* Harold *nor Allen works* there.

   Either the boys *or* their *sister has promised* to come.

   The chairman *or* the committee *members decide* on their next meeting time.

   Neither the students *nor* the *teacher wants* to make up the class they missed.

3. Always use singular verbs in certain constructions.

a. Use singular verbs with certain pronouns:

anybody	anyone	anything	another
everybody	everyone	everything	each
nobody	no one	nothing	either
somebody	someone	something	neither
	one		

   subject   *verb*

Everyone needs food, clothing, and shelter.

Nobody   *needs* to worry about ice storms in Jamaica.

The object of a preposition or a dependent clause does not change the verb form (Rule 1).

>   *main*
> *subject*   *dependent clause*   *verb*
> *Nobody* who raises chickens *thinks* chickens are smart.
>
>   *prepositional*
> *subject*   *phrase*   *main verb*
> *Nothing* of their plans *was known* to me.

b. Use singular verbs with uncountable (mass) nouns. Learn which words are countable and which words are uncountable in English. Countable/uncountable classification differs very much in different languages. (see **Countable and uncountable nouns**)

> *Gold was* discovered in California.
> The *money is* in the bank.
> The *water is* running.
> This *information is* difficult to understand.
> *Knowledge brings* understanding.
> Your *advice helps* us.

c. Use singular verbs with the *-ing* forms that are used as subjects of clauses (gerunds). (see **Countable and uncountable nouns**) A plural object after an *-ing* form does not affect the subject-verb agreement.

>   *object of*
> *subject*   *gerund*   *verb*
> *Designing* bridges *takes* great skill.
> *Picking*   apples   *is*   hard work.

A compound subject made up of *-ing* forms takes a plural verb like any other compound subject (see Rule 4 below).

> *Swimming, diving,* and *water-skiing are* water sports.

In informal style you may see plural *-ing* forms such as:

> His *doings are* beyond my understanding.

In formal writing, however, *doings* would not be used. A noun such as *activities* or *actions* is better.

d. Use singular verbs with a few special nouns that end in *-s*.

Diseases such as *measles* and *mumps:*

> *Measles is* a serious disease.

Subjects of study such as *economics* and *physics:*

> *Economics is* a difficult course.

Games such as *checkers* (*draughts*) and *chess:*

> *Checkers is* an easy game to learn.

Certain geographical names:

> *The United States is* a large country.

Other words thought of as a unit:

> The *news is* good today.
> *Molasses flavors* beans in some kinds of cooking.

e. Use singular verbs with quantities and numbers when they are thought of as a unit.

> Twenty *dollars is* not enough.
> Ten *pounds* of potatoes *is* usually sold in a bag.
> Five hundred *miles is* too far to drive in one afternoon.

f. Use a singular verb with the title of one book or article even when the words in it are plural.

> *Modern Short Stories is* the textbook you must buy.
> "Today's Heroes" *was* an article in yesterday's newspaper.

4. Use a plural verb with two or more nouns or pronouns joined by *and.*

compound subject	*verb*	
My *shoes* and tennis *racket*	*are*	in the car.
The *moon and stars*	*were*	not visible last night.
Grass and flowers	*grow*	fast in the summer.

Sometimes two nouns refer to the same person. If they do, use a singular verb.

| *subject* | *verb* | |
| The *secretary and treasurer was* | | Betty. |

5. Choose between a singular and a plural verb in certain constructions according to the meaning of the whole sentence.

a. Some words such as *some, all, half, none, more,* and *most* can be used in a phrase with singular or plural meanings.

SINGULAR: Some (*half, all, none, more, most, a lot*) of the food *has* been eaten.

PLURAL: Some (*half, all, none, more, most, a lot*) of the students *have* registered.

Look at the object following the preposition *of.* If a singular or an uncountable (mass) noun follows *of,* the verb is singular. If a countable plural noun follows *of,* the verb is plural. (see **Countable and uncountable nouns**) This construction is an exception to Rule 1a. The object of the preposition does affect the choice of the verb after the words listed above.

SINGULAR: *All* of the pie *was* eaten. (one pie—singular)
All of the rice *was* eaten. (uncountable or mass—singular)

PLURAL: *All* of the pies *were* eaten. (more than one pie)

b. Collective nouns stand for groups of more than one member. These groups are usually people or animals. Most collective nouns have both singular and plural forms: *team* and *teams.* The plural form always takes a plural verb. But the singular form may take a singular verb or a plural verb. Use singular verbs with most singular collective nouns if the group is acting as a unit, but use a plural verb if the members of the group are acting separately and individually.

	singular noun	*singular verb*	
Our	*team*	*is*	winning the game. (unit)

	singular noun	*plural verb*	
The	*team*	*have found*	jobs for the summer in different places, so they

will not be able to practice together again until fall. (individuals)

	plural noun	*plural verb*	
The	*members*	of the team *are*	playing in the tournament next week.

British usage and U.S. usage do not always agree. For example, in British usage, *government* may be thought of as the people who rule or as an institution. In U.S. usage, *government* is thought of as an institution.

	singular noun	*plural verb*	
BRITISH:	The *government*	*are*	resigning. (members of the government)

	singular noun	*singular verb*	
BRITISH AND U.S. USAGE:	The *government*	*is*	losing control of the situation. (institution)

Many specific collective nouns exist, especially for groups of animals and birds.

covey of quail   pride of lions

Some collective nouns are used often.

band	class	flock	orchestra
choir	club	group	team
chorus	company	herd	

Certain collective nouns always take plural verbs.

cattle	people	poultry	youth (can also be singular/
clergy	police	vermin	plural or uncountable)

The *cattle are* in the pasture.
The *youth are* willing to help the elderly.

6. All rules for subject-verb agreement apply to subject and verbs in dependent clauses.

subject   *prepositional phrase*   *verb*

If *either* of my brothers *wins* the race, I will be happy.

subject   *prepositional phrase*   *verb*

After *one* of those girls *has finished* with her book, let me use it.

In many dependent clauses, the relative pronoun is the subject of its own clause. Look at the antecedent of the relative pronoun in order to decide whether to use a singular verb or a plural verb. (The relative pronouns that can be used as subjects are *who, which,* and *that.* (see **Pronouns, relative**)

singular antecedent   *singular verb*

The *man who* always *catches* the largest fish is my father.

plural antecedent   *plural verb*

The *men who* always *catch* the largest fish are my uncles.

When *that* is the subject of the clause you can never leave it out unless you also leave out the verb that follows it.

singular antecedent   *singular verb*

The *test (that is)* being given tomorrow is difficult.

plural antecedent   *plural verb*

The *tests (that are)* being given tomorrow are difficult.

compound subject: plural antecedent   *plural verb*

Karen, Mary, and *Susan, who are* going to college this fall, need to find an apartment near the campus.

singular antecedent   *singular verb*

The *student who has* finished the work has left.

singular antecedent   *singular verb*

The library has two sections: the reference *room, which is* on

plural antecedent   *plural verb*

the first floor, and the *reading room and stacks, which are* on the second floor.

The antecedent can be the object of a preposition.

                                        plural   plural
                     preposition   antecedent   verb
This is an important decision   *like*   many *others that*   *are*   changing the educational institutions of our country.

                         singular   singular
            preposition   antecedent   verb
They rode   *with*   a   *friend   who*   *has*   a new car.

Allegory

An allegory is a story with a hidden meaning. The characters in the story represent something or someone else. In Aesop's fables and in George Orwell's *Animal Farm*, for example, the animal characters represent people. In Bunyan's *Pilgrim's Progress*, the main character on a journey represents an ordinary person in his struggles in life. The events (plot), characters, and setting in an allegory all have a second meaning. The metaphor in an allegory continues through the whole story. Sometimes an allegory is called an *extended* (long) metaphor. (see **Metaphor**)

The story of the wind and the sun that follows is an allegory. The story also illustrates personification, for the wind and the sun are able to have a conversation, a characteristic of people that the wind and the sun do not really have. (see **Personification**)

THE WIND AND THE SUN

One day the wind and the sun were having an argument about which of them was more powerful. The wind said that he was stronger than the sun because he could blow down trees, destroy buildings, and cause shipwrecks. But the sun disagreed, saying that his ability to make plants grow, ice melt, and water dry up showed that he was stronger and more important than the wind. While they were arguing, they saw a man walking down the road. The man was wearing a heavy coat. When the sun and the wind saw the man, they decided that they would use him as a test of their powers. The wind said that he could blow the coat off the man. The sun laughed at the wind, and agreed to let him test his powers first. If the wind succeeded in getting the man's coat off him, the wind would be more powerful.

The wind began to blow as hard as he could, but all that happened was that the man held his coat tighter and tighter around himself even when he could hardly stand up to the force of the wind. Finally the wind gave up and told the sun to try. Then the sun came out from behind a cloud and began to shine on the man. After struggling in the strong wind, the man was pleased to have calm sunshine, and he began to smile. He let go of his coat and began to swing his arms as he walked along. Soon he unbuttoned his coat. The sun shone stronger and stronger. As the man began to feel warmer, he unbuttoned his coat and then he opened it. Finally he became so warm that he took his coat off completely. The sun had proved that warm persuasion succeeds when cold force fails.

Aesop's Fables

Alliteration

Alliteration means repeating the same consonant sound in several syllables one after another or closely following. Alliterative sounds that are difficult to pronounce make a "tongue twister."

Peter Piper picked a peck of pickled peppers;
A peck of pickled peppers Peter Piper picked.

Alliteration is a device that is often used in poetry and prose.

The fair breeze blew, the white foam flew
The furrow followed free . . .
                    Samuel Taylor Coleridge

The great, grey, green, greasy Limpopo River . . .
                    Rudyard Kipling

Alliteration is used in many common set phrases:

fair or foul (good or bad)
safe and sound (unharmed)
through thick and thin (through all kinds of difficulties)
spick and span (very clean)
pretty as a picture (attractive)
kith and kin (family relationships)
health and wealth
friend or foe (friends and enemies)
sweet and sour
the fat is in the fire (the harm is already done)
as good as gold
as dead as a doornail

Allusion

An allusion is a reference to a fact that the writer thinks the reader already knows. Allusions can be made to matters of general knowledge such as sports, to characters and incidents connected with well-known works of literature, to historical events and characters, or to any fact the reader can reasonably be expected to know.

Classical and biblical allusions are very common in English literature, particularly in works that were written in earlier times. Since at one time Bible stories and Greek and Latin literature and mythology were studied by every schoolchild, at that time nearly all authors referred to characters and incidents from these sources. Knowing something about them is very helpful in understanding poetry and prose written in English.

He has the strength of Samson. (a strong man in the Bible)
He has the strength of Hercules. (a strong man in Greek mythology)

Alphabetizing

You need to understand alphabetizing in order to look up information you need in library card catalogs, encyclopedias, dictionaries, telephone directories, book indexes, and filing systems. You may also need to know how to put your own lists in alphabetical order for bibliographies and for filing systems. (see **Documentation**)

Two methods of alphabetizing are used. You need to understand both of them.

The Dictionary Method

The dictionary method follows alphabetical order exactly. Look at each letter in order.

Jones, *David*	*Da* comes before *D.E.* in the next entry
Jones, *D.E.*	*D.E.* comes before *Do* in the next entry
Jones, *Donald F.*	*F.* comes before *W* in Warren in the next entry
Jones, *Donald Warren*	*a* in Don*a*ld comes before *n* in Don*n*er in the
Jones, *Donner*	next entry

The Directory Method

The directory method follows alphabetical order in units. Look at each word or initial. Each unit of the name is considered before going to the next unit. A shorter unit always comes before a longer one if both begin with the same letter or letters.

FIRST UNIT	SECOND UNIT	THIRD UNIT	
Jones,	*D.*	E.	*D.* comes before *David*
Jones,	*David*		because it is shorter. The
Jones,	*Donald*	F.	rest of the list is the same
Jones,	*Donald*		as the dictionary method.
Jones,	*Donner*	Warren	

Uses of the Two Methods

As a general rule, shorter lists such as bibliographies use the dictionary method, but longer lists such as telephone directories and encyclopedias use the directory method. Some books use one system for the index and the other system for bibliographies.

Special Problems with Names

Alphabetize and look up names by the last name or family name.

1. Prefixes from foreign languages are not always treated the same in English. People who make lists try to treat the name in the way the person who bears the name would treat it, but some well-known people have had their names changed into English words. English spelling of many foreign names is very inconsistent.

A, a, al: usually put under *A,* but not always.

   Alhambra, The (palace in southern Spain): put under *A;* English article added.

   Alhazen (Arab mathematician): put under *A.*

but

Thomas à *K*empis is put under *K.*

d', de, D', and *De:* usually put under *D,* especially if capitalized, but usage varies.

   The name of *Descartes,* the philosopher, is spelled as one word in modern English, but his philosophy is called *Cartesian.*

   De Gaulle, Charles: put under *D.*

   de la Mare, Walter: put under *D* (sometimes a capital letter).

but

   de *Falla,* Manuel: put under *F.*

   de *La* Fontaine, Jean: put under *L.*

El: sometimes put under *E* and sometimes under the next word.

   El Capitaine (mountain in California): put under *E.*

but

   El *Cid:* put under *C.*

   El *Greco:* put under *G.*

L', La, Las, Le, and *Los:* usually put under *L.*

   La Fontaine, Jean de: put under *L.*

   Las Casas, Bartolomé de: put under *L.*

   Los Angeles, City of: put under *L.*

M' and *Mc:* sometimes alphabetized exactly following each letter of the word and sometimes listed as though spelled *Mac.*

   *M'*Clure could be listed as though spelled *Mac*Clure.

but not

   *M'*Lady Beauty Salon: *M'* stands for *my* in this phrase.

Mac (names beginning with *Mac* followed by a capital letter): sometimes alphabetized exactly following each letter of the word (both the dictionary and the directory method) and sometimes listed in a separate section before or after the general *M* listing (in some filing systems).

O': always put under *O.*

Van, van, van den, van der, and *von:* usually put under *V,* but sometimes under the family name.

   Vanderberg: spelled as an English word; put under *V.*

   van der Waals: spelled as a Dutch word; put under *W.*

   Jan van der Meer von Delft is known in English as Jan Vermeer: put under *V.*

2. The order of names is not the same in all languages. If you cannot tell which name is the family name, look for a comma. If there is no comma, the given name or names are first. If there is a comma, the family name is first.

Warren Jones: Jones is the family name; put under *J.*
Jones, Warren: Jones is the family name; put under *J.*

EXCEPTION: English usage follows the usage of Chinese and some other Oriental languages without a comma.

Mao Ze Dong (Chinese); put under *M*
Park Chung Hee (Korean); put under *P*

but

Masayoshi Ohira (Japanese); put under *O*

3. Hyphenated last names are usually alphabetized under the first letter of the first part of the hyphenated name.

Helen Stephenson-Rice: put under S.

Titles

Alphabetize and look up titles of books and chapters in books, magazines and newspapers, articles in magazines and newspapers, short stories, plays, movies, and music by the first word in the title after *A, An,* or *The.*

The Dangerous Journey	(leave out *The*)
comes before	(*a* in *Dangerous* comes before *o* in *Domino*)
A Domino Theory	(leave out *A*)

Special Problems

1. Alphabetize numbers as they would be put if they were spelled out: consider *40* as *forty.*

Fortune, X.J.	*u* before *y* in *forty* in the next entry
45 Tower Place	consider *forty-five,* and *five* is before *four* in the next entry
Forty-four Bells Cafe	*t* in *Forty* comes before *u* in *Forum* in the next
Forum Agency	entry

2. Do not consider apostrophes.

John's Grill	
Johns, G. W.	(dictionary method)

Johns, G. W.	
John's Grill	(directory method)

3. Abbreviations are usually alphabetized as they would be put if they were spelled out, except for *Mrs.* Titles such as *Dr., Mr., Mrs., Sir,* or *Capt.* are usually left out, but are sometimes included if two names are otherwise alike.

"*Mr.* Maxwell's Rescue": put as *Mister.*
Mt. Everest: put as *Mount.*
"*Mrs.* Robinson's Problem": put as *Mrs.*
St. Anne's Church: put as *Saint.*
Scott, *Rev.* Alfred J.: *Rev.* comes before *Sir.*
Scott, *Sir* Alfred J.: *A* comes before *M.*
Scott, Dr. Marvin: disregard title when names are different.

4. Filing systems are often set up for special purposes. They may follow special classifications that are useful to a particular business or organization.

Analogy _____

Analogy is comparison. Analogy may be *literal,* based on actual physical similarities, or *figurative,* based on limited similarities between things that are not really alike in most ways. Metaphors and similes are analogies. Analogies are often used in persuasion and argument. (see **Metaphor, Simile, Allegory,** and **Argument**)

People often compare life to a road through the mountains because both have their ups and downs.

Benjamin Franklin was in Paris when the first successful balloon flight took place. When asked what good such an invention was, Franklin answered, "What good is a newborn baby?" (No one knows how either a newborn baby or a new invention will develop.)

Anecdote _____

An anecdote is a very short story, often amusing, about a real person or event. Usually an anecdote is used to illustrate or support a generalization. (see **Substantiation**)

To illustrate the importance of continuing to try even after failure (a generalization), people sometimes tell the story of Robert the Bruce, who was a king of Scotland in the fourteenth century. Robert had been defeated six times by his enemies and was hiding from them. Watching a spider trying to attach its thread, he noticed that it kept trying even though it failed. After it had failed six times, Robert decided that if the spider could succeed on the seventh try, he too ought to try again. When the spider attached its thread on its seventh try, Robert was encouraged to go out to battle one more time, and this time he won the battle.

Anglicized Words

Anglicized words are foreign words that have been made into English words. Foreign words that have not been anglicized should be underlined in handwriting or typing and italicized in print. (see **Punctuation, underlining**) But when foreign words are considered to be English, do not mark them in any special way. Dictionaries show whether or not a word is considered foreign.

Sometimes knowing the anglicized form of a word is difficult. English-speaking people change foreign words to make them sound more natural in English just as people who speak other languages change English words to make them sound more natural in their languages. Words from languages that are very different from English are often changed a great deal. *El Uqsor* in Arabic, for example, has become *Luxor* in English. *Detroit* comes from the French word for *strait—étroit*, because it is "at the strait"; that is, it is on the banks of a narrow river that connects two lakes. You would probably not guess the origin of *Detroit* from its spelling, and you certainly would not guess it from its pronunciation.

Some words do not change their spelling in English even though they change their pronunciation. *Paris* is spelled the same in French and English, for example, but it is pronounced differently.

People do not always agree on how to spell words from another language. Some people think Greek words and names should be spelled more nearly the way Greeks pronounce them instead of the way English-speaking people have traditionally spelled them, following Latin spelling. People disagree particularly on the spelling of Arabic and Chinese words and words from other languages that have alphabets very different from English. Even after scholars have agreed on standardized spellings, you can find different forms in older books. Older spellings sometimes kept symbols that English does not use: *cañon* (from Spanish) is now almost always spelled *canyon*. Most English-speaking people understand the first form, however.

Antecedent

An antecedent is the word a pronoun stands for. Some pronouns are limited and can stand for only nouns or noun-equivalents with certain qualities. (see **Reference of the pronoun**)

Antonyms

Antonyms are words with meanings that are opposite to each other, such as *large* and *small, hot* and *cold,* and *good* and *bad.* Antonyms are sometimes formed with negative prefixes. (see **Word formation, prefixes**) Opposite meanings can also be shown by using words such as *no, not,* and *none.* (see **Negation**)

Apostrophe, see **Punctuation, apostrophe**

Appositive

An appositive is a noun, pronoun, or noun clause that comes directly after another noun and gives more information about it. Set appositives off from the rest of the sentence by commas if they are not necessary to identify the noun that they follow. If they identify the noun that they follow, do not use commas to set them off from the rest of the sentence. (see **Essential and nonessential modifiers** and **Punctuation, comma**)

	noun	*appositive*	
His	brother	*John*	left yesterday.
That	dog, a large	*collie,*	barked at us.
Two	books, both	*encyclopedias,*	are missing.

noun   *appositive*
We cannot find either of the missing *books,* the *encyclopedias.*

If you use a pronoun as an appositive, use the subject or object form, depending on how the word the pronoun stands for (the antecedent) is used in the clause.

subject,   *appositive—antecedent*
antecedent   *is subject*
Only two *students* from our team, *Beverly* and *I,* have a chance to win the race.

appositive—
antecedent is
object of   *object of*
preposition   *preposition*
The news brought hope to the *family, my parents, my brothers,* and *me.*

appositive—
direct   *antecedent is*
object   *object*
Mr. Peterson gave the distance *runners—Paul, Henry,* and *me*—clear directions before the start of the race.

Argument

Argument is writing or speech that presents both sides of an issue, but writing that clearly shows which side the writer thinks is correct. The opinion the writer supports is presented in the thesis statement. (see **Thesis statement**) An argument can try to make you do something and/or it can try to make you believe something. The points in favor of the writer's own opinion are called *pro;* the points against the writer's own opinion are called *con.* Argument is sometimes called persuasion. Persuasion, however, sometimes means presenting just the points in favor of the writer's or speaker's own opinion without presenting opposing ideas. A formal argument must show both sides of the issue.

Many persuasive devices can be used to convince other people to agree. Some of these devices are fair, but others are unfair and deceive people.

In writing argument, do the following:

1. Put all the cons before the pros; or take up each division of the issue, con and then pro.
2. Be sure you have more and/or stronger pro points than con points.
3. Put your strongest pro argument last.

Articles

A and *an* are indefinite articles that can be used only before singular countable nouns; *the* can be used before uncountable (mass) nouns and before countable plural nouns. No article, often called the zero article, identifies certain indefinite meanings of nouns. Articles are determiners and come before the nouns they modify. Except with ordinals such as *the first, second, third,* or *the last,* articles do not come directly before pronouns. (see **Determiners**)

The Indefinite Article

A OR an

A or *an* comes before a singular countable noun. *A* comes before a consonant sound, but *an* comes before a vowel sound. Choose according to pronunciation, not spelling. (see **Consonants**)

a ball	*an* apple	*a* university
a hospital	*an* eagle	*an* honest man
a car	*an* office	*a* year

Use *a(n)*

1. before an unidentified singular countable noun that is one example of its class, but the number *one* is not being emphasized.

A black dog is standing in the road.
(The emphasis is not on the number.)

One black dog is standing in the road.
(The emphasis is on the number one.)

2. before an unidentified singular countable noun that is representative of its class, as in a definition.

A dog is a domestic animal.

3. before a predicate noun after *to be* if no other determiner is used.

Mrs. Seckson *is a* good friend.
Man O'War *was a* famous racehorse.

4. with uncountable nouns to mean *a kind of*, or with *kind of*, or *certain*.

This man has *an honesty* that we all appreciate.
A greater unity is needed.
Literature of other countries gives us *an insight* into other cultures.

5. before *few* and *little* to mean *some but not many* (see **Confusing choices, few, a few**) Plural forms for *a(n)* are the zero article and *some*. (see below, pp. 52, 54)

The

The can be used with all nouns. Use *the* to identify a noun that shows

1. reference backward to a noun already mentioned.

A dog has been barking all day and here is *the* dog now, standing outside the gate.

2. reference forward to an identification soon to be made, often by modifiers following the noun.

The man *at the door* wants to speak to you.
The dog *that has been barking* all day has finally stopped barking.
Every student should know something about *the* history *of his own country*.

Use *the* before superlatives and before ordinal numbers. Put additional phrase modifiers after the noun.

This is *the best* cake *I have ever eaten*.
China has *the largest* population *of all countries in the world*.
Mr. Everest is *the highest* mountain *in the world*.
Charles Lindbergh was *the first* person *to fly the Atlantic alone*.

NOTE: Ordinal numbers used alone may have the zero article.

> She was first in her class.
> Our team is third in the standings.

3. context known to both writer and reader.

> Here comes *the* teacher. (one teacher known to the class)
> Turn on *the* light in *the* kitchen. (only one light in one kitchen)
> Have you been to *the* mountains recently? (mountains nearby that are known to everyone)
> They prefer to live in *the city*. (The reader, it is assumed, understands the difference between living in the country or suburbs and living in the city.)

4. identification of a class, especially in a generalization.

Followed by a noun, often singular:

> *The* child is the hope of the future.
> *The* nuclear threat is frightening.

Followed by an adjective (see **Adjectives, the + adjective**):

> *The* elderly are often lonely.
> *The* handicapped need access to public buildings.

5. the beginning of a phrase containing an appositive.

> This is my friend, *the* one I was telling you about.
> Do this experiment first, *the* experiment on page 29.

THE ZERO ARTICLE

Use the zero article (absence of an article)
  1. to refer to all members of a class.

> *Dogs* are domestic animals. (all dogs)
> Mary likes *dogs*. (all dogs)
> *Man* proposes; God disposes. (*man* in the sense of all human beings)

2. to distinguish one class from another.

> *Dogs*, not *squirrels*, are domestic animals.
> Mary likes *dogs*, not cats.
> *Men*, not *women*, are boxers.

3. to refer to an indefinite number but not necessarily to all members of a class.

> *Leaves* are beginning to fall. (many)
> *Engineers* make good salaries. (many)
> The edge of the field was marked by *trees*.

4. with plural nouns after *be*.

Most of my friends are *students*.
His sisters are *teachers*.

5. with institutions and practices felt to be unique.

School begins Monday. (a particular Monday)
Breakfast will be late tomorrow. (there will be only one breakfast tomorrow)
People are angry with *Congress*. (there is only one Congress in the country)

but

People are angry with *the* state legislature. (one of many)
People are angry with *the* city council. (one of many)

6. with set phrases, usually pairs, such as

man and wife
father and son
brother and sister
lock and key
sun, moon, and stars
heaven and hell
wind and rain
snow and sleet
go (come) home

7. with set prepositional phrases, such as

at war	in danger	on guard
at peace	in need	on purpose
at ease	in tears	on fire
at rest	in reply	on sale
at sea	in love	on vacation
at lunch	in difficulty	on time
		on duty
		on land (and sea)

by accident	out of control
by design	out of danger
by heart	out of date
by surprise	out of doors
by chance	out of order
by mistake	out of stock
by bus, plane, car	out of turn

You can find set phrases in dictionaries. Look the object word up if you are not sure of its use: *war, peace, danger,* and so on. Dictionaries written for nonnative speakers give more information about set phrases than other dictionaries do.

8. with nouns used in headlines in newspapers, captions in books, signs, labels, and the like.

PRISONER FREED
ENTRANCE TO PARKING
BEWARE OF DOG

Some

Use *some* for an indefinite amount with uncountable nouns.

He wants *some rice.*
She is taking *some instruction* in music now.
Mrs. Johnson gave us *some* good *advice.*
You can find *some information* about television shows in today's newspaper.

Any

Use *any* in place of *some* in questions and negatives. (see **Confusing choices, any, some, Negation** and **Questions**)

He doesn't want *any* rice.
She isn't taking *any* instruction in music now.
Mrs. Johnson didn't give us *any* good advice.
You cannot find *any* information about television shows in today's newspaper.

NOTE: *Any* may be used in the sense of "it doesn't matter which."

Any of the suits on this rack will fit you.
He has enough money to buy *any* car he wants.
Any doctor can tell you what long hours he works.

ARTICLES WITH PROPER NOUNS

Do not use an article with
    1. common nouns used as terms of address and therefore capitalized.

Thank you, *Mother.*
The patient is ready, *Doctor.*

    2. other proper nouns, except as noted below.

Use *a(n)*
    1. when using a proper noun to indicate the characteristics of the person named.

He is *a Hercules.* (very strong)
She is *a Florence Nightingale.* (a kind nurse)

2. to mean "a certain person whose name is."

A *Dr. Jones* called this morning.
A *Mr. Johnson* is looking for you.

Use *the*
   1. for a family name in the plural.

   The Hendersons have moved.
   The Smiths came this evening.

NOTE: Do not use an apostrophe in plural family names that are not possessive.

   2. to distinguish two people who have the same name.

   The *George Brown* who teaches here is not the *George Brown* you knew in college.

   3. when the article is accepted as part of a geographical name.

COUNTRIES:	the Netherlands	the United States or the U.S.
	the Philippines	the Soviet Union or the U.S.S.R.
SEAS AND OCEANS:	the Black Sea	the Pacific (Ocean)
	the Red Sea	the Atlantic (Ocean)
	the Indian Ocean	the Baltic (Sea)
	the North Sea	the Mediterranean (Sea)

Ocean or *Sea* is always part of the name in the list on the left, but you may leave it out in the list on the right. Do not use *the* with names of individual lakes, but *the Great Lakes* means collectively Lake Superior, Lake Huron, Lake Michigan, Lake Erie, and Lake Ontario.

RIVERS:	the Amazon	the Mississippi
	the Ganges	the Nile
MOUNTAIN RANGES:	the Alps	
	the Andes	
	the Rockies or the Rocky Mountains	
	the Himalayas or the Himalaya Mountains	

Most individual peaks do not have *the* in their name, but *the Matterhorn* does.

   4. when the article is accepted as part of any kind of proper name.

SHIPS:	the *Arizona*	the *Grof Spee*
	the *Queen Elizabeth* II	the *Norway*
NEWSPAPERS:	*The Times*	*The Times of India*
	The New York Times	but *Time* (magazine)

NOTE: Names of ships and newspapers are printed in italics. Show this in writing or typing by underlining.

HOTELS:	The Hilton The Cloisters	The Sheraton The Marriott
COLLEGES AND UNIVERSITIES:	the University of Michigan the University of Southern California	

When the identifying name of a college or university is first, do not use *the*.

Harvard University
Indiana University
Concordia College

OTHER ORGANIZATIONS AND INSTITUTIONS:	the United Nations the National Gallery	the Museum of Natural History the Rose Bowl

but

Central Park Soldiers' Field	Carnegie Hall Memorial Stadium

You cannot tell about many proper names except by learning the usage in each case: for example, the Grand Canyon, but Grand Coulee Dam. (For articles with adjectives, see **Adjectives, the + adjective.**)

Aspect

Aspect is a term some grammarians use to describe different ways of thinking about action and time. English tenses have the following aspects:

1. A perfect aspect, which makes a statement about an act being completed or not completed (commonly called the perfect tenses).

2. A continuous/progressive aspect, which makes a statement about the progression or continuation of an act (commonly called the continuous/progressive tenses).

> *past tense,*
> *perfect aspect,*
> *or past perfect*
> *tense*

Charles *had drunk* his coffee this morning (an action completed in the past) when the phone *rang*. (past tense, a single action that happened after the first action—*had drunk*—was completed)

> *past tense,*
> *progressive/continuous*
> *aspect, or past*
> *progressive/continuous*
> *tense*

Charles *was drinking* his coffee this morning (an action going on, not completed, in the past) when the phone *rang*. (past tense, an interruption of an uncompleted action)

Perfect and continuous/progressive verb forms are used in the present, past, and future, and can be combined. A past perfect continuous/progressive form is possible, for example:

> He *had been drinking* his coffee when the phone *began* to ring. (emphasis on the duration of *had been drinking*)

(For detailed discussion of perfect and continuous/progressive forms, see **Tenses.**)

Auxiliary Verbs

The auxiliary verbs combine with other verbs to make all the tenses except the present and the past. *Be, have,* and *do* operate in special ways in clauses in the same ways that modals operate. (see **Operators**)

Most forms of the auxiliaries can be contracted with a noun or pronoun (he's) and/or with *not* (he isn't). (see **Contractions**)

Be (am, is, are, was, were) may be the main verb in the clause, or as an auxiliary it may combine with the present or past participle of another verb.

Have

Have may also be the main verb in the clause or as an auxiliary it may be part of a verb phrase in which a past participle must be used. In British usage, *have* as a main verb is usually an operator, but in American usage *have* requires *do* as an operator when *have* is the main verb.

Have AS MAIN VERB

QUESTIONS AND SHORT ANSWERS:	He *has* a dog. *Does* he *have* a dog? Yes, he *does*. What *does* he have?
NEGATIVES WITH CONTRACTION AND TAG QUESTION:	He *doesn't have* a dog, *does* he?
AFTER *so:*	He *has* a dog. and so *does* she.
AFTER *but:*	He *has* a dog. but she *does* not.

Do

Do may be the main verb in the clause or it may be the auxiliary or it may be both. If *do* is the main verb, use *do* as the operator with it when you need one.

Do AS MAIN VERB

QUESTION AND
SHORT ANSWER: He *does* many things in his spare time. *Did* he *do* that? Yes, he *did*.

WH QUESTION: What *does* he *do?*

NEGATIVE WITH
CONTRACTION AND
TAG QUESTION: He *doesn't do* that often, *does* he?

AFTER *so:*   He *does* many things and *so does* she.

AFTER *but:*   He *does* his work well, but she *does* not.

Always use the simple present (bare infinitive) form of the main verb after any form of *do*.

Do AS OPERATOR
She *collects* stamps.

QUESTION AND
SHORT ANSWER: *Does* she *collect* stamps? Yes, she *does*.

WH QUESTION: What *does* she *collect?*

NEGATIVE WITH
CONTRACTION AND
TAG QUESTION: She *doesn't collect* stamps, *does* she?

AFTER *so:*   She *collects* stamps, and so *does* her sister.

OTHER TENSES

PAST (WITH *did*):   She *collected* stamps.
Did she *collect* stamps?
What *did* she *collect?*
She *didn't collect* stamps, *did* she?
She *collected* stamps, and so *did* her sister.

FUTURE (WITH
will):   She will *collect* stamps.
Will she *collect* stamps?
What *will* she *collect?*
She *will* not *collect* stamps, *will* she?
She *will collect* stamps, and so *will* her sister.

B

Be

Be is the most irregular verb in English. Since it is used more than any other verb, both as the main verb in a clause and as an auxiliary in forming tenses and the passive voice, you must learn all of its parts and how to use them.

Principal Parts of Be

INFINITIVE	PRESENT SINGULAR	PAST SINGULAR	PAST PARTICIPLE	PRESENT PARTICIPLE
(to) *be*	I *am* happy.	I *was* happy.	*been*	*being*
	You *are* happy.	You *were* happy.		
	He/she/it *is* happy.	He/she/it *was* happy.		
	PLURAL	**PLURAL**		
	We/you/they *are* happy.	We/you/they *were* happy.		

Be usually has a predicate complement following it, such as the words *happy* (adjective) in these examples, or a word, phrase, or clause showing place.

Be *in Other Tenses*

PRESENT PERFECT, SINGULAR

I *have been* happy.
You *have been* happy.
He/she/it *has been* happy.

PLURAL

We/you/they *have been* happy.

PAST PERFECT, SINGULAR

I *had been* happy.
You *had been* happy.
He/she/it *had been* happy.

PLURAL

We/you/they *had been* happy.

FUTURE, SINGULAR
I *will* (shall) *be* happy.
You *will* (shall) *be* happy.
He/she/it *will* (shall) *be* happy.

PLURAL
We/you/they *will* (shall) *be* happy.

FUTURE PERFECT, SINGULAR
I *will* (shall) *have been* happy.
You *will* (shall) *have been* happy.
He/she/it *will* (shall) *have been* happy.

PLURAL
We/you/they *will* (shall) *be* happy.

NOTE: The distinction between *shall* and *will* for emphasis (I/we *shall* and you/he/she/it/they *will* in nonemphatic use, but you/he/she/it/they *shall* in emphatic use) is not generally observed in the United States. *Will* and *shall* are often but not always interchangeable. (see **Modals**)

Be as a main verb is not usually used in a continuous (progressive) tense unless it is used in the sense of "behaving." Form the continuous tenses with the same forms of *be* you use when it is a main verb + *being.*

PRESENT CONTINUOUS, SINGULAR
I *am being* difficult.

You *are being* difficult.
He/she/it *is being* difficult.

PLURAL
We/you/they *are being* difficult.

PAST CONTINUOUS, SINGULAR
I *was being* difficult. (behaving in a difficult manner)
You *were being* difficult.
He/she/it *was being* difficult.

PLURAL
We/you/they *were being* difficult.

Be *as an Auxiliary Verb*

Use the correct form of *be* in verb phrases to make all tenses except the simple present, past, and future. (see **Tense**) Use forms of *be* with the past participle of the main verb to make the passive voice. (see **Voice**)

PRESENT PASSIVE, SINGULAR
I *am* surprised.
You *are* surprised.

PLURAL
We/you/they *are* surprised.

PAST PASSIVE, SINGULAR
I *was* surprised.
You *were* surprised.

PLURAL
We/you/they *were* surprised.

FUTURE PASSIVE, SINGULAR
I/you/he/she/it will *be* surprised.

PLURAL
We/you/they will *be* surprised.

Meanings of Be *as a Main Verb*

1. As a linking verb, *be* joins a subject to a predicate adjective that describes the subject or to a predicate noun that restates the subject **or** gives additional information about it. (see **Predicate complements**)

        predicate
subject   *noun*
Martha is a student.

        predicate
        adjective
Alfred is   tall.

A pronoun that follows *be* should be in the nominative case (see **Case**)

        predicate
subject   *nominative*
   It   is I (he, she we, they)

Many people use *it is me/him/her/them,* however, especially in speech, or avoid the construction.

2. Without a complement, *be* can mean to *exist.*

I think; therefore, I *am.* (exist)

3. *Be* can mean to *live, stay,* or *arrive* in a specific place. In this meaning it is usually followed by an adverb.

He *is* here. (single-word adverb)
He *is* in Chicago. (prepositional phrase)
They *are* at work. (prepositional phrase)

4. With the infinitive of another verb, *be* has a future meaning of intention, obligation, or permission.

She *is to finish* her work before she leaves.
Charles *is* not *to go* out tomorrow.

5. *Be* followed by *to* can mean *to go to* or *to visit.*

We have *been to* Japan several times.
Has he *been to* the park today?

6. Use *be* to show age. Never use *have.*

The child *is* ten years old.
How old *are* these children?
Sarah *will be* twenty-one next Monday.

7. Never leave out *be* when it is the main verb in the clause. Although in many other languages you can leave out *be,* in English you must have a subject and finite verb form to have a complete sentence. (*You* can be understood in commands; see **Commands**)

Where *are* the books? The books *are* on the table.
What *is* this? This *is* a pine tree.

Bracket, see Punctuation, bracket

Capitalization _____

1. Use a capital letter to begin every sentence. Do not use a figure to begin a sentence, but write the figure in words or put it in a different place in the sentence.

INCORRECT: 7 people came.

CORRECT: Seven people came.

INCORRECT: $10,000 is missing.

CORRECT: Ten thousand dollars is missing.

INCORRECT: 60 percent of all traffic accidents involve drivers who have been drinking.

CORRECT: Sixty percent of all traffic accidents involve drivers who have been drinking.

or

Drivers who have been drinking are involved in 60 percent of all accidents.

2. Use a capital letter to begin a direct quotation that begins in the middle of the sentence as well as one that starts at the beginning of the sentence. (see **Direct speech**)

BEGINNING: "Come as quickly as you can," he said.

MIDDLE: He said, "Come as quickly as you can."
They asked, "Where can we get something to eat?"
The bus driver said, "You must have exact change."

If the words that show who is speaking (dialogue guide) come in the middle of a sentence of the direct quotation, do not put a capital letter at the beginning of the part of the direct quotation that continues the sentence.

CONTINUING   "Come," he said, "*as* quickly as you can."

QUOTATION: "Where," they asked, "*can* we get something to eat?"

                    "I cannot make change," the bus driver said; "*you* must have exact change."

Put a capital letter at the beginning of the continuing quotation if it is a new sentence.

"Come," he said. "We can go now."
"Where can we get something to eat?" they asked. "We are hungry."
"I cannot make change," the bus driver said. "You must have exact change."

Do not use a capital letter to begin an indirect quotation. (In an indirect quotation, the speakers words are reported but not repeated exactly; see **Reported speech**)

He told us *to* come as quickly as possible.
They asked *where* they could get something to eat.
The bus driver said *that* he could not make exact change.

3. Capitalize the pronoun *I* but not *me, my, myself,* or *mine.*

The book *I* found in *my* desk is not *mine.*

4. Capitalize proper names and words formed from proper names. Capitalize people and their titles. Use periods after titles that are abbreviations. Do not use periods after titles that are not abbreviations. Use commas between names and titles that follow names. (see **Abbreviations**)

Dr. Marian Harvey
    or
Marian Harvey, M.D.
    or
Marian Harvey, Ph.D.

Mr. John Smith or John Smith, M.A.
Mrs. Arthur Moore
Ms. Jane Brown
Miss Anne Martin (Note: no period after *Miss*)
Sir Henry Thornton
Governor Johnston
Aunt Mary and Uncle George
Professor Jones
Major Cummings
Alexander the Great (Note: *the* is not capitalized)
the Elizabethan Age
a Christian civilization
Buddhist philosophy

Capitalize titles when they refer to specific people, but not when they refer to one person in a larger class.

> He is a *p*rofessor at the university. (one of many professors)
> She is a *m*ajor in the army. (one of many majors in the army)

Capitalize titles of relationship when a specific person is being spoken to or is referred to by title.

> Aren't you listening, *M*other?
> Has *F*ather come home yet?

Do not capitalize titles of relationship when a personal pronoun comes before them.

> Have you seen *my* aunt?
> The man you spoke to is *his* uncle.
> I wrote a letter to *my* mother yesterday.

Capitalize geographical names and words formed from them.

Paris, France	French culture
Bombay, India	Indian food
Accra, Ghana	Afro-Americans
Montreal, Canada	Canadian students
Asia	Asian studies
the United States	the U.S. government
the United Kingdom	British traditions

NOTE: *The* is rarely capitalized before geographical names, but capitalize it in The Hague.

Capitalize titles of books, magazines, articles, short stories, compositions, plays, movies, television shows, and music, but do not capitalize articles, conjunctions, or prepositions unless they are the first word of the title. For rules about underlining (italics) and quotation marks, see **Titles.**

> *The Advanced Learner's Dictionary* (a book)
> *A Dictionary of Musical Terms* (a book)
> "A New Look at Old Age" (an article)
> "Learning by Doing" (an article)
> "Ten Minutes to Doomsday" (an article)
> *The Marriage of Figaro* (an opera)
> *The New York Times* (a newspaper)
> *Time* (a magazine)

Capitalize names of particular college courses but not the name of the discipline unless it is a language.

> He is taking *H*istory 101
> Many colleges require students to take courses in American literature.

American is capitalized because it comes from *America,* but *literature* is not capitalized because it is not the name of a specific course.

> She is writing a paper for her *world history* course.
> Arthur is taking Chemistry III this quarter.
> Have you registered for Math 205?

Capitalize names of the deity, religions, and religious bodies.

> Christian/Christianity   the First Baptist Church
> Jewish/Judaism   Mormon
> Islamic/Islam   St. John's Lutheran Church
> Hindu/Hinduism   Protestant
> God (but *gods* if plural)   Allah

Capitalize dates, months, days of the week, holidays, historic periods, and events.

> January, February, and so on   Easter
> Sunday, Monday, and so on   Passover
> New Year's Day   the Middle Ages
> Thanksgiving   the Civil War

Do not capitalize names of the seasons: spring, summer, autumn, fall, winter.

Capitalize names of the planets, stars, and constellations.

> Jupiter   Venus   Gemini
> Mars   Saturn   Orion
> Sirius   the Pleiades   Mercury

Do not capitalize earth, moon, or sun.

5. Capitalize the first letter of a line of poetry.

> When lilacs last in the dooryard bloom'd,
> And the great star early droop'd in the western sky in the night,
> I mourn'd, and yet shall mourn with ever-returning spring.
> *Walt Whitman*

6. Capitalize the first word of every point of an outline, a list, or the legend (explanation of the symbols) of a map.

Products of North America

I. Plant products
    A. Food
        1. Grain
        2. Vegetables
        3. Fruit
    B. Nonfood
        1. Lumber
        2. Cotton
        3. Tobacco

  II. Mineral products
   A. Metals
    1. Iron
    2. Copper
    3. Silver
    4. Gold
   B. Fuels
    1. Petroleum
    2. Coal

  7. Capitalize *north, south, east,* and *west* and compound words made from them when they refer to recognized specific regions or are part of a proper name. Do not capitalize *north, south, east,* and *west* and compound words made from them when they mean directions.

> They are attending school in the South.
> The *N*ortheast has severe storm warnings tonight.
> Miss Collins is an expert on the *M*iddle *E*ast.
> Mr. and Mrs. Adams go *s*outh every winter to avoid the cold weather.
> Canada is *n*orth of the United States and Mexico is *s*outh of it.
> North Dakota and South Dakota are *w*est of Minnesota.
> The copying machines are along the *n*orth wall of the library.
> When you come to the next corner, turn left and drive *e*ast for two miles.

NOTE: Put *north* and *south* first in compound single words: *northeast, northwest, southeast,* and *southwest.* Compass terms may have two words such as *east by northeast.*

> The wind is out of the *northeast.*
> Many people like the dry climate of the *Southwest.*

  8. Treatment of prefixes with proper names is not consistent. Look in a dictionary to be sure when to use capital letters and hyphens.

antichrist	anti-Semite
transatlantic	post-World War II
subarctic	Postimpressionism
Precambrian	post-Pleistocene
pre-Christian	pro-American
Pre-Raphaelite	premedical
pre-Socratic	pre-engineering

Case _____

  Case means the differences between words that are the subjects of a clause (nominative case), words that are objects (objective case), and words that show possession or similar relationships (possessive or genitive case).

Nouns

In modern English nouns have a different form for the possessive case, but they show no difference between the subject and object forms. Make the possessive of a noun by adding -*'s* to a noun that does not already end in -*s*, and by adding only an apostrophe to a noun that already ends in -*s*. (see **Punctuation, apostrophe**)

COMMON (SUBJECT AND OBJECT) FORM	POSSESSIVE FORM
Gerald	Gerald's cat (singular)
Sue	Sue's book (singular)
The men	The men's pay (plural)
The girls	The girls' coats (plural)
	The boys' activities (plural)

Pronouns

Personal pronouns, compound indefinite pronouns (*everyone, somebody,* and so forth) and the relative pronoun *who* change according to their case. (See **Pronouns** for complete tables.)

NOMINATIVE	OBJECTIVE	POSSESSIVE
I	me	my, mine
who	whom	whose
somebody	somebody	somebody's

NOTE: Although many people use *who* for both subject and object forms in spoken English, make the correct distinction between *who* and *whom* in formal writing. Look at each clause to see how the relative pronoun is used in order to decide which form to use. Do not let words that come between the relative pronoun and the rest of its own clause confuse you.

subject   *verb*

He asked us *who* we thought *would win.*

Who is the subject of the dependent clause in the sentence and *would win* is the verb. *We thought* are words that come between the subject and verb and do not change the case of *who*.

Put *he/him, she/her,* or *they/them* in place of *who/whom,* as in the following example.

subject   *verb*

 Who do you suppose *is* the winner?
(*He/she* is the winner.)

object   *subject verb*

This is the girl *whom* we think the *judges chose* to be first. (The judges chose *her.*)

These are the men *who* their employer thinks *are* good workers. (*They* are good workers.)

Do not let a preposition before a relative pronoun make you think that the relative pronoun should always be *whom*. Look at the clause to see whether *who* is the subject or object in its own clause.

<pre>
               preposition subject   verb
The decision   about   who   can register for the course will be made
</pre>
tomorrow.

The entire dependent clause in the sentence above is *who can register for the course*. The entire clause is the object of the preposition about *of*. *Who* is the subject in its own clause. Therefore you must use the subject form, *who*.

<pre>
               preposition direct object subject verb
The decision   about   whom   we   ask will be made tomorrow.
</pre>

Whom is the direct object in its own clause. You must use the object form, *whom*.

<pre>
                                        preposition subject verb
This book company will send a catalogue   to   whoever asks for
</pre>
one.

The entire clause *whoever asks for one* is the object of the preposition *to*. You must use the subject form, *whoever*. *Whoever* is the subject in its own clause.

Cause and Effect

English has many constructions to express cause and effect (sometimes called cause and result). To add variety and exactness to your writing, learn to use several of them correctly. You need to understand all of them.

Clauses

It was raining.   I opened my umbrella.

When you read these two statements you know that they are probably related to each other. You must show the reader exactly how they are related. Your first idea will probably put the effect (result) first.

EFFECT (RESULT)   CAUSE
I opened my umbrella   *because* it was raining.

The normal pattern of the English sentence puts the *because* clause (the dependent clause) after the independent clause. For sentence variety you can invert the order and put the *because* clause first:

CAUSE	EFFECT (RESULT)
Because it was raining,	I opened my umbrella.

When you put a dependent clause at the beginning of the sentence, put a comma after the dependent clause since you have now changed the normal order of the sentence. Similar sentences with an independent clause followed by a dependent use *since* and *as*. (see **Clauses**)

EFFECT (RESULT)	CAUSE
I opened my umbrella	*since* it was raining.
	as it was raining.

NOTE: Although you can put *for* in place of *since*, and *as* in the two sentences above, *for* cannot be used in a sentence that you invert. (see below, p. 70)

Inverted

CAUSE	EFFECT (RESULT)
Since it was raining,	I opened by umbrella.
As it was raining,	

Phrases

You can show cause and effect with prepositional phrases. They can come at the end of the sentence or at the beginning. Put a comma after a prepositional phrase at the beginning of the sentence if it has four words or more. (see **Punctuation, comma**)

EFFECT (RESULT)	CAUSE
I opened my umbrella	*because of* the rain.
	on account of the rain.
	in order to protect myself from the rain.

Inverted:

Because of the rain,	
On account of the rain,	I opened my umbrella.
In order to protect myself from the rain,	

BE CAREFUL: Do not confuse *because* and *because of*. You must put a subject and verb after *because*. You must put a noun or another word that can replace a noun after *because of*, but you must not put a finite verb after *because of*. (see **Finite verb**)

PREPOSITIONAL PHRASES:	*preposition*	*object of preposition*
	Because of the wet	*weather,* I carried an umbrella.
	Because of	a *report* of the storm, I carried an umbrella.
	Because of	*hearing* a report of the storm, I carried an umbrella.

	subject	*verb*	
CLAUSES:	*Because*	*I*	*heard* a report of the

storm, I carried an umbrella.

Because the rain was starting, I carried an umbrella.

Some sentence patterns using *-ing* forms are very formal. You are likely to see and use them in the natural and social sciences:

CAUSE	RESULT
The effect of the rain was	a *lowering* of the temperature.
The result of the rain was	

(Note that this construction emphasizes that cause and effect are impersonal results of natural forces.)

The rain was *the cause of* my opening my umbrella.
The rain *resulted in*   my opening my umbrella.
It rained, *resulting in*   my opening my umbrella.
It rained, *causing* me *to* open my umbrella.

An implied cause/result can be expressed by an *-ing* absolute form. (see **Absolutes**)

The rain *starting* to become heavier, I opened my umbrella.
The rain *beginning,* I opened my umbrella.

Two Independent Clauses (Compound Sentences)

So and *for* can join two independent clauses. If the clause showing cause comes first, put *so* between the clauses. If the clauses showing effect (result) comes first, put *for* between the clauses. You cannot invert these constructions.

CAUSE	EFFECT (RESULT)
It was raining,	*so* I opened my umbrella.
EFFECT (RESULT)	CAUSE
I opened my umbrella,	*for* it was raining.
CAUSE	EFFECT (RESULT)
There was a flood,	*so* I had to move out of my house.
EFFECT (RESULT)	CAUSE
I had to move out of my house,	*for* there was a flood.

Put a comma before *for* and *so* when they are used as coordinating conjunctions to join two independent clauses. Both words can be used in other ways. (see **Coordinating conjunctions, Prepositions,** and **So**)

More Formal Construction

Some other compound sentences are more formal in style. They cannot be inverted. In the sentences below, two independent clauses are joined by adverbs. You must put a semicolon between independent clauses joined by adverbs. (These adverbs are sometimes called conjunctive adverbs.)

CAUSE	EFFECT (RESULT)
	therefore, I opened my umbrella.
It began to rain;	*as a result,* I opened my umbrella.
	consequently, I opened my umbrella.

Notice some of the word combinations used in writing about cause and result. You must get these right:

Too much rain *resulted in* a flood. It rained too much, *resulting in* a flood.

My move $\begin{cases} \textit{was a result of} \\ \textit{resulted from} \end{cases}$ the flood.

I was *forced to* move $\begin{cases} \text{by the flood.} \\ \text{because of the flood.} \end{cases}$

The flood *forced me to* move.
The flood *caused me to* move.

NOTE: *Force* and *cause* used in the active voice must be followed by objects, usually personal objects (personal pronouns or proper names). (see also **Confusing choices, result from, result in**)

Make and *have* can have causative meanings. Both have several constructions.

Use *make* with an adjective in the pattern required by the adjective. (see **Adjectives, constructions that follow the verb**)

The storm *made* him *afraid to* go.
The storm *made* him *afraid of going.*
The storm *made* him *afraid that he would* get wet.

Make can be followed by an adjective by itself.

The storm *made* him *afraid.*
The storm *made* him *late.*

Use *make* with an object followed by a bare infinitive.

The storm *made him leave* early.
The dean *made* the *students wait* outside.

Use *have* with an adjective (see **Adjectives, constructions that follow the verb**) or with a past participle.

John *had* his hair *trimmed.*
We *have* just *had* a new house *built.*

Use *have* with an object followed by a bare infinitive.

> Emma *had everyone come* to her party.
> Paul *has Stephanie buy* the tickets.

Use *have* with an object followed by an *-ing* form.

> Emma *had everyone coming* to her party.
> Paul *has Stephanie buying* the tickets.

Double comparatives show cause and effect. (see **Adjectives, comparison**)

> The *more* it storms, the *more* fearful he is.

Many verbs have a causative idea in them. These verbs are often closely connected with or identical to adjectives.

VERB		ADJECTIVE
(to) anger	means	to make angry
clean	means	to make clean
curl	means	to make curly
delay	means	to make late
ease	means	to make easy
dirty	means	to make dirty
empty	means	to make empty
fill	means	to make full
quiet	means	to make quiet
wet	means	to make wet

A few verbs have intransitive forms (forms that do not take direct objects) that are similar in form to transitive forms that are causative. (The verbs do not correspond in all their meanings.)

INTRANSITIVE	TRANSITIVE (CAUSATIVE)
fall, fell, fallen, falling	fell, felled, felled, felling
The tree *fell* over.	The lumberjack *felled* the tree.

In some pairs of verbs that are often confused, the transitive form can be considered a causative in some meanings.

INTRANSITIVE	TRANSITIVE (CAUSATIVE)
lie, lay, lain, lying	lay, laid, laid, laying
The books *are lying* on the table.	*Lay* the books on the table. (cause them to lie)
rise, rose, risen, rising	raise, raised, raised, raising
The river *rose* two feet last night.	The heavy rains *raised* the level of the river two feet last night. (caused it to rise)
shine, shone, shone, shining	shine, shined, shined
After he polished his shoes, the leather *shone*.	He *shined* his shoes. (caused them to shine)

sit, sat, set, sitting
The cake *is sitting* on the table.

set, set, set, setting
Set the cake on the table. (cause it to sit)

Some causative verbs are formed with the prefix *en-*.

act	becomes	enact
camp	becomes	encamp
code	becomes	encode
danger	becomes	endanger
dear	becomes	endear

Some causative verbs are formed with endings (suffixes).

in *-en*

awak*en*	rip*en*
deaf*en*	sadd*en*
light*en*	straight*en*
loos*en*	wid*en*

NOTE: *En*light*en* has *en* both as a prefix and as an ending.

in *-ify*

ampl*ify*	just*ify*
beaut*ify*	lique*fy* (note spelling)
de*ify*	pur*ify*
dign*ify*	sanct*ify*
divers*ify*	sat*isfy*
fort*ify*	simpl*ify*

in *-ize*

central*ize*	mechan*ize*
equal*ize*	modern*ize*
immun*ize*	popular*ize*
international*ize*	symbol*ize*
italic*ize*	vapor*ize*
legal*ize*	visual*ize*
local*ize*	

Chronological Order _____

Chronological order is the order of time. It is putting events in the order in which they happened, beginning with the event that happened earliest and continuing to the event that happened last.

Chronological order in the future begins with present time or with an imagined event at some time in the future and goes in imagination farther and farther into the future.

Reverse chronological order moves backward in time, beginning with the present or with the event nearest the present, then the event before that, and finally ending with the event farthest back from the present in time.

Use a combination of tense and time words to make chronology clear to your reader.

Tense

Use the past tense for writing normal and reverse chronological order. To show that an event happened before another event in the past, use the past perfect tense.

past
Father punish*ed* Wayne yesterday.

past   *past perfect*
Father punish*ed* Wayne yesterday because he *had thrown* a rock through Mrs. Smith's front window *the day before.*

Terms Used with Chronological Order

In addition to the usual words that express time periods such as *second, minute, hour, day, month,* and *year;* the words *decade* and *century* are often used with ordinal numbers.

the fifth day of May (May 5)
the fifth decade of this century (1940–1950)
The fifth century (A.D. 400–499/499–400 B.C.)

Periods of time are often indicated by the article and a date followed by *'s.* Some styles add the *-s* without an apostrophe.

the 1940's—the decade from 1940 to 1949
the 1500's—the century from 1500 to 1599
the change from one century to another—from 1799 to 1800

Time words that introduce dependent clauses:

when, before, after, while, since

Time words that are often interrupters:

now	later	simultaneously
nowadays	earlier	previously
next	formerly	subsequently
then	concurrently	first

Additional time words and phrases:

previous, previous to, previously
early
at the same time as
every (year, month, day, etc.)
every other (means skipping every second day, week, month, etc.)

Time words that are prepositions:

in (the first half of the century)	during (1950)
at (the beginning of the century)	before (1950)
prior to (1950)	after (1950)
since (1950)	previous to (1950)
between (1950 and 1960)	

Since means from a stated time up to the present. It is usually used with the present perfect tense. *After* can be used with the past or past perfect tense.

> *After* World War II many colonies of the European countries *became* independent. *Since* then, these countries *have* formed their own governments.

Classification _____

Classification is organizing things into groups according to the ways they are alike and sometimes according to the ways they are different. You can often classify the same information in more than one way. Educational institutions in the United States, for example, could be classified according to different features.

level of education:	preschool, elementary, secondary, and postsecondary
financial support:	public or private
control:	government and private, and private into secular and religious
purpose:	practical, liberal, technical, professional
age of students:	children, adolescents, adults

Choose the method of classification that helps you develop your thesis statement or the idea you want to explain.

Classification often uses the language of comparison (see **Comparison and contrast**)

ADJECTIVES	NOUNS	VERBS
major	classes	divide into
important	categories	fall into
less important	kinds	classifies as/into
unimportant	types	group (something)
main	divisions	into
primary	classifications	put into
secondary	aspects	
significant	qualities	
	characteristics	
	parts	

Clauses _____

A clause is a group of words that has a subject-verb combination in it. The verb must be a main or finite verb form. The *-ing* or the infinitive forms cannot be the main verb.

INCORRECT:	The girl *to run* down the street (fragment)
INCORRECT:	The girl *running* down the street. (fragment)
CORRECT:	The girl *is running* down the street.
	The girl *runs* down the street.

Embedded clause is a term sometimes used for subordinate parts of the sentence that do not always have subject-main verb combinations. (see **Subordinating and reducing**) Here, however, *clause* means a group of words that has a subject and a main verb.

Independent clauses

Independent clauses (also called main clauses) can be punctuated as separate sentences. They may be long or short. Each independent or main clause has one subject-verb combination in it.

> Running down the street chasing the bus to school, *Greg shouted* loudly after it to stop and pick him up.

There is only one subject-main verb combination in the sentence above: *Greg shouted.* Other words in this sentence that are verb forms are *running, chasing,* and *to stop* and *pick up.* None of these forms can be the main verb in the sentence, however. (see **Finite verbs**)

INDEPENDENT CLAUSE:	*Greg ran* down the street.
INDEPENDENT CLAUSE:	*Greg chased* the bus down the street.
INDEPENDENT CLAUSE:	*Greg shouted* at the bus driver to stop for him.
INDEPENDENT CLAUSE:	*Greg will be* late to work.
INDEPENDENT CLAUSE:	The next *bus will stop* to pick Greg up.

The sentences above are independent clauses. They have a subject and a verb. They do not have a subordinating conjunction or relative pronoun that would make them dependent.

Dependent Clauses

Dependent clauses (also called subordinate clauses) cannot be punctuated as complete sentences except in direct quotations in some transitional uses.

1. A dependent clause must be attached to an independent clause.

More than one dependent clause can be attached to the same independent clause.

       dependent clause   *independent*
                                                  clause
When the alarm *clock rang,*   the *boy saw*

       dependent clause
that *it was* time to get up.

A dependent clause may come in the middle of an independent clause.

      independent
        clause
The boy got up.

      dependent clause
The boy *who was sleeping* got up.

2. A dependent clause may be marked or unmarked. If it is marked, the first word in the clause is a *relative pronoun* or a *subordinating conjunction.* In an unmarked clause, *that, which,* or *who(m)* is left out. The only markers that can be left out are *that, which,* and *who(m),* and they can be left out only in certain constructions as explained under adjective clauses and noun clauses. (All WH-words can be used to introduce dependent clauses.)

              marker
This is the story   *that*   she read.
This is the story she read. (unmarked: *that* is left out)

           marker
They said   *that*   they were going.
They said they were going. (unmarked: *that* is left out)

3. A dependent clause acts in the sentence like an adjective, an adverb, or a noun.

Adjective Clauses

Like a single-word adjective, an adjective clause modifies a noun or pronoun.

           dependent
             clause
          (adjective)
This is the story *that she read.*
(*that she read* modifies *story*—it tells which story)

           dependent
             clause
          (adjective)
John is the boy *who remembered.*
(*who remembered* modifies *boy*—it tells which boy)

An adjective clause in English usually comes immediately after the noun or pronoun it modifies. In the following sentence, *that we liked very much* modifies *bears*.

> The story about the bears *that we liked very much* is in this book. (We liked the bears.)

To make *that we liked very much* modify *story*, put it directly after *story*.

> The story *that we liked very much* about the bears is in this book. (We liked the story.)

The marker for an adjective clause is called a relative pronoun.

Adverb Clauses

Like a single-word adverb, an adverb clause tells when (time), where (place), how (manner), why (cause), and to what extent (degree). (see **Adverbs**) An adverb clause can also show cause, concession, condition, contrast, and purpose.

> *independent clause*   *dependent clause*
> We had already gone   when Charlotte came.

In normal word order, the adverb clause follows the independent clause as in the sentences above. If the adverb clause comes first in the sentence, however, the adverb clause is followed by a comma. (see **Punctuation, comma**)

> *dependent clause*   *independent clause*
> When Charlotte came,   we had already gone.

The marker for an adverb clause is sometimes called a subordinating conjunction or a relative adverb. If you leave out the marker you change the adverb clause into an independent clause and change the basic structure of the sentence. (see **Sentence structure**)

Noun Clauses

A noun clause can replace a single-word noun, a pronoun, or a noun phrase as subject of the sentence:

> *noun phrase*
> *His speech* is difficult to understand.

> *noun clause*
> *Whatever he says* is difficult to understand.

as direct object of the verb:

> *noun*
> She knew *the truth.*

> *noun clause*
> She knew *what he had really said.*

as object of a preposition or following a two-word verb:

> *pronoun*
> They voted for *her.*

> *noun clause*
> They voted for *who(m)ever they liked* best.
> (Use whomever in formal writing.)

as predicate nominative (sometimes called subject complement) after *to be* or another linking verb:

> *noun clause*
> His belief is *that things will improve.*
> It seems *that things are improving.*

A noun clause is necessary to the basic structure of its sentence and cannot be left out.

Words that can introduce noun clauses:

1. *that* (can be left out in a noun clause used as direct object and after "it is + adjective . . .")

> *direct object*
> He said *(that) he was coming.*
> It is strange *(that) he is coming.*

That can never be left out if it is the subject of the clause.

2. WH-words: *who, whose, whom, what, which, why, how, when, whether* (and *if* when it means *whether*). Most of these words also have a form which adds *-ever: whoever, whatever, whichever,* and so on. Noun clauses beginning with WH-words are usually indirect questions. (see **Reported speech**)

> *noun clause*
> He knows *who broke the window.*
> They do not know *what to do.*

Connecting Words That Join Clauses

Two independent clauses can be joined in two ways.

1. Two independent clauses can be joined by a comma and a coordinating conjunction (*and, but, or, for, nor, yet, so*).

INDEPENDENT CLAUSE	COORDINATING CONJUNCTION	INDEPENDENT CLAUSE
The alarm clock rang,	*and*	Mark got up.
The alarm clock rang,	*so*	Mark got up.
The alarm clock rang,	*but*	Mark did not get up.
The alarm clock rang,	*yet*	Mark did not get up.
Mark got up,	*for*	the alarm clock rang.

2. Two independent clauses can be joined by a semicolon. An interrupter may be added to the second clause to show more clearly the relation between the ideas in the two clauses. (Single-word interrupters are often called conjunctive adverbs.)

INDEPENDENT CLAUSE	INDEPENDENT CLAUSE
The alarm clock rang;	the boy got up.
The alarm clock rang;	*therefore,* the boy got up.
The alarm clock rang;	*consequently,* the boy got up.
The alarm clock rang;	*as a result,* the boy got up.
The alarm clock rang;	*nevertheless,* the boy stayed in bed.
The alarm clock rang;	*however,* the boy stayed in bed.

Interrupters are movable; they may be put in the beginning, in the middle, or at the end of the clause. They must be separated from the rest of their own clause by a comma or commas. (see **Interrupters**)

> The alarm clock rang; the boy, therefore, got up.
> the boy got up, therefore.

The Meaning of Connectors

The following connectors show *effect* or *result* in the second clause.

Coordinating conjunction:

> It was raining,   *so* I carried an umbrella.

Interrupters:

> It was raining;   *therefore,* I carried an umbrella.
> It was raining;   *consequently,* I carried an umbrella.
> It was raining,   *as a result,* I carried an umbrella.
> It was raining,   *thus* I carried an umbrella.
> It was raining;   *accordingly,* I carried an umbrella.

The following connectors show *contrast* in the second independent clause.

Coordinating conjunction:

> One of her eyes was blue,   *but* her other eye was green.
> One of her eyes was blue,   *yet* her other eye was green.

Interrupters:

> One of her eyes was blue;   *however,* her other eye was green.
> One of her eyes was blue;   *on the other hand,* her other eye was green.
> One of her eyes was blue;   *nevertheless,* her other eye was green.
> One of her eyes was blue;   *even so,* her other eye was green.
> One of her eyes was blue;   *by/in contrast,* her other eye was green.

The following connectors show *addition* of more facts or ideas to the facts or ideas stated in the first clause.

Coordinating conjunction:

> He was rich,   *and* his brother was rich.

Interrupters:

> He was rich;   *also* his whole family was rich.
> He was rich;   *furthermore,* his whole family was rich.
> He was rich;   *in addition,* his whole family was rich.
> He was rich;   *moreover,* his whole family was rich.
> He was rich;   *in fact,* his whole family was rich.
> He was rich;   his whole family was rich *too.*

NOTE: *Too* usually comes in the middle or at the end of a clause. Words of four letters or fewer are not usually set off by commas.

The following connectors can be used to introduce an *illustration* or *example* in the second independent clause.

Interrupters:

> He seemed very rich;   *for example,* he owned three cars.
> He seemed very rich;   *to illustrate,* he owned three cars.
> He seemed very rich;   *in fact,* he owned three cars.
> He seemed very rich;   *for instance,* he owned three cars.
> He seemed very rich;   *for one thing,* he owned three cars.

Other connectors introduce *more illustrations and examples* after the first one.

> for another thing
> secondly
> thirdly
> finally
> at last
> He was rich; *for one thing,* he owned three cars. *For another thing,* he always wore the most expensive clothes.

The following connectors can be used to show *choice* or *alternatives* stated in two independent clauses.

Coordinating conjunction:

> You must pay a fine;   *or* you must go to jail.
> He did not pay a fine;   *nor* did he go to jail. (negative alternative)

Interrupters:

> You must pay a fine;   *otherwise,* you must go to jail.
> You must pay a fine;   *if not,* you must go to jail.

The following connectors show *emphasis.*

Interrupters:

> She was a beautiful girl;   *indeed,* she was the most beautiful girl I have ever seen.
>
> She was a beautiful girl;   *in fact,* she was the most beautiful girl I have ever seen.

The following connectors show *repetition* and *explanation.*

Interrupters:

> He seemed very rich to us;   *in other words,* he appeared very wealthy.
> He seemed very rich to us;   *that is,* he appeared very wealthy.

The following connector introduces the clause that tells the *cause.*

Coordinating Conjunction:

> I carried an umbrella,   *for* it was raining.

The following connector can be used to show that *addition* and *alternatives* are both possible. When both addition and alternatives are possible, *and/or* can be used, especially in scientific and legal writing.

> The checks in this joint account must be signed by Harold Lawson *and/or* they must be signed by Jane Lawson.

SUBORDINATING CONJUNCTIONS

The idea in an independent clause may be modified or further explained by a dependent clause. (see **Subordination**) An adverb dependent clause can be introduced by a subordinating conjunction. A subordinating conjunction is different in several ways from a coordinating conjunction. (Sometimes certain subordinating conjunctions are called relative adverbs.)

1. A clause that begins with a subordinating conjunction cannot be punctuated as a separate sentence. If it is a separate sentence, it is incorrect.

independent clause	*independent clause*
The alarm clock rang.	Mark got up.
Mark cooked breakfast.	Mark ate breakfast.

dependent clause	*independent clause*
When the alarm clock rang,	Mark got up.
After Mark cooked breakfast,	he ate it.

| INCORRECT: | When the alarm clock rang. (fragment) |
| INCORRECT: | After Mark cooked breakfast. (fragment) |

2. Some subordinating conjunctions can also be prepositions. Look at the sentence to see how it is constructed. Then decide what kind of verb forms and punctuation you need. (see **Prepositions**)

prepositional phrase
Since my arrival here, I have made many friends.

dependent clause
Since I arrived here, I have made many friends.

The preposition form of *because is because of*. Do not confuse these forms. A preposition must be followed by a noun, pronoun, or noun-form such as the *-ing* form.

Because the alarm clock rang, Mark got up.
Because of the ringing of the alarm clock, Mark got up.

Not all subordinating conjunctions can also be prepositions.

| INCORRECT: | *If* lack of protein, the body does not develop well. |
| CORRECT: | *If* the body lacks protein, it does not develop well. |

Common Subordinating Conjunctions

*after	because	in order that	*till
although	*before	once	*until
	-*er* (comparative adjective + *than*)		
as	even though	rather than	when, whenever
as far as	except that	*since	where, wherever
as if	how	so that	while
as long as	if	sooner than	
as though	in case	though	

The words preceded by an asterisk (*) can be prepositions. The other words on the list cannot be prepositions.

FORMAL FORMS: in as much as, whereas, whereby, whereupon

The following words can be used in similar sentence patterns as absolutes with or without *that*. They usually come at the beginning of the sentence.

admitting (that)	presuming (that)
assuming (that)	providing (that)
considering (that)	seeing (that)
given (that)	supposing (that)
granted (that)	
granting (that)	

Admitting we have made mistakes, we can try to do better in the future.
Admitting that we have made mistakes, we can try to do better in the future.
Granted xy equals *yz*, then *ax* equals *ay*.
Granted that xy equals *yz*, then *ax* equals *ay*.

Coherence

Coherence means that all parts of a composition are clearly related to each other in order to explain one idea or give one impression. If all the parts of your composition are arranged in order, if the relationship between your ideas is clear, and if everything you have written is relevant to your subject, your composition will have unity or coherence. You must have coherence between all the sentences in one paragraph and between paragraphs.

In order to test what you write, ask these questions:

1. *Pronouns:* Does each personal pronoun have a clear antecedent in its own sentence or in the sentence just before? Have you used any pronouns without antecedents? Does each personal pronoun agree with its antecedent in number and gender? (see **Reference of the pronoun**) Have you used the same point of view in the whole composition, or have you shifted from first- to second- to third-person pronouns without a reason? (see **Point of view**)

2. *Adverbs:* Do adverbs (single words, phrases, and clauses) show relationships between ideas clearly? Do you need more adverbs? Have you used the right word to show the meaning you want? (see **Adverbs, Clauses,** and **Transitions**)

3. *Conjunctions:* Have you used conjunctions where they are needed? Have you used the right word to show the meaning you want? (see **Conjunctions, Clauses,** and **Transitions**)

4. *Repetition of structure (parallel structure):* Have you used the same grammatical structure for similar ideas or for ideas of the same importance? (see **Parallel structure**)

5. *Repetition of words:* Have you repeated key words, especially nouns, so that the reader easily remembers what you are writing about?

6. *Synonyms:* Have you used synonyms in their correct meaning? (see **Connotation** and **Context**)

7. *Order:* Have you arranged your ideas in a clear order? (see **Chronological order, Logical order, Spatial order,** and **Outlining**)

8. *Relevance:* Have you kept to the point? Do you have any detail or illustration that is not directly related to the topic sentence of your paragraph or to the thesis statement of your whole composition? (see **Relevant ideas, Topic sentence,** and **Thesis statement**)

Colloquialisms

A colloquialism is a word or phrase that is used in speech but not in formal writing. Sometimes words begin as slang, become colloquialisms, and after some time become acceptable as standard English. British usage and American usage are not always the same. When you are not sure about usage of a word, look it up in a standard dictionary. Some dictionaries use the label *informal* and others use the label *colloquial*. (see **Usage labels**)

Colloquialisms or informal usage can be grammatical structures or words.

COLLOQUIAL STRUCTURE:	*What* did you do that *for?*
FORMAL:	*Why* did you do that?
COLLOQUIAL STRUCTURE:	Alison remembers *who* she saw yesterday. (*who/whom* distinction)
FORMAL:	Alison remembers *whom* she saw yesterday.
COLLOQUIAL STRUCTURE:	Harry *can't* remember where he left his books. (contractions)
FORMAL:	Harry *cannot* remember where he left his books.
WORDS:	*cop* (informal) for *police officer* *kid* for *child* *a shrinking violet* for *a person who is shy or timid*
	Short forms of words for complete forms *exam* for *examination* *gonna* for *going to* *math* for *mathematics* *tech* for *technical* or *technology* *wanna* for *want to*

Colon, see **Punctuation, colon**
Comma, see **Punctuation, dash**

Comma Splice

A comma splice or a comma fault is a serious error in connecting two independent clauses. Do not connect independent clauses by a comma alone without a coordinating conjunction (*and, but, or, nor, for, yet,* and *so*).

independent clause

INCORRECT: Robert has never been to New York,

independent clause

he has been to Los Angeles, however.

Do not be confused by *however*. Putting *however* between the two clauses does not correct the sentence because *however* is not a coordinating conjunction. A word like *however*, which is called an interrupter or a conjunctive adverb cannot join independent clauses unless you also use a semicolon. Some other words like *however* are *also, too, then, therefore, furthermore, thus,* and *for example*. (see **Interrupters**)

independent clause

INCORRECT: Robert has never been to New York, however,

independent clause

he has been to Los Angeles.

Correct a comma splice in one of four ways:

1. Put a semicolon between two independent clauses.

independent clause

CORRECT: Robert has never been to New York;

independent clause

he has been to Los Angeles, however.

2. Put a comma and a coordinating conjunction between independent clauses.

independent clause

CORRECT: Robert has never been to New York, but

independent clause

he has been to Los Angeles.

In a series of independent clauses, put a coordinating conjunction between the last two clauses. (see **Punctuation, comma**)

independent clause

Robert has never been to New York,

coordinating
independent clause *conjunction*
he has never been to Chicago,   and

independent clause

he has never been to St. Louis.

3. Put a period and a capital letter between independent clauses, making them separate sentences.

independent clause

CORRECT: Robert has never been to New York.

independent clause

He has been to Los Angeles, however.

4. Make one of the independent clauses into a dependent clause or into another subordinate construction. (see **Clauses** and **Subordination**)

dependent clause

CORRECT: Although Robert has never been to New York,

independent clause

he has been to Los Angeles.

participial phrase

CORRECT: Never having been to New York,

independent clause

Robert has often been to Los Angeles.

A *run-on sentence* is exactly like a comma splice except that the comma is left out: there is no punctuation at all between independent clauses. (see **Run-on sentences**)

independent clause

INCORRECT: Robert has never been to New York however,

independent clause

he has been to Los Angeles.

or

independent clause

INCORRECT: Robert has never been to New York

independent clause

he has been to Los Angeles, however.

Commands _____

Use the imperative form of the verb without *to* for impersonal commands. (This is the same form as the simple verb form or bare infinitive.) *You* is understood as the subject and rarely stated.

Use adverbs to show time in commands.

Be quiet	now.
	for ten minutes.
Mail these letters	at once.
	this afternoon.
Finish problem five	tomorrow morning.
	before you attempt problem six.

Use *do* for emphasis.

Do be quiet.
Do mail these letters.

Use *do not* for negation (prohibition).

Do not mail these letters now.
Do not attempt problem six before you finish problem five.

Many commands in English do not use the infinitive form of the verb. Polite requests, especially, use questions and statements that are interpreted as commands. Commands using only the infinitive are impersonal. They are usually used in speaking to groups and in writing. In conversation use *please* to soften the force of an imperative verb.

You can choose from many different ways to make a command or request.

IMPERSONAL:	(Please) open the door (please).
MORE POLITE:	(Please) will you open the door (please)?
MORE POLITE:	(Please) would you open the door (please)?
EXTREMELY POLITE (a command, not a request for information):	(Please) would you like to open / mind opening the door (please)?
POLITE COMMAND:	You can be opening the door while I . . .
POLITE NEGATIVE COMMAND:	Must you open the door now? (means Please don't)

Let + a personal object and the bare infinitive can show permission or a polite command.

$$\text{Let} \begin{cases} them \\ him \\ Sara \\ us \end{cases} \text{go in now.}$$

Let us often contracts to *let's* in speech.

> *Let's* go in now.

NOTE: *Allow* and *permit* are followed by a personal object + *to*. In this construction, *allow* and *permit* are more formal than *let*.

$$\left. \begin{array}{l} Allow \\ Permit \end{array} \right\} \text{me } to \text{ help you.}$$

Comparison and Contrast _____

Although *comparison* is often used as a general term to indicate both likenesses and differences, when both terms are used, *comparison* means likenesses and *contrast* means differences. The phrase "There is no comparison between . . . and. . . ." implies that the differences are very great and that there are almost no similarities at all.

Organizing ideas of comparison and contrast can be done more than one way. You can organize according to your subject divisions, or you can use the likenesses and the differences as main divisions. Choose the best method of organization for the material you have. One possible method of organization is

Japan and Canada

I. Japan
  A. Geographical location
    1. Islands
    2. In the western Pacific/Asia
    3. In the northern hemisphere
  B. Culture
    1. Ancient
    2. Oriental
    3. Unified
II. Canada
  A. Geographical location
    1. Mainland
    2. North America
    3. Northern Hemisphere
  B. Culture
    1. European-based
      a. French
      b. English
      c. Others
    2. Varied

Another possible method of organization is

Japan and Canada

I. Similarities
  A. Geographical
    1. Northern hemisphere
    2. Mountains
    3. Coastal areas
    4. Seas
  B. Political
    1. Democratic
    2. Parliamentary
    3. Interests in the oceans
II. Differences
  A. Geographical
    1. Size
    2. Island as opposed to mainland
    3. Latitude of northern Canada

B. Cultural
   1. Unity as opposed to diversity
   2. Languages
   3. Population density

Grammatical Structures That Show Likenesses

Like and *as*: *Like* is a preposition, but *as* introduces clauses, although sometimes the verb in the clause introduced by *as* is left out. (see **Adjectives, comparison**)

Use an object pronoun after *like*.

$$
\text{David}
\begin{cases}
\text{acts} \\
\text{behaves} \\
\text{is} \\
\text{thinks} \\
\text{looks}
\end{cases}
\begin{matrix}
\textit{like his father.} \\
\textit{like him.}
\end{matrix}
$$

Use a subject pronoun after *as*.

David is   *as*
$\begin{cases} \text{handsome} \\ \text{tall} \\ \text{hard-working} \end{cases}$
     as his father (is).

David works   *as*
$\begin{cases} \text{much} \\ \text{hard} \\ \text{many hours} \end{cases}$
     as his father (does).

David can work as hard as his father (can).

Verb forms are repeated at the end of the clause according to the rules for negatives and questions. Use the verb in the main clause if it is a modal or an auxiliary. Replace all other verbs with a form of *do*. (see **Operators**) Since *as* introduces a clause, a pronoun following it that is the subject of a clause must be a subject pronoun even if the second verb is left out.

David liked that movie *as* much *as we* did.
David is *as* tall *as he* (is).

If you repeat the verb, you will not use the wrong pronoun with this structure. Use a possessive form after *as* if you have used a possessive form in the first part of the comparison.

David's habits are *the same as his* father's (habits) (are).
His father's habits are *the same as his* (habits) (are).

The word following the possessive (habits) and the second use of the verb (are) can be put in or left out. You must use a verb in the second part, however, if the person or tense changes. (see **Operators**)

Words that show likenesses:

> The book for English 112 is *the same as* the books for English 11.
>
> Sally's friends *are* the same as her sister's *were*, but not the same as her sister's *are* now.

the same (as)	all, every (for more than two)
alike	likeness
similar (to)	similarly
equal (to)	
equally	in the same way
neither (for two things)	in the same manner
both (for two things)	as well as
each	

> David's and his father's habits are *the same.*
> *similar.*
> *alike.*

Alike always comes after the word it modifies. (see *Adjectives, word order*)

> They are *equally* industrious.
> David *as well as* his father is industrious.
> *Both* are industrious.
> *Each* of them is industrious.
> *All* the members of the family are industrious.
> *Every* member of the family is industrious.

(See **Agreement of subject and verb** for explanation of *David as well as his father is, each is, all are,* and *every member is.*)

> There is a *likeness* *between* the habits of David and his father.
> *similarity* their habits.
>
> Their *similar* habits show how *alike* they are.
>
> *In the same way,*
> *In the same manner,* both work hard.
> *Similarly,*

You cannot use *likely* to mean *in the same way* because it always means *probable* or *probably.*

Use adverb modifiers to make the meaning of adverbs clearer.

Almost and *nearly* show that the likeness is not absolute.

> David is *almost* as tall as his father.
> *nearly*

Plainly, surely, clearly, indeed, really, just, exactly, and *definitely* emphasize the likeness.

David is $\begin{matrix} just \\ exactly \end{matrix}$ as tall as his father.

Verb forms that show likenesses:

... is similar to ... in ...
... is like ... in
... is identical to ... in ...
... resembles ... in ...
compare ... and ...
... has a similar ... to ... 's.
... and ... are alike in ...
             the same
... and ... have the same ...
             similar

Norway *is similar to* Sweden *in* its climate.
Norway *is like* Sweden *in* climate.
Norway *is nearly identical to* Sweden *in* climate.
Norway *resembles* Sweden *in* climate.
Norway *has* a climate *similar to* that of Sweden.
Norway and Sweden $\begin{matrix} are\ the\ same \\ alike \end{matrix}$ in climate.
Norway and Sweden *have similar* climates.

NEGATION

Structures that show differences (below) can be used negatively to show likenesses.

David is *not unlike* his father. (They are alike.)
Norway and Sweden are *not dissimilar* in climate. (They are similar.)

Grammatical Structures That Show Differences

Structures that show likenesses can be used to show differences in negative structures. (see **Negation**) Adjectives and adverbs can be compared to show differences between two things (*-er, more*) or between more than two things (*-est, most*). (see **Adjectives, comparison**)

Negatives with *like* show differences:

David does *not* $\left\{ \begin{matrix} look \\ act \\ behave \\ think \end{matrix} \right\}$ $\begin{matrix} prepositional \\ phrase \end{matrix}$ *like* his father.
                                 like him.

David is *not like* his father.
          like him.

Comparatives, followed by *than*:

David is tall*er than*   his father (is).
he (is).

David works hard*er than*   his father (does).
he (does).

David can work hard*er than*   his father (does).
he (does).

David liked that move more *than* we did.

A negative verb with *the same as* shows differences:

David's habits are *not the same as* his father's.
This book for English 112 is *not the same as* the one for English 111.

Modifiers that show differences:

different (from) . . .*in*   dissimilar (from, to) . . . *in*
unlike   opposite (to, from)
inferior (to)   in contrast with
differently   distinct from

Japan is *different from* Canada *in* population density.
          unlike
Japan is on the *opposite* side *of* the globe from Canada.
David's experience is *inferior to* his father's.
Japan's imports are *distinct from* those of Canada.
In contrast with Canada, Japan must import petroleum products.

NOTE: Be sure to use the correct prepositions after adjectives.

Verbs that show differences:

differ from . . . in . . .)
contrast (with . . . in . . .)
separate
distinguish (between, among . . . and . . .)
Japan *differs* from Canada   *in many ways.*
Japan and Canada *differ*
Japanese life *contrasts with* Canadian life *in* many ways.
We can *distinguish between* the unified society of Japan and the pluralistic
society of Canada.

Nouns that show differences:

The { difference
contrast
variation
dissimilarity } between life in Canada and life in Japan is clear.

Other words that show differences:

> but (conjunction and preposition)
> however (interrupter)
> nevertheless (interrupter)
> on the one hand . . . on the other hand (interrupter)
> one . . . another . . . (determiner and pronoun, singular countable)
> some . . . other . . . (determiner, plural countable)
> some . . . others . . . (pronoun, plural countable)

Complements

A complement is a word that is necessary to complete the meaning of a verb. In normal word order a complement follows the verb. (see **Inverted word order**)

	linking verb	*predicate adjective*	
Barbara	is	friendly.	

	transitive verb	*indirect object*	*direct object*
Barbara	gave	Charles	the ball.

	transitive verb		*direct object*	*objective complement adjective*
Barbara	found		the work	difficult.

	transitive verb		*direct object*	*objective complement noun*
The committee	elected		Barbara	chairperson.

A linking verb must be followed by a predicate adjective, and a predicate noun, a pronoun, or an adverbial complement. (see *Be*) A transitive verb in its active form must be followed by a direct object. (see **Voice**) Some transitive verbs can also be followed by indirect objects, and some can be followed by objective complements. Intransitive verbs are not followed by predicate adjectives or nouns or by direct objects.

Depending on the verb and its meaning, a transitive verb may be followed by different combinations of complements.

		direct object only	
George found a		kite.	

	indirect object	*direct object*	
George found	us	a kite.	

		direct object	*objective complement*
George found		Henry	difficult.

Depending on the meaning of the sentence, the same word may be a transitive or linking verb.

              transitive   *direct object*
Arthur   grew   roses.

              linking   *predicate adjective*
Arthur   grew   fat.

Depending on the meaning of the sentence, the same word may be an intransitive or a transitive verb.

              intransitive
The car   ran   well.

             transitive *direct object*
Ben   ran   his car   into a telephone pole.

(see **Indirect object, Predicate complement, Sentence patterns, Verbs, kinds of,** and **Voice**)

Concession

Concession admits (concedes) that although something is true or accepted, another part of the problem or another viewpoint exists. (see **Argument, Clauses, adverb, Conjunctions,** and **Interrupters**)

INTERRUPTERS	**RELATIVE ADVERBS**
after all	although
all the same	though
at any rate	even though
however	
in any case	**PREPOSITIONS**
in spite of that	in spite of
nevertheless	despite
still	

COORDINATING CONJUNCTION
but
yet

It is very cloudy today; { however / all the same, / in spite of that, / nevertheless, / still, } it may not rain at all.

{ Although / Even though / Though } it is very cloudy today, it may not rain at all.

In spite of the clouds, it may not rain at all.

It is cloudy, but/yet it may not rain at all.

Conditional Sentences _____

Clauses after *if* show whether the writer or speaker thinks that the stated result is possible (real), or that the result is impossible or unlikely (unreal or contrary to fact). Use *would* in the result clause when the result is unreal or contrary to fact.

Real Conditions

Use the present, present perfect, or past tense after *if* or *unless*. Use the present, past, future, or a command in the result clause.

CONDITION	RESULT
present *tense*	*future* *tense*
If you *brush* your teeth every day,	you *will have* fewer cavities.
If you *drive* carefully,	you *will have* fewer accidents.

Unless means *if you do not.*

If you *do not brush* your teeth, *Unless* you brush your teeth,	you *will have* many cavities
If you *do not drive* carefully, *Unless* you drive carefully,	you *will have* an accident.

After an *if* clause in the present tense, the verb in the result clause can be present tense also, or it can be a command.

PRESENT	PRESENT
If you *help* me now,	you *are* a true friend.
If you *get* the right answer,	you *understand* this problem.
	COMMAND
If you *understand* this problem,	*show* me how to do it.
If Carl *calls* today,	*tell* me at once.

Perfect and continuous forms can be used after *if* in real conditions.

If you *have finished* reading my book, please return it.
If Jim *is sleeping*, you should wake him.

PAST	PAST
If Pam *found* a job,	she was happy.
If they *showed* him the way,	he found the right office.
If Carl *called* yesterday,	you forgot to tell me.
	FUTURE
If she *found* a job,	she will be happy.
If she *did* not *find* a job, *Unless* she *found* a job, }	she will be unhappy.
If they *did* not *show* him the way, *Unless* they *showed* him the way, }	he will not find the right office.

If + should means that a result is possible.

> *If* it *should* rain tomorrow, be sure to close the windows.

Unreal or Contrary-to-Fact Conditions

Use *would* in the result clause to show an unreal condition.

PRESENT/FUTURE RESULT

Use *if +* the past tense and *would* in the result clause to show that the result is impossible or unlikely to happen in the future. (see **Modals, would**)

CONDITION	RESULT
(past tense)	*(would + main verb)*

If you *brushed* your teeth carefully, you *would have* fewer cavities. (*Meaning:* You do not brush your teeth; you will not have fewer cavities.)
If you *drove* carefully, you *would* not *have* so many accidents. (*Meaning:* You do not drive carefully and you do have many accidents.)
If you *helped* me, you *would be* a true friend. (*Meaning:* I do not think that you will help me; therefore you are not a true friend.)

Use *were* in place of *was* in unreal conditions. (see **Mood**)

> *If* I *were* (never *was*) you, I would never do that.
> *If* the truth *were* known, public opinion would change.
> *If* wishes *were* horses, all beggars would ride.

Even though you will sometimes hear *was* following *if* in conversation, use *were* in formal writing.

> *Would* can be used after *if* when it means *be willing to.*

> *If* you *would* stop talking for a minute, I would be able to finish this lesson. (*Meaning:* You are not willing to stop talking and I will not be able to finish this lesson.)
> *If* Martha *would* save her money, she would be able to go home for summer vacation. (*Meaning:* Martha is not willing to save and she will not be able to go home for summer vacation.)

NOTE: *Unless* is not usually used in unreal (contrary-to-fact) conditions.

CONDITIONAL	RESULT
(past tense)	*(would + verb)*

If you *did* not *brush* your teeth carefully, you would have many cavities. (*Meaning:* You do brush your teeth carefully, and, therefore, you do not have many cavities.)
If you *did* not *drive* carefully, you would have many accidents. (*Meaning:* You drive carefully, and, therefore, you do not have many accidents.)

PAST RESULT

Use *if +* the past perfect tense and use *would have +* past participle in the result clause to show unreal conditions and results in the past.

CONDITIONAL	RESULT
(past perfect tense)	(would have + *past participle*)

If you *had brushed* your teeth carefully, you *would have had* fewer cavities. (*Meaning:* You did not brush your teeth carefully at some time in the past, and you had some cavities as a result.)

If you *had* not *driven* so carefully, the accident *would have been* much worse. (*Meaning:* Because you drove very carefully, the accident was not too bad.)

Inverted word order in unreal conditions: You can leave out *if* and put *had, were,* or *should* first in the clause. (This is a formal style, used in writing more than in speech.)

Had you brushed your teeth more carefully, you would not have had so many cavities.
Had you driven more carefully, you would not have had an accident.
Were the truth known, public opinion would change.
Should it rain tomorrow, the meeting will be held in the auditorium.

Punctuation: Punctuate *if* clauses like other dependent clauses. Put a comma after an *if* clause at the beginning of the sentence, as in all the examples above. When the *if* clause follows the result clause, do not separate it from the result of the sentence by a comma. *If* clauses usually come at the beginning of the sentence. (see **Punctuation, comma**)

You will have fewer cavities if you brush your teeth carefully.
You would have had fewer cavities if you had brushed your teeth carefully.

Other words that can introduce conditional clauses must be followed by the same verb forms as *if*. (*That* can be left out when it is not the subject of the clause it begins.)

in case (that)	suppose/supposing (that)
in the event (that)	on condition (that)
provided/providing (that)	whether or not
so/as long as	

In case our team wins, it will be the new champion.
In the event the plane arrived late, we would miss our connection.
Provided that you buy the groceries, I will cook dinner.
So long as he does not bother me, I will not bother him.
Supposing that he had been found guilty, he would have gone to prison.
On condition that she comes to every meeting, she has permission to attend the seminar.
Whether or not it rains, the game will be played as scheduled.

NOTE: Other meanings of *if* are not conditional. *If* can be used to mean *when.*

If you heat water to 100°C, it will boil.

Even if can mean *although.*

> *Even if* he has lost all his money, he is still cheerful.

If can replace *whether* in informal style.

> We are unsure *if* (whether or not) he will come.

Shortened clauses with *if: If so* and *if not* can replace complete clauses.

> It may rain today. *If so* (if it rains), you will need your umbrella.
> You must pay your library fines. *If not* (if you do not), you will not be allowed to graduate.

Confusing Choices

Diction as it is used in composition means choosing the correct word. The choices listed below are problems of diction, spelling, and grammar that often cause confusion. Not all possible meanings are given for every word, but only the meanings or uses that are often confused.

Accept, except

Accept is a verb that means *receive* or *approve*; *except* is a preposition that means that everything following it is left out of the statement.

> I *accept* (*receive*) your apology.
> Everyone will go *except* Bob. (Bob is *not included.*)
> Your application has been *accepted.* (approved)
> Handicapped students are *excepted* from physical education courses. (*not included* in the requirement to take physical education courses.)

According to, accordingly

According to means *on the authority of* (someone); *accordingly* at the beginning of a clause means *as a result* or at the end of a clause it means *in a suitable manner.*

> *According* to the weatherman, it will rain tonight.
> It may rain tonight. *Accordingly,* you may need your umbrella. (as a result)
> It may rain tonight. You should dress *accordingly.* (in a suitable manner)

Advice, advise

Advice is an uncountable noun that means a *suggestion* as to how someone should act or think; *advise* is a verb meaning to *suggest,* give an opinion, or recommend.

> Pearl's *advice* to wait was helpful. (noun)
> Pearl *advised* us to wait. (verb)

Affect, effect

Affect is a verb that means *to change* or *influence; effect* may be a verb that means *to cause* or *bring about,* or it may be a noun that means *the result.*

> Lack of sleep *affects* my work. (verb)
> The protests *effected* a change in the bus route. (verb)
> The *effect* of the protests was a change in the bus route. (noun)

After, afterward, afterwards

After is a preposition or subordinating conjunction that means *later than something; afterward* or *afterwards* is an adverb that means *later. Afterward* and *afterwards* can be used in the same way.

> Charles came *after* me. (preposition)
> Charles came *after* I did. (conjunction)
> Charles came first, and I came *afterward*(*s*). (adverb)
> *Afterward*(*s*) I came. (adverb)

Ago, before, earlier (see also *for, since*)

Ago, before, and *since* show the relation of one point in time to another. Use *ago* in connection with past time to mean *a point in time before now.* Use *before* to show action or time *prior to* another action or time. Use *earlier* to show time before something that has already happened or will happen. Use *for* and *since* to introduce a period of time, never a point in time. *Now* is not a reference of *before* and *earlier* unless it is so stated.

> Christine moved to Portland ten years *ago*. (before now)

> *Before* Christine *moved* to Portland (past tense shows past reference of *before*) she *had lived* in San Francisco. (past perfect tense shows a time prior to the time of *moved*) Christine *will wait* six months *before* she *goes* back to San Francisco to visit her mother. (After a future tense, *before* + *present* tense shows *future* action) (see **Tense, present**) *Earlier* (before a time already stated) she *had lived* in Los Angeles.

> In 1870 Charles' great grandfather moved to Kansas. *Before* that, he *had come* to the United States from Sweden. Earlier, even *before* coming to the United States, he *had worked* for a photographer in Sweden. *Later* in Kansas he *took* pictures of settlers who *began* to farm there. Charles *learned* about his great grandfather three years *ago* [*before now*] when one of his aunts *wrote* down the history of their family.

All, all of, whole

(For uses and word order of *all* and *all of,* see **Determiners.**) Do not use *all of* if *all* is acceptable. (see **Wordiness**) Use *whole* as an adjective between the article and the noun to mean *complete, not divided,* or *entire,* and after the noun to mean *in one piece.* Use *all* to mean the *total,* divided or undivided. (If *the* comes before the noun, put *all* before *the.*)

> *All* students who drive must have parking stickers. (not *all of the*)
> Bill ate *all the* cake, *all four* pieces.
> Bill ate *the whole* cake, *all of* it. (total)
> Bill ate the biscuit *whole.* (undivided, in one piece)

NOTE: Use *all of* before pronouns: *all of it, all of us, all of you, all of them.*

All ready, already

All ready means *completely prepared; already* means *by now* or *by a certain time.*

> Jan is *all ready* to go. (prepared)
> Jan has *already* gone. (by now)
> Yesterday Jan had *already* gone before I came. (by then)

All right

Always spell *all right* as two words, never as *alright.*

> Mildred got the answers *all right.* (correct)
> The parking attendant told us that it would be *all right* to leave our car in the driveway. (permitted)

All together, altogether

All together means *everything or everyone in one place or group;* *altogether* means *completely.*

> The class went *all together* to the mountains on the same bus. (*in one group*)
> The decision is *altogether* wrong. (completely)

Allusion, illusion

An *allusion* is a reference to something already known; an *illusion* is something imagined, not true. *Allude* is a verb.

> Shirley has the *illusion* that she is beautiful when she is not.
> The speaker made an *allusion* to the wisdom of Solomon.

Already, yet

Already means *by now* or *by a certain time; yet* means *now* or *by a certain time* and is used in negatives and questions in the present perfect and past perfect tenses. Do not use *yet* with the past tense in the same clause. (see **Negation**)

> The Harrisons have *already* come. (*by now*)
> The Harrisons had *already* arrived when I came. (*by then*)
> The Harrisons have *not* come *yet*. (*by now*—with present perfect tense)
> The Harrisons had *not yet* arrived when I came. (by then—with past perfect tense)

As a conjunction, *yet* can mean *however*. (see **Conjunctions**)

Amount, number

Use *amount* to refer to uncountable nouns. Use *number* to refer to countable plural nouns. (see **Countable and uncountable nouns**)

> Penny bought a large *amount* of bread. (uncountable)
> Penny bought a *number* of items on her grocery list. (countable)

Another, other, others (see **Determiners**) (For *one another*, see *each other* below.)

Use *another* (1) before singular countable nouns and (2) before *one*. Use *other* (1) before countable nouns; (2) following *the, all,* or *every*; and (3) before countable nouns.

> Ted wants *another cup* of coffee. (countable, singular)
> He wants *another one*. (countable, singular)
> He wants *the other one*. (countable, singular)
> *Every other cup* is broken. (countable, singular)
> *All other cups* are broken. (countable, plural)
> Ted prefers this coffee to *other kinds*. (countable, plural)
> He really doesn't like *other coffee*. (uncountable)
> Is there *other* (a different kind of) *coffee* that will please Ted? (uncountable)

Use *other* or *the others* as a pronoun to replace countable nouns.

> There are several *other plates*. Look for *the others*. (countable, plural)
> Paul went on the first bus with some of the children, but Wilma waited to go with *the others*. (countable, plural)

Any, some

Any and *some* can be adjectives or pronouns. Use *some* in positive statements; use *any* in negation and in questions. *Some* can also be used in questions when agreement is expected or in an invitation or request. *Any* can also be used in positive statements after *if* or to express doubt. Use compounds such as *anyone, anybody, someone,* and *somebody* in the same ways. (see **Negation** and **Questions**)

Ted doesn't want *any* coffee.
Ted, do you want *some* coffee? (positive answer expected)
Ted, do you want *any* coffee? (negative answer expected)
Would you like to have *some* coffee? (invitation to have coffee)
We *cannot* stop to drink *any* coffee now.
If you want to get *any* coffee, buy it now.
I don't think there is *any* coffee in the house.
I doubt that there is *any* coffee in the house.

Anybody and *anyone; any body, any one*

Use *anybody* and *anyone* as indefinite pronouns in questions and negation. (see **Pronouns, indefinite**) Use *any body* as a noun, *body* modified by *any*. Use *any one* as a pronoun, *one* modified by *any*.

Can *anyone/anybody* help? (it does not matter who)
Sharon's hair is limp; it does not have *any body*.
Bring me a pen from my desk. It doesn't matter which color; *any one* will do.

Any more, anymore

Use *anymore* as an adverb in questions and negations to mean *no longer*.
Use *any more* in questions and negatives to mean *none in addition*.

We never eat chocolate *anymore* because Carl is allergic to it. (no longer)
Harry does not want to eat *any more* chocolate. (none in addition—he has already eaten some)

As if, as though, like

As if and *as though* are conjunctions. Use *as if* and *as though* to introduce clauses. Use *like* as a preposition to introduce a prepositional phrase. (*Like* can also be a verb—see *like, please* in this section.)

Elizabeth feels $\begin{array}{c}\textit{as though}\\\textit{as if}\end{array}$ she is lost.
Coffee does not taste *like* tea.
Sweet potatoes taste *like* pumpkin.

At, in, on (time) (see **Prepositions, time**)

Use *at* with specific times of the day.

at 10:15, *at* night, *at* dinner (time)

Use *in* with more general times.

in 1903, *in* two weeks, *in* a $\begin{array}{c}\text{month}\\\text{day}\\\text{week}\\\text{year}\end{array}$, *in* March

Use *on* with days and dates.

> *on* Saturday, *on* May 23, *on* the weekend (British: *at* weekends)

At, in, on (place) (see **Prepositions, space**)

Use *at* with a point in space.

> *at* the airport, *at* school, *at* home

Use *on* with a surface.

> *on* the street, *on* the table, *on* the floor

Use *in* with three-dimensional space.

> *in* the box, *in* the house, *in* a city,

The choice of preposition may change according to what is in the writer's or speaker's mind.

> *at* the store (location)
> *in* the store (within a building)
> sitting *on* the sofa (not enclosed)
> sitting *in* an easy chair (back and arms around the body)

Because, because of

Use *because* as a conjunction to introduce a dependent clause. Use *because of* as a preposition to introduce a prepositional phrase. (see **Cause and effect**)

> *dependent clause*
> Gene needs to wear a raincoat *because* it may rain.

> *prepositional phrase*
> Gene needs to wear a raincoat *because* of the rain.

Bear, bore, born and *bear, bore, borne*

Use *born* as the past participle when *bear* means *carry* or *endure*. Use *borne* as the past participle when *bear* means *give birth to*. Use *born* to mean *be brought into existence*.

> Marshall has *born* his sorrows bravely. (endured)
> Today machines *bear* the burdens that were once *born* by men.
> Mary has *borne* a son. (given birth to)
> The new*born* baby was only a few hours old.
> Strength is sometimes *born* out of difficulties.

Before, ago (see *ago, before*)

Beside, besides

Beside is a preposition that means *next to; besides* can be an adverb or preposition that means *in addition* or a preposition that means *except.*

preposition
The kitten is sleeping *beside* her mother. (next to)

preposition
Besides milk we need eggs. (in addition to)

adverb
Besides, we need eggs. (in addition)

preposition
Everyone *besides* Tom will be there. (except)

adverb
I really want to stay home tonight; *besides,* I have already seen that movie. (in addition)

Between . . . and . . . , from . . . to . . .

Always use *between* with *and* and use *from* with *to* when separating pairs of dates.

Between 1750 *and* 1800 rapid change took place.
From 1750 *to* 1800 rapid change took place.

Choice (*choices, choose*) and *device* (*devices, devise*)

These words have a change in spelling (*c* to *s*) and sound (*s* to *z*) like that in *advice, advise. Choose* also has a vowel change. (see **Nouns, spelling**)

Do, make

Do and *make* are verbs with similar meanings, but you cannot usually use one in place of the other. *Do* is an operator, but *make* is not. (see **Operator**)

Do the work.
     the dishes. (also *wash* the dishes)
     the house or housework. (also clean house or clean the house)
     the laundry. (but *wash* the clothes)
     research.

do + *ing* forms:

do the cleaning.
     the gardening.
     the ironing.
     the painting.
     the driving, etc.

Do is often used with abstract ideas.

> do business (buy or sell)
> one's best or worst, the best you can
> one's duty
> a favor
> good (charitable activities)
> well (make satisfactory progress)
> harm
> justice

An object after *do* can change the meaning of the verb.

$\begin{cases} \text{This medicine} \\ \text{A vacation} \\ \text{A rest} \end{cases}$ will *do you good.* (improve your sense of well-being)

Your picture does not *do you justice.* (show you as good or as beautiful as you are)

The book review does not *do the book justice.* (show it as good as it is)

In a question, *do* can mean to carry on a trade, occupation, or profession.

> What does Penny *do?* (What is her occupation?)
> She *is* a teacher now, but she *was* a student until last year. (*Do* is not always used in the reply.)

Make often means to create or produce something that was not there before.

> *make* a bargain (agree)
> the bed (straighten sheets and blankets for a neat appearance)
> a cake (also *bake* a cake)
> believe (imagine)
> an error, a mistake
> a fire
> (a) noise
> a statement
> war

Make + a noun can sometimes replace a verb related to the noun; using the single-word verb is better in writing because the phrase is wordy. (see **Wordiness**)

> *make* an agreement (with or about)   or   agree (to or with)
> an announcement (of)   announce
> an answer (to)   answer
> an attempt (to)   attempt (to)
> a beginning (of)   begin (to)
> a decision (to, about)   decide (to, about)
> a discovery (of)   discover
> an end (to)   end
> an offer (of, for)   offer (to)

a profit (from)	profit (from)
a promise (to, about)	promise (to)
progress (in, with)	progress (in)
a search (for)	search (for)
a start (on, in + ing)	start (to)
a stop (for, to)	stop (for, to)
a turn	turn
a vow (to)	vow (to)

Some meanings are limited to one form only.

She started the engine. (not *made a start*)
Columbus discovered the New World. (not *made the discovery of*)

Make can be followed by an objective complement (*make* + noun or object pronoun + adjective or noun)

                          direct   objective
                          object   complement
The people *made   him   president.* (noun)

                                  direct   objective
                                  object   complement
Getting out of school early *made* the *children   happy.*   (adjective)

Make can be a causative verb before another verb. (*make* + object — noun or pronoun + bare infinitive) (see **Cause and effect**)

                          direct
                          object   verb
The thunder *made* everyone *run* into the building.
The coach *made* his team *train* six hours a day.
Fear of the police *made* the thief *run* away.

Each, every, everyone, all

Use *each* and *all* as pronouns or adjectives. Use *each* and *every* before *one* and before singular nouns. Use *all* before plural countable nouns.

SINGULAR FORMS

Each ⎫
Every ⎰ child has a seat now.

(negative: no one)
(negative: no child)

Each one ⎫
Every one ⎬ has a seat now.
Everyone ⎭

(negative: not one)
(negative: not one)
(negative: no one)

Everyone and *everybody* are indefinite pronouns. *All* and *each* do not have similar one-word forms. Use *everyone* for people only. Do not use *everyone* before *of*, but use *every one*.

Everyone in the class went on the bus.

Every one
Each one of the students went on the bus.

Although *every* and other words made with it must be followed by a singular verb *in writing, every* is close in meaning to *all;* you will often *hear* a plural verb with it. Use *single* as an intensifier with *every.*

> *Every* plate was broken, *every single* one.

Use *each* when persons or things are thought of separately.

> *All* the plates were broken, but *each one* had been broken at a different time.

PLURAL FORMS
> *All* (the) children have seats now. (negative: no children, none of the children)

NOTE: *All the* children is more definite than *all* children. Use *all the* children when the individual members of the group are known.

> *All* children in the world need enough to eat.
> *All the* children on this bus have their lunches with them.

Each other, every other, one another

Each other and *one another* are reciprocal pronouns: Each of two or more persons or things does something to the other one.

> The lovers held *each other's* hands.
> The cats snarled at *each other.*

Some people prefer to use *each other* for two persons or things and *one another* for more than two.

> At the class reunion, many old friends greeted *one another.*

Every other can be the singular of *all others*, or it can mean *every second one* before countable nouns.

> The car was not out of gas. We looked for *every other* possibility, but we could not find what the trouble was.
> Write on *every other* line. (skip lines 2, 4, 6, 8, etc.)
> Take this medicine *every other* day. (Monday, Wednesday, Friday, etc.; or Tuesday, Thursday, Saturday, Monday, etc.)

Every day, everyday

Every day is an adverb meaning the same as *each day* (see above). Spelled as one word, *everyday* is an adjective meaning *usual* or *common.*

> We have the newspaper delivered *every day.*
> Carl works *every day* except Sunday.
> These are my *everyday* clothes. (not special)
> Not finding a place to park is an *everyday* problem. (common)

Except, accept; see accept, except

Few, only a few, a few

Few and *only a few* mean *not many* or *not enough*, emphasizing the lack of something; *a few* means a small number, but does not imply a lack or insufficiency. *Only a few* can replace *few*.

$\begin{Bmatrix} Few \\ Only\ a\ few \\ Not\ enough \end{Bmatrix}$ people came to the meeting, so we had to reschedule it for next week.

A few people came to the meeting, so we were able to finish our business. (not many, but enough)

We found $\begin{Bmatrix} few \\ only\ a\ few \end{Bmatrix}$ apples on the apple trees, so we left them for the birds. (not enough to pick)

We found *a few* apples on the trees, so we picked what was there. (enough to pick)

NOTE: The difference between *few* and *a few* is also found between *little* and *a little.* (see below, p. 111)

For, since

Use *for* before a period of time with all tenses. Use *since* only before a specific point in time with reference to *now*, relating past to present. (see **Prepositions, time**)

Hundred, hundreds (also *thousand(s), million(s)*, and so on)

Do not change the adjective *hundred* to a plural form after a number. Use *hundreds, thousands, millions*, and so on only as indefinite pronouns (often followed by *of* + a noun or pronoun).

AS NUMBERS
Two hundred men were there.
More than *two thousand* students voted for student president.
Over *six hundred* people were moved out of the flooded area.

AS INDEFINITE PRONOUNS
Hundreds (*of* people) lined up to get tickets to the concert.
Thousands (*of* bees) swarmed after their queen.

Its, it's

Its is a personal pronoun like *his; it's* is a contraction of *it is*. Use *its* to mean *of it*. Avoid using *it's* in formal writing.

Professor Hill's discovery is remarkable, but *its* practical value must be proved. (the value *of it*.)
The dog has buried *its* bone. (*of it*)
It's (*it is*) true that a storm is coming.
A decision has been made, and *it's* going to be a popular one.
The flight attendant said, "*It's* time to buckle your seat belts."

Lay, laid, laid and lie, lay, lain

Use *lay, laid, laid* as a transitive verb (with a direct object) to mean *put* or *place*. Use *lie, lay, lain* as an intransitive verb (no direct object) to mean *recline*. Do not confuse *lie, lay, lain* with *lie, lied, lied*, an intransitive verb that means *say something that is not true*.

PRESENT TENSE
Criminals *lie* when they are caught.
Children *lie* in the grass to watch the clouds.

direct object
Librarians *lay* the *guides* to the library on a table near the entrance.

PAST TENSE
The thief *lied* to the police. (from *lie*—told something not true)
The boy *lay* on his back in the grass. (from *lie*—recline)
The librarian *laid* the papers on the table. (from *lay*—put)

PRESENT CONTINUOUS/PROGRESSIVE
The criminal *is lying* about his burglaries.
The children *are lying* on their backs in the grass, watching the clouds.

direct object
The librarian *is laying* some guides to the library on a table near the entrance.

PRESENT PERFECT
The thief *has lied* about his burglaries.
Father *has lain* down for a short nap.

direct object
The librarian *has laid* some instruction booklets on the table.

Like, please

One meaning of *like* is *find pleasant;* as a verb *please* can mean *make someone happy*. A person or personal pronoun must be the subject of *like* but the object of *please* in its active form.

subject
Robert *likes* chocolate cake.

but

object
Chocolate cake always *pleases* Robert.

subject
Most *children* like candy.

but

object
This candy *pleases* the *children*.

Please (verb) is often used in the passive with a subject that refers to a person.

> Robert *is pleased with* the cake.
> The *children are pleased with* the candy.

Formal announcements often use *it pleases* someone *to* . . .

> *It pleases us to* announce the opening of a new store.

Little, only a little, a little

Little and *only a little* mean *not much* or *not enough,* emphasizing the lack of something; *a little* means *a small amount,* but does not imply lack or insufficiency. Use these words before uncountable (mass, noncount) nouns instead of *few, a few,* and *only a few.*

$\begin{cases} Only\ a\ little \\ Little \\ Not\ enough \end{cases}$ thought has been given to the problem, and no solution has been found.

After a little thought has been given to the problem, a solution will be found.

$\begin{cases} Only\ a\ little \\ Little \\ Not\ enough \end{cases}$ milk is left for tomorrow.

A *little* milk is left; it will be enough for tomorrow.

Loose, lose, loss

Do not confuse the spelling of *loose* (*let go* or *untie*) and *lose* (*fail to find*). Use *lose* as a verb. Use *loss* as a noun meaning *the result of losing.* Use *loose* as an adjective (rarely as a verb).

> The gate is open and the horses are *loose.* (set free or strayed away)
> We may *lose* them if they are not found soon. (fail to find)
> *Losing* them would be a great *loss.*
> You must pay attention and not *lose* your place in the music. (fail to find)
> Walter's bicycle lock is *loose* (not held together securely), but no one has stolen the bicycle yet.

Many, much

Use *many* before or to replace countable plural nouns (adjective and pronoun); use *much* before or to replace uncountable nouns (adjective and pronoun). (see **Countable and uncountable nouns**)

> The *number* of children in school is increasing; *many* more *children* are enrolled today than were enrolled twenty years ago.
> The *amount* of *sunshine* in winter is less than in summer; there is *much* more *sunshine* in the summer.

Must, have to, ought to, should (see **Modals**)

Use *must* to show necessity (the strongest meaning). Use *have to* for the past of *must* (nearly as strong). Use *ought to* and *should* to show obligation and moral necessity, not as strong as *must*.

> Drivers *must* (have to) stop at red lights to avoid collisions.
> Drivers *ought to* (should) obey the speed limit to keep from having accidents.
> We *had to* pay a deposit before our telephone was installed.

Numbers, a number, the number

Use *numbers of* to mean *many* or *very many* (with a plural verb). Use *a number* to mean *some* or *many* (followed by *of* + a plural noun, it takes a plural verb). Use *the number* to mean quantity (followed by *of* + a plural noun, it takes a singular verb).

> *Numbers of* birds *are* roosting in the trees by the school. (many birds)
> *A number of* birds *are* roosting in the trees by the school. (a group, but it does not contain as many birds as in *numbers of*)
> *The number of* birds that can live in this cage *is* four.
> *The number of* birds that are roosting in the trees by the school *is* impossible to count.

Passed, past

Use *passed* as the past tense and past participle of *pass* (this past participle is never used as an adjective before a noun). Use *past* as an adjective, an adverb, a preposition or a noun.

> Time *passed* (by) slowly. (past tense)
> Our troubles have *passed*. (past participle)
> We saw the city hall as we drove *past*. (adverb)
> We drove *past* the city hall. (preposition)
> The days of summer are *past*. (predicate adjective)
> The *past* can never come back. (noun)
> The *past* few days have gone by quickly. (adjective)

People, person(s)

Both *people* and *person(s)* are pronouns that stand for human beings; both have plural meanings but only *person* can be used in the singular. Use *people* only as a plural noun with a plural verb. Use *person* as singular and *persons* as plural.

> $\left\{\begin{array}{l}\text{Ten}\\\text{Many}\\\text{Fifty}\end{array}\right\}$ $\left\{\begin{array}{l}\textit{people}\\\textit{persons}\end{array}\right\}$ are waiting.
> One *person* is waiting.

Principal, principle

Notice the difference in spelling. Use *principal* as an adjective or a noun to mean *chief* or *the most important one*. Use *principle* as a noun to mean *rule, belief,* or *law of nature.*

> Miss Blake is the *principal* of Roosevelt School (head teacher)
> The *principal* actor in the play was very good. (most important one)
> The Mayor's *principal* interest was getting re-elected. (chief)
> Make honesty your *principle*. (rule)
> People who take their religion seriously have strong *principles*. (moral beliefs)
> The *principles* of gravity never change. (laws of nature)

Principal sometimes means a sum of money that has been invested.

> Many people try to spend their interest without using any of the *principal* of their investments.

Remember, remind

Both are regular verbs. Use *remember* to mean *recall.* Use *remind* to mean *cause to recall.*

> Oscar did not *remember* his dental appointment until the dentist's secretary called to *remind* him.
> *Remind* me (make me remember) to pay the electric bill tomorrow

Result from, result in

Use *result from* to mean *caused by.* Use *result in* to mean *cause.*

> The fire *resulted from* (was caused by) faulty wiring.
> The fire *resulted in* (caused) damage to the building.
> Freezing temperatures *resulted in* (caused) ice on the lake.
> Ice on the lake *resulted from* (was caused by) freezing temperatures.

Rise, rose, risen and raise, raised, raised

Use *rise* as an intransitive verb (without a direct object) to mean *go higher.* Use *raise* as a transitive verb (with a direct object) to mean *make something higher.*

> Smoke *rises*. (goes higher)
> Eagles *rise* from the cliffs to hunt their prey. (go up)
>
>   *direct*
>   *object*
> Every morning the students *raise* the *flag*. (make it go up)
>
>   *direct*
>   *object*
> If you study hard, you can *raise* your *grades*. (make them go up)

Shine, shined, shined and *shine, shone, shone*

Use *shine* with a direct object to mean *make shining;* use *shine, shone, shone* without a direct object to mean *give off light or brightness.*

direct
object

Peter *shined* his shoes until they *shone.*
The sun *shone* all day today.

Sit, sat, sat and *set, set, set*

Use *sit* to mean *put oneself on a chair or on a flat place with one's back upright* or *to remain in one place.* (*Sit* is never used in English to mean *reside* or *live* in a place.) Use *set* to mean *place* or *put;* it must be followed by a direct object except with fowl or birds to mean *incubate eggs.*

The children are *sitting* quietly in their classroom.
Susan *sits* too much; she needs more exercise.

direct object

Louis *set* the   coffee pot   on the table.

direct object

Where has Tim *set* down his new   schedule?
The hen has been *setting* for a week.

Some time, sometime, and *sometimes*

Some time means *an indefinite amount of time; sometime* means *at a time not specifically stated;* and *sometimes* means *occasionally.*

Dr. Prentiss will be able to give you *some time* at 3:00 this afternoon. (amount of time is uncertain)

Dr. Prentiss will see you for fifteen minutes *sometime* this afternoon. (exact time of the appointment is uncertain.)
Dr. Prentiss has *sometimes* seen Marcia Blake. (occasionally, not regularly)

Stationary, stationery

Stationary (adjective) means *not movable; stationery* (noun) means *writing paper.*

The new lights for the tennis courts are permanent and *stationary.* (not movable)
We need to order some new *stationery.* (writing paper)

Still, already, yet, and *however*

Still and *yet* can replace each other in meaning when they mean *however.*

Gerald is weak in mathematics; $\genfrac{}{}{0pt}{}{\textit{still}}{\textit{however}}$ he is strong in English.

Gerald is weak in mathematics, *yet* he is strong in English.

Note punctuation differences in the two sentences above. (see **Clauses, connectors**)

In any tense *still* can show that something continues or continued longer than expected and *already* can show that it begins or began sooner than expected. In this sense, when *yet* replaces *already* in negative statements, it corresponds to *still* in positive statements.

This ice cream is *still* frozen (longer than expected); I thought it would be melted $\genfrac{}{}{0pt}{}{\textit{by now.}}{\textit{already.}}$

This ice cream is melted *already* (sooner than expected); I thought it would *still* (*up to now*) be frozen.

This ice cream has not melted *yet*. (up to now)

The baby is *still* crawling. (longer than expected)
The baby is *already* walking. (sooner than expected)
The baby is *not* walking *yet*. (not as soon as expected)

Still, any more, any longer, no longer

Still means *up to now; not . . . any more, not . . . any longer,* or *no longer* replace *still* in negative statements. (see **Negation**)

Are you *still* going to Paris in June?

No, I am *not* planning that trip $\left\{ \genfrac{}{}{0pt}{}{\textit{any more.}}{\textit{any longer.}} \right.$

I am *no longer* planning to go to Paris in June.

Struck, stricken

Both *struck* and *stricken* are past participles of *strike*. Use *struck* in the sense of *a physical blow*, but use *stricken* to show *emotion* or *illness*.

The speeding car has *struck* a telephone pole.
The rebels have *struck* a blow for freedom.
The thoughtless daughter has been *stricken* with grief since her mother died.
Before a vaccine was developed, thousands of people were *stricken* by polio every year.

Such, such a

Both *such* and *such a* come before a noun that is modified, coming before an adjective that modifies the same noun. Use *such a* before singular countable nouns. Use *such* before uncountable and plural countable nouns. A phrase or clause beginning with *as* or a clause beginning with *that* can follow the nouns. (see **Determiners** and **Countable and uncountable nouns**)

	ADJECTIVE	SINGULAR NOUN	
Such a	(cold)	day	as today made Lucy shiver.
Such a	(happy)	child	made every one laugh.

		UNCOUNTABLE NOUN	
Such	(unselfish)	friendship	as Mary's is hard to find.
Such	(good)	food	as this is fit for a king.

		COUNTABLE PLURAL	
Such	(difficult)	problems	as we are doing now are too hard for me.

Andy makes *such* (long) telephone calls *that* his phone is always busy.

That, which, and *who, whom, whose*

That, which, and *who, whom, whose* are relative pronouns. Some writers use *that* and *which* in the same way in essential adjective clauses. In the United States many writers prefer using *that* to introduce essential adjective clauses. Use *which* but never *that* to introduce adjective clauses that are nonessential. Use *who, whom,* or *whose* in both essential and nonessential clauses to refer to people. Some writers use *that* to refer to people but never *which*. (see **Pronouns, relative**)

This, that, these, those

Use *this* (singular) and *these* (plural) to refer to or modify someone or something nearer in space or time or just mentioned. Use *that* (singular) and *those* (plural) to refer to something farther away in space, time, or thought. (see **Pronouns, demonstrative**)

Do you prefer *this* cake or *that* pie?
These pictures are much clearer than *those* we were looking at earlier.

Their, there, they're

Their is the third person plural possessive pronoun; *there* is an adverb or an expletive; and *they're* is the contraction for *they are.*

All the employees brought *their* families to the company picnic. (possessive)
There is a new motorcycle parked behind the gym. (adverb)
Dick's new motorcycle is parked over *there* behind the gym. (adverb)

They're too late to get into the concert now because the doors have already been closed. (they are)

NOTE: Avoid beginning a written sentence with the expletive *there*. (see **Expletives**)

Wear, were, we're, where

Wear means *to have clothing or something else on the body; were* is the past tense of *be* in all except the third person singular; *we're* is the contraction for *we are;* and *where* means *in what place?* or *in that place.*

> Alan wonders what to *wear* today.
> The clowns *were* funny.
> *We're* early today.
> *Where* are you going?
> Sally found her coat *where* she had left it.

Weather, whether

Weather means conditions related to the climate; *whether* means *if* (something happens) . . . *or not.* In informal writing, do not leave out *or not* after *whether.*

> The *weather* today is better than predicted.
> *Whether* it rains or *not,* the game will be played.

What . . . for? and why?

Use *why?* in formal writing. *What . . . for?* is informal and can be used in conversation. NEVER SAY "*Why* are we doing this *for?*" or "*What for* are we doing this?" If you use *why,* do not use *for.* Never put *what* and *for* together at the beginning of a clause. (*What for?* can be used to mean *why?* as a short question only if no clause completes the construction and the meaning is "*What is the purpose of?*")

> *What* are we helping him *for?* (informal)
> *What* are we standing in line *for?* (informal)
>
> *Why* are we helping him? (formal)
> *Why* are we standing in line? (formal)

Your, you're

Your is the second person possessive pronoun; *you're* is the contraction for *you are.* Avoid *you're* in formal writing.

> Where is *your* car? (car belonging to you)
> Why have all of you forgotten *your* money? (money belonging to you)
> *You're* on time, neither late nor early. (you are)

Conjunctions _____

Conjunctions join ideas by joining grammatical structures. You must know the different kinds of conjunctions in order to punctuate sentences correctly and in order to express your ideas in the most effective way.

Coordinating conjunctions are *and, but, for, or, nor, yet,* and *so.* Coordinating conjunctions join grammatical structures of the same kind: words to words, phrases to phrases, and clauses to clauses. (see **Coordinating conjunctions**)

WORD: Rice *and* potatoes are common foods.

PHRASE: Today travelers go by plane *or* by bus.

CLAUSE: Many trees lose their leaves in winter, *but* evergreen trees do not.

Correlative conjunctions are pairs of conjunctions that are used together.

both . . . and   not only . . . but also
either . . . or   neither . . . nor

Correlative conjunctions must be followed by the same grammatical structures. (see **Parallel structure**)

             noun
INCORRECT: *Either* the *meat* was tough to begin with *or*

      adjective
      overcooked.

          noun   *pronoun*
CORRECT: *Either* the *meat* was tough to begin with *or it*
      was overcooked.

Subordinating conjunctions introduce dependent clauses. For examples of their use and their listing according to meanings, see **Clauses, connectors.**

Conjunctive adverbs show relationships between ideas but are not grammatically necessary in the clause. (see **Interrupters**)

Connecting Words _____

Connecting words show relationships between the ideas in words, phrases, and clauses. (see **Adverbs, Clauses, Connectors, Interrupters,** and **Transitions**)

Connotation

Connotation means the emotional, social, or moral value that is associated with a word. For example, calling someone a pig is insulting because dirt or gluttony is associated with pigs. Be careful because people do not always agree about the connotation of words, and dictionaries do not always give enough information so that you can easily choose which word to use. *Woman*, *lady*, and *female*, for example, can all refer to the same person, but the associated meanings are different. *Female* and *woman* are biological facts, but *lady* has had social and class differences connected with it. Animals and objects have different connotations in different cultures. In English

a hawk	is warlike
a dove	is peaceful
a turtle	is slow
a pig	is fat or dirty or greedy (*pigheaded* means stubborn)
a mule	is stubborn
a donkey	is patient
a fox	is crafty
a snake	is evil
an apple	is connected with temptation

Among English-speaking people a rabbit may be associated with good luck (a rabbit's foot is considered lucky), poor performances at games (especially in Britain), reproduction, and speed. In parts of Africa, a rabbit is associated with cleverness. Color connotations also differ very much from one culture to another. To English-speaking people, for example, *green* may be associated with the following:

a traffic light	We have the *green light* (we can go forward with our plans).
envy	Matthew's new sailboat made all his friends *green* (with envy).
lack of experience (an inexperienced person is called a *greenhorn*)	Wars are not won with *green* (inexperienced) troops or with a *greenhorn* in command.
nausea	She was so seasick she turned *green* (nauseated).
skill in gardening (a *green* thumb)	Mr. Bentley has a *green thumb;* his roses are always beautiful.
flourishing or vigorous	Ernest always kept *green* the memory of his dead father.

Consonants

Consonants are sounds that are not vowels and the letters that stand for these sounds. (The letters that stand for vowels are *a, e, i, o, u,* and sometimes *y.*) When you use an indefinite article, put *a* before a word beginning with a consonant sound but put *an* before a vowel sound. (see **Vowels**)

h sometimes has a consonant sound and sometimes a vowel sound.

h AS A CONSONANT	*h* AS A VOWEL
a happy day	*an* honest man
a helping hand	*an* honor student

At the beginning of a word, *y* is always a consonant.

a year
a yellow rose
a young kitten

Context

Context means the setting of a word. The setting (the whole clause, sentence, or paragraph) tells you the specific meaning a word has if more than one meaning is possible. The word *fine,* for example, can be used in different meanings and as different parts of speech.

ADJECTIVE:	He is a *fine* boy. (good)
ADJECTIVE:	It is a *fine* day. (pleasant—not raining)
NOUN:	He had to pay a *fine* at the library. (penalty)
VERB:	The judge will *fine* you for speeding. (charge or penalty)
ADJECTIVE:	*Fine* print is difficult to read. (narrow, small)

A word that is appropriate in one context may not be suitable in another. *Tiny,* for example, means very small, but you would not usually use it with *mansion.* The word *boy* is usually insulting when used for an adult male, but calling someone *a good old boy* can be complimentary when it means a person is a friendly fellow. To go *out with the boys* means to go to an all-male party or activity. *Old boys* can mean men who once attended the same school. (see **Connotation** and **Denotation**)

Contractions

Contractions are shortened forms of verbs that represent the sounds of speech. Contractions are written to show subject-verb combinations or negative-verb combinations. Avoid using them in formal writing. (see **Style**)

With Pronouns

I'm—I am
I've—I have
I'd—I had or would
I'll—I will or shall
You're, we're, they're, who're—You, we, they, who are
You've, we've, they've, who've—You, we, they, who have
You'd, we'd, they'd, who'd—You, we, they, who had or would
You'll, we'll, they'll, who'll—You, we, they, who will or shall
he's, she's, it's, who's—he, she, it, who is (sometimes he, she, it, who has)
he'd, she'd, it'd, who'd—he, she, it, who had or would
he'll, she'll, it'll, who'll—he, she, it, who will or shall
let's—let us

With Negatives

Ain't is considered colloquial or nonstandard. Do not use it in writing with any noun or pronoun. *Aren't I?* is sometimes used for *am I not?*

I, you, we, they, who don't—do not
                haven't—have not
I, we, you, he, she, it, they, who didn't—did not
                    hadn't—had not
You, we, they, who aren't—are not
              weren't—were not
He, she, it, who isn't—is not
            doesn't—does not
            hasn't—has not
            wasn't—was not

All nouns and pronouns can be used with the following forms (modal + *not*):

won't—will not
wouldn't—would not
can't—cannot
couldn't—could not
mustn't—must not
shouldn't—should not
mightn't—might not (rare)
needn't—need not (rare in U.S.)
oughtn't—ought not (rare)

In direct quotations, *-'s* is sometimes used after a proper name to show *is.*

"John*'s* a good friend," he said. (John is a good friend.)

Never use a positive contraction of a personal pronoun + *be, have, do,* or a modal as the last word of a clause. Negative contractions, however, are common at the end of a clause.

Virginia is my friend.	Yes, *she is.* (NEVER Yes, *she's.*)
	No, she *isn't.*
I'd go.	Yes, *I would.* (NEVER Yes, *I'd.*)
	I *wouldn't.*

Contrary-to-Fact Statements _____

Use a past or past perfect verb in a contrary-to-fact statement (sometimes called *nonreal*). Use *were* instead of *was* in a statement that is not true and is not likely to be true. (see **Subjunctive**)

After *as if* or *as though*:

Marie gives orders as though she *were* a queen.
Donald is only ten, but sometimes he talks as though he *were* twenty.

After *wish* when it introduces a statement that is untrue:

He wishes he *were* home in Japan instead of studying here. (He is not in Japan.)
They wish they *had made* the team. (They did not make the team.)

NOTE: Many people do not use these forms in speech except in the phrase "If I *were you.*" Formal writing requires them, however.

Coordinating Conjunctions _____

Coordinating conjunctions join two or more words, phrases, or clauses in the *same* grammatical category.

and	for
but	so
or	yet
nor	and/or

NOTE: *For, so,* and *yet* are sometimes used in other ways in a sentence.

Meaning

Do not confuse the meanings of the coordinating conjunctions. (see **Clauses, connectors**)

And shows addition:

> Two *and* four make six.

But shows contrast:

> Two and four make six, *but* two and three make five.
> They bought eggs and bread, *but* they forgot to buy milk.

Or and *nor* show choice, separation, or negative addition.

> Two and four *or* five and one make six.
> They had enough money for eggs *or* bread, but not enough for both.
> They did not buy eggs, *nor* did they buy bread.

Nor must follow *not* or *neither*. It is used in formal writing. Note that it is followed by an operator and the word order of a question. (see **Negation**)

So shows result:

> They didn't have enough money to buy milk, *so* they bought only eggs and bread.

For shows cause:

> They bought only eggs and bread, *for* they did not have enough money to buy milk.

Yet shows contrast:

> They bought eggs and bread, *yet* they forgot to buy milk.

For and *yet* are rarely used in speech in this construction, but they are often used in formal writing.

And/or means that what follows may be an addition to or a substitution for the previous statement. *And/or* is not used in a formal literary style, but it is often used in scientific writing:

> Her letters are poorly typed. She needs a new typewriter *and/or* a new secretary.
> The glassware is not clean. He needs a new dishwasher *and/or* better procedures.

Agreement

When *and* joins parts of the subject of a sentence, the verb is plural (see **Agreement of subject and verb**):

> The *boys and* their *father are* going together.

When *or* or *nor* joins parts of the subject of a sentence, the verb agrees with the part of the subject closest to it:

> Neither the boys *nor* their father *is* going.
> Neither Father nor our uncle *nor the boys* are going.

Punctuation

When a coordinating conjunction joins two main clauses, put a comma before the coordinating conjunction. But when a coordinating conjunction joins two words, phrases, or subordinate clauses, do not put a comma before the conjunction unless there is another reason for it. (see **Punctuation, comma,** and **Clauses, connectors**)

> They bought bread and milk, but they forgot to buy eggs.
> They had enough money for eggs and bread or for eggs and milk.

Compound Constructions

Coordination means putting ideas into equal grammatical constructions that are called *compound*. Ideas in equal constructions should be of equal importance. If the ideas do not have the same importance, put the less important one in a less important (subordinate) construction. (see **Subordination**)

Use coordinating conjunctions and correlative conjunctions (*either . . . or, neither . . . nor, not only . . . but also*) to join constructions of equal importance. (See **Parallel structure** for special problems with correlative conjunctions.)

1. Join words:

> *compound subject*
> *Paris, Rio de Janeiro, and Tokyo* are three cities I would like to visit.

> *compound verb*
> Andrew *played* in a band *and took* one math course last summer.

> *compound   compound*
> *compound subject   verb   verb*
> *Andrew and Peter   played*   together in a band *and took* one math course last summer. (Both parts of the subject act in both parts of the verb. Compare the compound sentences below.

> *compound*
> *direct object*
> Phyllis found her *books and coat* that she had left in the car.

> *compound*
> *predicate adjective*
> Annie is   *tall and slender.*

> *compound*
> *infinitives*
> The children want to *go and play* now.

> *compound object of preposition*
> I have an art class on *Monday, Wednesday, and Friday.*

2. Join phrases:

> *compound verb*
> *phrases*
>
> Andrew *had been playing* in the band for several months

> *compound verb*
> *phrases*
>
> *and had been taking* a math course, too.

> *prepositional*   *prepositional*
> *phrase*   *phrase*
>
> I have an art class *on Monday but* not *on Tuesday.*

> *gerund phrase*   *gerund phrase*
>
> *Driving through heavy traffic and finding a parking place* took Jane longer than she had planned.

> *compound adverb phrases*
>
> The bus is crowded *early in the morning and late in the afternoon.*

> *compound infinitive phrases*
>
> We decided *to go* now *and to see* as much as possible.

3. Join clauses:

Compound sentences are independent clauses joined by coordinating conjunctions.

>   *independent clause*   *so*
>
> Andrew *played* in the band last summer, *but* Peter *has* just joined it.
>   *and*

>   *independent clause*
>
> **CORRECT:**   Phyllis left her books in the car, *and*

>   *independent clause*
>
> she *left her coat in the library.*

Compound sentences that have the same subject in both clauses are likely to be wordy. Reduce the number of words in the sentence above by changing to a compound object.

>   *compound direct object*
>
> **IMPROVED:**   Phyllis left her *books* in the car *and* her *coat* in the library.

Dependent clauses can be joined by coordinating conjunctions.

>   *dependent clause (noun)*
>
> Discovering (that) the distance was too far *and*

> *dependent clause (noun)*
>
> (that) the time was too short, we decided not to drive to Florida.

>   *dependent clause (adverb)*
>
> When the experiment has been completed *and* (when)

>   *dependent clause (adverb)*
>
> the results have been published, Walter should get a promotion.

To avoid wordiness reduce coordinate clauses whenever possible. (see **Wordiness**)

CORRECT:	*dependent clause* If you have your test sheets *and*
	dependent clause if you have your pencil, you may begin to write now.
IMPROVED:	*compound object* If you have your test sheets and pencil, you may begin to write now.

Countable and Uncountable Nouns _____

Countable and *uncountable* refer to different kinds of nouns. Count-*able* nouns are sometimes called *count nouns*. Uncountable nouns are sometimes called *noncount* nouns or *mass* nouns. Nouns can be countable in one meaning and/or usage and uncountable in another meaning and/or usage.

COUNTABLE NOUNS	UNCOUNTABLE NOUNS
have singular and plural forms	have only one form
take singular or plural verbs according to their use as singular or plural	take singular verbs
can have *a, an,* or *one* before them as modifier in the singular	cannot have *a, an,* or *one* before them as modifier
can have *many* or *few* before them as modifier in the plural	can have *much* before them as a modifier
can have *some* before them as modifier only in the plural	can have *some* before them as a modifier
can have *number of* before them only in the plural	can have *amount of* before them

(see **Agreement of subject and verb, Articles, Determiners, Number,** and **Pronouns, indefinite,** and **quantity**)

Certain kinds of nouns are usually countable.

1. Names of persons, animals, plants, insects, and the like, and their parts:

PERSONS	ANIMALS	PLANTS	INSECTS	PARTS
a boy	a cat	a cactus	an ant	an ankle
a girl	a dog	a bush	a butterfly	a bone
a man	a horse	a flower	a caterpillar	a face
a student	a mouse	an oak	a fly	a head
a teacher	a tiger	a potato	a mite	a nose
a wife	a wolf	a rose	a tick	an ear
a woman	a zebra	a tree	a wasp	a wing

2. Objects with a definite shape:

a ball	a car	a house	a street	a typewriter
a building	a door	a mountain	a tent	an umbrella

3. Units of measurement (for length, area, weight, volume, temperature, pressure, speed, and so on) and words of classification. Uncountable nouns can be measured or classified:

a basketball	a foot	a square foot,	a drop	a kind	a bit
a gram	a meter	meter	a degree	a type	an item
an inch	a pound	a cubic inch, centimeter		a piece	a part

Classifications in society:

a family	a country	a language
a clan	a state	a word
a tribe	a city	a phrase

4. Some abstract words:

a help	an invention	a rest
a hindrance	a nuisance	a scheme
an idea	a plan	a taboo

Certain kinds of nouns are usually uncountable.
  1. Names of substances and materials:

FOOD	MATERIALS AND METALS	NATURAL QUALITIES
bread	copper	lightness
cake	cotton	darkness
chocolate	dacron	heaviness
meat	grass	brightness
spaghetti	iron	dullness and other words in
spinach	rayon	*-ness*
butter	steel	luminescence
cheese	wood	adolescence

2. Names of liquids, gases, and substances made of many small particles:

LIQUIDS	GASES	GRAINS AND OTHER SOLIDS MADE OF MANY SMALL PARTICLES
coffee	air	barley
milk	carbon dioxide	rice
oil	oxygen	sugar
tea	smoke	popcorn

3. Names of languages: Arabic, English, Chinese, French, Japanese, Russian, Spanish, Swahili, Welsh.

4. Most *-ing* forms. Exceptions include *building, feeling, dealing, wedding,* and *helping* when it means a portion of food; a *saving* is an economy, but *savings* is an amount of money; *furnishings* is always plural. (see **Gerunds**):

camping	hiking	parking	studying
clothing	learning	shopping	trying
dancing	lightning	smoking	waiting

5. Many abstract nouns, including words in *-ness, -ance, -ence,* and *-ity,* which are usually abstract and uncountable:

beauty	ignorance	peace	serenity
equality	importance	plenty	selfishness
happiness	obsolescence	sanity	verbosity

Many words that are countable in other languages are uncountable in English:

advice	courage	leisure	permission
anger	damage	luck	photography
applause	(harm)	luggage	and other
baggage	dirt	melancholy	disciplines in
behavior	education	money	*-aphy*
cash	equipment	moonlight	poetry
chaos	fun	mud	progress
chess and	furniture	music	publicity
names of	garbage	news (plural	rubbish
other games	harm	form but	safety
and sports	hospitality	takes singular	violence
china (dishes)	information	verb)	weather
conduct	laughter		

When uncountable nouns are measured or classified, they follow *of.*

a *piece of* cake	an *amount of* leisure	a *bottle of* milk
a *slice of* bread	five *pounds of* sugar	a *yard of* cloth

Piece, bit, and *item* can be used with many words. Other similar words can be used with only a few uncountable nouns.

a *slice of* bread, cake, meat	a *blade of* grass, wheat
a *bar of* chocolate, copper, candy	a *grain of* rice, barley, wheat
a *sheet of* paper, ice	a *lump of* coal, sugar

Many words have both countable and uncountable meanings. Substances, materials, activities, and abstract ideas often have countable meanings when one item or one specific example is meant.

COUNTABLE	UNCOUNTABLE
an activity, activities	activity
an agreement, agreements	agreement
an art, arts (a method of doing something)	art
a beauty, beauties (a person or thing that is beautiful)	beauty
a bone, bones (piece or pieces)	bone (substance)
a brick, bricks	brick (substance)
a business, businesses (a particular activity or activities)	business (activity)
a cake, cakes	cake (substance)
a chocolate, chocolates (a piece, pieces of candy)	chocolate (substance)
a cloth, cloths (a piece or pieces)	cloth (substance)
a decision, decisions (action or actions)	decision
a duty, duties (one requirement or requirements)	duty
a fire, fires (one or more examples)	fire (substance)
a glass, glasses (for liquid); (eye) glasses	glass (substance)
a hair, hairs (one or more strands)	hair (substance and collectively for all the hairs on one person's head)
a history, histories (one or more accounts or events)	history (study of the past)
an honor, honors (act or acts of respect)	honor (abstract)
a hope, hopes (an expectation)	hope (abstract)
an iron, irons (for pressing clothes, changing a tire, and so on)	iron (substance)
a kindness (a good deed or deeds)	kindness (abstract)
a language, languages (English, Chinese, and so on)	language (activity)

COUNTABLE AND UNCOUNTABLE NOUNS

COUNTABLE	UNCOUNTABLE
a light, lights (lamp or lamps or one source of light)	light (substance)
a material, materials (a substance; especially of cloth)	material
a noise, noises (one or more sounds)	noise (usually unpleasant sound)
a pain, pains (one or more feelings)	pain (collective)
a paper, papers (sheet of paper, a composition, a newspaper)	paper (substance)
a pity (something unfortunate)	pity (emotion)
a pleasure, pleasure (thing or things that give happiness)	pleasure (emotion)
a silence, silences (a period or periods of time without sound)	silence (lack of sound)
a space, spaces (empty place or places)	space (the expanse of the universe)
a stone, stones (a piece or pieces)	stone (substance)
a success, successes (a person or event)	success (abstraction)
a thought, thoughts (one instance)	thought (abstraction)
a time, times (an occasion, occasions)	time (collective)
a trade, trades (a skill, an exchange)	trade (business)
a traffic, traffics (dealing, dealings)	traffic (business; the number of vehicles)
a war, wars (a particular instance)	war (activity)
a wine, wines (a kind of)	wine (substance)
a work, works (of art, of an author)	work (effort or employment activity)
a worry, worries (one or more instances)	worry (activity)

Some words have similar forms, one countable and the other uncountable.

COUNTABLE	UNCOUNTABLE
clothes (plural only)	clothing
dance(s)	dancing
furnishings (plural only)	furniture
laugh(s)	laughter, laughing
machine(s)	machinery
moonbeam(s)	moonlight
payment(s)	pay
permit(s)	permission
sunbeam(s)	sunlight
use(s)	usefulness

When a prefix is added, some words that are countable become uncountable and some that are uncountable become countable.

COUNTABLE	UNCOUNTABLE
*in*decision	decision
*in*equality, *in*equalities	equality (abstraction)
	*in*equality (abstraction)
justice(s) (person only)	justice (abstraction)
an *in*justice, *in*justices (action)	*in*justice (abstraction)

D

Dash, see **Punctuation, dash**

Definition

A definition places something in a class or category and then shows how it is different from everything else in that same class or category.

Definitions may be short and objective, as they are in a dictionary, or longer and personal, as in an extended definition of democracy. You may state them in the singular, *a table,* or in the plural, *tables.*

CLASS	HOW IT IS DIFFERENT
A table is a piece of furniture	to eat, work, or write on. (by function)
or	
Tables are pieces of furniture	made of hard material such as wood, glass, or metal. (by material)
	with a flat top supported by legs or a pedestal. (by shape)

A negative definition tells what something is not.

A table is a piece of furniture	not intended for sleep. (function)
or	not made of cloth. (material)
Tables are pieces of furniture	that are not spherical. (shape)

Denotation

Denotation is the dictionary definition of a word. To use a word correctly, however, you must know if special circumstances affect its use or meaning. *Pretty*, for example, means *attractive in appearance*, but use it in that sense only for a child or young girl or young woman. Do not use it for a man or older woman. You can use *pretty boy* for a dog or a horse, but not usually for a person except jokingly. (Sometimes *pretty* replaces *very* in informal use: *That's pretty good.*) *Faithless* and *unfaithful* both mean *lacking in faithfulness*, but only *unfaithful* is used specifically to refer to a married person who has sexual relations with someone besides the marriage partner. (see **Connotation** and **Context**)

D

Description

Description gives a mental picture of something, usually according to what can be seen, but any impressions of the other senses—smell, taste, hearing, and touch—make description more vivid and therefore more effective. Location of the person, object, or scene being described is usually important in description. (see **Spatial order**)

Good description is specific and concrete. Use words that are precise and accurate. Avoid words that are general and trite.

Determiners

Determiners modify nouns and gerunds (and sometimes pronouns), but the nature of the noun—countable, singular; uncountable; or countable, plural—tells which determiner is possible. (see **Countable and uncountable nouns**)

Determiners always come before the nouns they modify. Other modifiers can come between a determiner and the noun it modifies. (see **Adjectives, order of**)

Use only one determiner before any one noun unless one of the determiners is in a prepositional phrase.

> *my*
> *some* books—*some* of *those* books
> *their*

"Predeterminers" (*all, both,* and *half*) are explained at the end of this section, pp. 135–136. See **Confusing choices** for special problems with some pairs of determiners: **a lot,** lots, lots of; **all,** all of, whole; **another,** other; **any,** some; **any body,** any one, anybody, anyone; **any more,** anymore; **each,** every, everyone, all; **each other,** every other; **few,** a few; **little,** a little; **one,** another, other, others.

Table of Determiners

	NOUN-SINGULAR COUNTABLE (takes singular verb)	NOUN-UNCOUNTABLE (takes singular verb)	NOUN-PLURAL COUNTABLE (takes plural verb)
Article	the, a, an, no	the, zero (no) article, no	the, zero (no) article, no
Possessive Pronoun Forms	my, our, your, his, her, its, their	my, our, your, his, her, its, their	my, our, your, his, her, its, their
Relative Pronoun Forms	whose, which(ever), what(ever)	whose, which(ever), what(ever)	whose, which(ever), what(ever)
Demonstrative Pronoun Forms	this, that	this, that	these, those
Indefinite Pronoun Forms	one, any, some, every, each, either, neither, (the) other, another	some, any, much, enough, more, most, (the) other, such, little, less, least, the amount (of)	some, any, both, many, enough, more, most, other, such, few, fewer, fewest, the number (of)
Cardinal Numbers	one		two, three, etc.
Ordinal Numbers	(the) first, second, third, etc., (the) last	(the) first, second, third, (the) last	(the) first, second, third, (the) last
Possessive Proper Nouns	John's, Mary's, Washington's	John's, Mary's, Washington's	John's, Mary's, Washington's

NOTE: *Zero article* in the table of determiners means that an uncountable noun or a plural noun is possible with no determiner or with only a pre-determiner before it. (see **Articles**)

DETERMINER		KIND OF NOUN
The	*book* is here.	(singular, countable)
Our	*books* are here.	(plural, countable)
Some	*day* they will come.	(singular, countable)
Some	*milk* is on the table.	(uncountable)
	Milk is on the table.	(uncountable)
Some	*books* are on the table.	(plural, countable)
Whatever	*milk* was left on the table has turned sour.	(uncountable)
This	*book* is on the table.	(singular, countable)
This	*milk* has turned sour.	(uncountable)
	Books are on that table, not magazines.	(plural, countable)
These	*books* are on the table.	(plural, countable)
Every	*book* on the table is for sale.	(singular, countable)
Enough	*milk* is on the table for all of us.	(uncountable)
Enough	*books* are on the table for all of us.	(plural, countable)
Mary's	*book* is on the table.	(singular, countable)
Washington's	*advice* is needed.	(uncountable)

You can put an *of* phrase after the indefinite pronoun forms. The meaning is the same with or without the *of*.

Any of the books will do.	(singular, countable)
Some of the milk is on the table.	(uncountable)
Some of the books are on the table.	(plural, countable)
Enough of the milk is on the table.	(uncountable)
Enough of the books are on the table.	(plural, countable)

NOTE: *Each* can be followed by *one,* but *no* + *one* becomes *none* or *not one.*

Each (one) of the books is on the table.	(singular, countable)
None (not one) of the books is on the table.	(singular, countable)

Predeterminers

Predeterminers that modify nouns come before determiners. They can be used without an *of* phrase to modify a noun.

ALL, BOTH, HALF

All the boys are here.
Half a loaf is better than none.
Both the children are asleep.
Half these apples are rotten.
Half this milk is spoiled.
All his children are here.
All John's children are here.
All whose names are called must come forward.

In a related construction, *all, both,* or *half* can be followed by an *of* phrase.

Half of these apples are rotten.
Half of this milk is spoiled.
All of his children are here.
All of John's children are here.

NOTE: After *of* use *those whose* instead of *whose* by itself

All of those whose names are called must come forward.

With an *of* phrase, these words can modify a pronoun as well as a noun.

All of the boys (them) are here.
Half of the loaf (it) is better than none.
Both of the children (them) are asleep.

WORD ORDER OF PREDETERMINERS: *All* and *both* can come after the noun or pronoun they modify.

The *people all* have problems.
They all have problems.
The *children both* are here.
They both are here.

Words showing multiplication can be predeterminers only. Do not use them with an *of* phrase or put them after the word that they modify.

CORRECT:	Double that salary will be too much.
INCORRECT:	Double *of* that salary will be too much.
CORRECT:	Four times the number of people were killed by hurricanes this year as compared to last year.
INCORRECT:	Four times *of* the number of people were killed by hurricanes this year as compared to last year.
CORRECT:	Twice the number that we expected registered today.
INCORRECT:	Twice *of* the number that we expected registered today.

But you can put an *of* phrase after *number*. Always use a plural noun or pronoun after *number of*.

CORRECT: *Twice* the number of students that we expected registered today.

NOTE: *Doubled, tripled,* and so on can follow the noun they modify.

That salary *doubled* will not be enough.

FRACTIONS

Fractions can be predeterminers and can also be used with an *of* phrase. Put a hyphen between the number parts of a fraction, but not after an article.

One-fourth (of) the class was absent.
One-third (of) my income goes for rent.

One in a fraction can be replaced by *a* and sometimes by *the,* as in

We will come in *a* half hour, but we still have *a* half mile to go.
You don't know *the* half of it.

Dialogue _____

Dialogue is spoken English written down. In dialogue the speaker's exact words are reported or imagined. Quotation marks separate a speaker's exact words from the explanations of the person speaking and comments on how the speaker feels. (see **Direct speech**)

A dialogue reports the conversation of two or more people. A monologue reports what one person says.

Diction _____

Diction can mean clear pronunciation if you are discussing speech, but in writing, diction means *choosing the correct word.* Many times you must choose between words that are spelled or pronounced nearly the same. Some words have meanings that are similar but not exactly the same. If you are not absolutely sure which word to use or how a word is spelled, look it up in a dictionary. (see **Confusing choices** for a list of words that often cause difficulty.) You must also use the correct form of a word. If you have difficulty telling which form is the adjective, adverb, noun, or verb form, see **Word formation, endings**.

Dictionaries

As your English improves, you should use English-English dictionaries rather than bilingual dictionaries to help you learn to think in English. Two dictionaries written especially for people who are not native speakers of English are especially helpful: the *Oxford Advanced Learner's Dictionary of Current English* and the *Longman Dictionary of Contemporary English*. Both these books give a great deal of grammatical information that is not in dictionaries for native speakers, and they also use words in phrase and sentences so that you can see other words such as prepositions or adverbs that must be used with the word you are looking up. These dictionaries tell you whether nouns are countable or uncountable, and give much more information about slang uses and connotation than dictionaries for native speakers do. Because they contain so much information about grammar and syntax, they do not have as many word entries as other dictionaries of the same size. You also need a dictionary written for native English speakers in order to have a longer word list for which definitions are given.

Direct Object

A direct object follows an active verb. Somebody or something (subject) acts in some way (verb) on somebody or something (direct object). (see **Voice**)

SUBJECT	VERB	DIRECT OBJECT
Mary	threw	the ball.
Mary	bought	some ice cream.
Mary	loves	John.

The direct object is something or somebody different from the subject except for the rare direct object that is a reflexive pronoun. (see **Pronouns**)

SUBJECT	VERB	DIRECT OBJECT	
John	hit	a ball (it)	over the fence.
John	hit	himself (reflexive pronoun)	on the elbow.

The direct object can be a noun, a noun phrase, an object pronoun, a noun clause, an *-ing* form, or an infinitive.

SUBJECT	VERB	DIRECT OBJECT
Mary	threw	the ball. (noun)
Mary	bought	some ice cream. (noun phrase)
Mary	bought	it. (pronoun)

Mary	bought	whatever we wanted. (noun clause)
Mary	likes	eating ice cream. (*-ing* form)
Mary	likes	to eat ice cream. (infinitive)

An indirect object can show *to* or *for* whom the action is done. (see **Indirect object**)

Direct Speech

Writers in English have two ways of showing what people say or write: *direct* speech and *reported* speech. Reported speech is sometimes called indirect speech. (see **Reported speech**)

Direct speech is a written record of someone's exact words. A phrase that identifies the speaker or writer can come either before or after the quotation. This phrase is sometimes called a *dialogue guide*. Direct speech is sometimes called *direct quotation* or *quoted speech*.

| | *quotation* | *dialogue guide* |
| DIRECT SPEECH: | "We want to go," | the students said. |

or

	dialogue guide	*quotation*
REPORTED SPEECH:	The students said, "We want to go."
	The students said that they wanted to go.

Punctuating Direct Speech

1. Put quotation marks (sometimes called inverted commas) around the speaker's exact words. Double quotation marks are usually used in the United States. (see **Punctuation, quotation marks**)

"We want to go," the students said.
"Tomorrow is a holiday," Kay told us.

2. Put a capital letter at the beginning of the speaker's exact words. The speaker's exact words (direct quotation) may begin at the beginning of the sentence,

"We want to go," the students said.
"Tomorrow is a holiday," Kay told us.

or the speaker's exact words (direct quotation) may begin in the middle of the sentence,

The students said, "We want to go."
Kay told us, "Tomorrow is a holiday."

3. Use a comma, a question mark, or an exclamation point to separate the speaker's exact words from the rest of the sentence. Do not use a period to separate the direct quotation from the phrase telling who speaks unless there are several sentences together in a longer passage (see below, rule 5).

> "We want to go," the students said.
> "May we go?" the students asked.
> "Help!" the students shouted.

NOTE: The phrase telling who speaks does *not* begin with a capital letter if it is not at the beginning of the sentence, even if it follows a question mark or an exclamation point.

4. Always put periods and commas inside (to the left of) the second part of the pair of quotation marks.

> "We want to go," the students said.
> The students said, "We want to go."

5. When the exact words of more than one speaker are written together, a special format is used. Indent at the beginning of the line to show a change of speaker.

FIRST SPEAKER:	"Peter, will you return these books to the library for me when you go there to work on your research paper this afternoon?" Sue asked. "I cannot take them back today, and they are due now."
SECOND SPEAKER:	"Will tonight be soon enough?" Peter answered. "I have to report for the first meeting of the track team this afternoon, but I plan to go to the library tonight, and I can take them for you then."
FIRST SPEAKER:	"That will be fine; thanks a lot," Sue said.
THIRD SPEAKER:	"If you do Sue a favor," Jan said, "then you can ask her to help you study for your chemistry test next week, Peter. Maybe she can help me, too."
FIRST SPEAKER:	"Of course, I could never refuse to help my friends," Sue agreed.

6. Always use a verb in the phrase that tells who is speaking in formal written English. Do not use a name followed by a colon without a verb unless you are writing or copying a play. People who write plays follow a special format.

7. When the dialogue guide (phrase telling who is speaking) interrupts the speaker's exact words, do not put a capital letter at the beginning of the continuation unless a new sentence begins there.

> "We want to go as soon as we can because we are afraid the game will be over before we get there," the students said.
> "We want to go as soon as we can," the students said,
>
> *continuation of the speaker's exact words in the same sentence*
> "because we are afraid the game will be over before we get there."

"Connie, come here," Aunt Marian said.

continuation
"Connie," Aunt Marian said, "come here."

8. You can invert the order of words in the dialogue guide when they come within the direct quotation or at the end of it. Normal word order is always correct, however.

NORMAL WORD
ORDER:
subject   verb
"We are the ones who are coming," *Charlotte said.*

INVERTED WORD
ORDER:
verb   subject
"We are the ones," *said Charlotte,* "who are coming."
"We are the ones who are coming," *said Charlotte.*

NORMAL WORD
ORDER:
"No one else knows as much as Ellen," *Margaret said.*

INVERTED WORD
ORDER:
"No one else," *said Margaret,* "knows as much as Ellen."
"No one else knows as much as Margaret," *said Ellen.*

9. Use ellipses (three spaced periods) to show that you have left out part of a direct quotation. (see **Punctuation, ellipses**)

"My purpose," wrote Wordsworth about the language of his poetry, "was to imitate and . . . adopt the very language of men."

NOTE: When you use a quotation from a written source, do not indent the beginning of the quotation if it comes in the middle of a paragraph of your own writing.

10. Use brackets around your own explanation within a quotation.

"My purpose [in choosing a poetic style] was to imitate and . . . adopt the very language of men," Wordsworth wrote.

Do

Do is both a main verb and an auxiliary (helping) verb. For uses of *do* as a main verb compared with *make,* see **Confusing choices, Do and Make.** For uses of *do* as an auxiliary (helping) verb, see **Auxiliary verbs, Operators,** and **Verb phrases.** For contracted forms of *do,* see **Contractions.** *Do* has irregular forms: *does, did* (past), and *done* (past participle).

Documentation _____

Documentation means giving credit to your sources for ideas, interpretations, and facts that came from someone else. Footnotes show the source of quotations, paraphrases, and facts that are not your own information each time you use such material in a paper. A bibliography is a list of all the sources you have used in your paper or a list of sources someone else has prepared for you to use when you want to find out more about a subject.

Although footnote and bibliography forms are not the same, the facts you need in documentation are mainly the same for both footnotes and bibliographies. Be sure to write down these facts when you first find the information:

1. The author of the book or article
2. The exact title of the book or article
3. The date of publication
4. Additional information *for a book*
   a. page number(s) on which you found *each item* of relevant information
   b. volume number if the book is part of a series
   c. name of the company that published the book
   d. place where the book was published (if several cities are mentioned, use the first one listed)
5. Additional information *for a magazine*
   a. exact name of the magazine or journal
   b. number of the volume and issue if this information is given (volume numbers are often given in Roman numerals)
   c. page number(s) on which you found each item of relevant information
   d. page number(s) on which the article begins and ends

The way you use your information depends on the discipline (subject) you are writing for. The humanities (languages, literature, history, speech, art, and music) usually use the same format although there are variations in it. The MLA Style Sheet is used more than any other guide in the humanities. Sciences and social sciences use formats that are very different from the humanities format. Find out the format that is required for the discipline for which you are writing, get the handbook or style sheet that is recommended, and follow it *exactly*.

Failure to provide the documentation that is needed in a research paper is called plagiarism. Plagiarism is a serious error in scholarship whether it is intentional or unintentional. (see **Plagiarism**)

Differences between footnote and bibliography forms in the humanities:

FOOTNOTES

Put the author's first name first.

Separate the items of information by commas.

Indent the first line of each entry.

Put the place and date of publication for books in parentheses.

Number the footnotes in sequence.

Give the page references for books and articles.

Put footnotes in order of appearance in the paper.

BIBLIOGRAPHY

Put the author's last name first.

Separate the items of information by periods.

Indent the second and subsequent lines of each entry.

Do not number the entries.

Give the page numbers for the beginning and end of articles only, but do not give page numbers for books.

Put bibliographical entries in alphabetical order according to the author's last name.

Terms and Abbreviations Used in Documentation

Style sheets and handbooks no longer advise the use of all abbreviations and terms below, but you need to understand and recognize them when you see them in older books and journals.

Some of these abbreviations are sometimes written in italics, but they are usually treated as English words now, so do not underline them unless your style sheet tells you to do so.

anon.	anonymous—author unknown or not given
c., ca., or circa	about—used with estimated dates
cf.	*confer*—compare or consult
ch., chs./chap., chaps.	chapter, chapters
cite	give as a reference
diss.	dissertation
ed.	editor, edited by, edition
e.g.	*exempli gratia*—for example
et al.	*et alia*—and others (more than one author, but only one is named)
f.	and the following page
ff.	and the following pages
ibid.	*ibidem*—in the same place; it means that this reference is the same as the one immediately above.
idem	the same
i.e.	*id est*—that is

l., ll.	line, lines
loc. cit.	*loco citato*—in the place cited (already mentioned)
MS, MSS	manuscript, manuscripts
N.B.	*Nota Bene*—take note
n.d.	no date of publication given
n.p.	no place of publication given
op. cit.	*opere citato*—in the work (book or article) already cited (mentioned)
p., pp.	page, pages
passim	here and there throughout the pages already mentioned
rev.	revised
[sic]	thus—used to identify an apparent error and show that the source has been copied correctly (always put this word in brackets, not parentheses)
tr., trans.	translator, translated by, translation
v., vv.	verse, verses
vv.	verses
vol., vols.	volume, volumes

Footnotes

Footnotes show the source of ideas, interpretations, and facts that come from someone else, or they sometimes explain more fully a difficulty in the text. Footnotes are put at the bottom of the page. You must give credit to anyone whose ideas or facts are used in your footnotes unless the material you use is common knowledge accepted without disagreement by everyone who knows about your subject. You can generally assume that information in dictionaries and encyclopedias is common knowledge. If you find the same information without documentation in several books, you can usually assume that the information is common knowledge to scholars in that field, and you do not have to document it either. *Reference notes* are put in parentheses in the text. *End notes* are put at the end of the paper.

Explanatory footnotes give additional comment or information related to the text that the author considers helpful but less important. Although you often see explanatory footnotes in books, do not use them unless you are sure that they are acceptable. Some editors and teachers allow their use, but others dislike them.

Footnotes can be made for nonprint sources such as interviews, television and radio programs, speeches, movies, and records. Look up the correct forms to use in the handbook or style sheet of your discipline.

Bibliography

A bibliography may be published separately or at the end of a book or article. When you are asked to compile a bibliography for a research paper, you must give a list of all the materials that appear in your footnotes (sources cited) or a list of all the materials you have found, whether or not you have used them in your footnotes (sources consulted).

Arrange a bibliography alphabetically, according to the author's last name. If the name of the author is not known, the article or book is alphabetized by its title. (see **Alphabetization**) Sometimes bibliographies show the difference between primary sources and secondary sources. A *primary source* in art or literature is the piece of art or literature that you are discussing. In other disciplines, the primary source could be research data, diaries of people involved in events, or records written at the time the events happened.

A *secondary source* is a report or an explanation of the primary source or a commentary on it. Since secondary sources do not all have the same value, you must use your own judgment to evaluate them when they disagree. What is the scholar's reputation and bias? What is the date? Documentation? Is the publication a scholarly one or a popular one?

An *annotated bibliography* is a list of books and articles on a subject with all the necessary publication information, but also with a brief summary of the information in the book or article and a comment about the interpretation or bias the author brings to the subject.

Else

Else means *other* or *more*. It always follows the word it modifies. It can modify a compound pronoun—*anyone, somebody, everything,* and so on—or it can modify a WH-word that starts a question. *Else* can have a possessive form when it refers to a person.

> If anybody *else* tries to sit here, we will be too crowded.
> Everyone *else* remembered. Why didn't you?
> We have looked everywhere for the missing child. What *else* can we do? Is there anywhere *else* to look?
> Who *else* is coming?
> This umbrella is Dan's; that one is someone *else's.*
> Who *else's* work is not finished yet?

Following *or, else* means *otherwise* or *if not.*

> Run fast, *or else* put up your umbrella to keep from getting wet.
> Pay the rent, *or else* move out of the apartment.

Emphasis

Show emphasis by several methods.

1. Move words, phrases, and clauses from their normal position to emphasize them. (Never put *always* or *ever* [unless *ever since* or *ever after*] at the beginning or end of a statement, but *always* can come at the beginning of a command.)

Move an adverb, adverb phrase, or adverb clause to the beginning of the sentence for emphasis.

The doctor is ready to see you *now*.
Now the doctor is ready to see you.

Pamela drinks three cups of coffee *every morning*.
Every morning Pamela drinks three cups of coffee.

Jerry was disappointed *when he lost the race*.
When Jerry lost the race, he was disappointed.

Move *so* to the beginning of a sentence that has a *so . . . that* construction and put the verb before the subject to emphasize the word that follows *so*.

The *arguments* were *so* convincing *that* we finally agreed to the proposal.

       verb   *subject*
So convincing *were* the *arguments that* we finally agreed to the proposal.

Put the direct object at the beginning of the clause.

I always enjoy *this beautiful scene*.
This beautiful scene I always enjoy.

He took *what he could*.
What he could, he took.

Put the predicate nominative at the beginning of the clause.

The new mayor is the hope of the city.
The hope of the city is the new mayor.

More tutoring is what I need.
What I need is more tutoring.

2. Use *do, did,* or *does* to emphasize the verb.

The children learn quickly here.
The children *do* learn quickly here.

Brenda has her own room now.
Brenda *does* have her own room now.

We need to clean house.
We *do* need to clean house.

3. Use *ever* as a separate word after a WH-word for emphasis.

What did you do?
What *ever* did you do?

How did he do that?
How *ever* did he do that?

E

4. Use emphasizing words with care. Often a statement is stronger without them, especially in writing. (see **Very**)

ADJECTIVES	ADVERBS
certain	certainly
clear	clearly
definite	definitely
great	greatly
perfect	perfectly
total	totally
absolute	absolutely
the very	very
real	really
	indeed
	quite
	truly

Truly, really, and *very* can come between a determiner and an adjective.

This is a serious mistake.

       truly
This is a *really* serious mistake.
       very

You are wrong.
You are *certainly* wrong.

This is a mistake.
This is *definitely* a mistake. (adverb)
This is a *definite* mistake. (adjective)

5. Use certain words and phrases to emphasize negatives.

not, none, any, *at all*
not *by any means*
none *whatever*
never *again*
not *one*
not *a single one*

We have run out of bread. (uncountable)
We do not have any *at all*.
There is none *whatever*.
We cannot find any *by any means*.
We have no apples. (countable)
We have none *whatever*.
We have none at all, *not one*.
We do not have a *single* one.
We may never have *any more*.

6. Use a possessive or object pronoun according to the emphasis you want when you use an -*ing* form, gerund, or participle. (see **Gerund**)

7. Use the passive voice when the actor is unimportant. (see **Passive verbs**)

Enough _____

When *enough* is used as an adverb, it must follow the adjective or adverb that it modifies. It means *as much* or *as many as necessary*, or *to the necessary degree*.

>   *adjective*
> Chris is   *old*   *enough* to go to school.

>   *adverb*
> The firemen came   *soon* *enough* to save the house from burning down.

>   *adverb*
> Mrs. Peterson has worked *long* *enough* to retire.

When *enough* is used as an adjective, it must follow a countable singular noun, but it can come before or after an uncountable or a countable plural noun.

>   *adverb*
>   *countable*
>   *singular*
>   *noun*
> He is   *man*   *enough* to face his problems.

>   *uncountable*
>   *noun*
> The distance runners have *enough determination* to finish the race.

> or

>   *uncountable*
>   *noun*
> The distance runners have *determination enough* to finish the race.

>   *uncountable*
>   *noun*
> Do you have *enough*   *money*   for your plane fare?

>   *uncountable*
>   *noun*
> Do you have   *money*   *enough* for your plane fare?

>   *countable*
>   *noun*
> He has done *enough experiments* to finish the course.

>   *uncountable*
>   *noun*
> He has done *experiments enough* to finish the course.

When *enough* is a pronoun, it means *a sufficient amount or number.*

pronoun
The children ate *enough* to satisfy themselves.

pronoun
Since the plums have been ripe, we have had *enough* of them to make jam.

pronoun
We have made many friends, *enough* to keep us from being lonely here.

Essential and Nonessential Modifiers _____

Modifiers such as adjectives, participial phrases (*-ing* forms), and dependent clauses may be either *essential* or *nonessential.* (Some grammars use the terms *restrictive/nonrestrictive* or *limiting/nonlimiting* for this difference.)

Essential modifiers are necessary to identify the word they modify. They tell "which one." Nonessential modifiers give additional information about something that is already identified. A proper name is almost always complete identification, so additional information about somebody or something called by a proper name is almost always nonessential.

Do not set off essential modifiers from the rest of the sentence by a comma or a pair of commas. Set off nonessential modifiers from the rest of the sentence by a comma or a pair of commas. (see **Punctuation, commas**)

ESSENTIAL:	My neighbor who likes to swim hates rainy days. (*who likes to swim* tells which neighbor.)
NONESSENTIAL:	Dr. Brown, who likes to swim, hates rainy days.
ESSENTIAL:	Students who need a receipt may apply here. (Some students need a receipt.)

Putting commas in the sentence above changes the meaning from *some students* to *all students.*

NONESSENTIAL:	Students, who need a receipt, may apply here. (All students need a receipt.)
ESSENTIAL:	Drivers in the city who obey traffic laws have fewer accidents. (Some drivers in the city obey traffic laws; only these drivers have fewer accidents.)
NONESSENTIAL:	Drivers in the city, who obey traffic laws, have fewer accidents. (All drivers in the city obey traffic laws and have fewer accidents than drivers outside the city.

In spoken English the difference between essential and nonessential modifiers is shown by a change in intonation and by slight pauses before and after nonessential modifiers. Show these pauses in your writing by using a comma or commas to show nonessential modifiers.

ESSENTIAL:	My brother James is a student here. (I have more than one brother. One is named James. That one is a student here.)
NONESSENTIAL:	My brother, James, is a student here. (I have only one brother; his name is James. He is a student here.)

Essential modifiers tell which one.

ESSENTIAL:	The word *receive* is often misspelled.
ESSENTIAL:	The planet Pluto is the planet in the solar system that is the farthest from earth.

Do not set off the *-self* pronouns with commas.

I *myself* will go.
The drivers *themselves* could not avoid the accident.

CLAUSES: (see **Pronouns, relative**) An essential clause can begin with *that*, it can begin with its own subject if *that* is left out, it can begin with a WH-word, or it can begin with a preposition followed by a WH-word. If you can use either *that* or *which,* use *that* in essential clauses in formal writing (British usage allows *which*).

	ESSENTIAL CLAUSE	
that	The man *that* I told you about	is here.
that left out; subject begins the clause	The man *I* told you about	is here.
WH-word	The man *whom* I told you about	is here.
preposition + *WH*-word	The man *of whom* I spoke	is here.

A nonessential clause begins with a WH-word or with a preposition followed by a WH-word.

	NONESSENTIAL CLAUSE
WH-word	Joyce Harris, *who(m)* I saw yesterday, asked about you. (Use *whom* in formal writing.)
WH-word	Joyce Harris, *who* came back from vacation yesterday, asked about you.
WH-word	Joyce Harris, *whose* mother is in the hospital, left early today.
preposition + *WH*-word	Joyce Harris, to *whom* I sent an invitation to our party, asked about you.
WH-word	Chicago, *which* is known as the windy city, gets the wind off Lake Michigan.

Although proper names are usually followed by nonessential modifiers, proper names that stand for more than one person, place, or thing can be identified by essential modifiers. Put *the* before the proper noun to indicate one specific item out of more than one.

ESSENTIAL: The Miami *that is in Ohio* is a smaller city than the Miami *that is in Florida.*

ESSENTIAL: That is the Joe Green *who is the football player,* not the Joe Green *who is the singer.*

Exclamation point, see **Punctuation, exclamation point**

Expletive

An expletive is a meaningless word or filler, usually at the beginning of a sentence. (Sometimes *expletive* means an oath or a violent or profane word used to express strong feeling.) *There* and *it* can be expletives in the sense of fillers. Putting the true subject of the clause at the beginning makes a better written sentence. (see **It**)

Always use a singular verb after *it.*

CORRECT: It is useless to go now.
IMPROVED: To go now is useless.

CORRECT: It has been a short vacation.
IMPROVED: Our vacation has been short.

Use *it* to begin a sentence about the weather.

CORRECT: It is raining/snowing/hot/cold, and so on.

Use a singular verb after *there* if the noun following the verb is singular; use a plural verb if the noun following the verb is plural. Put the true subject at the beginning of the clause if possible.

       singular
CORRECT: There *is* no *one* here to help.
IMPROVED: No *one is* here to help.

       plural
CORRECT: There *are* many *students* standing in line.
IMPROVED: Many *students are* standing in line.

Explicit Material

Explicit means clear or well-explained. When you write exposition, do not expect your readers to guess what you mean, but state your ideas clearly in logical order. If you write fiction (novels and short stories), you expect your readers to enjoy using their imaginations. But when you are explaining something or persuading someone, your explanation must be clear and complete. (see **Argument, Exposition,** and **Implicit**)

Exposition _____

Exposition means explanation. The adjective form is *expository*. Most academic writing is mainly exposition or argument, which is similar to exposition. Exposition is one of the four kinds of prose discourse; the other three are *description* (adjective: descriptive), *narration* (adjective: narrative), and *argument* (adjective: argumentive or argumentative). Exposition is usually arranged in logical order. Illustrations or examples may be in chronological order or spatial order, but the underlying pattern is almost always some kind of logical order. (see **Argument, Description, Logical order,** and **Narration**)

Fiction

Fiction is a story that is partly or completely imaginary. A prose story that is not long enough to be published as a separate book is called a *short story*. A prose story long enough to be published separately is called a *novel*. (A short novel is sometimes called a *novella*.) (see **Prose**)

Three elements in fiction are the *plot* (what happens), the *characters* (the people), and the *setting* (where the story takes place). A few pieces of fiction have animals instead of people for characters (these are sometimes called *fables*), and science fiction often has characters that are not human.

The *theme* of a short story or novel is the underlying idea or truth that is illustrated by the story, such as the relation between humanity and evil, the relation between humanity and the forces of nature, or the reactions of people to changes in society. The theme is usually implicit rather than explicit; that is, the author shows what the story means through the plot, characters, and setting, but does not tell you its meaning directly.

A *historical novel* is based on well-known events in history that actually happened. The author fills in characters, details of action, and motivation that are not recorded in historical accounts by making reasonable inferences and imagining events that historians did not record. The adjective *fictional* is commonly used to describe something that is not factual but a product of the imagination.

Although sometimes people think of fiction only as novels and short stories, poetry and drama which tell stories are also fiction. Thus in a broad sense of the word *fiction*, any narrative that includes imaginary elements is fiction.

154

Figures of Speech _____

Figures of speech explain or suggest by using words and ideas differently from their literal meanings. *Figurative language* is language that uses many figures of speech.

Apostrophe—direct address of an abstract quality (see **Personification**)

Climax—arranging ideas in order of importance. (see **Logical order**)

Hyperbole—an extreme exaggeration

Irony—saying the opposite of what is really meant (see **Irony**)

Metaphor—comparing qualities of two things that are basically different (see **Metaphor**)

Personification—giving human qualities to things that are not human (see **Personification**)

Repetition—using the same word, form, or idea more than once (see **Repetition**)

Simile—comparing one quality of two things that are basically different, explicitly, using *like* or *as* (see **Simile**)

Finite Verb _____

A finite verb is a verb form or forms that can be used as the main verb in a clause. (see **Clause**) A finite verb may be just one word or it may be several words together in a finite verb phrase.

A finite verb can show tense, voice, mood, and aspect. In order to show all these different meanings, a finite verb phrase can include modals and auxiliaries as well as the head verb (the head verb carries the dictionary meaning). (see **Aspect, Mood, Tense,** and **Voice**) In the present tense, with *be* in the past tense, and in all verb phrases that use present or past forms of *be*, verb forms also show number. (see **Agreement of subject and verb**)

PRESENT TENSE,
ACTIVE VOICE: John *throws* the ball.

PAST TENSE,
ACTIVE VOICE: John *threw* the ball.

PRESENT TENSE,
PROGRESSIVE/
CONTINUOUS ASPECT: John *is throwing* the ball.

PRESENT TENSE,
PASSIVE VOICE: The ball *is thrown* (by John).

PRESENT TENSE,
ACTIVE VOICE,
INDICATIVE MOOD,
(STATEMENT):   John *throws* the ball.

PRESENT TENSE,
IMPERATIVE MOOD,
(COMMAND):   *Throw* the ball.

F

Aspect

Aspect is sometimes used to distinguish the perfect and continuous/progressive verb forms. Many grammars, however, treat the perfect and progressive forms as tenses rather than as separate aspects.

> The children *learn* easily. (present)
> The children *have learned* easily. (present perfect)
> The children *are learning* easily. (present continuous/progressive)

Few verbs can be used in all the possible forms of a finite verb. Only active verbs have direct objects, for example. Some verbs are never used as commands.

Agreement

A finite verb must agree with its subject in person and number. (see **Agreement of subject and verb**)

Tense

Show tense in a finite verb phrase only in the head word (main verb), the modal, the auxiliary, or *be*. (*Be* is listed separately from the auxiliaries *have* and *do* in the table.)

> John *goes*. John *went*. John *will go*.
> John *can* go. John *could* go.
> John *is* going. John *was* going.
> John *has* to go. John *had* to go.
> John *wants* to go. John *wanted* to go.

Do not repeat the tense in an infinitive that follows the finite verb.

INCORRECT:	Leslie *liked* to *walked* to the office.
CORRECT:	Leslie *liked* to *walk* to the office.
INCORRECT:	My sister *did* not find time to *studied* last night.
CORRECT:	My sister *did* not find time to *study* last night.

Do not repeat the tense in the head verb after *do, does,* or *did.* (This form of the head verb is called the simple or bare infinitive form.)

INCORRECT:	My sister *did* not *found* time to study last night.
CORRECT:	My sister *did* not *find* time to study last night.
INCORRECT:	Leslie *did* not *walked* to the office.
CORRECT:	Leslie *did* not *walk* to the office.

Word Order

Put the words in a verb phrase in the required order. Form verb phrases in the order given below for a statement, starting at the left. Most phrases will be made of two or three words. (See **Inverted order, Operators,** and **Questions** for changes in word order in special circumstances.)

	MODAL^T (not)	+ AUXILIARY^T (not)	+ be^T (not)	+ *ing* FORM	+ HEAD VERB: base or past participle	+ OBJECT and/or INF/GER
They 1.	could				go.	
2.	will				go.	
3.	will		be	going.		
4.			are	going.		
5.			were	going to	walk.	
6.	will				have	to go.
7.	might	have	been		found.	
8.	might	have	been	hiking.		
9.			are	being	taught	to obey.
10.	may	have	been	asking		her to come.
11.			are	being	examined.	
12.		did			find	the report.

1. *T:* Only these three forms marked *T* can show tense in a finite verb phrase. Show tense in only *one* of these forms. Working from left to right on the chart above, you can

show tense by changing *will, shall,* or *may* to *would, should,* or *might* if one of these words is in the clause

or

use *will* or *shall* to show future tense

or

show tense by changing *have* or *do* to *had* or *did*

or

show tense by changing *be* to *is, are, was, were,* or *been.*

2. *Not:* Working from left to right on the table, you can put *not* after the modal if there is one (*may not*)

or

put *not* after any form of *have* or *do* if there is no modal (*have not* or *do not*)

or

put *not* after *be* if there is no modal, no *have,* or no *do* (*is not, are not, were not*)

3. *Have, did,* and *be* can be head verbs. You can use them as the head verb and as the auxiliary in the same sentence.

He *has* (aux) *had* (head verb) to work hard.
She *did* (aux) not *do* (head verb) her work.
They *are* (aux) *being* (head verb) difficult.

4. Use the head verb only once. In a finite verb phrase, you can use the base (simple, bare infinitive) form **or** the *-ing* form **or** the past participle of the head verb.

5. Do not put more than one *-ing* form in any one finite verb phrase except after *going to be.*

6. With *going* as a semi-auxiliary in the future and intentional meaning, add *to.*

7. After certain base forms, you can add an infinitive or gerund. (see **Infinitive/-*ing* choice**)

Format

Format is the way something looks on a piece of paper. Format is fixed by the way people usually arrange words, sentences, paragraphs, outlines, and titles on each page. Format changes for different purposes. In handwritten paragraphs, for example, you should indent from the left-hand margin at the beginning of each paragraph in formal composition. In typed business letters, however, you should not indent from the left-hand margin, but you should leave extra space between your paragraphs. Outlines, documentation in the humanities, documentation in the sciences, business writing, and newspapers all have different required formats. In this handbook you will find the accepted format for academic writing except where a note explains other styles. (see **Business writing, Outlining, Style**)

Use one side of the paper only for typed or handwritten compositions.

If you write on lined paper with a red-line margin, be sure the red line is at the left side of the paper.

If you write on looseleaf notebook paper, be sure the holes are at the left side of the paper.

The correct format of a term paper or a research paper includes the following separate sheets of paper:

Title page: This should carry the title of the paper, your name, your instructor's name, the course, and the date.

Thesis statement and outline and as many additional pages as you need for the outline. (Sometimes an outline is not required.)

Composition: Always start your composition on a new page; use a clean sheet of paper after you have finished your outline.

Documentation: If footnotes are required, you may be told to put them at the bottom of the page they document, in parentheses in the text, or all together at the end of the paper. If a bibliography is required, put it last. (see **Documentation**)

A long paper must usually be typed and presented in a folder. Follow the instructions you are given.

Fragments _____

A fragment is a group of words that looks like a sentence, but it is not. A capital letter begins the group of words, and a period ends it. But in between the capital letter and the period, some part that is necessary has been left out or put in a wrong form, resulting in a fragment. A sentence fragment is a serious error in composition.

A dependent clause that is not attached to an independent clause is a fragment. (see **Clauses**)

A subordinating word such as *that*, the WH-words, and the subordinating conjunctions (*after, because, if,* and so on) make a clause dependent. (However, WH-words can introduce questions of only one clause. (see **Questions, Relative pronouns, Subordinating conjunctions, and WH-words**)

INCORRECT:	1. *When* Charles came to visit us. (*fragment*)
INCORRECT:	2. *If* Margaret has missed the first bus today. (*fragment*)
INCORRECT:	3. *That* Harold told us about. (*fragment*)
INCORRECT:	4. *Who* was looking for a new apartment. (*fragment*)

The first two sentences above can be corrected by leaving out the subordinators (in these sentences the subordinators are subordinating conjunctions).

	independent clause
CORRECT:	1. Charles came to visit us.

	independent clause
CORRECT:	2. Margaret has missed the first bus today.

Leaving out the subordinators does not always correct sentences, however. Sentences 3 and 4 can be corrected only by changing *that* and *who* (relative pronouns) to personal pronouns.

CORRECT:	3. Harold told us about *it*.
CORRECT:	4. *She* was looking for a new apartment.

It and *she* refer to an unknown antecedent in a longer passage. Since sentence fragments are usually written as part of a longer passage, they can often be attached to the sentence that comes before them or to the sentence that comes after them, keeping the subordinating word. You put in the subordinator because it showed the meaning you wanted when you first wrote the sentence. That meaning is important. Keep subordinating words in your sentence if possible when correcting them.

dependent clause
1. When Charles came to visit us,

independent clause
he brought us some flowers.

dependent clause
CORRECT: 2. If Margaret has missed the first bus today,

independent clause
she will have to take a later one.

independent clause   *dependent clause*
3. This is the book   that Charles told us about.

independent clause
4. My sister Helen is the one

dependent clause
who is looking for a new apartment.

2. A statement that begins with a capital letter and ends with a period is a fragment if it does not have a subject and/or a finite (main) verb. Verbals (*-ing* and *to* + verb) cannot be the main verb in a clause.

FRAGMENTS
Margaret missing the first bus today.
Margaret to miss the first bus today.

An *-ing* form or an infinitive can be changed to a finite verb.

CORRECT: Margaret $\begin{cases} \text{will miss} \\ \text{missed} \\ \text{has missed} \\ \text{is going to miss} \end{cases}$ the first bus today.

Verbal phrases can also be attached to an independent clause or a sentence before or after them.

CORRECT: Margaret, missing the first bus today, was late to work.

CORRECT: Margaret was sorry to miss the first bus today.

INCORRECT: Margaret's alarm clock did not wake her up this morning and she left her apartment later than usual. *Missing* the first bus today.

CORRECT: Margaret's alarm clock did not wake her up this morning and she left her apartment later than usual, missing the first bus today.

Do not punctuate prepositional phrases as sentences, even when they have verbals in them. Always connect them to an independent clause.

INCORRECT:	Margaret *as a result of missing the first bus.* She was late to work.
CORRECT:	As a result of missing the first bus, Margaret was late to work.
INCORRECT:	Margaret was late to work. Even after running to the bus stop.
CORRECT:	Margaret was late to work even after running to the bus stop.

NOTE: Sentence fragments are very common in spoken English. They are acceptable in a written record of actual speech, but avoid them in formal writing unless you are recording the exact words that someone has actually said.

Function Words

Function words make writing clear by showing relationships between ideas. These words can be used with different subjects. Function words join ideas within one sentence, between sentences, and between paragraphs. Sometimes they are called *transitions* or *continuity*. (The subject or ideas you are writing about are stated in *content words*.)

Function words show *order*.

order of time (see **Chronological order**)
order of space (see **Spatial order**)
numerical order—first, second, third, last, finally, another, a second, the final, the last
order of importance—the first, second, third, and so on; the chief, main, primary, secondary, and the like.

a more
the most
the least
a less
} {
significant
notable
influential
prominent
vital
essential
important
necessary

Function words *introduce illustrations and examples.* (see **Substantiation**)
Function words show *logical connection.*

likenesses and differences (see **Comparison and contrast**)
reasons, causes, and results (see **Cause and effect**)

(See also **Clauses** and **Interrupters** for correct punctuation of function words.)

Fused sentences, see **Run-on sentence**

G

Gender

Most nouns in English have the same form for male and female. The only pronouns that show sex distinction are *he* and *she* and the other forms related to them. *It* shows that sex is unknown, absent, or unimportant. English has few words with two related forms, one for male and the other for female. Some words, however, are sex-related. They can be used for only one sex.

Some Words with Masculine and Feminine Forms

MASCULINE	FEMININE
man	woman
widower	widow
host	hostess
god	goddess
steward	stewardess
waiter	waitress
lion	lioness

Some Words That Can Be Used for One Sex Only

People

father	mother
husband	wife
boy	girl
son	daughter
uncle	aunt
brother	sister
nephew	niece
gentleman	lady

Animals, Birds, and Fowl

MALE	FEMALE	COMMON WORD
bull, steer*	cow	cattle
stallion, gelding*	mare	horse
boar	sow	pig, hog
ram	ewe	sheep
buck	doe	deer
cock, rooster, capon*	hen	chicken
gander	goose	goose
drake	duck	duck

* Used for a male that has been castrated.

Some people object to words for occupations and professions that are marked to indicate sex differences. *Flight attendant* is preferred to *steward* and *stewardess,* for example. (See **Women, terms referring to**)

Adjectives do not change to show gender. Possessive pronouns, however, must show the sex of the person they stand for (antecedent), never the sex of the noun they modify.

masculine   *masculine feminine*
   Ralph   brought   *his*   *mother* some roses. (*his* refers to *Ralph*, not to *mother*)

feminine   *feminine masculine*
   Lucy   found   *her*   *brother* in the library. (*her* refers to *Lucy*, not to *brother*)

G

Generalization _____

A generalization is a statement that is true for more than one specific instance or one which links the common characteristics of separate facts. Generalizations do not always have to be absolutes; that is, they do not have to be true in every possible instance. Statements that are true most of the time can be generalizations. In science, however, a generalization is a conclusion drawn from many different observations that all give the same result. Scientific generalizations are often called laws. In composition, a generalization that states the main idea of an entire composition is called the thesis statement. (see **Thesis statement**) A generalization that states the main idea of a paragraph is called the topic sentence. (see **Topic sentence** and **Paragraph**)

A calculator works faster than the human brain.
Hurricanes can be very destructive.
Successful societies adapt to their physical environments.

The generalizations above are very broad. They can be limited by specific modifiers or by substituting specific terms for general ones.

> Hurricanes *in the Caribbean* have caused great damage *in the last ten years.* (modifying)
>
> Hurricanes in the Caribbean have caused *great property damage and loss of life* in the last ten years. (substituting *great property damage and loss of life* for damage)

The specific examples given to illustrate a generalization are called *supporting details, evidence,* or *substantiation.* They may be facts and/or opinion. For a generalization about hurricanes, facts based on written reports or personal experience are required.

Gerunds _____

Gerunds are *-ing* forms of the verb that are used as nouns. Gerunds name actions. (see **Nouns**)

SUBJECT:	*Learning* the new bus schedule is easy.
	Making new friends can be difficult.
PREDICATE NOMINATIVE:	My student job this year is *working* in the library.
	Paul's favorite sport is *running.*
DIRECT OBJECT:	Paul likes *running.*
	Jim enjoys *playing* golf.
OBJECT OF A PREPOSITION:	Paul likes most sports *except fishing.*
	Some people are afraid *of speaking* in public.
OBJECTIVE COMPLEMENT:	The police officer considered the offense *speeding.*
	The teacher called the children's play *learning.*

Although gerunds are used in a clause as nouns, they keep the qualities of verbs. Gerunds can be followed by direct objects, indirect objects, adverb modifiers, and predicate adjectives if their meaning allows these constructions.

		direct
GERUND FOLLOWED BY	*gerund*	*object*
DIRECT OBJECT:	*Learning* the new bus *schedule* is easy.
	Making	new *friends* can be difficult.

NOTE: When an article or an adjective modifies the gerund, the gerund is followed by a prepositional phrase instead of by a direct object.

MODIFIERS BEFORE A GERUND:	*modifier gerund*	*prepositional phrase*

Constant learning of new bus schedules is annoying.

The building   of a lasting friendship can take a long time.

GERUND FOLLOWED BY INDIRECT OBJECT:	*indirect object*

Giving Jim new golf clubs would please him.

Buying Paula new shoes is expensive.

GERUND FOLLOWED BY ADVERB MODIFIER:	*adverb modifier*

Learning quickly is easier for Pat than for Steve.

Eating   fast is bad for the digestion.

GERUND FOLLOWED BY PREDICATE ADJECTIVE:	*predicate adjective*

Feeling happy makes Ray sing.

Being kind can be difficult.

Use a possessive pronoun before a gerund. Using an object form of the pronoun changes the meaning and emphasis of the sentence. Use an object pronoun if the *-ing* form is a participle that modifies the pronoun.

OBJECT PRONOUN FOLLOWED BY PARTICIPLE:	

We heard *the dog barking.*

We heard *it barking.* (emphasis on *it—barking* modifies *it*)

We saw *John sleeping.*

We saw *him sleeping.* (emphasis on *him—sleeping* modifies *him*)

POSSESSIVE PRONOUN FOLLOWED BY GERUND:	

We heard the *dog's barking.*

We heard *its barking.* (emphasis on *barking—its* modifies *barking*)

We were annoyed by *John's sleeping.*

We were annoyed by *his sleeping.* (emphasis on *sleeping—his* modifies *sleeping*)

Many compound nouns are made from a gerund and another noun. They usually show the *purpose* to which the head noun is put.

a drinking fountain—a fountain for drinking
an ironing board—a board for ironing
a parking lot—a lot for parking
a swimming pool—a pool for swimming

Have

Have is both a main verb and an auxiliary (helping) verb. It is also used in many idiomatic phrases.

As a main verb, *have* has many different meanings. Many of its meanings are related to possessing, getting, accepting, and causing someone to do something, but there are many others also. Look up *have* in a dictionary if you see it used in a way that you do not understand.

For uses of *have* as an auxiliary (helping) verb, see **Auxiliary verbs, Negation, Operators, Questions,** and **Tense.**

For word order of *have* in verb phrases, see **Finite verbs.**

For special uses of *have* (*have to, had better*), see **Modals.**

For the use of *had* to replace *if* in inverted contrary-to-fact clauses, see **Inverted word order.**

For contracted forms of *have*, see **Contractions.**

Homonyms, see **Spelling**

Hyphen, see **Punctuation, hyphen**

I

Idiom

An idiom is a phrase or word used in a special meaning that you cannot understand just from knowing the dictionary definition and the grammar of the parts. Many two-word verbs are idiomatic. *To bear up*, for example, means *to have courage*. Most idioms are formed with prepositions, but usually you cannot decide which preposition to use according to logic. You *agree to* something, for example, but you *agree with* someone. To *differ from* is *to be different*, but to *differ with* is *to disagree*. You can look up and study idioms in special books of idioms and in dictionaries written for students of English as a second language.

Idiomatic usage means using words and phrases in the forms commonly used whether or not these forms appear to be the only logical ones. English-speaking people say "the *lesser* (not less) of two evils," "a ten-*foot* (not feet) pole," and "he *is* (not *has*) ten years old." We can say that a person eats "*like* a pig" to mean greedily, or "*like* a bird" to mean not very much, but we say that someone "*has* an eagle eye" to mean that he or she has excellent vision.

Image

An image is a picture formed in the reader's mind. A *literal image* is a description or suggestion of actual physical qualities.

A *figurative image* uses metaphor or simile to bring a picture into the reader's mind that compares things that are not basically similar. For example, a poet who compares his lady to a rose is thinking of her beauty, softness, or fragrance; but he does not expect the reader to think of thorns, pruning, or the short life of the blossom in relation to his love. A figurative image is successful when the writer and reader think of the same qualities. (see **Metaphor**)

Imagery is the use of images, both literal and figurative, in speech and writing.

> *Literal Images*
> I knew a man . . .
> This man was of wonderful vigor, calmness,
>   beauty of person,
> The shape of his head, the pale yellow and white
>   of his hair and beard, the immeasurable
>   meaning of his black eyes . . .
> He was six feet tall, he was over eighty years
>   old . . .   *Walt Whitman*

> *Figurative Images*
> There is a garden in her face
> Where roses and white lilies grow;
> A heav'nly paradise is that place,
> Wherein all pleasant fruits do flow [grow]
> There cherries grow which none may buy
> Till cherry-ripe themselves do cry.
>   *Thomas Campion*

In the poem above, the poet compares a woman's face to a beautiful garden and her lips to cherries which can be taken only when she herself agrees to be kissed.

> All the world's a stage,
> And all the men and women merely players.
> They have their exits and their entrances;
> And one man in his time plays many parts,
> His acts being seven ages.
>   *William Shakespeare*

In the passage above, a play is a metaphor for life. Although you may imagine a real stage in your mind when you read the passage, Shakespeare's purpose was not to fill your mind with the physical details of a stage, but to explain ideas about life.

Literal and figurative images can be used together. In the passage below, personification is mixed at first with literal images. At the end of the eleventh line the images change. From that point on in the second stanza, *sun, air,* and *night* are personified. In the last stanza, the evening scene becomes a metaphor for death.

A late *lark twitters* from the quiet skies;	*literal imagery: sound*
And from the west,	
Where the *sun, his day's work* ended,	*personification intro-*
Lingers as in content,	*duced*
There falls on the *old, gray city*	*literal imagery: sight*
An influence *luminous* and serene,	
A *shining* peace.	
The smoke ascends	*literal imagery continues*
In a rosy-and-golden haze. The spires	
Shine, and are changed. In the valley	
Shadows rise. The lark sings on. The sun,	*personification mixed*
Closing *his* benediction,	*with literal imagery*
Sinks, and the darkening *air*	
Thrills with a sense of the *triumphing night—*	
Night with *her train* of stars	
And *her great gift* of sleep.	
So be my passing!	*metaphor for death*
My task accomplished and the long day done,	
My wages taken, and in my heart	
Some late lark singing,	
Let me be gathered to the quiet west,	
The sundown splendid and serene,	
Death.	

Implicit Ideas

An implicit idea is one that is not stated directly but that can be guessed, deduced, or inferred from the facts that are given. The opposite of *implicit* is *explicit*. (see **Explicit**) The noun form is *implication* and the verb is *imply.*

An *implication* is the idea or judgment that is suggested. An *inference* is the conclusion that is drawn from the suggestion. The *writer or speaker implies* and the *reader or listener infers.*

If you see an ambulance driving down the street with its siren going and its lights flashing, you can *reasonably infer* that it is going to an accident where someone has been injured or to help someone who is ill. You do not know for certain, however. Other reasons are possible: the ambulance crew might be testing their equipment or rushing to get a cup of coffee. The first inference is more likely and reasonable, however, if you have no other evidence.

Some words imply actions or results that they do not explicitly state.

George *refused* to pick up the letter. (Although *refuse* means unwilling-ness, a mental state, it implies that he did not do the action of picking up the letter.)
George *delayed* picking up the letter. (George did not pick up the letter on time. He may not have picked it up yet. We do not know for sure.)
George *was delighted* to pick up the letter. (Although *delighted* refers to George's mental state, it implies that he picked up the letter.)

Indentation

Indentation means leaving space at the beginning of a line of writing or print. Indenting is a sign that some kind of a change is beginning.

1. Indent at the beginning of each *paragraph*. In some styles, skip a line or leave space between paragraphs in addition to or instead of in-denting. (see **Style, business writing**)

2. Indent in *direct quotation* whenever the speaker changes. (see **Direct speech**)

3. Indent in an outline every time the idea or detail goes to a more specific level. (see **Outlining**)

Indirect Object

An indirect object is always part of a clause in which the main verb is an active verb. The indirect object is almost always the person *to* whom or *for* whom something is done.

active verb	indirect object	direct object
Mary threw	*John*	the ball.

In the sentence above the indirect object comes before the direct object. It can also come after the direct object, following *to* or *for*. Most verbs can have the indirect object in either place.

active verb	direct object	indirect object
Mary threw	the ball	*to John.*

	indirect object	direct object
Mary brought	*Fred*	a sandwich.

	direct object	indirect object
Mary brought	a sandwich	*for Fred.*

An object pronoun can be an indirect object.

indirect
object

Mary threw *him* the ball. (more common word order)

indirect
object

Mary threw the ball to *him.* (possible word order)

A nonpersonal indirect object is possible with verbs such as *give, owe, pay,* and *send.*

indirect   *direct*
object   *object*

Frank paid the *bank* the amount that he owed.

Word Order of Indirect Objects

1. With most verbs, if the *direct object* is a *noun,* the indirect object can be put either before it or after it.

SUBJECT	ACTIVE VERB	INDIRECT OBJECT	DIRECT OBJECT	INDIRECT OBJECT
Paul	gave	Jane	the book.	
Paul	gave	her	the book.	
Paul	gave		the book	to her.

2. If the *direct object* is a *pronoun,* the indirect object usually comes after the direct object.

direct
object
pronoun

Paul gave   *it*   to her.
Wilma bought *them* for John.

3. If either the direct object or the indirect object is long or has many modifiers, it usually comes last. Put an indirect object that is modified by a clause or a long phrase after the direct object.

direct
object   *indirect object*

Paul gave   the book to the *girl who was waiting for it.*
Terry cooked dinner for *the Boy Scout troop.*

Put a direct object that is a noun clause or that has an adjective clause in it after the indirect object.

indirect
object   *direct object*

Paul gave   *the girl*   the book that he had just bought.
Terry cooked *the Boy Scouts* a dinner that they would never forget.
Wilma asked   *them*   what the answer was.

indirect
object   *direct object*

The teacher explained to *the class* whatever they had difficulty understanding.

Avoid putting both a long direct object and a long indirect object in the same sentence. If you do, you are likely to confuse the reader.

4. Certain verbs must have *to* or *for* with the indirect object. The *to* or *for* phrase usually comes after the direct object. (For exceptions, see rule 3 above.) Some of the most common of these verbs are:

> *admit:* She admitted her mistakes *to* her mother.
> *communicate:* The dean communicated the decision *to* the student.
> *announce:* The judges announced the winner *to* the crowd.
> *dedicate:* The football team dedicated the game *to* their injured teammate.
> *describe:* The tourist described the beautiful view *to* (*for*) us.
> *entrust:* They entrusted their money *to* their best friend.
> *explain:* The professor explained the problem *to* (*for*) him.
> *indicate:* The guide indicated the way *to* me.
> *introduce:* Albert will introduce you *to* his friends.
> *mention:* Charlotte forgot to mention her accident *to* her husband.
> *outline:* The director outlined the work *to* (*for*) us.
> *prescribe:* The doctor prescribed medicine *for* the patient.
> *propose:* The chairman proposed a new plan *to* the committee.
> *prove:* The lecturer proved his theory *to* the audience.
> *recommend:* My friends have recommended this restaurant *to* me.
> *repeated:* I will repeat the problem *to* (*for*) you one more time.
> *report:* The new members of the team reported *to* the coach today.
> *return:* My brother returned the book *to* me.
> *suggest:* The doctor suggested a vacation *to* him.

5. If a WH-word is the indirect object in a clause, the sentence will be a question. In that case, follow the word order for questions. (see **Questions**)

	indirect object	*direct object*
INFORMAL:	*Who(m)* did Terry cook dinner for?	
FORMAL:	For *whom* did Terry cook dinner?	

6. With some verbs, the indirect object can become the subject of a passive sentence. (see **Passive verbs**)

	indirect object	*direct object*
ACTIVE:	Paul gave Jane	the book.
	Wilma asked them what the question was.	

	subject	
PASSIVE:	Jane was given the book (by Paul).	

or

The book was given to Jane (by Paul).
They were asked what the question was.

Indirect speech and **Indirect questions,** see **Reported speech**

Infinitive

The infinitive is the form of the verb that follows *to*. In every verb except *be*, the same form is used in the present tense for all persons except the third person singular. (see *Be*)

I, you, we, they *run;* but he run*s*.
I, you, we, they *have;* but he *has*.

Use the infinitive phrase (*to* + infinitive)
  1. as a noun:

SUBJECT OF THE CLAUSE:	*To know* Donna well is difficult.
PREDICATE NOMINATIVE:	To know Donna well is *to love* her.
DIRECT OBJECT:	Ed hates *to study*.

After *prepositions,* however, use *-ing* forms except after *but, except,* and *about.*

	object of preposition	
INCORRECT:	*After* to study Ed turned out the light.
INCORRECT:	*Before* to get a driver's license, you must pass a test.
	object of preposition	
CORRECT:	*After* studying, Ed turned out the light.
CORRECT:	*Before* getting a driver's license, you must pass a test.
CORRECT:	If you want to drive, you have no choice *but* *except*
	object of preposition	
	to get a driver's license.
	object of preposition	
CORRECT:	My sister is *about* to get her driver's license.

2. to modify a noun or pronoun:

	noun modifier
CORRECT:	*Permission to drive* depends on getting a driver's license.
	noun modifier
CORRECT:	Ed's *ability to study* is greater when he has a quiet

pronoun   modifier
place in *which* *to do* it.

3. to *complete it is* + *adjective* (see **Adjectives, constructions that follow the verb** and *It*):

	adjective infinitive
CORRECT:	Sometimes it is *difficult* *to get* a driver's license.
	adjective infinitive
CORRECT:	It is not *easy* *to learn* another language well.

In formal writing, leave out *it is* and move the infinitive phrase to the beginning of the clause. An *-ing* form can also be the subject of the clause.

	subject
IMPROVED:	*To get* a driver's license is sometimes difficult.
	Getting a driver's license is sometimes difficult.
IMPROVED:	*To learn* another language well is not easy.
	Learning another language well is not easy.

4. to *complete many verb constructions*:

Some verbs must be followed by an infinitive phrase (with *to*), some verbs can be followed by an *-ing* form, and some verbs can be followed by a *bare infinitive* (without the *to*). Some verbs can be followed by either an infinitive phrase or by an *-ing* form. (see **Infinitive/-*ing* choice**)

Verb followed by an infinitive phrase:

> Mr. Jefferson *needs to leave* now.
> Ben *offered to finish* the experiment today.

Verb followed by an infinitive phrase or by an *-ing* form:

> Mrs. Parker *likes to go* shopping on Saturdays.
> Mrs. Parker *likes going* shopping on Saturdays.

Use the *bare infinitive* (simple verb form)

a. after modals:

Ed $\begin{Bmatrix} \text{must} \\ \text{can} \\ \text{will} \end{Bmatrix}$ *study* in California next year.

The weather $\begin{Bmatrix} \text{will} \\ \text{could} \\ \text{might} \end{Bmatrix}$ *be* worse tomorrow.

b. after *do, does,* or *did* if the main verb in the clause cannot be an operator (see **Operators**):

QUESTION:	Why *did* Ed *study* in Texas last year?
NEGATIVE STATEMENT:	Ed *did not study* in New York last year.

QUESTION: Why *does* everyone *love* Donna?

NEGATIVE
STATEMENT: Marcia *does not love* Donna.

c. after certain verbs that can be followed by the bare infinitive (see **Infinitive/-ing choice**):

John's brother *let* him *borrow* his car.
The bank *made* both of us *sign* the check.

Infinitive/-*ing* Choice _____

Some verbs may add an infinitive to complete the meaning of the main verb, but others may add an -*ing* form. Deciding whether to use the infinitive or the -*ing* form is difficult. You may also need to put in a person or a pronoun referring to a person. A few verbs use all constructions, but most verbs do not use them all. With some verbs a different construction changes the meaning.

1. *Infinitive (to + verb) Constructions*

a. An infinitive form can follow the main verb. The subject of the main verb is also the subject of the infinitive.

subject + verb + infinitive
Susan   likes   to go.
Mary   wanted   to go.

b. An infinitive form can follow a noun or pronoun that is not the subject of the main verb. (If the stated subject of an infinitive is a pronoun, that pronoun must be an object pronoun.)

                  pronoun
subject + verb + noun or + infinitive
Susan   wants   *us*   to go.
Mary   wanted   *John*   to go.

c. An infinitive form can follow a noun or pronoun that is not the subject of the main verb, as in **b**, but the only infinitive form that can be used with these verbs is *to be*. (See **Objective complement** for a similar construction without *to be*.)

Susan considered the book *to be* useless.
Mary declared Paul *to be* the winner.

A few verbs follow the patterns shown in **a**, **b**, or **c** except that you must leave out the *to*. These verbs are noted in the lists as *bare* infinitives.

Table 1. Some Verbs That Can Be Followed by Infinitives

*advice (b)	enable (b)	learn (a)	report (b)
*allow (b)	encourage (b)	let (b bare)	request (b)
appoint (b)	expect (a,b)	*like (a,b)	*require (b)
ask (a,b)		*listen to	resolve (a)
*attempt		(b bare)	return
	fail (a)	love (a,b)	["go back"] (a)
	*fear (a)		return
*be (a)	*feel (c)		["take back"] (b)
*bear (a)	*find (c)	make (b bare)	
beg (a,b)	*forbid (b)	manage (a)	say (a)
*begin (a)	force (b)	mean	*see (b bare)
believe (c)	*forget (a)	["intend"] (a,b)	seem (a)
bother (a)			send (b)
	go "purpose" (a)	need (a,b)	*start (a)
call on (b)	guess (c)	neglect (a)	stop (a)
care (a)		notify (b)	suppose (c)
cause (b)	happen (a)		
challenge (b)	*hate (a,b)	offer (a)	teach (b)
choose (a,b)	hear (a bare)	order (b)	tell (b)
claim (a)	help (ab,b bare)		tempt (b)
come (a)	hesitate (a)	*permit (b)	tend (a)
command (b)	hire (b)	persuade (b)	think (c)
compel (b)	hope (a)	plan (a)	train (b)
consent (a)		pledge (a)	trust (b)
consider (c)	*imagine (c)	*prefer (a,b)	try (a)
*continue (a)	induce (b)	prepare (a)	
	inform (b)	pretend (a)	
dare (a,b)	instruct (b)	promise (a)	*understand (c)
decide (a)	intend (a,b)	prove	urge (b)
declare (c)	invite (b)	(a with *to be*, c)	used to (a bare)
demand (a)			
*deserve (a)	judge (c)	*quit (a)	wait (a)
desire (a)			want (a,b)
determine (a,c)	know (c)	refuse (a)	warn (b)
discover (a,c)		*remember (b)	wish (a,b)
drive (b)	lead (b)	remind (b)	

* These verbs can also be followed by an *-ing* form (see Table 3). See notes following Table 3 about *remember/forget* and verbs of the senses.

NOTE: Modals are not included in this table. (see **Modals**)

More Constructions That Must Be Followed by the Infinitive

1. *Purpose:* Many verbs can be followed by *in order to*. Sometimes *in order to* is shortened and becomes *to*. In expressing purpose, both *to* and *in order to* are followed by an infinitive.

Robert hired a boat *to go* on the lake.
Robert hired a boat *in order to go* on the lake.
The men escaped *to* avoid punishment.
The men escaped *in order to* avoid punishment.

2. *Complement: be* + adjective + infinitive. After an adjective following the main verb *be* (and sometimes after other linking verbs) an infinitive phrase can be used. (see **Adjectives** and **Infinitives**) Constructions that follow the verb.

	verb	*adjective*	*infinitive*
The results of this experiment	are	difficult	to get.
This book	is	easy	to understand.
Our friends	were	pleased	to see us.
My friends	were	disappointed	to miss you.

3. *After WH-words:* If a WH-word follows the main verb, an infinitive phrase can follow the WH-word and include the meaning of *can* or *should*. (see **Reported speech**). The two classes of these verbs are shown by *a* and *b*.

a. The subject of the main verb is also the subject of the infinitive.

subject +	*verb*	+ *WH-word*	+ *infinitive*	
They	asked	*which*	book *to buy*.	(they can/should buy)
We	are deciding	*when*	*to go*.	

b. The subject of the main verb is not the subject of the infinitive, but another noun or pronoun before the WH-word is the subject of the infinitive. If the subject of the infinitive is a pronoun, use an object pronoun.

subject +	*verb*	*noun or* + *pronoun* +	*WH-word*	+ *infinitive*	
They	asked	*us*	which	book *to buy*.	(we can/should buy)
We	are advising	*them*	what	*to do*.	(they can/should do)

Table 2. Some Verbs That Can Be Followed by WH-Word + Infinitive

advise(b)	forget (a)	know (a)	*show (b)
ask (a,b)			
	guess (a)	learn (a)	teach (a,b)
consider (a)			tell (a,b)
	hear (a)	*observe (a)	think (a)
decide (a)		remember (a)	
discover (a)	imagine (a)		understand (a)
	inform (b)	say (a)	
*explain (a)	*inquire (a)	see (a)	*wonder (a)

* These verbs are not in Table 1. All other verbs in this list also appear in Table 1.

2. -ing *Forms*

Many verbs can be followed by -*ing* forms.

a. The -*ing* form can follow directly after the main verb.

subject +   verb   + -ing form
John   delayed   *going.*

b. The -*ing* form can follow a noun or pronoun different from the subject of the main verb. If the word before the -*ing* form is a pronoun, use a possessive form. (see **Gerunds**)

subject +   verb   + pronoun + -ing form
John   delayed   his   *going.*
Martha appreciated   his   *helping* her.

Use the possessive form of nouns also in formal writing.

Martha appreciated *John's* helping her.

Use the object pronoun after verbs of the senses.

Martha watched *him* washing the car.
Martha noticed *him* cleaning the lab.

Table 3.   Some Common Verbs That Can Be Followed by -*ing* Forms

admit (a)	endure (a,b)	keep (a)	propose (a)
*advise (a,b)	enjoy (a,b)	keep from (a)	put off (a,b)
*allow (a)	escape	keep (him)	
appreciate (a,b)	["avoid"] (a)	from (a)	*quit (a)
*attempt (a)	excuse (b)		
avoid (a)		*like (a,b)	recall (a,b)
	favor (a,b)	*listen to (b)	regret (a)
*be (a)	*fear (a,b)	love (a,b)	*remember (a,b)
*bear	*feel (b)		*require (a)
["endure"] (b)	*find (b)	mean	resent (a,b)
*begin (a)	finish (a,b)	["signify"] (a,b)	resist (a,b)
	*forbid (a,b)	mind	resume (a,b)
complete (a)	*forget (a,b)	["object to"] (a)	risk (a,b)
consider (a)		miss (a)	
*continue (a)			save (a,b)
	get ["start"] (a)		*see (b)
defend (b)	go—activity (a)	need (a)	stand (a,b)
defer (a)		neglect (a)	*start (a,b)
delay (a)			stop (a,b)
deny (a)	*hate (a,b)		suggest (a,b)
*deserve (a)		object to (a,b)	
despise (a)	*imagine (a,b)	omit (a,b)	
detest (a,b)	intend (a)		*try (a)
dislike (a,b)	intend (a)	*permit (a)	
dread (a,b)	investigate (b)	postpone (a,b)	*understand (b)
		*prefer (a)	

* These verbs can also be followed by an infinitive (see Table 1). See notes below about *remember/forget* and verbs of the senses.

PROBLEMS IN CHOOSING BETWEEN THE INFINITIVE AND THE -ing FORM

1. The *-ing* form can be used after prepositions. (Since words can introduce either a prepositional phrase or a clause, be careful not to use an *-ing* form as the only verb form in a clause.)

	subject	*verb*	*-ing form*
CORRECT:	He	fears	going.

	subject	*verb*	*preposition*	*-ing form*
CORRECT:	He	is afraid	of	going.

	subject	*verb*	*infinitive*
CORRECT:	He	is afraid	to go.

	infinitive
INCORRECT:	Before *to go* she will see you.

	preposition *-ing form*
CORRECT:	Before going she will see you.

(*Before* is a preposition.)

	subordinating conjunction *subject* *verb*
CORRECT:	Before she goes, she will see you.

(*Before* is a subordinating conjunction.)

2. *For* can introduce an infinitive with a stated subject.

> They are waiting *for us to go.*
> (*Us* is the subject of *to go.*)

3. Sometimes *to* can have an *-ing* form following it instead of an infinitive. How can you tell which form to use? Ask this question: Can I put *that thing* or *that one* after *to*? or can I use *do that* after *to*?

	He became used to *that one.* (If *that one* works, use *-ing* form.)
	He became used to *working* hard.
INCORRECT:	He used to *that one.* (*That* one does not follow; try *do that.*)
CORRECT:	He used to *do that.*
CORRECT:	He used *to work* hard. (If *do that* works, use the infinitive.)

4. Some phrases with *to* must be followed by an *-ing* form if a verb form is used with them.

accustom(ed) to going	look forward to going
adapt(ed) to going	pay (paid) attention to going
adjust(ed) to going	put a stop to going
agreeable to going	preferable to going
change(d) from .. to ..	resistant to going
(in) contrast(ed) to going	solution to losing
introduce(d) to driving	submit(ted) to training
limit(ed) to going	superior to going

NOTE: In a comparison, put the *-ing* form both before and after the adjective if possible. (see **Parallel structure**)

> *Going* up a ladder is easier than *coming* down.
> *Succeeding* is preferable to *failing*.

5. You can use either the infinitive or *-ing* form after *forget* and *remember*, but the meaning is different. The *-ing* form shows *memory* of action before the time of the action of the main verb.

> Frank remembers *going*. (Frank has a memory that he went.)
> Frank forgot *having borrowed* the book. (Frank had no memory that he had already borrowed the book.)

The infinitive shows *action* or *lack of action* after the main verb.

> Frank remembered to go. (Frank remembered and then he went.)
> Frank will forget to go. (Frank will not go.)

6. You can use either *an* infinitive or an *-ing* form with verbs of the senses. The subject of the infinitive or *-ing* form is usually expressed. *To* is always left out. The bare infinitive emphasizes the completion of a single act; the *-ing* form shows a process and/or emphasizes the duration of the action.

subject	*verb*	*object/subject*	*infinitive*	*-ing*
Brenda	saw	him	go	/ going.
	will hear			
	is watching			

(*Him* is both the object of *saw* and the subject of *go* or of *going*.)

Verbs of the senses that follow this pattern:

feel	observe
hear	overhear
listen to	see
look at	smell

see **Gerund** and **Participle**

Interjections _____

An interjection is a word that shows strong comment or emotion. An interjection is not a grammatical part of its clause, and it is always followed by an exclamation mark or a comma. (see **Punctuation, exclamation mark**)

> Oh! There you are.   *or*   Oh, there you are.
> Well! Where were you?   *or*   Well, where were you?
> Help! The baby fell in the lake!

Do not confuse *oh* with *O*. Use *oh* as an exclamation. Use *O* in formal direct address, in prayer, and in literary usage (often in poetry and personification). Always capitalize *O* and never put a punctuation mark directly after it.

> O God, grant our prayers.
> O mighty ocean waves.
> O powerful western fallen star!

Interrupters

Interrupters are transitional words or phrases. They are often called *conjunctive adverbs*. They

1. show the relationship between ideas within a sentence or between sentences.
2. cannot replace coordinating conjunctions between independent clauses unless you use a semicolon between the clauses.
3. are often set off by commas within their own clause (single words of four letters or fewer are not usually set off by commas).
4. are movable within their own clause although they are most often put at the beginning.

(see **Clauses, connecting words**)

Frequently Used Interrupters

TO ADD INFORMA-TION AND REASONS	TO SHOW CAUSE AND EFFECT	TO EXPLAIN, GIVE REASONS
also	accordingly	actually
besides	as a consequence	admittedly
equally	as a result	certainly
further	consequently	for example
furthermore	then	in fact
in addition	therefore	indeed
moreover	thus	really
too		of course
	TO CONTRAST	that is
TO COMPARE	however	
by comparison	instead	
likewise	in spite of that	TO SUMMARIZE
similarly	anyhow	in all
	nevertheless	in a word
TO SHOW ORDER	on the contrary	in brief
first, second, . . .	on the other hand	briefly
finally	otherwise	in short
last	still	in summary

	TO SHOW CHRONOLOGICAL ORDER	
subsequently	then	first
later	now	formerly
next	nowadays	earlier
after that	concurrently	previously
afterwards	simultaneously	before that

NOTE: *Actually, indeed,* and *in fact* introduce something you believe is true. If what is written earlier is not true, these words show contrast.

BE CAREFUL: The most common writing errors with interrupters are comma splices and run-on sentences. Interrupters alone cannot join independent clauses. You must put a semicolon or a comma and a coordinating conjunction between the clauses in addition to the interrupter. (see **Clauses** and **Comma splices**)

Differences between Coordinating Conjunctions and Interrupters

COORDINATING CONJUNCTIONS

PUNCTUATION AND WORD ORDER:

1. Put a comma before a coordinating conjunction that joins clauses, but

2. Do not separate a coordinating conjunction from the rest of its own clause with a comma.

3. Put a coordinating conjunction first in its clause when using it to join clauses.

INTERRUPTERS

1. Put a semicolon between two or more independent clauses if a coordinating conjunction is not used, and

2. Separate an interrupter from the rest of its own clause with a comma or commas if it is a long word.

3. Move an interrupter within its own clause for emphasis and rhythm.

EXAMPLES OF COORDINATING CONJUNCTIONS AND INTERRUPTERS

RESULT:

Jeff left his apartment very dirty when he moved out of it, *so* he lost his deposit.

Jeff left his apartment very dirty when he moved out of it; *consequently,* he lost his deposit.

TIME:

Jeff moved out of his apartment last week, *and* later he moved in with Warren.

Jeff moved out of his apartment last week; *subsequently,* he moved in with Warren.

EXPLANATION:

Marian thought she had lost her keys; *actually,* she had left them in the door.

CONTRAST:

Marian thought she had lost her keys, *but* she found them later.

Marian thought she had lost her keys; *however,* she found them later.

Marian thought she had lost her keys; she found them later, *however.*

FURTHER EXPLANATION: All the club members agree to the proposal, and they are very happy about it.

All the club members agree to the proposal;
in fact,
indeed, } they are very happy about it.
actually,

CONTRAST: We thought we had enough money for the trip Saturday, *but* everyone must pay more.

We thought we had enough money for the trip Saturday; *in fact,* *actually,* everyone must pay more.

Inverted Word Order

Inverted word order means moving a word, phrase, or clause out of its usual position in a sentence. (see **Conditional sentences, Direct speech, Emphasis, Operators,** and **Questions**)

Inversions in Poetry

Poets often invert and repeat grammatical elements for emphasis and for rhythm. If you have difficulty understanding a poem, find the grammatical parts and rearrange them in normal word order in a paraphrase.

Under the wide and starry sky,
Dig the grave and let me lie,
Glad did I live and gladly die,
    And I laid me down with a will.
    Robert Louis Stevenson

Paraphrase: Dig my grave and let me lie under the wide and starry sky. I live and die gladly and I laid myself down willingly.

Let me not to the marriage of true minds
Admit impediments.
    William Shakespeare

Paraphrase: Do not let me admit that there are impediments (obstacles) to the marriage of true minds.

Irony

Irony means using a word in a sense that is the opposite of its usual meaning, usually for a humorous effect or for emphasis. Calling a very large person by the nickname "Tiny" is ironic, for example. If a friend makes a stupid mistake and you say, "That was very intelligent," you are using irony. Irony is used in the nursery rhyme, "A Ten O'Clock Scholar":

> "Why do you come so *soon?*
> You used to come at ten o'clock,
> And now you come at noon."

Soon is used to emphasize the idea that the "scholar" has come very late indeed.

Irrelevant Material

Irrelevant material is something that is not to the point and not related to the subject you are writing about. Although what you write may be true and interesting to you, do not use it unless it is directly related to the development of your topic sentence and thesis. (see **Relevant material**)

It, Impersonal Use

Use *it* as the subject of the sentence in impersonal constructions that show temperature, weather, and time.

> It is hot.
> It is raining.
> It is getting late.
> It is too early to go now.
> It is time to go now.

It sometimes replaces a subject that comes later in the sentence.

> It is true that Gerald is my brother.
> (That Gerald is my brother is true.)
> It is impossible to decide now.
> (To decide now is impossible.)
> It is a good idea to find out now.
> (To find out now is a good idea.)

Using *it is* . . . is often wordy. Avoid this construction in formal writing if you can. Put the true subject in the subject position at the beginning of the sentence. Do not use *it* to refer to the whole idea of a clause. (see **Pronoun, reference**)

INCORRECT: Because Kathy oversleeps, she has to drive too fast on her way to work; *it* is so dangerous I am afraid to ride with her.

Improve the sentence above by putting *her driving* in place of *it*.

IMPROVED: Because Kathy oversleeps, she has to drive too fast on her way to work; *her driving* is so dangerous I am afraid to ride with her.

INCORRECT: When children watch too much violence on TV, *it* may affect their behavior.

In the sentence above, *it* has no antecedent (word that it stands for). Improve the sentence above by rewriting it completely.

IMPROVED: Watching too much violence on TV may affect children's behavior.

Intransitive verbs, see **Verbs, kinds of**

Irregular verbs, see **Verbs, irregular forms**

Italics

Italic type is a typeface or style of printing that is slanted to the *right*. Titles, foreign words and phrases, and words, letters, and numbers used as such are usually printed in italics. In typed or handwritten material, show italics by underlining. (see **Punctuation, underlining**)

Jargon

Jargon usually means the special language of a group that people outside the group do not understand. Trades and professions have specialized terms that people who work in the field know. When you are writing for a general audience, however, avoid jargon and use terms that everyone understands. Even when the word is a common one, a specialized meaning makes it jargon.

SPECIAL ACTIVITY	WORD	SPECIALIZED MEANING
theater	the boards	the stage
architecture	setoff	a flat projection from a wall
medicine	carrier	a person who transmits a disease but does not get it
music	beat	a regular unit of rhythm
physics	beat	an amplified pulse caused by superimposing sound waves of different frequencies
golf	ace	a hole in one
physics	ace	a quark

L

Linking verbs, see **Verbs, kinds of**

Literary Terms _____

Terms used to discuss literature are listed alphabetically. (see **Allegory, Alliteration, Analogy, Figures of speech, Image, Irony, Metaphor, Personification, Repetition,** and **Simile**)

Logical Order _____

Logical order is the arrangement of facts and ideas according to importance, comparison and/or contrast, cause and effect, and argument.

Importance

When you arrange ideas in order of importance, put the least important ideas or evidence at the beginning and the most important ideas or evidence at the end of your composition. This arrangement is sometimes called *climactic* order.

Comparison and Contrast

In comparison and contrast you show likenesses and differences in two or more things. Put all the likenesses together and put all the differences

J

L

together, or organize around the people, things, or ideas to be compared and contrasted. (see **Comparison and contrast**)

Cause and Effect

Arrange cause and effect according to reasons. Answer the stated or implied question *why* with *because* stated directly or indirectly. (see **Cause and effect**)

Argument

When you organize an argument in a formal paper, give the reasons for and the reasons against a belief or an action. The points in favor of the belief or action are called the *pro;* the points against the belief or action are called the *con.* You can organize an argument by separating the parts of the argument and giving the *con* and *pro* for each one, or by giving all the *cons* first and then all the *pros*, ending with the strongest *pro*. Usually *con* points are given before *pro* points.

If you find you have stronger *con* points than *pro* points, change sides or write on a different subject.

Markers

Markers are endings and other changes in words that show a change in their meaning and use in the sentence. Regular markers in English are spelled -*s*, -'*s*, and -*s*' on nouns and -*s*, -*ed*, and -*ing* on verbs. The unmarked form of a word is often called the *base word*.

NOUN: *Boy* (unmarked) can be changed to boy*s*. (plural)
boy'*s*. (singular possessive)
boys'. (plural possessive)

VERB: *Walk* (unmarked) can be changed to
walk*s* (third person singular, present tense)
walk*ed* (past and past participle)
walk*ing* (present participle and gerund)

Markers can be irregular. (see **Number** and **Verbs, irregular**) Always look in a dictionary if you have any doubt about the correct form. If no irregular form is shown after the base form in the dictionary, you can assume that changes in the word are regular.

Clause Markers

A word that introduces a dependent clause is sometimes called a clause marker. Other terms are often used to identify special kinds of clause markers. *Relative pronouns* introduce dependent clauses that function as nouns or adjectives. *WH-words* introduce direct and indirect questions. *Subordinating conjunctions* introduce dependent clauses that function as adverbs. (see **Clauses, dependent** and **WH-words**)

Everyone knows someone *who** talks too much. (relative pronoun)
Catch the hat *that* is blowing down the street. (relative pronoun)
The hikers asked *where** the trail began. (subordinating conjunction)

Mass nouns, see Countable and uncountable nouns

Metaphor

A metaphor is a comparison that shows similarities in things that are basically different. A distinction is made between a *metaphor,* which compares without using *like* or *as;* a *simile,* which uses *like* or *as* in the comparison; and *personification,* which gives human qualities to something that is not human, usually an abstract idea. (see **Image, Personification, Simile**)

METAPHOR: The trees are sentinels guarding the road to the old house.

or

The trees, sentinels standing at attention, guard the road to the old house.

The ship plows through the waves.

SIMILE: The trees are *like* sentinels guarding the road to the old house.

or

The trees, standing *as* sentinels, guard the road to the old house.

The ship goes through the waves *like* a plow.

Metaphors are often used in poetry and prose.

She dwelt among the untrodden ways . . .
A violet by a mossy stone . . .
          William Wordsworth

Thou art thy mother's glass
[You are your mother's mirror].
          William Shakespeare

Love is a star to every wandering bark [ship].
          William Shakespeare

Hope is a good breakfast, but it is a bad supper.
          Francis Bacon

* These are also WH-words.

Quarry the granite rock with razors, or moor the vessel with a thread of silk; then may you hope with such keen and delicate instruments as human knowledge and human reason to contend against those giants, the passion and the pride of man.

John Henry Cardinal Newman

If we do not make common cause to save the good old ship of the Union on this voyage, nobody will have a chance to pilot her on another voyage.

Abraham Lincoln

A *dead* metaphor is a word or expression that has been used so much that its original figurative meaning has been forgotten: *skyscraper*, for example.

A *mixed* metaphor is a figure which begins with one comparison but changes to another one in an illogical way.

The cold *hand* of death *quenched* her thirst for life.

A hand cannot quench thirst; only some kind of drink can relieve thirst.

A *worn-out* metaphor has been used so much and for so long that it has lost the impact it once had. The first person who compared teeth to pearls had a good idea, but today, hundreds of years later, the idea has lost its freshness. Writers have been comparing a government to a ship for thousands of years. The idea was fresher when Sophocles used it than when Lincoln did in the quotation above. Avoid using worn-out metaphors in your own writing.

Modals

Can, could, may, might, shall, should, ought to, will, would, and *must* differ in form and meaning from other verbs. (The modal forms of *need* and *dare* are used so rarely in the United States that they will not be considered here.) Related verb phrases are *be able to, have to, had better, used to,* and *be used to.*

Forms and Constructions of Modals

Modals:
1. do not add *-s* in the third person singular present.
2. have no *-ing* form.
3. can show the future (except *can* in the sense of ability) and some show the past by using adverbs.
4. Act as operators. (see **Operators**)
5. can never be followed directly by another modal.
6. must be followed by bare infinitives (simple forms) of other verbs in verb phrases.

MODALS

Most modals can be contracted with *not* and some can be contracted with the pronoun. (see **Contractions**)

Back-shift in reported speech is irregular and differs in some cases for different meanings of the same verb.

Meanings of Modals

Modals show many meanings that are shown by the subjunctive or another mood in many other languages. They generally do not show a happening or event but show thoughts about actions: Permission, for example, means that you are allowed to do something but not necessarily that you do it.

PERMISSION: *May* we cook? (Do you object? or Is there a regulation against cooking?)

ADVISABILITY: *Should* we cook? (Is cooking a good idea?)

NECESSITY: *Must we cook?* (Are we required to cook?)

The questioners are not necessarily cooking at the time they ask the questions above. We do not know for sure whether or not they will cook in the future, although the implication here of *may* is that they want to cook, and if the answer is "yes," they probably will cook. The implication of *must* is that the questioners do not want to cook, and if the answer is "no," they probably will not. (see **Implicit ideas**)

Adverbs often show the time setting of modals.

COULD (in the meaning of *ability*)
Terry could cook tomorrow. (future)
Terry could cook every day. (present habitual)
Terry could cook yesterday. (past)

The tense of other verbs in the sentence can also show the time setting.

Terry could *cook* while the children *are getting* dressed.
Terry could *cook* well when he *came* to see us last summer.

Without an adverb, modals can mean "now and in the future."

We should respect our parents. (present and future)

Although the *can/could, may/might, will/would,* and *shall/should* pairs sometimes have a present/past relation, *could, might, would,* and *should* have separate meanings that do not always correspond to the "present" part of the pair.

can AND could

Can and *could* are used mainly for ability, possibility, and permission.

1. *Ability* (*is able to, is capable of,* and sometimes *knows how to*)

Be able to can replace *can* if more precise tense distinctions are needed, and must be used for *capability* in the future.

> *can* in the present and future
> > negative and positive
> > > (is able to)

Rosa *can* do these problems easily, but Jerry *cannot*. (Note spelling of *cannot*).

Sandy *can* start working tomorrow.

Do not use *can* in the future for learned ability.

Roger *will be able to* swim better when he takes more lessons.

Mr. Porter *will be able* to use the computer after he finishes the training course.

Rosa *will be able* to do these problems easily on the test tomorrow, but Jerry will not.

Back-shift into reported speech in the past.

He thought that Rosa could do these problems easily.

PAST:	At one time Rosa could (was able to) do these problems by herself.
PAST NEGATIVE:	At one time Rosa could not (was not able to) do these problems by herself.

2. *Possibility* with *can* and *could* (something may happen if conditions are suitable)

No one is perfect; everyone *can* make mistakes. (Mistakes are possible.)
Even good cooks *can* turn out bad food at times. (It is possible sometimes to turn out bad food.)

Could in place of *can* in the present and future meanings of possibility shows doubt, not a change in tense. (see **Conditional sentences**)

Even good cooks *could* turn out bad food at times. (possible but not very likely)
The dean *can* see you at 2:30. (a definite possibility for an appointment)
The dean *could* see you at 2:30. (Perhaps an appointment might be arranged.)
Our team *can* win the volleyball match. (Winning is a definite possibility.)
Our team *could* win the volleyball match. (Winning is unlikely but possible if certain conditions are met.)

In all the sentences above with *could*, a conditional *if*-clause is implied.

Even good cooks *could* turn out bad food if . . .
The dean *could* see you at 2:30 if . . .
Our team *could* win the volleyball match if . . .

Negatives with possibility show that something is *impossible*.

> The results of this experiment *cannot be correct.* (The results are impossible.)
>
> The results of this experiment *cannot* be correct. (The results are impossible.)

(for uses of *could* after *if* and *unless,* see **Conditional clauses**)

Past possibility: *could* + adverb(s) and/or a finite verb in the past:

> *adverb*
> The dean *could* see you *yesterday.*

> *past verb*
> The dean *could* see you but you *broke* your appointment.

> **BACK-SHIFT AFTER**
> **REPORTED SPEECH:** At one time people thought that ships sailing too far west *could* fall off the edge of the earth.

Past condition contrary to fact: *could* + *have* + past participle:

> When the flood came, the water *could have risen* higher than it did (something could have happened but it did not); the damage *could have been* worse.
>
> Everyone complained about the heat yesterday, but it *could have been* hotter. (Even hotter weather was possible.)

> **NEGATIVE:** The judge *could not have* sent him to jail just for getting a parking ticket.
>
> It *could not have snowed* in Zanzibar.

3. *Permission* with *can* and *could* (*be allowed to, be permitted to, have permission to*) Although many authorities have preferred *may* to *can* to show permission, even in much formal writing both are used in the present and future to show permission. See below under *may* for differences in its use in the past.

> Anyone with a library card from the main library *can* borrow books from the branch libraries.
>
> You *can* hand in your composition tomorrow instead of today if you need to revise it.

Past, *could* (usually with an adverb or with a clause that has a verb in the past tense) shows that permission was given at some time in the past but is no longer given under the conditions described.

> *At one time* anyone *could* travel without a passport. (but not now)
>
> *Once* anyone *could* buy land here, but now no one can.

Permission can also be shown by *have permission to, is permitted to,* and *was allowed to. Have permission to* means that permission is necessary and has been granted. *Are permitted to* and *is allowed to* mean that special permission is not necessary.

> At one time anyone *was allowed to* (could) swim in the Warner's lake, but now the only people who *are allowed to* (can) are those who *have permission.*

OTHER USES OF *can* AND *could*

In polite questions, *could* is considered more polite than *can.*

> *Can* you see me now?
>
> *Could* you see me now? (more doubt and thus more possibility of an easy refusal)

Polite commands with *can* put the speaker on the same level as the person to whom the command is given.

> You *can* finish typing this letter while I make a phone call. (politely, "Finish typing this letter.")

may AND *might*

May and *might* are used mainly for permission and possibility.

1. *Permission* with *may:* Although *may* and *can* are usually interchangeable, some authorities prefer *may* in formal writing. *Might* is sometimes used to show the past, but it is often replaced by *could.* Adverbs and other verbs make the time reference clear.

> *present*
> You *may* wait here *now* until the doctor can see you.

> *past, reported speech*
> The nurse *told* them that they *could* (*might*) wait in the waiting room.

> *future*
> You *may* come back at ten o'clock *tomorrow.*
> You *may* remind me again *next week.*

Past permission is not shown with *might.* (see *could*, permission, above)

2. *Possibility* with *may* and *might*:

> My car *may* need new tires.
> The answer to this problem *may* not be correct.
> Causes of the poor test results *may* be understood later.

Might shows more doubt than *may* does (see *could*, above).

> My car *might* need new tires.
> The answer to this problem *might* not be correct.
> Causes of the poor test results *might* be understood later.
> We *might* go to Florida this winter, or we *might* go to Texas instead.

NOTE: *May* and *might* in the meaning of possibility are not generally used in questions. *Can* and *could* are usually used.

Past possibility (not yet certain): *may* + *have* + past participle:

> They *may have found* a solution to the problem.
> Warren and Sally *may have had* an accident.

May becomes *might* or *could* in the past:

> He thought that his car *might* need new tires.
> He found that his car *could* need new tires.

(see **Conditional clauses** for *might* following *if* and *unless*)

will AND *would*

1. *Agreement* with *will* (with a personal subject only, in all tenses):

> I *will* (agree to) help you.
> We *will* sign the contract immediately.
> I *will* be there at 10:15 tomorrow. (a definite appointment)

2. *Polite commands, offers,* and *invitations* (*Would* shows more doubt.) (see **Commands**):

> *Will* you please open the door for me.
> *Would* you please open the door for me. (even more polite)
> *Will* (*would*) you like another cup of coffee?
> *Will* you come to dinner at my house tomorrow?

(See **Conditional clauses** for *would* following *if* or *unless* [They *would if* they *could*, but they *cannot*.].)

Past habitual with *would* shows an action repeated in the past. You can often use *would* instead of *used to*.

> When we were children, we *would* often *make* our mother angry by pretending to quarrel. We *would disagree*, we *would complain* about each other, and sometimes we *would* even *wrestle* and *pretend* to hit each other. We *would do* all these things just to get our mother's attention.

3. *Prediction* with *will*, also a statement of natural law, especially in scientific and technical writing, shows a result that is likely or certain.

> Water *will* freeze at 0° Celsius (32°F). (It always freezes. . . .)
> When these chemicals are mixed, the reaction *will* be as follows. (The reaction is always. . . .)
> Boys *will* be boys. (Boys always behave a certain way.)

shall AND *should*

Questions in the first person: *shall* is used in questions before *I* or *we* in the sense of "would you like me to?"

Shall (should) I close the door now?
Shall (should) we go to Florida next spring?
Shall (should) I fix lunch now?

Should (above) shows more doubt or uncertainty on the part of the speaker. It can also introduce a question of advisability. (see below)

should AND *ought to*

Advisability and *obligation* can be shown with *should* and *ought to*.

GENERAL TRUTHS: Children *should* be respectful to older people.
        Children *ought to respect* older people.
        Drivers *should* be careful when it rains.
        Drivers *ought to* be careful when it rains.

Ought to is rarely used in the negative:

Children *should not* be disrespectful to older people.
Drivers *should not* be careless when it rains.

Show definite time with adverbs of time or tenses of other verbs:

Tomorrow you *should* pay the gas bill.
Tomorrow you *ought to* pay the gas bill.
Jonathan *should* be making better grades than he *is*.
Jonathan *ought to* be making better grades than he *is*.

SPECIAL USES OF *should*

After verbs of command and request, *should* + main verb can be used instead of the subjunctive. (see **Subjunctive**)

The commander ordered that the flag (*should*) fly at half mast.
Government regulations require that the price (*should*) be cut.

NOTE: A more common sentence pattern uses the infinitive for commands and requests.

The commander ordered the flag *to be flown* at half mast.

WITH *should* OR
SUBJUNCTIVE: The police directed that *we* (*should*) *take* the detour.
WITH INFINITIVE: The police directed *us to take* the detour.

Should can replace *if* in conditional sentences.

If she comes early, tell me.
Should she *come* early, tell me.

If Herb finds shoes that fit him, he will buy them.
Should Herb *find* shoes that fit him, he will buy them.

(see **Conditional sentences** for *should* following *if* and *unless*)

must AND *have to*

Have to can replace *must* in the positive; *had to* replaces *must* in the past. *Necessity:*

> You *must* (*have to*) pass a test before you enter the computer course.
>
> You *must* (*have to*) pay for all your groceries at the cash register.
>
> Alan and Martha *must* (*have to*) get a marriage license before the wedding. (*will have to* is possible)

Past Necessity is shown by *had to.*

> Irvin *had to* take an eye test before renewing his driver's license.
> Theresa *had to* buy five books this term.

Lack of Necessity (does not need to) is shown by *do not have to.*

> PRESENT: We *do not have to* (do not need to) buy many books this term.
>
>   George *does not have to* work because his father gives him enough money to go to school.
>
> PAST: Doris *did not have to* pay as much as she expected to repair her car.
>
>   I *did not have to* hand in my composition last week.

Prohibition—must + negative:

> Pedestrians *must not* cross the expressway except on the bridge.
> Marilyn *must not* throw trash in the parking lot.

Logical Necessity—Must can indicate a deduction or an inference from the facts given in the present, past, and future.

> PRESENT
> He has many accidents; he *must* be a careless driver.
>
> She came in with her umbrella dripping; it *must* be raining outside.
>
> My answer to problem two is wrong; I *must* be using the wrong formula to solve it.

NOTE: *Must* in a question such as *Must you go?* implies *I don't want you to go.*

> PAST (*must* + *have* + PAST PARTICIPLE):
> You *must have studied* hard to get such good grades.
>
> He *must have had* many accidents to lose his driver's license.

> FUTURE:
> If the main verb is *be*, use *must* + *be*. If the main verb is not *be*, use *must* + *be* + *going to* + main verb.

be AS THE MAIN VERB:

Everyone in the play practiced late today; the dress rehearsal *must be* to-morrow.

OTHER VERBS AS MAIN VERBS:

Andy is looking everywhere for his new tennis racquet; he *must be planning* to play tennis this afternoon.

Clara cleaned house today; she *must be going to have* company.

The sky is clear and the temperature is dropping fast; it *must be going to* freeze tonight.

RELATED PHRASES

Be able to—see above under *can* (can follow a modal)

Have to—see above under *must* (can follow a modal)

Had better—shows advisability and means nearly the same as *should* and *ought to,* but with the idea that the advice is suitable or advantageous. A bad result may follow if the advice is not taken. Even though the form is past, it is used only with a present meaning. *Had better* is always followed by the bare infinitive.

You *had better move* your houseplants indoors before a freeze, or they will die.

Becky *had better get* new tires for her car before she has an accident.

Used to + infinitive shows habitual action in the indefinite past. Do not use a time phrase beginning with *since* with *used to.* Often the same idea can be shown by *would* in the past. (See above for *would* and see **Tense, present** for habitual present.) *Used to* cannot follow a modal.

Travelers *used to* cross the Atlantic by ship and then take a train, but these days they fly all the way.

When I was a small child, I often *used to* argue with my brother, but now we agree most of the time.

People *used to* believe that the earth was flat, but now we know that it is a sphere.

When we were children, we often *used to* make our mother angry by pretending to quarrel. We *used to* disagree, we *used to* complain about each other, and sometimes we *used to* wrestle and pretend to hit each other. We *used to* do all these things just to get our mother's attention.

Be used to + -*ing* form or a noun or pronoun means *be accustomed to.* The tense is shown on *be.*

Our cat *is used to sleeping* in a basket.

People who *are used to drinking coffee* when they get up in the morning do not like to go without it.

When I lived in northern Canada I *was used to* cold weather, but now that I live in southern Florida, I *am used to* the heat.

Meanings of Modals and Related Phrases

ABILITY/CAPABILITY
can (cannot)— present and future

could (could not)—present and past

ADVISABILITY
shall I? should I?—questions

should
(should not)— present, past, and future

had better (had better not)— present

DEDUCTION/INFERENCE
must (must not)—present, past, and future

INTENTION/INSISTENCE
shall (shall not)— (future meaning)

will (will not)— (future meaning)

be going to (not be going to)— present, past, and future

NOTE: Past intention is usually shown with *want* or *desire*.

NECESSITY/OBLIGATION
must (must not)—present and future

have to (not have to)— present, past, and future

ought to
(ought not)— present, past, and future

should
(should not)— present, past, and future

need to
(need not)— present, past, and future

to be (see *Be*)— present, past, and future

OFFER
will (will not)—future

would like
(would not like)— present and future

OPPORTUNITY
REALIZED: can
(cannot)— present tense

be able to
(not to be able to)— present, past, and future

NOT REALIZED: could have—past

PERMISSION
may (may not)—present and future

can (cannot)— present and future

could
(could not)— past

let + personal object— present and future

POSSIBILITY/IMPOSSIBILITY
can (cannot)— present and future

could
(could not)— present and future

may (may not)—present and future

might
(might not)— present and future

could have
(could not have)— past

may have (may not have)— past

might have
(might not have)— past

PREDICTION/NATURAL LAW
will (will not)—present and future

PROHIBITION
must not—present and future

NOTE: Also shown by *do not, no +ing* form,
it is forbidden to, and
it is unlawful to.

REPEATED ACTION IN THE PAST
would (would not)—past

used to—past

NOTE: Habitual action in the present is shown by the present tense.

Modifiers

Modifiers affect the meanings of other words in some way. Nouns can be modified by adjectives, articles, determiners, participles, and infinitives. Verbs can be modified by adverbs, which can also modify adjectives and other adverbs. Phrases and clauses can modify both nouns and verbs, but their word order in the clause may be different from the word order of a one-word modifier. Noun forms can modify other nouns, both in their common forms and in their possessive forms. Certain forms of pronouns can modify nouns.

The word that is modified is often called the *head word*. Words that come before the head word are called *premodifiers*. Words that come after it are called *postmodifiers*.

Some Examples of Modifiers of Nouns

Kind of Modifier	Premodifier	Headword-Noun	Postmodifier
Article Determiner	The or this	horse ...	
Predeterminer (plural only)	All the	horses ...	
Possessive Noun (Proper)	Ruth's	horse ...	
Possessive Pronoun	Her	horse ...	

In the following examples, you must use a determiner in the singular, and you may use one in the plural, depending on the meaning of the sentence. *The* as shown in the table is one of many possible determiners. (see **Determiners**)

Kind of Modifier	Premodifier	Headword-Noun	Postmodifier
Possessive Noun (Common)	(The) girl's	horse	
Single-Word Adjective	(The) big	horse	
Adjective of Comparison	(The) slower	horse	or slower than mine
	(The) fast	horse	or as fast as mine
	(The)	horse	alone
Intensive Pronoun	(The)	horse	itself
Prepositional Phrase	(The)	horse	in the pasture
Adjective Clause	(The)	horse	that she bought
Noun	(The) show	horse	
Noun, Appositive	(The)	horse,	the mare,
Infinitive	(The)	horse	to buy
Present Participle	(The) working	horse	
	(The)	horse	running away
Past Participle	(The) trained	horse	
	(The)	horse	found yesterday

Although predicate adjectives and predicate nouns modify nouns and pronouns that are the subject of the clause, they are usually called complements, not modifiers. (see **Predicate complements**)

See **Adjectives, order of** for a chart of the word order when several premodifiers modify the same noun.

Some Examples of Modifiers of Verbs (All modifiers of verbs can be called adverbs.)

Kind of Adverb	Verb	Adverb
Single Word	(He) ran	quickly.
Prepositional Phrase	(He) ran	down the street.
Clause	(He) ran	when he saw us.

See **Adverbs** for other examples of words that adverbs can modify and for the word order of adverbs in a clause.

Mood

Four terms have traditionally been used to describe the different ways verbs can express an idea:

> the indicative—makes a statement. (see **Statement**)
> the imperative—gives a command. (see **Commands**)
> the interrogative—asks a question. (see **Questions**)
> the subjunctive—shows a condition contrary to fact, such as an unreal statement after *if*, a command, a request, or necessity. (see **Contrary-to-fact Statements, Conditional Sentences,** and **Subjunctive**)

Some grammars use *mode* instead of *mood* to show the differences in the way the verb idea is expressed. Many languages make changes in the verb form to show the ideas such as obligation, permission, and necessity that English can show by using modal and auxiliary verbs before the main verb. (see **Modals** and **Auxiliary verbs**)

Be *used in different moods*

indicative (a statement)

> Frances *is* a good student.

imperative (a command)
> *Be* a good student.

interrogative (a question)

> *Is* Frances a good student?

subjunctive (a statement after *if* that is not real)

> If Frances *were* not a good student, she would leave school. (She *is* a good student.)

Were is usually used in written nonreal statements after *if* for all persons.

N

Narration

Narration means telling a story. A narration may be a short anecdote used as a part of an explanation (expository writing), or it may be a story told for its own sake, as in fiction (short stories and novels) or in history and biography. Narration is one of the four kinds of prose (description, argument, and exposition are the other kinds). *Narrative* is used as the adjective form and also as another noun form meaning *narration*. Narration usually uses chronological order. (see **Fiction** and **Chronological order**)

Negation

Negation shows disagreement, denial, absence of somebody or something, or an opposite idea or quality.

Formation of a Negative Clause (see **Operators**)

1. Put *not* directly after all operators (all forms of *have* and *do* acting as auxiliaries and after *am, is, are, was, were, shall, should, will, would, can, could, may, might, must,* and *ought*). (see **Contractions**)

Deborah *will do* the work.	She *will not* do it. She *won't* do it. *She'll not* do it.
Russell *is walking* to work today.	He *is not* walking to work today. He *isn't* walking to work today. *He's not* walking to work today.

Word Order: Put *not* after the first modal or auxiliary in a verb phrase. (see **Finite verbs, table of word order**)

NOTE: In speech, using *not* as a separate word instead of in a contraction emphasizes the negative idea. In formal writing, avoid using contractions.

    2. Make the negative of all other verbs with the required form of *do* and *not* or the contracted forms *don't, doesn't,* or *didn't.*

> They *do not* see you very often these days.
> They *don't* see you very often these days.
> She *does not* walk to work every day.
> She *doesn't* walk to work every day.
> They *did not* find the lost dog.
> They *didn't find* the lost dog.

Tag questions are always positive following negative statements and negative following positive statements. (see **Tag questions**)

    In negative questions, keep *-n't* with the operator when you move the operator to the beginning of the clause. (see **Questions**)

> Do*n't* they see you often these days?
> Does*n't* he walk to work every day?
> Did*n't* they find the lost dog?

The strong form of *not* follows the subject in formal writing.

> Do they *not* see you often these days?
> Does he *not* walk to work every day?
> Did they *not* find the lost dog?

WH-questions also keep *-n't* with the operator (the verb that follows the *WH*-word) or put *not* after the subject.

> Why is*n't* he on time?
> Why is he *not* on time?

Answers to Negative and Positive Questions

Negation in English is related to the positive statement. English-speaking people agree or disagree with the underlying positive statement, not with a negative question, even if the only statement they hear or see is negative.

AFFIRMATIVE STATEMENT:	Chris likes to eat bananas.
AFFIRMATIVE QUESTION:	Does Chris like to eat bananas?
AFFIRMATIVE ANSWER:	Yes, he does. (agreement)

NEGATIVE ANSWER:	*No,* he doesn*'t.* (disagreement)
NEGATIVE QUESTION:	Chris doesn*'t* like to eat bananas, does he?
AFFIRMATIVE ANSWER:	Yes, he does. (agreement—he likes to eat bananas)
NEGATIVE ANSWER:	*No,* he doesn*'t.* (disagreement—he does not like to eat bananas)

Notice that *yes* is always followed by a positive verb, and that *no* is always followed by a negative form. Use the same answer for both the affirmative and negative question. The following answers are likely to be misunderstood.

INCORRECT:	No, he does. (disagreement with the question because he likes to eat bananas)
INCORRECT:	Yes, he doesn't. (agreement with the question because he does not like to eat bananas)

Other Negative Words and Double Negatives

Since formal English rarely puts more than one negative word into one clause, you must remember which words in English have this negative effect.

not (in the verb, and modifying words other than the verb)
nor (see **Conjunctions**)
neither, nor (see **Conjunctions**)
unless (see **Conditional sentences**)

no	nobody	rarely	hardly
never	nothing	seldom	scarcely
none		barely	

CORRECT	INCORRECT
No one is ever here.	*No* one is *never* here.
There is *no* way to do that.	There's *not no* way to do that.
They do *not* have much money.	They *don't* have *no* money.
They have *hardly any* money.	They *don't* have *hardly any* money.

Words beginning with negative prefixes, such as *nonaligned* and *nonexistent,* although they have a negative meaning, may be used with other negatives in the same clause. (See **Word formation, prefixes,** for more examples with a negative meaning.)

Our country is *not non*aligned, but has treaties with other countries.
One can*not* say human kindness is *non*existent.

Without and certain verbs of negative meaning such as *fail* or *lack* can occur in the same clause with the negative words listed above.

> He is *not* without his faults. (He has some faults.)
> They do *not* lack water. (They have enough water.)
> The first experiment did *not* work, and the second one failed, too.

Either is used in negative statements and answers after *not* to indicate an additional negative item or idea.

> Do Mary and Margaret both want bananas?
> Mary doesn*'t* want any, and Margaret doesn*'t*, either.
> The first experiment did *not* give the expected results, and the second one did *not, either*.

Neither is used in a similar construction, omitting *not* in the second clause.

> The first experiment did *not* give the expected results, and *neither* did the second one.

NOTE: *Either* and *neither* are more often used as correlative conjunctions. (See **Parallel structure** and **Emphasis** for other adverbs used to emphasize negative ideas.)

To make the negative command, put *don't* or *do not* before the main verb.

Pick up the book.	Do *not* pick up the book.
	Don*'t* pick up the book.
Let him pick up the book.	Do *not* let him pick up the book.
	Don*'t* let him pick up the book.
Someone open the door.	Do *not* (let) anyone open the door.
	Don*'t* (let) anyone open the door.

NOTE: *Someone* changes to *anyone* in the negative sentence. *Not* follows *let's* or *let us*.

Let's open the door.	Let's *not* open the door.

Public signs often state negative commands as *no* before an *-ing* form.

No smoking	*No* running	*No* standing	*No* loitering

Stop has the sense of negation.

> Stop smoking (do *not* smoke) Stop pollution (do *not* pollute or allow others to pollute)

Transferred Negatives

After some verbs such as *think, believe,* or *expect,* the *not* can move from the *that* clause in which it logically belongs to the main clause.

MAIN CLAUSE:	I do *not* think that you have tried very hard to finish this work.
	means
that CLAUSE:	I think that you have *not* tried very hard to finish this work.
MAIN CLAUSE:	She does *not* believe that you care about her as much as you say you do.
	means
that CLAUSE:	She believes that you do *not* care about her as much as you say you do.

The *that* may be omitted in a noun clause used as a direct object if it is not the subject of its own clause. (see **Clauses, dependent**)

Negatives and Style

Contractions are used in speech and informal writing, but the strong form of *not* is often very formal and disturbs the rhythm of the sentence. Writers, therefore, often express the negative idea in other ways when they do not want to write in a very formal style.

Why is*n't* he on time? (informal)
Why is he *not* on time? (formal) = Why is he *late?* (less formal, less emphatic)
They do*n't* have much money. (informal)
They do *not* have much money. (formal) = They have *hardly any* money. (less formal)
The stars are*n't* visible. (informal)
The stars are *not* visible. (formal) = The stars are *in*visible. (formal or less formal)

Non-count nouns, see **Countable and uncountable nouns**

Nouns

Nouns are words that name things such as persons, animals, places, ideas, and institutions. A noun can be the subject of a clause. Nouns are sometimes called *substantives*, a term that means any word or group of words that can be used as the subject of a clause: a noun, a pronoun, a noun phrase, a gerund, a gerund phrase, or an infinitive phrase.

Kinds of Nouns

COUNTABLE AND UNCOUNTABLE (see **Countable and uncountable nouns**)

PROPER NOUNS AND COMMON NOUNS

Proper nouns are names of particular people, places, or things. They are capitalized. All other nouns are *common* nouns.

> *George Allen* attends *Lakeview College.*
> *Monday, June* 15, is *Marilyn Morgan*'s birthday.

Proper nouns take articles or determiners only if two or more people, places, or things have the same name.

> My brother is named Bill Johnson and my cousin is also named Bill Johnson. *The Bill Johnson* who lives across the street from me is my brother.

Common nouns can be classified into abstract nouns and concrete nouns. (see **Abstract** and **Concrete**) *Abstract* nouns name ideas, emotions, qualities, and processes: justice, beauty, happiness, length, weight, classification. *Concrete* nouns name persons or things that can be known directly through the senses; ball, boy, bread, chair, heat, noise, fire, smoke, ice, water, and so on.

COLLECTIVE NOUNS

Collective nouns are special nouns that stand for a group of people, animals, birds, or insects. Collective nouns take singular or plural verbs depending on whether the group acts as a unit (singular) or as separate individuals (plural). (see **Agreement of subject and verb**)

Some collective nouns for people are

army	choir	congregation	police
audience	chorus	group	team
band	clan	orchestra	troop
brigade	class	patrol	youth

Some collective nouns for animals, birds, and insects are

a herd of cattle, sheep, goats	a hive of bees
a flock of birds, chickens	a swarm of ants, bees, flies

Spelling of Nouns

Most nouns are *regular* in spelling the plural. Add -*s* to the end of the singular form.

boys, boys	book, books	pencil, pencils

Add -*es* to make plurals of nouns that end in -*s* or in a similar sound (*ch, sh-, tch, x,* and *z*).

bun*ch*, bunch*es*	pat*ch*, patch*es*	fo*x*, fox*es*

(See **Spelling** for irregularities in nouns ending in *-ch, -s, -sh, -tch, x,* and *z,* in *-o,* and in *-y.*)

Some nouns are *irregular* in spelling plurals.

1. A final *-f* or *-fe* becomes *-ves* in some nouns (some of the *-f* nouns are related to a verb in *-ve*).

NOUN IN *-f*	PLURAL NOUN	VERB
calf	calves	calve
belief	beliefs (regular plural)	believe
elf	elves	—
half	halves	halve
hoof	hooves (also hoofs)	—
knife	knives	knife
leaf	leaves	—
life	lives	live
loaf	loaves	—
proof	proofs	prove
relief	reliefs (rare in plural)	relieve
self	selves	—
shelf	shelves	shelve
thief	thieves	thieve (thieving common; other forms rare)
wife	wives	—
wolf	wolves	wolf

NOTE: *Roof* is regular.

2. Most nouns in *-th* have regular plurals.

NOUNS IN *-th*	PLURAL	VERBS IN *-the*
breath	breaths	breathe
cloth	cloths	clothe
	(*clothes* is a different noun that means *clothing*)	
tooth	teeth	teethe
wreath	wreaths	wreathe

3. Some old English plural forms are still used.

man, men
woman, women
fireman, firemen
workman, workmen, and other compounds with *-man*
mouse, mice
louse, lice
goose, geese

child, children
ox, oxen
brother, brethren (religious use only—brothers in other uses)
foot, feet
tooth, teeth

4. Some nouns can keep the singular form in a collective plural meaning.

ANIMALS, BIRDS, AND FISH

Mr. Parker hunts
{
deer.
pheasant.
elephant.
duck.
}

He catches
{
trout.
perch.
bluefish.
}

TREES AND PLANTS (GRAINS)

The Allens planted
{
pine
oak
wheat
corn
rye
sorghum
barley
}
on their farm this year.

PEOPLE

Everyone—*man, woman,* and *child*—is affected by air pollution.
Student and *teacher* alike signed the petition.

5. Some Latin and Greek plurals are used. Writers in science often use the Greek or Latin forms even though most writers use English plurals.

Words Keeping Foreign Plurals (Always use the foreign plural if there is no entry under English plural.)

SINGULAR	FOREIGN PLURAL SCIENTIFIC USE	ENGLISH PLURAL GENERAL USE

Words ending in *-a* in the singular and *-ae* in the plural:

amoeb*a*	amoeb*ae*	amoeb*as*
alumn*a*	alumn*ae*	
antenn*a*	antenn*ae*	antenn*as*
formul*a*	formul*ae*	formul*as*
nebul*a*	nebul*ae*	nebul*as*

Words ending in *-ex* or *-ix* in the singular and *-ices* in the plural:

ap*ex*	ap*ices*	ap*exes*
append*ix*	append*ices*	append*ixes*
cerv*ix*	cerv*ices*	cerv*ixes*
ind*ex*	ind*ices*	ind*exes*

Words ending in *-is* in the singular and *-es* in the plural:

analy*sis*	analy*ses*
ax*is*	ax*es*
bas*is*	bas*es*
cris*is*	cris*es*
diagno*sis*	diagno*ses*
hypothe*sis*	hypothe*ses*
neuro*sis*	neuro*ses*
oa*sis*	oa*ses*
parenthe*sis*	parenthe*ses*
synop*sis*	synop*ses*
the*sis*	the*ses*

Words ending in *-on* in the singular and *-a* in the plural:

criteri*on*	criteri*a*
phenomen*on*	phenomen*a*

Words ending in *-um* in the singular and *-a* in the plural:

agend*um*—also agend*a*	agend*a*	
bacteri*um*	bacteri*a*	
dat*um*	dat*a*	
curricul*um*	curricul*a*	curricul*ums* (error, errors)
errat*um*	errat*a*	
medi*um*	medi*a*	(*mediums* has a different meaning)
memorand*um*	memorand*a*	memorand*ums* (often memo, memos)
strat*um*	strat*a*	
symposi*um*	symposi*a*	symposi*ums*

Words ending in *-us* in the singular and *-i* in the plural:

bacill*us*	bacill*i*	
cact*us*	cact*i*	cactu*ses*
fung*us*	fung*i*	fungu*ses*
nucle*us*	nucle*i*	
radi*us*	radi*i*	
stimul*us*	stimul*i*	
syllab*us*	syllab*i*	syllabu*ses*
termin*us*	termin*i*	

Words ending in *-im* in the plural (from Hebrew):

cherub	cherub*im*	cherub*s*
seraph	seraph*im*	seraph*s*

Some nouns with regular plural spelling do not have a singular form. (These nouns take plural verbs when they do not follow a preposition.)

Nouns that can follow *a pair of*:

binoculars
glasses (eyeglasses)
pants
pliers
pajamas

scales
  (countable in other meanings)
scissors
shorts
tights
tongs
trousers
tweezers

Some nouns are never used in the singular or preceded by a number:

archives
arms (weapons)
belongings
clothes
congratulations
credentials
earnings
looks (appearance)
manners (courteous behavior)
misgivings
odds
particulars (details)
premises

proceeds
quarters (place to live)
regards
remains
resources
riches
shortcomings
suds
surroundings
thanks
valuables
whereabouts

Some nouns have a plural form but a singular meaning (they take singular verbs):

checkers (draughts)
chess
economics
mathematics
means
measles
metropolis

molasses
mumps
news
physics
series
statistics
tennis

People has a singular form but always takes a plural verb. (See **Agreement of subject and verb** for more about irregular forms.)

Uses of Nouns

See each of the headings below in its own section for more examples of nouns used in different ways in a clause.

1. Subject

subject
Father just came.

2. Predicate nominative

> *predicate*
> *nominative*
> Mr. Jefferson is my   *father.*

3. Direct object

> *direct*
> *object*
> The children love their *father.*

4. Indirect object

> *indirect*
> *object*
> The children gave their *father* a hug.

5. Object of a preposition

> *object of*
> *preposition*
> We are waiting for our   *father.*

6. Objective complement

> *objective*
> *complement*
> Sally never called her stepfather   *father.*

7. Appositive

> *appositive*
> Mr. Jefferson, the   *father*   of one of our students, is here now.

8. Possessives (see **Punctuation, apostrophe** and **Case**):

Father's car is out of gas.

9. Modifier of another noun (see **Adjectives, order of**)
   modifier

A *father* figure is important to a child's psychological development.

Endings of Nouns

Certain endings are common on nouns. Do not confuse words that have the same root but that have endings that show they are different parts of speech.

> *noun*
> The newspaper article contained informa*tion* about Latin America.

> *adjective*
> An informa*tive* article about Latin America was in the newspaper today.

(see **Word formation, suffixes,** for a more complete list of noun endings)

Number, Singular and Plural _____

English grammar usually shows the difference between one and more than one. *One* is called singular; *more than one* is called plural. Nouns that can be either both singular or plural are called *countable*. Certain nouns that English-speaking people think of as abstract or as masses are usually singular in English. These nouns are called *uncountable* or *mass nouns.* To be sure about the way English uses a word, look it up in a reference book such as the *Oxford Advanced Learner's Dictionary* or the *Longman Dictionary of Contemporary English.* (see **Countable and uncountable nouns** and **Agreement of subject and verb**)

Numbers, Use in Formal Writing _____

Numbers should usually be spelled out in the text of formal writing if you can spell them in one or two words: *seventeen, forty-one, two hundred, nine thousand,* and so on.

Put a hyphen between the parts of compound numbers from twenty-one through ninety-nine and between the parts of fractions. (see **Punctuation, hyphen**)

Never begin a sentence with figures. If the number is long, rewrite the sentence so that the number is not the first word.

INCORRECT:	9,725 people visited the exhibit last month.
CORRECT:	Last month 9,725 people visited the exhibit.
	Forty-two people visited the exhibit yesterday.

If you have both long numbers and short numbers in the same sentence or list, use figures for all of them.

CORRECT:	Last month 9,725 people visited the exhibit, and yesterday 42 people visited it.

Objective Complement _____

An objective complement modifies or gives additional information about a direct object. An objective complement always follows a direct object. Only a few transitive verbs can take objective complements.

	SUBJECT	VERB	DIRECT OBJECT	OBJECTIVE COMPLEMENT
ACTIVE:	The club	elected	Helen	treasurer. (noun)
PASSIVE:	Helen	was elected		treasurer. (noun)
ACTIVE:	We	found	the baby	crying. (adjective)
PASSIVE:	The baby	was found		crying. (adjective)
ACTIVE ONLY:	Charles	made	his mother	happy. (adjective)
ACTIVE ONLY:	The training	made	the team	a winner. (noun)

Some of the verbs that can be followed by a direct object and an objective complement are listed in the following chart.

VERBS THAT CAN BE FOLLOWED BY A DIRECT OBJECT + A NOUN OR AN ADJECTIVE	VERBS THAT CAN BE FOLLOWED BY A DIRECT OBJECT + A NOUN ONLY	VERBS THAT CAN BE FOLLOWED BY A DIRECT OBJECT + AN ADJECTIVE
believe	appoint	color (it) red, ...
call	elect	cut (it) short
consider	name	force (it) open
declare		hold (it) open
find		kick (it) loose
imagine		knock (it) open
keep		paint (it) blue
leave		pull (it) tight
make		push (it) shut
pronounce		set (it) right
report		wash (it) clean
think		work (it) loose

These verbs can also be followed directly by the adjective if the noun object is followed by a long modifier: We forced *open the door that was blocking the way.* Compare separable two-word verbs. (see **Two-word verbs**)

NOTE: Two other constructions similar in meaning to the objective complement are possible with some verbs: *as* or *to be* sometimes follow the direct object. A few verbs can be followed by a direct object + objective complement, by a direct object + *as,* and by a direct object + *to be.* Some verbs can be followed by two of these structures, and some verbs can be followed by only one. (See **Infinitive/-*ing* choice** for verbs that can be followed by a direct object + *to be.*

O

Some verbs that can be followed by a direct object + *as* are listed below.

                                 direct
                                 object
The club elected John treasurer. (*Treasurer* is the objective complement.)
                      to be treasurer.
                      as treasurer.

                          direct
                          object
The judge declared the burglar guilty. (*Guilty* is the objective complement.)
                      to be guilty.

                          direct
                          object
Mrs. Johnson accepted the money *as* a gift.

Some verbs can be followed by a direct object + *as*:

accept + dir. obj. + as	interpret + dir. obj. + as
acknowledge + dir. obj. + as	know + dir. obj. + as
classify + dir. obj. + as	recognize + dir. obj. + as
characterize + dir. obj. + as	regard + dir. obj. + as
consider + dir. obj. + as	report + dir. obj. + as
define + dir. obj. + as	take + dir. obj. + as
describe + dir. obj. + as	treat + dir. obj. + as
intend + dir. obj. + as	use + dir. obj. + as

              accepted
              interpreted
              considered   *direct*
              recognized   *object*   an insult. (noun)
The coach   regarded   my remarks as   rude. (adjective)
              reported
              took
              treated

Objects, Kinds of _____

Direct objects and indirect objects follow transitive verbs in the active voice. Prepositions are followed by objects. Direct objects can take objective complements after a few verbs. (see **Direct objects, Indirect objects, Prepositions,** and **Objective complements**)

Pronouns used as objects must be the object form (objective case). (see **Case**)

Gerunds and infinitives can take objects in the same way the base verb does when it is the main verb in the clause.

Gerunds and infinitives can replace single-word objects. (see **Gerunds** and **Infinitives**)

Noun clauses can replace single-word objects. (see **Clauses, noun**)

Operators _____

An operator (sometimes called a *special* verb) is a verb form that can come first in a question: it is an auxiliary or a modal. An operator does special things in a clause. (see *Be, Do,* **Modals, Negation,** and **Questions**)

AUXILIARIES *(can also be the main verb)*

be: *am, is, are, was, were*

have, has, had (an operator when it is an auxiliary but rarely an operator as main verb in the United States)

do, does, did (replaces or is used with all verbs that are not operators when an operator is needed)

MODALS *(can be followed by the bare infinitive of another verb)*

can, could

may, might

shall, should

will, would

must

need (an operator mainly in British usage)

dare (mainly British usage)

ought (rarely an operator; usually replaced by *should* in questions)

When verb phrases that are semi-auxiliaries or semi-modals have an operator as part of the phrase, use the word already in the phrase as the operator.

In *be going to, be* (*is*) acts as operator:

Is he going to find his book?

In *had better, had* acts as operator:

*Had*n't she better come now?

In a positive question, *had better* would be replaced by *should*:

Should she come now?
She *had* better buy a new car.
Should she buy a new car?

Constructions Requiring an Operator

1. Questions (see **Questions**)

YES/NO QUESTIONS

a. *With an operator already in the statement:*

STATEMENT: Flora *will* come with us tomorrow.
QUESTION: *Will* Flora come with us tomorrow?

STATEMENT: Patrick *is* looking for a new job.
QUESTION: *Is* Patrick looking for a new job?

STATEMENT: The student assistants *were* pleased with their new schedule.
QUESTION: *Were* the student assistants pleased with their new schedule?

STATEMENT: We *must* go now.
QUESTION: *Must* we go now?

b. *Without an operator already in the statement:*

PRESENT TENSE

If the verb already in the statement is

third person singular—use *does* + *infinitive*
all other persons—use *do* + infinitive

PAST TENSE

All forms—use *did* + *infinitive*

Never put the past form of the main verb after *did*.

STATEMENT: Flora *came* with us yesterday.
QUESTION: *Did* Flora *come* with us yesterday?

STATEMENT: Patrick *changes* jobs often.
QUESTION: *Does* Patrick *change* jobs often?

STATEMENT: The student assistants *liked* their new schedule.
QUESTION: *Did* the student assistants *like* their new schedule?

                                          dependent clause
STATEMENT: They *think* (that) they should go now.

                                          dependent clause
QUESTION: *Do* they *think* (that) they should go now?

NOTE: The verb in the independent clause changes to make the question. The verb in the dependent clause does not change.

Short answers to *yes/no* questions must use the operator that is in the question.

QUESTION:	*Will* Flora come with us tomorrow?
SHORT ANSWER:	Yes, she *will*. or No, she *won't* (*will* not).
QUESTION:	*Is* Patrick looking for a new job?
SHORT ANSWER:	Yes, he *is*. or No, he *isn't*.
QUESTION:	*Were* the student assistants pleased with their new schedules?
SHORT ANSWER:	Yes, they *were*. or No, they *weren't*.
QUESTION:	*Must* we go now?
SHORT ANSWER:	Yes, we *must*. or No, we *mustn't*.
QUESTION:	*Did* Flora come with us yesterday?
SHORT ANSWER:	Yes, she *did*. or No, she *didn't*.
QUESTION:	*Does* Patrick change jobs often?
SHORT ANSWER:	Yes, he *does*. or No, he *doesn't*.
QUESTION:	*Do* the student assistants like their new schedule?
SHORT ANSWER:	Yes, they *do*. or No, they *don't*.
QUESTION:	*Do* they think (that) they should go now?
SHORT ANSWER:	Yes, they *do*. or No, they *don't*.

WH-QUESTIONS

If the WH-word is the subject of the clause, or if it modifies the subject, do not change the verb form to make the question.

	subject	verb	
STATEMENT:	Charles	*wants*	to see me.
WH- QUESTION:	*Who*	*wants*	to see me?
STATEMENT:	The red car	*made*	me think of Mary.
WH- QUESTION:	*What*	*made*	me think of Mary?
STATEMENT:	Your dog	*barked*	last night.
WH- QUESTION:	*Which* dog	*barked*	last night? (*Which* modifies the subject.)
STATEMENT:	Pat's book	*fell*	off the table.
WH- QUESTION:	*Whose* book	*fell*	off the table? (*Whose* modifies the subject.)

If the WH-word is used as anything besides the subject or a modifier of the subject, use an operator in the question.

a. *With an operator already in the statement:*

STATEMENT:	He *will* leave tomorrow. (*Will* is an operator.)

	subject		
WH- QUESTION:	*When will*	he	leave tomorrow?

	subject		
WH- QUESTION:	*Why will*	he	leave?

b. *Without an operator already in the statement:*

STATEMENT: He leaves tomorrow.

	subject		
WH- QUESTION:	*How does*	he	leave?

	subject		
WH- QUESTION:	*What does*	he	do when he leaves?

TAG QUESTIONS

Use an operator in a tag question, a shortened question form at the end of a statement. If the statement is positive, the tag question is negative. If the statement is negative, the tag question is positive. (Tag questions are rarely used in formal writing. Contractions are usually used in tag questions in speech.)

a. *With an operator already in the statement (a negative statement always has an operator):*

Flora *is* coming with us, *isn't* she? (*is* she *not*?)
Flora *isn't* coming with us, *is* she?

The student assistants *were* pleased with their new schedules, *weren't* they? (*were* they *not*?)
The student assistants *weren't* pleased with their new schedules, *were* they?

We *must* go now, *mustn't* we? (*must* we *not*?)
We *mustn't* go now, *must* we?

b. *Without an operator already in the statement:*

Flora *came* with us yesterday, *didn't* she? (*did* she *not*?)
Flora *didn't* *come* with us yesterday, *did* she?

Patrick *changes* jobs often, *doesn't* he? (*does* he *not*?)
Patrick *doesn't* *change* jobs often, *does* he?

The student assistants *like* their new schedules, *don't* they? (*do* they *not*?)
The student assistants *don't* *like* their new schedules, *do* they?

2. Negation

a. *With an operator already in the positive statement, put* not *after the operator* (see **Adverbs, order of**):

Flora *will not* come with us tomorrow.
Patrick *is not* looking for a new job.
The student assistants *were not* pleased with their new schedule.
We *must not* go now.

b. *Without an operator in the positive statement, use* do, does, *or* did. *Never put the past form of the main verb after* **did**.

Flora *did* not *come* with us yesterday.
Patrick *does* not *change* jobs often.
The student assistants *do* not *like* their new schedule.
They *do* not *think* (that) they should go now.

3. As a repeating verb

After *so* in a shortened clause:

a. *With an operator already in the first clause:*

Flora *will* come tomorrow, and *so will* Patrick.
Patrick *is* looking for a new job, and *so am* I. (Use the form of *be* that agrees with the subject of the clause the operator is in).
The student assistants *were* pleased with their new schedule, and *so was* Dr. Jackson.
We *must* go now, and *so must* everyone else.

b. *Without an operator already in the first clause:*

Flora *came* yesterday, and *so did* Patrick.
Patrick *changes* jobs often, and *so does* Paul.
The student assistants *liked* their new schedule, and *so did* Dr. Jackson.
They *think* (that) they should go now, and *so does* Roger.

After *as* or *than* in a comparison an operator must be used, or the verb may be left out if the meaning is clear without it. (see **Adjectives, comparison**)

Flora *is* as quick as Patrick (*is*). (*quicker than*)
Flora *came* as soon as Patrick (*did*). (*sooner than*)
The lab assistants *were* as pleased as Dr. Jackson *was*. (*more pleased than*)
The lab assistants *liked* their new schedule as much as Dr. Jackson *did*.

If the number or tense changes after *so* in a shortened clause or after *as* or *than* in a comparison, you must repeat the verb in its correct form.

Flora *is* as unhappy today as Patrick *was* yesterday. (change in tense)
Ted and Patrick *are* as happy today as Flora *was* yesterday. (change in tense and number)
Flora *was* happy yesterday, and so *were* Ted and Patrick. (change in number)
Flora is happier today *than* Ted *was* yesterday. (change in tense)

After *neither* or *nor*:

Flora *did not finish* yesterday, and *neither did* Patrick.

The student assistants *did* not *like* their new schedule, *nor* did Dr. Jackson.

4. In parallel structure after *not only* (see **Parallel structure**)

Not only was the young girl beautiful, but she *was* also a talented musician.
Not only did the authorities decide to build more schools, but they also *raised* teachers' salaries.

Outlining

An outline is a brief and orderly way of showing how ideas, facts, illustrations, and examples are related to each other. It is a guide to make sure your ideas are arranged in an order that seems logical to people who speak English.

In a *topic outline,* none of the points are complete sentences.

In a *sentence outline,* all the points must be complete sentences.

The format of an outline must not be changed. You must use letters and numbers in the conventional way and you must indent correctly if you want to make your ideas clear.

FIRST LEVEL:	Show the main divisions in your outline by using Roman numerals: I, II, III, . . .
SECOND LEVEL:	Show the subdivisions under each Roman numeral by using capital letters: A, B, C, . . .
THIRD LEVEL:	Show supporting details for each subdivision by using arabic numbers: 1, 2, 3, . . .
FOURTH LEVEL:	If you need additional details, use lower-case letters: a, b, c, . . .

Put Roman numeral I approximately one and a half inches from the left-hand edge of the page, inside the red line if you have one on your paper. Indent to the right when you go to a more specific level; move back to the left when you go to a more general level. Be sure all points of the same level are lined up under each other. More specific levels are called "lower levels." The highest, most general, most abstract level is called level one and uses Roman numerals. This level shows the major divisions of your outline. (see **Abstraction**)

Facts on Which to Base an Outline

In my country, private and public (government-supported) education both exist in the cities, but there are only small public schools in rural areas because few people live there. Many parents are not satisfied with public education. All public education is day and coeducational. Parents who can afford to do so send their children to private schools of different kinds. All postsecondary education is public and coeducational. Parents who can afford to do so often send their children out of the country for their university education. All public business education is postsecondary, but some private business schools exist on the secondary level. Parents choose secondary schools for their children mainly according to their children's abilities and test scores. Only students with very high test scores and grades can get into government-supported schools that prepare them for university studies. Universities have faculties for the professions of law, medicine, dentistry, veterinary medicine, and engineering. There are also colleges for teachers, nurses, and technical-vocational training.

A Topic Outline

	Education in My Country	
Title		
First Level	I. Elementary education	(1st major division)
Second Level	A. Public education	(1st subdivision of I)
Third Level	1. Village schools	(example of A)
	2. City schools	(example of A)
Second Level	B. Private education	(2nd subdivision of I)
Third Level	1. Religious schools	(example of B)
	2. Parents' associations	(example of B)
	3. Schools for profit	(example of B)
First Level	II. Secondary education	(2nd major division)
Second Level	A. Public education	(1st subdivision of II)
Third Level	1. Technical-vocational schools	(example of A)
	2. Preparatory schools	(example of A)
Second Level	B. Private education	(2nd subdivision of II)
Third Level	1. Business schools	(example of B)
	2. Technical-vocational schools	(example of B)
	3. Preparatory schools	(example of B)
Fourth Level	a. Boys' schools	(example of 3)
	b. Girls' schools	(example of 3)
First Level	III. Postsecondary education (public)	(3rd major division)
Second Level	A. Business schools	(1st subdivision of III)
	B. Technical-vocational schools	(2nd subdivision of III)
	C. Teacher-training schools	(3rd subdivision of III)
	D. University professional schools	(4th subdivision of III)
Third Level	1. Law faculty	(example of D)
	2. Medical faculty	(example of D)
	3. Dental faculty	(example of D)
	4. Veterinary faculty	(example of D)
	5. Engineering faculty	(example of D)

1. Not all of the facts appear in the outline. Some facts are not relevant to the subject, such as the fact that many students study outside their own country. Use only facts that are relevant. (see **Relevant material**)

2. Indent all the numbers of the same kind and all the letters of the same kind the same distance from the left-hand margin.

3. Do not write any complete sentences in a topic outline; therefore, do not put a period at the end of each point in the outline.

4. Always divide when you go to a lower level. If you do not have at least two points, put the information in parentheses, as in III, where *public* is an explanation but not a subdivision.

5. Use parallel structure whenever possible, but use another noun form if you need to. In I B 3, *schools for profit* is correct. *Profitable schools* appears to be more parallel, but it would not be true, because it is possible for a school to be organized for the purpose of profit but to be unprofitable. (see **Parallel structure**)

6. Do not use the title as Roman numeral one. If you do, you will not be able to think of a Roman numeral two. An outline gives the divisions and subdivisions of your subject as you explain it in your title. Your title must be separate from your outline.

7. Put periods after the numbers and letters that show the divisions of the outline.

8. Facts can be arranged more than one way according to the emphasis you want to give them. Instead of arranging the facts on education according to elementary, secondary, and postsecondary education, this outline could have two major divisions: public and private. Then it could develop elementary, secondary, and postsecondary subdivisions under these two major divisions:

    I. Private education
       A. Elementary schools
       B. Secondary schools

   II. Public education
       A. Elementary schools
       B. Secondary schools
       C. Postsecondary schools

9. You do not need to have the same number of points in all subdivisions. In the first outline, for example, I and II both have subdivisions A and B, but III has subdivisions A, B, C, and D.

A sentence outline has the same format as a topic outline, but each point must be a complete sentence. The topic outline for "Education in My Country" can be developed into complete sentences.

A Sentence Outline

Title   **Education in My Country**

I. Elementary education is well developed in my country.
   A. Public elementary schools are everywhere.
      1. Village elementary schools have been built in rural areas.
      2. Many elementary schools have been built in cities.
   B. Private elementary schools have been organized in cities.
      1. Religious organizations have built boarding schools.
      2. Parents' associations have built boarding schools.
      3. Private individuals have built day schools for profit.

II. Most secondary schools are in cities.
   A. Public secondary schools are mainly in the cities.
      1. Technical-vocational schools train boys and girls together for careers.
      2. Preparatory schools prepare boys and girls for university entrance examinations.
   B. Private secondary schools have several purposes.
      1. Private business schools train boys and girls separately for business careers.
      2. Technical-vocational schools train boys for careers.
      3. Preparatory boarding schools prepare boys and girls for university entrance examinations in separate schools.

III. Public postsecondary schools are located near the largest cities.
   A. Business schools prepare students for careers on a higher level than secondary business schools do.
   B. Technical-vocational schools train higher-level technicians.
   C. Teacher-training schools prepare teachers for elementary and secondary schools.
   D. Nursing schools train nurses and nurses' aides.
   E. Three universities prepare students for the professions.
      1. Three law faculties prepare lawyers for the bar examination.
      2. Two medical faculties prepare doctors for their examinations.
      3. One dental faculty prepares dentists for their examinations.
      4. One veterinary faculty prepares veterinarians for their examinations.
      5. Three engineering faculties prepare engineers and architects for their examinations.

    In order to write a sentence outline, you must decide exactly what you are going to say about each point in your outline. A sentence outline is more complete and gives more information than a topic outline, but you can usually write a topic outline much faster. Each kind of outline has advantages and disadvantages. Choose the one that is suitable for the writing you will do.

P

Paragraph _____

A paragraph is a unit of thought that has several or many sentences in it.

The *length* of a paragraph varies according to the purpose of the writing. Academic writing, business writing, journalism, and scientific and technical writing have different purposes. They may, therefore, require paragraphs of different lengths. In academic writing a developing or body paragraph is often 75 to 125 words long. Sometimes it is much longer. (see **Style**)

The *organization* of a paragraph depends on the purpose of the writing. In a short paper, each major point in an outline may be developed into a paragraph. In a very long paper, several paragraphs may be necessary to develop one point. Arrange your ideas clearly in the order that is the most suitable. (see **Chronological order, Logical order, Outline,** and **Spatial order**)

The *topic sentence* of a paragraph tells what the paragraph is about and how the ideas are developed. A topic sentence can be put any place in the paragraph, but putting it at the beginning guides the development. (see **Topic sentence**)

The *appearance* of a paragraph is important. In handwriting, indent the first line of each paragraph. *Do not indent every time you begin a new sentence.* Leave margins on both sides of the paper. If you are writing on looseleaf notebook paper, write so that the holes are in the left-hand margin. Use blue or black ink on white paper. (see **Format**)

Three kinds of paragraphs make up every formal composition. An *introductory paragraph* begins the paper, stating what the paper is going to be about in the form of a thesis statement. *Body paragraphs* develop the thesis statement. A *concluding paragraph* restates the thesis, usually in different words, and shows briefly how the development relates to it. Sometimes short *transitional* paragraphs join the ideas in the body paragraphs, but many writers include transitional elements in the body paragraphs. (see **Transitions**)

Parallel Structure

Parallel structure means repeating the same grammar patterns to show that the ideas in them have the same importance. Putting sentences and longer passages into parallel structure requires thinking ahead. Because the writer or speaker must plan parallel structures before writing or speaking, parallel structure is rarely used in informal speech, but it is used mainly in formal writing or in speeches that are carefully written out before they are given. Coordinating conjunctions usually join parallel structures. (see **Coordinating conjunctions**)

Parallel Structure with Single Words or with Phrases

With *-ing* forms:

PARALLEL: Evelyn likes hik*ing*, swimm*ing*, and bicycl*ing*.

With infinitive phrases:

PARALLEL: Evelyn likes *to hike, to swim*, and *to ride* a bicycle.

Do not mix the forms.

NOT PARALLEL: Evelyn likes *to hike, to swim*, and *riding* a bicycle.

NOTE: Although the verb *like* can be followed either by the *-ing* form or by an infinitive phrase, use the same form in one sentence to keep the structure parallel.

Use *to* before all verbs or only before the first one.

NOT PARALLEL: Evelyn likes *to hike, to swim*, and *ride* a bicycle.

PARALLEL: Evelyn likes *to hike, swim*, and *ride* a bicycle.

Do not mix prepositional phrases and *-ing* forms.

NOT PARALLEL: Anthony liked to spend his time *studying* in the library, *working* in the biology laboratory, and *at* soccer games.

PARALLEL: Anthony liked to spend his time *in the library, in the biology laboratory*, and *at the soccer games*.

Parallel Structure with Clauses

NOT PARALLEL:	Anthony was happy *when he was studying math, working on his biology experiments,* or *to watch soccer games.*
PARALLEL:	Anthony was happy *when he was studying math, when he was working on his biology experiments,* or *when he was watching soccer games.*

A parallel structure that begins with clauses must keep on with clauses. Do not change to another pattern or change the voice of the verb from active to passive or from passive to active.

PARALLEL:	*Whoever requests* my allegiance, *whoever demands* my loyalty, *whoever requires* my trust— that leader must be *both wise and trustworthy.*

Parallel independent clauses make a special kind of compound sentence that is called a *balanced sentence.* The structures in its parts are the same.

NOT BALANCED:	The hare was *fast* but erratic; the *slow* tortoise was persistent.
	independent clause
BALANCED:	The hare was fast but erratic;
	independent clause
	the tortoise was slow but persistent.

The sentence above is grammatically correct, but it is not *balanced* because the adjective *fast* follows the verb in the first clause and *but* emphasizes the idea of contrast. The adjective *slow* comes before the noun in the second clause, however, and *but* is left out. Both sentences are compound sentences, but only the first one is balanced.

NOT BALANCED:	A wise leader does not ask for loyalty but gets it; when a foolish leader demands loyalty, he fails to get it.
BALANCED:	A wise leader does not ask for loyalty but gets it; a foolish leader demands loyalty and fails to get it.

Lists after a colon:

NOT PARALLEL:	Use your dictionary for the following purposes: to find word *meanings, pronunciation, spelling,* and *looking up* irregular forms. (*Looking up* cannot be the object of *find.*)
PARALLEL:	Use your dictionary for the following purposes: to find word *meanings, pronunciation, spelling,* and irregular verb *forms.*

(PARALLEL example shown with labels: noun — *meanings,* noun — *pronunciation,* noun — *spelling,* noun — *forms)*

PARALLEL: Some punctuation marks are rarely used: *slashes,* the *periods* of ellipsis, and *brackets.*

PARALLEL: Use the library for the purposes for which it was intended: *reading, studying,* and *looking* up information, not for *talking* and *sleeping.*

Use correlative conjunctions in pairs.

both . . .and . . .
either . . . or . . .
neither . . . nor . . .
not . . . but . . .
not only . . . but also . . .

                    noun   *noun*
              Both   *and*

PARALLEL: *Neither* the parents *nor* the children enjoyed *Not only*   *but also* the program.

Either the parents *or* the children will attend, but not both.

                                        noun
The program was attended *not* by the parents *but*
                  noun
(only) by the children.

Put the same structure directly after each correlative conjunction.

                                infinitive
NOT PARALLEL: Julia has decided *neither*   *to go*   to Miami *nor*
     prepositional
     phrase
to Chicago.

                                        prepositional
                                        phrase
PARALLEL: Julia has decided to go *neither*   *to Miami*   *nor*
     prepositional
     phrase
to Chicago.

                            noun
PARALLEL: *Neither* the *results* of the first experiment *nor* the
     noun
results of the second one were the results we expected.

                            noun
PARALLEL: *Not only* the *parents* enjoyed the program, *but* the
     noun
children enjoyed it also.

Do not change the verb from active to passive or from passive to active.

                          active
NOT PARALLEL: Both the parents *enjoyed* the program, and also it
     passive
was enjoyed by the children.

<table>
<tr><td></td><td>*passive*</td></tr>
</table>

NOT PARALLEL: Not only *was* the program *enjoyed* by the par-
                                        active
                ents, but the children *enjoyed* it too.

                                        passive
PARALLEL: Not only *was* the program *enjoyed* by the par-
                                        passive
                ents, but it *was enjoyed* by the children too.

                                        active
PARALLEL: Not only did the parents enjoy the program,
                        passive
                but the children enjoyed it too.

Paraphrase

Paraphrasing is rewriting using different words. When you paraphrase something that someone else has written, you state it in your
own words. If you copy the words of the original author exactly, you are
not paraphrasing; you are quoting and you must use quotation marks.
(see **Direct speech**)

Do not put paraphrases in quotation marks. Paraphrases should be
your own words, *but* they are *not your own ideas*. In a documented
paper, therefore, paraphrases must have footnotes in the same way that
direct quotations must have footnotes. (see **Documentation**)

You may sometimes need to paraphrase something that you yourself
have written by writing the same idea in different words. Many writers
do this in the conclusion of a formal paper when they paraphrase their
thesis statement. Paraphrasing does not develop your ideas, however; it
only restates them. (see **Wordiness**)

Parentheses, see **Punctuation, parentheses**

Participles

Participles are forms of the verb that are used in verb phrases to
form tenses.

He was *walking* many miles.
   has *walked*

Or they can be adjectives.

The man *walking* down the street seems *tired*.

Present participles and *past participles* are special forms of the verb.

Make present participles by adding *-ing* to the present form of the
verb according to regular spelling rules. Make past participles of regular

verbs by adding *-ed* to the present form according to regular spelling rules. (see **Spelling**) Learn the past participles of irregular verbs. (see **Verbs, irregular**)

Uses of Participles (see **Tense**)

In verb phrases, use a form of *be* + a present participle to form the continuous/progressive tenses.

> is *walking*. (present continuous/progressive)
> The man was *walking*. (past continuous/progressive)
> will be *walking*. (future continuous/progressive)

Use a form of *have* + a past participle to form the perfect tenses.

> has *walked*. (present perfect)
> The man had *walked*. (past perfect)
> will have *walked*. (future perfect)

Use past participles to form the passive voice of transitive verbs.

> is *seen* often. (present passive)
> has been *seen* often. (present perfect passive)
> The man was *seen* often. (past passive)
> had been *seen* often. (past perfect passive)

As adjectives, present participles show that the time of the action of the participle is the same as the time of the action of the main verb.

> The man *walking* down the street *seems tired*. (*Walking* and *seems tired* are happening at the same time.)

Perfect participles show that the time of the action of the participle was *before* the time of the action of the main verb.

> The man, *having walked* for several miles, *seems* tired.
> *Having walked* for several miles, the man *seemed* tired. (*Having walked* happened before *seemed tired*.)

Past participles also show that the action of the participle has already happened, but the emphasis is on the present state or condition rather than on the action in the participle.

> The dish *broken* into a dozen pieces cannot be mended.
> The money *found* on the street was soon claimed.

Participial phrases can include a subject, complement(*s*), and adverbs.

> (Peter)
> SUBJECT: We left *him* sleeping. (Use an object pronoun for the subject of a participle.)

NOTE: The main verb in the sentence above is *left*, which can be followed by an *-ing* form. Some verbs can be followed by only an *-ing* form, other verbs can be followed by only an infinitive form, and still others by either form (sometimes with a change in meaning). (see **Infinitive/-*ing* choice**)

If the main verb in the clause can be followed by either a present participle or a gerund, choose the form that gives the emphasis you want. (see **Gerund**)

Participle: Use an object pronoun. The emphasis is on the object.

> *emphasis*
> *on*
> *object   present*
> *pronoun participle*
> We watched *him   running.*

Gerund: Use a possessive pronoun. The emphasis is on the gerund.

> *emphasis*
> *possessive   on*
> *pronoun   gerund*
> We watched *his   running.*

Object: Participles made from transitive verbs can take direct and indirect objects.

> *direct*
> *object*
> *Finding* the *course* too difficult, Penny decided to drop it.

> *indirect   direct*
> *object   object*
> *Lending Doris* the *book,* Joe told her she could keep it for a week.

Predicate Complement: Participles made from linking verbs can take predicate nominatives and predicate adjectives. (*Being* is often left out.)

> *predicate*
> *adjective*
> (Being)   *sad*   about losing the game, the team dressed quietly.

> *predicate*
> *nominative*
> (Being) the   *home*   of his childhood, the house held many memories.

Adverb Modifiers: Participles can be modified by single words, phrases, and clauses.

> *single-word adverb*
> *quickly,*

> Returning the papers   *prepositional phrase*   Robert thanked Anne for the
> *with a smile,*

> *adverb clause*
> *as soon as he could,*
> chance to look at them.

Absolute phrases are formed with participles. (see **Absolutes**)

> The rain *having* already *begun,* we decided to spend the afternoon at home.

> Jobs *being* difficult to find, Pat decided she would have to move.

NOTE: Participles and participial phrases are often reduced forms of dependent clauses. (see **Subordinating and reducing** and **Wordiness**)

Common Errors with Participles

Do not write *dangling participles,* participles that do not modify a noun in the same clause. Participles at the beginning of the clause usually modify the subject.

DANGLING:	*Having* already *chosen* a new bicycle, the old one was put up for sale. (What does *having chosen* modify? It cannot modify *the old one* since bicycles cannot choose.)
CORRECT:	*Having* already *chosen* a new *bicycle, Max* put *his* old one up for sale. (*Having chosen* now modifies *Max.*)
DANGLING:	*Finding* no coffee in the cupboard, tea was used instead. (*Finding* cannot modify *tea.* There is no word in the sentence for *finding* to modify.)
CORRECT:	*Finding* no coffee in the cupboard, the *cook* used tea instead.

Do not write *fragments* by using the *-ing* form by itself as the main verb in the sentence. Use a form of *be* in the continuous/progressive tenses. (see **Fragments**)

	participle alone
FRAGMENT:	The cherry trees *blossoming* in the spring.
CORRECT:	The cherry trees *are blossoming* this spring.
	The cherry trees *were blossoming* last month.
	The cherry trees *have been blossoming.*
	Cherry trees *blossom* in the spring.
FRAGMENT:	The wind *blowing* the branches nearly to the ground.
CORRECT:	The wind *is blowing* the branches nearly to the ground.
	The wind *was blowing* the branches nearly to the ground.

Do not confuse the past and past participle forms of irregular verbs when those forms are not the same. (see **Verbs, irregular,** groups 1 and 4)

INCORRECT:	The painters *done* the work.
CORRECT:	The painters *did* the work.
	The painters *have done* the work.
INCORRECT:	The chorus *sung* the song.
CORRECT:	The chorus *sang* the song.
	The chorus *has sung* the song.

Do not use infinitives after verbs that require *-ing* forms or use *-ing* forms after verbs that require infinitives. (see **Infinitive/-ing choice**)

INCORRECT:	We *enjoy to go* to the movies.
CORRECT:	We *enjoy going* to the movies.
INCORRECT:	We *want going* to the movies.
CORRECT:	We *want to go* to the movies.

Word Order of Participles

Use participial phrases that are nonessential modifiers before or after the words that they modify. Use participial phrases that are essential modifiers only after the words that they modify. (see **Essential and nonessential modifiers**)

A nonessential modifier *does not identify* the word it modifies or tell *which one*. Use commas to separate nonessential modifiers from the rest of the clause.

> nonessential modifier
> *Finding the course too difficult,* Pat dropped it.
> Pat, *finding the course too difficult,* dropped it.

An essential modifier *identifies* and tells *which one*. Do not separate essential modifiers from the rest of the clause with commas.

> essential modifier
> The money *found on the street* was soon claimed by the man who had lost it.

Participles Used as Adjectives

Most participles cannot come between an article or determiner and the word they modify.

In standard English you would not say *the sung song,* but you can say *the lost child.* Participles such as *lost,* when used as adjectives, can also be modified by words such as *very, more, most, less,* and *least.* (Adjectives that can be modified by these words are sometimes called *gradable.*) (see **Adjectives**) These participles can also follow *be* and be used as objective complements.

-ing FORMS	PAST PARTICIPLES
alarming	alarmed
amazing	amazed
amusing	amused
astonishing	astonished
boring	bored
	broken
	closed
confusing	confused
damaging	damaged
	defeated
disappointing	disappointed
	(different meanings)
distinguishing	distinguished
disturbing	disturbed
embarrassing	embarrassed
encouraging	
entertaining	
exciting	excited
fascinating	fascinated
finishing	finished
frightening	frightened
	honored
interesting	interested
lasting	
	limited
	lost
	murdered
	organized
pleasing	pleased
promising	
	recorded
rewarding	
satisfying	satisfied
shocking	shocked
	spoken
surprising	surprised
tiring	tired
wearing (in the sense of *tiring*)	worn
worrying	worried

Some other words in *-ing* that show purpose can be used before nouns but cannot be modified by *very*: clothes that are used *for hiking*, or fields that are used *for playing*, for example. Such words include *running, riding, swimming,* and *flying.*

Before a noun:

> The *disturbing* news shocked everyone.
> The *disturbed* crowd began to shout.

After *be*:

> The news was *disturbing*.
> The people were *disturbed*.

As an objective complement:

> The police found the boys *disturbing* the peace.
> The doctor declared the criminal *disturbed*.

With *very*:

> The news was *very disturbing*.
> The people were *very disturbed*.

Notice the difference in meaning in the *-ing* and *-ed* forms after *be*. The *-ing* form can be completed by a personal object.

> The news was *disturbing me*.
> The day was *boring me*.
> My coach was *encouraging me*.
> My sister was *embarrassing me*.

With the *-ed* form, the meaning is passive. Something is happening to the subject.

> I was *disturbed*.
> I was *bored*.
> I was *encouraged*.
> I was *embarrassed*.

Particle

Particle is sometimes used to mean a short word, especially a conjunction or a preposition that is used to complete a construction but that is not the most important element in it. An *adverbial* particle is the second part of some two-word verbs: find *out*, make *up*, sign *off*, and so on.

Parts of Speech

Parts of speech are the classes into which words are put according to their grammatical uses. The same word is sometimes used as different parts of speech without any change in form. Endings (suffixes) added to the base form or root of the word often show changes in the part of speech, however. (see **Word formation**)

The following sections related to parts of speech are in the text in alphabetical order: **Adjectives, Adverbs, Articles, Conjunctions, Determiners, Interjections, Nouns, Prepositions, Pronouns, Two-word verbs,** and **Verbs.**

Passive Verbs _____

A passive verb is a form of transitive verb: The subject receives the action instead of acting. Many active verbs can be changed into passive verbs, but not all can. Most passive verbs can be changed into active verbs. Although passive verbs used carelessly make writing dull and wordy, passive verbs have specific uses:

1. When the actor is unknown, unimportant, or obvious, or wishes to be unknown.
2. In certain styles of scientific writing.
3. In writing about disasters and accidents if the result or the victim is more important than the cause.

	active
CORRECT:	Club members adopted the new rules in 1980.
	passive
CORRECT:	New club rules were adopted in 1980.
	active
CORRECT:	I completed the experiment to show the relation between nutrition and growth.
	passive
CORRECT:	The relation between nutrition and growth was shown.
	active
CORRECT:	A flood destroyed Mr. Johnson's house.
	passive
CORRECT:	Mr. Johnson's house was destroyed by a flood.

The emphasis in the sentences above is different. In the last pair of sentences, for example, the first one emphasizes the flood, but the second emphasizes the destruction of the house. Someone involved in flood control might write the first sentence. Mr. Johnson or his insurance agent might write the second one. (see **Voice**)

Formation of the Passive

Make the passive from a form of *be* + the past participle of the main verb.

Passive Voice of *Destroy*

TENSE		SINGULAR / PLURAL		PAST PARTICIPLE OF MAIN VERB
Present	The house(s)	*is*	*are*	destroyed.
Present Perfect		*has been*	*have been*	destroyed.
Past		*was*	*were*	destroyed.
Past Perfect		*had been*	*had been*	destroyed.
Future		*will be*	*will be*	destroyed.
Future Perfect		*will have been*	*will have been*	destroyed.
Present Progressive		*is being*	*are being*	destroyed.
Past Progressive		*was being*	*were being*	destroyed.

All passive and all continuous/progressive forms have some form of *be* in them.

By + an agent after a passive verb gives the same information that the active subject gives in the active voice. You can leave this information out in the passive voice.

PRESENT:

PASSIVE
past participle
The experiment *is completed* (by Mary).

ACTIVE
Mary *completes* the experiment.

PRESENT PROGRESSIVE:

PASSIVE
The experiment *is being completed* (by Mary).

ACTIVE
Mary *is completing* the experiment.

PAST:

PASSIVE
The experiment *was completed* (by Mary).

ACTIVE
Mary *completed* the experiment.

PAST PROGRESSIVE:

PASSIVE
The experiment *was being completed* (by Mary).

ACTIVE
Mary *was completing* the experiment.

Passive infinitives are possible with some verbs.

After a storm the roof needs *to be inspected* for damage. (direct object)
To be struck by lightning is a frightening experience. (subject)
This engine was the first one *to be made* entirely of plastic. (adjective)

Passive gerunds are possible with some verbs.

> *Being chosen* captain of the team is a great honor. (subject)
> The thief was afraid of *being discovered.* (object of a preposition)
> His goal, *being elected* president of the club, was achieved last month. (appositive)

Passive participles are possible with some verbs. In the present tense, *being* is often left out, and *having been* or *had been* is sometimes left out of perfect participial phrases that are passive.

> *(Being) chosen* captain of the team, Susan was happy to accept the honor.
> *(Having been) chosen* captain of the team last year, Susan expected to be elected again.
> *(Being) made* entirely of plastic, the engine was carefully tested.

With some verbs, the indirect object can become the subject of the passive.

		indirect object	*direct object*
ACTIVE:	Don sent	Mary	a letter.
PASSIVE:	A letter was sent (by Don) (to Mary).		
PASSIVE:	Mary was sent a letter.		

Period, see **Punctuation, period**

Person

As a grammatical term, *person* means the way the writers express their ideas: as their own (first person), directly to the reader (second person), or as ideas of others (third person). Pronoun forms that show these differences are called personal pronouns. (see **Pronouns, personal** and **Point of view**)

Most *nouns* show the plural by adding *-s.* (see **Nouns**)

	FIRST PERSON	SECOND PERSON	THIRD PERSON
SINGULAR:	I	you	he, she, it
	me	you	him, her, it
	my	your	his, her, its
	myself	yourself	himself, herself, itself
	mine	yours	his, hers, its
PLURAL:	we	you	they
	us	you	them
	our	your	their
	ourselves	yourselves	themselves
	ours	yours	theirs

Besides the forms of *be,* the only *verb* form that changes to show person is the third person singular in the present tense: I, you, we, they *walk,* but he, she, it *walks*. Put an -*s* on the end of all third person singular verbs in the present tense except modals, *have*, and *be*. (See *Be* for its irregular forms in the present and past tenses; see **Agreement of subject and verb;** and see **Spelling** for rules about adding -*s* to nouns and verbs.)

Personification

Personification gives nonhuman things the qualities, abilities, or emotions of people. Personification often uses abstract ideas; these abstract ideas are often capitalized. (see **Apostrophe**)

How rarely *Reason guides* the stubborn choice.
Samuel Johnson

And the *sun looked* over the mountain's rim.
Robert Browning

. . . *earth took* him to her stony care.
William Butler Yeats

. . . *Love fled*
And *paced* upon the mountains overhead
And *hid his face* amid a crowd of stars.
William Butler Yeats

Phrase

A phrase is two or more words that work together as a unit and/or as the same part of speech. The main word in a phrase is sometimes called the *head* word. A clause has a subject-finite verb combination, but a phrase does not have both a subject and a finite verb. A noun phrase can be the subject of a clause, however, and a verb phrase can be the main verb of a clause. Verb phrases can be finite or nonfinite; that is, they can be the main verb of a clause (finite); or they can be infinitives, participles, or gerunds (nonfinite). Other phrases are prepositional phrases and adverbial phrases. (see **Nouns, Verbs, Prepositional phrases, Infinitive,** and **Adverbs**)

A noun phrase is a noun and its modifiers.

NOUN PHRASE: *The large white house* was sold yesterday.

A (finite) verb phrase includes all the finite verbs in one clause.

VERB PHRASE: The house *has been sold.*

A nonfinite verb phrase includes an infinitive, a gerund, or a participle and its object and modifiers, if any.

INFINITIVE PHRASE:	The house *to be sold* is across the street.
GERUND PHRASE:	*Selling the house* may be difficult.
PARTICIPIAL PHRASE:	*Having sold the house,* he was happy.
	Found guilty of breaking into the house, the thief went to jail.

A prepositional phrase includes a preposition and the noun or noun phrase that is its object.

PREPOSITIONAL PHRASE:	The house *on the next corner* has been sold.

An adverbial phrase can be a prepositional phrase used as an adverb.

PREPOSITIONAL PHRASE:	The house has been sold *since last week.*

or an adverb and another adverb that modifies it.

ADVERB PHRASE:	They sold the house *very quickly.* (*Quickly* modifies *sold* and *very* modifies *quickly.*)

Plagiarism

Plagiarism means using someone else's ideas or facts without giving credit to that person. If you quote directly from a newspaper, book, or magazine without giving the source of the quotation in a footnote or bibliography, you have plagiarized. But even if you rewrite the idea in your own words, you must give credit to whoever originally wrote or said what you are using in your own paper. Facts that are general knowledge (George Washington was the first president of the United States) or statements on which most experts agree (Shakespeare was a great dramatist) do not require you to give sources. But when authorities on the subject that you are writing about disagree, or when the facts that you are using are not general knowledge, you must show where the ideas, criticism, and facts that you use came from. Plagiarism can also mean using a paper written originally by someone else and handing it in as your own work. Most schools, colleges, and universities have severe penalties for plagiarism; it is considered cheating.

Point of View

Point of view shows whether the writer is speaking directly (*I*), or to the reader (*you*), or about someone or something else (*he, she, it,* or *they*). (See **Tone** for Point of view in the sense of *attitude*.) Pronouns, nouns referring to people, and names establish the point of view:

	SINGULAR	PLURAL
FIRST PERSON:	I	we
SECOND PERSON:	you	you
THIRD PERSON:	he, she, it	they

Most academic and journalistic writing is done in the third person singular, and most academic writing is done in the present tense. Since the third person singular, present tense verb has an *-s* ending, you must be especially careful to use the correct forms: he agree*s*, she think*s*, Professor Armstrong state*s*, and so forth. (see **Agreement of subject and verb**) Sometimes you may choose the point of view in which to write, but you must be *consistent*; you must not change, but keep writing in the same point of view all through your paper unless you have a good reason to change. You must make your changes very clear to the reader. The following paragraph contains several unnecessary changes.

Visiting Paris for the first time is an exciting experience. I[1] could hardly wait to see the Eiffel Tower. As our[2] bus came from the airport into the center of the city, you[3] could not see it, but they[4] all kept trying. You[5] must see the Eiffel Tower to see Paris.

> [1]I—first person, singular
> [2]our—first person, plural
> [3]you—second person
> [4]they—third person, plural
> [5]you—second person

The following paragraphs maintain a consistent point of view.

First-time visitors[1] to Paris always want to see the Eiffel Tower as soon as possible. Coming into the city on the bus, they[2] look for it but cannot see it although they[3] keep trying. The Eiffel Tower, most tourists[4] think, is the most important sight to see in Paris.

> [1]visitors—third person, plural
> [2]they—third person, plural
> [3]they—third person, plural
> [4]tourists—third person, plural

The first time I[1] landed at the Paris airport, I[2] could hardly wait to get into the city to see the Eiffel Tower. As my[3] bus was going into the city, I[4] kept looking out the window, hoping to catch sight of it. I[5] thought that the Eiffel Tower was the most important thing to see in all of Paris.

> [1]I—first person, singular
> [2]I—first person, singular
> [3]my—first person, singular
> [4]I—first person, singular
> [5]I—first person, singular

Possessives

Two constructions can show *possession* or source. A construction that follows *of* is easy to make. The construction with *-'s* or *-s'* is sometimes confusing. (Some grammars call possessive forms *genitives*.)

Nouns

APOSTROPHE + *s* OR APOSTROPHE ALONE

Nouns can be changed to the possessive by adding *-'s* or, if the word already ends in *-s*, by adding an apostrophe by itself. (See **Punctuation, apostrophe** for more about the apostrophe with possessive forms.)

's AND *'* FORMS

the dog's bark (singular)	Curtis' friend (plural)
a day's work (singular)	the Johnsons' house (plural)

of PHRASE AFTER NOUNS NOT RELATED TO PEOPLE

the tires *of the car*	the roof *of the house*
the surface *of the road*	the leaves *of the tree*

CHOICE BETWEEN *'s* AND *of* POSSESSIVE FORMS

1. Nouns connected with people and human activity usually take the *'s* form:

proper names: Abraham Lincoln's speech
personal nouns: the girl's dress
collective nouns: the team's success
nouns relating to human activity: the body's ability
geographical names: Canada's history
institutions: the University's budget, the museum's members

2. Many phrases of time take the *'s* form:

a month's pay	two weeks' vacation
a year's work	season's greetings

3. Certain idioms take the *'s* form:

our money's worth	an arm's length

4. Higher animals can take the *'s* form:

a dog's life	the kitten's cry
the horse's mane	the cat's meow

The noun following an *'s* possessive can be left out if the context makes the meaning clear.

Martha's course is harder than Grace's. (Grace's course)
Paul's dog is well trained, but Kevin's is not. (Kevin's dog)
They bought their furniture at Scott's. (Scott's furniture store)

Double possessives using both *of* and the *'s* form are common with proper nouns when the reference is definite and personal.

a novel of Conrad's	a friend of my father's
a symphony of Beethoven's	a painting of Picasso's

Double possessives are also possible with pronouns (see below).

a friend of mine	a book of hers

Pronouns

Two forms of pronouns are possessive: one form goes before the noun the way the *'s* noun form does, and the other form follows *of*. (see **Pronouns, possessive**)

my friend	a friend of mine
our friends	friends of ours
his friends	friends of his

Predicate

Predicate means the verb phrase and all the complements and modifiers connected to it. A predicate can be just a single word, or it can include several words in a verb phrase, objects or predicate nominatives and their modifiers, and adverbs in the form of single words, phrases, and clauses. (see **Adverbs**, **Verb phrase**, and **Complements**)

SUBJECT	PREDICATE
The boy	laughed.
The boy	laughed and ran away.
The boy	laughed at the cat.
The boy	caught the ball.
The boy	tried to catch the ball.
The boy	tried to reach the ball that was rolling across the playground.
The boy	tried to reach the ball that was rolling across the playground but slipped and fell.

Predicate Complements

Predicate complements (also called subjective complements) of two kinds follow linking verbs (also called copulas). (see **Verbs, kinds of**)

Predicate nominatives are nouns or noun substitutes that restate the subject.

Predicate adjectives modify the subject.

Common linking verbs are *be, become, appear, feel, look, remain, rest, seem, smell,* and *taste.*

SUBJECT	LINKING VERB	PREDICATE COMPLEMENT
The house	is	a mansion. (noun restates *house*)
The house	appears	large. (adjective describes *house*)
The house	seems is appears feels	empty. (adjective describes *house*)
The apple	looks seems smells tastes	rotten. (adjective describes *apple*)
The answer	is still	*what I told you yesterday.* (noun clause restates *answer*)
Your prize	will be	*whatever you choose.* (noun clause restates *prize*)

Other verbs can be linking in special meanings, usually when they mean *became.*

The food *grew* cold.　　My uncle *fell* sick.　　The house *stands* empty.
The weather *turned* bad.　Our dream *came* true.　The milk *went* sour.
The children *ran* wild.　　*Get* ready.

Use adjective forms after linking verbs: The weather turned *bad*, not *badly.* (see **Adjective/adverb choice**)

NOTE: Adverbs of place can complete the meaning of *be*. (see **Be, meanings**)

The bread is *on the table.*　　　　　*Here* is your paper. (inverted)

Prefixes, see Word formation, prefixes

Prefixes

Prepositions show relationships in time and space and relationships between ideas (logical relationships). Many words that can be used as prepositions can also be used as adverbs, but not all of them can. A preposition in a prepositional phrase is always followed by a noun, a pronoun, or another word that can replace a noun, such as an *-ing* form (gerund). Always use an object form of a personal pronoun after a preposition.

	preposition		*noun*
Robert put the book	*on*	the	*table.*
Robert went	*with*		*Carol.*

		pronoun
Robert went	*with*	*her.*

noun
With practice Priscilla learned to ski.

-ing form/
gerund
With training the dog learned to obey.

Prepositions of Space and Movement

Most of the following prepositions can be used for both space and movement, depending on the meaning of the rest of the sentence.

above	by	off
across	by (the edge/	on
against	side of)	opposite
along	down	out
alongside	far (away) from	out of
among	from	outside
around	as (far) as	over
at	in	past
away from	in back of	round
before	in front of	through
behind	inside	throughout
below	inside of	to
beneath	in the middle of	towards
beside	into	under
between	near	underneath
beyond	next to	up

Do not put *of* after another preposition unless the dictionary shows it. Do not, for example, write *off of* or *behind of*. When the *of* can be used or left out, leave it out.

Many preposition forms can be used as adverbs, but not all of them can. Some of the adverb forms must have another preposition added: *Away* and *far* are adverbs, but *away from* and *far from* are prepositions.

Shirley is waiting *outside* the door. (prepositional phrase used adverbially)
Shirley is waiting *outside*. (adverb)

The prepositional phrase gives more information than the single-word adverb.

Some adverbs are very similar to but not exactly the same as related prepositions.

The taxi was waiting *near the hotel.* (prepositional phrase)
The taxi was waiting *nearby.* (adverb)

Learn the set phrases with prepositions of space.

Harriet lives	*in* Denver. (a city)
	in Colorado. (a state or province)
	on Green Avenue. (street without a number)
	at 261 Green Avenue. (street with a number)
	in Room 261 or Apartment 210-A. (specific room or apartment)
Harriet's friend lives	*in* Canada. (country)
	at or *away from* home.
	on a farm.
	in a dormitory, apartment, house, student hostel.
	in poverty, wealth, a city, a suburb, a town, a village.
	in the South, West. (region or section)
The plane landed	*in* Chicago.
	at O'Hare Airport.
	at the Chicago airport.

Harriet lives at 261 Green Avenue, Denver, Colorado.
The plane landed at O'Hare Airport, Chicago.
We are going to visit my cousin *in* Denver.

He is	*in* college.
	at the university.
We are going	*across* the Rocky Mountains.
	across the Mississippi River.
	across the desert.
Their house is (located)	*on* the beach.
	on the ocean.
	at the shore.
	in the mountains.
	on the river, bay, lake.
	in the desert.
	on the plains.

NOTE: When you do not put a preposition between different pieces of information about place, use a comma. (see **Punctuation, comma**)

Use *between* to show a location that has two points of reference, but use *among* to show a location that has more than two points of reference.

Our house is *between* the house of the Andersons and the house of the Simpsons.
My car is parked *among* hundreds in the parking lot, *between* Joe's car and Cliff's car.

Use *to* to show directions in some phrases.

perpendicular *to*	*to* the north, south, east, west
horizontal *to*	next *to*

but

north, south, east, west *of* the library

NOTE: Compound compass directions made of two words are written as one word and always begin with *north* or *south*. Precise directions for navigation are usually given in degrees.

northeast	southeast	east by northeast
northwest	southwest	west southwest

Do not capitalize points of the compass when they mean direction. (see **Capitalization**)

Prepositions that show space and movement often introduce essential information that tells *which one*. These phrases are adjective phrases and follow the noun or pronoun they modify.

The buses *in the city* run every ten minutes.
The houses *on the bay* were damaged by the hurricane.

Prepositions of Time

after	prior to
as (late) as	since (+ point in time)
before	to
during	till
for (+ period of time)	until
in	up to
on	upon

Most prepositions of time cannot be used as single-word adverbs in the way that prepositions of space and movement can. *After, before, since,* and *until* can introduce dependent adverb clauses, however. (see **Clauses, adverb**)

Since can be used as a single-word adverb.

The dogs chased the cat, and the cat has not been seen *since*.

During, for, and *since* have special uses. *During* and *for* are followed by a period of time. *During* means *while the event or period is in progress*. *For* marks the *length* of time or an *appointed* time.

This tree has been here *for* two hundred years.
Ted will wait *for ten* minutes; then he will leave.
He waited *for* an hour.

but

Pat has an appointment *for* 3:00.
During the 1960s many nations of Africa became independent.
We sat on the grass *during* the concert in the park. (during the time of the concert)

Since marks the *beginning* of a period of time. It can be used with a point in time and mean *from that time until now*. As a preposition, *since* is usually used with the present perfect or the present perfect continuous/progressive tense in the main clause.

> Pat *has been waiting since* 2:30.
> *Since* 1960 many nations of Africa *have become* independent.
> We *have been sitting* on the grass *since* 5:00 waiting for the concert to start.
> *Since* finding a new roommate, Martha *has been* happier.

NOTE: As a conjunction, *since* is used with a perfect or present tense in the *main clause* when it refers to time. (There are no tense restrictions when it means *because*.)

> I *have been* very busy *since* I saw you last week.
> It *is* at least ten years *since* Carl rode a horse.

Learn the set phrases of time.

Paul always comes	as *early/late/soon* as possible.
	at ten o'clock. (specific time)
	on time.
	late for class.
	in time for class.
	up to fifteen minutes late.
	after ten o'clock.
	before ten o'clock.
Paul waited/did not come	*until* (*till*) ten o'clock.
	on (*upon*) the hour. (minute, day)
returned	*a year to the day* after his first appointment. (exactly)
	a minute to the hour. (exactly)
Paul visited Canada	*in* 1980. (year)
	in May. (month)
	on May 18. (date)
	on Wednesday. (day of the week)
	in the morning, afternoon, evening, daytime, the night.
	at noon, midnight, night.
	period of time
Great social changes have taken place	*in/during* the past ten years, the past decade, and the past century.
	specific time
	since 1960, then, that time.

Prepositions That Show Logical Relationships

The following examples deal with some common problems with prepositions, but they do not cover all meanings of each preposition. Use a
dictionary written for students of English to study and learn additional
meanings.

1. Use *of* to show the relationship between a part or parts and the
whole. (When *one* comes before *of*, *one* is the subject of the clause and
takes a singular verb even though the noun after *of* must be plural. (see
Agreement of subject and verb)

One *of* our friends has a car.
One *of* the best methods is the one that you used yesterday.

but

Much *of* the water is polluted. (uncountable)

Plural nouns must be replaced by plural pronouns.

One *of them* has a car.
One *of them* is the one that you used yesterday.
Many *of them* have cars.
Ten *of them* are missing.
Some *of them* are here.

An uncountable noun can follow *of* and can usually be replaced by *it*.

Some of the *rice* (*it*) has been burned.
Much of the *advice* (*it*) that I get is useless.
All of the *news* (*it*) is good today.
None of the *information* (*it*) was helpful.
Chris is a doctor *of* dentistry.
Bart is a professor *of* biology.

2. Learn the uses of *of*, *out of*, and *from* to show origin and material.

Willis is a citizen *of* Australia.
Sara is a student *from* Mexico. (Her home is in Mexico.)
George is a student *of* Mexico. (He studies about Mexico.)
They are residents *of* the United States.
Amanda is a doctor *from* Massachusetts. (Her home is in Massachusetts.)
Amanda is a doctor *of* medicine. (kind of doctor; see above)
The desk is made *of/from/out of* wood.
This cloth comes *from* India; it is made *of/from/out of* silk.
This jam is made *of/from/out of* strawberries.
Butter is made *of/from/out of* cream.

Of can also show material or content.

We bought a basket *of* tomatoes. (Tomatoes were in the basket.)
We bought a basket *of* straw. (The basket was made out of straw.)

3. Use *for* to show *purpose.*

Thelma is going *for* an interview tomorrow.
Larry needs a new case *for* his camera.

4. Use *on* and *about* to show a *subject.*

I just bought a book *on/about* botany.
Walter has read many articles *on/about* opera.

5. Use *except* and *but* to show *omission.*

No one *but/except* Catherine saw the new schedule.
Everyone is ready *except/but* Arthur.

6. Use *by* and *with* to show an agent and *without* to show the lack of an agent.

They traveled *by* foot, car, plane, train, etc.
The small boy tied his shoes *by* himself.
                              without any help.
                              with no help from anyone.

(See **Voice** for special uses of *by* and *to* with transitive verbs.)

7. To show *cause* use *on account of, because of, owing to,* and *due to.*

Owing to
Due to
On account of $\Big\}$ his age, he could not get the job he wanted.
Because of

Do not confuse *because of* with *because.* *Because* introduces a dependent clause; it must be followed by a subject and verb.

　　　　　subject verb
Because　he　was too young, he could not get the job he wanted.

preposition
Because of his age, he could not get the job he wanted.

8. Use *besides, together with, as well as, with,* and *in addition to* to *add* ideas and information. Do not confuse *beside* and *besides.*

Three teams *besides/in addition to/together with/as well as* ours played in the tournament.

(*Besides* is usually the best choice to avoid wordiness.)

The teams *with* their supporters filled the gym.

9. Use *without* to show lack or omission.

Without their supporters, the teams played in an empty gym.

10. Use *in spite of* or *despite* to show concession.

Despite
In spite of the bad weather, our trip to the mountains was a success.

Many people are cheerful *in spite of* their problems.

11. Use *like* to show similarities. Use *as* as a preposition only when it means *in the role of*. Otherwise, use *as* as a conjunction. (see **Adjectives, comparison**)

Like father, *like* son.
He looks *like* his father, walks *like* his father, and eats *like* his father.

 preposition   *preposition*
Now I am speaking not   *as*   your doctor but   *as*   your friend.

 conjunction   *conjunction*
She is not   *as*   friendly   *as*   her brother is.

12. Do not confuse *to* as a preposition with *to* in the infinitive phrase. (see **Infinitive**)

Prepositions of space are often used in a figurative sense to show logical relationships.

What are the reasons *behind* your proposal?
Cliff's reputation is *above* reproach.
The costs have gone *above/beyond* the estimate.

Prepositions with Adjectives and Verbs

Use only certain prepositions with certain verbs and adjectives. Learn the correct prepositions when you add new verbs and adjectives to your vocabulary. Many verbs have very different meanings when combined with prepositions and adverb particles. (see **Adjectives** and **Two-word verbs**)

Participial Prepositions

A number of *-ing* forms can be followed by nouns or pronouns in a construction similar to that of a prepositional phrase.

barring	excepting	regarding
concerning	pending	respecting
considering		

Barring a delay, the package should arrive Monday.
Concerning your parking violation, you will have to pay the fine by the date below.
Excepting only those with a doctor's excuse, all students must register for physical education.

You will often see these phrases in business letters.

Grammatical Structure of Prepositional Phrases in a Clause

1. When you use a prepositional phrase as an adjective, put it directly after the word that it modifies.

> *adjective*
> *prepositional phrase*
> The *principal of my high school* (*of my high school* modifies principal)

> *adjective*
> *prepositional phrase*
> is the *man   with the cane.* (*with the cane* modifies man)

2. When you use a prepositional phrase as an adverb, put it at the beginning or at the end of the clause it is in.

> *adverb*
> *prepositional phrase*
> The Thompsons planted trees *along their driveway.*

> *adverb*
> *prepositional phrase*
> *Along their driveway* the Thompsons planted trees.

Put a comma after a long prepositional phrase or phrases (four words or more) at the beginning of a clause. (see **Punctuation, comma**)

> *Along the curving driveway,* the Thompsons planted trees.
> *Along the driveway leading to the house,* the Thompsons planted trees.

3. Prepositions can introduce noun clauses, especially in formal writing. (see **Clauses, noun**)

> *preposition   noun clause*
> The club is giving free tickets   *to   whoever asks for them.*

> *noun clause*
> The president will give the job *to whomever he chooses.*

4. Prepositions often come at the end of a clause in speech and in informal writing, but writers avoid putting them at the end of a clause in formal writing. (see **Style**)

> **INFORMAL SPEECH:**   We *don't* know *who* the package was delivered *to.*
>
> **FORMAL WRITING:**   We *do not* know *to whom* the package was delivered.

Prepositions and adverbs that are part of two-word verbs often come at the end of a clause. (see **Two-word verbs**)

> The firemen put out the fire.
> They put it out. (*It* cannot follow *out.*)
> Will was annoyed with Allen.

EMPHASIS ON ONE: Allen was the one (that) Will was annoyed *with*.
FORMAL: Allen was the one *with whom* Will was annoyed.

5. Only three prepositions can be followed by an infinitive phrase: *but, except,* and *about.* Other prepositions can be followed by *-ing* forms if the meaning allows them.

We had no choice *but to go.*
We had no choice *except to go.*
They were *about to leave* when their friends came.

They had no hope *of leaving* early.
Charles is helpless *about doing* his own cooking.
Wendy has been waiting for an answer ever *since applying* for the grant.

Principal Parts of Verbs _____

The principal parts of verbs must be used only in certain ways.

Use the **simple form** (the same as the bare infinitive)
1. as the main verb in the clause (add a final *-s* in the third person, singular, present tense—*be* and *have* are irregular):

They *see* that they have a great deal of work these days. (statement, independent clause)
See the balloon! (command)
Mary always speaks to us when she *sees* us. (statement, dependent clause)

2. directly after modals and forms of *do*:

They *will see* their friends at the lake.
They *can see* the answer by looking in the back of the book.
They *must see* the truth of that statement.
They *had better see* the director today.
Did you *see* the director yesterday?

3. after *to*:

They used *to see* us often.
They have *to see* the director today.
They wanted *to see* the director.

Use the **past** as the main verb, past tense:

They *saw* us yesterday.

NOTE: All regular and some irregular English verbs have the same form for the past and past participle, but some irregular verbs have a different form for the past. (see **Verbs, irregular**)

Use the **past participle**
1. after *has, have,* or *had*:

They *have seen* us many times.
They had seen us already before we saw them.
She *has* not *seen* us yet.

2. as an adjective:

The man *seen* in the bank was not the thief.
Stars *seen* at night are not the only stars in the sky.
The Southern Cross, *seen* by early explorers from Europe, was a new constellation Europeans had never observed before.

3. in passive forms after the verb *to be* (see **Passive verbs**):

They *are* often *seen* at the concerts.
She *is seen* there every day.
He *has been seen* here many times.
The dog *was never seen* again.
She likes to *be seen* in public places.

Use the **present participle** (*-ing* form)
1. in the continuous/progressive tenses after some form of *be*:

Mary will *be seeing* the doctor again tomorrow.
She *is seeing* the doctor often these days.

NOTE: The verb *see* and other verbs of the senses are not usually used in the continuous/progressive tenses. Here, however, *see* means *visit;* therefore, the continuous tenses are possible in the two sentences above.

2. as an adjective:

Seeing the accident, the man stopped to help the victims.

3. as a noun (gerund):

Seeing is believing.

Negative forms change in the present tense and the past tense. Use a form of *do* + *not* + bare infinitive. (see **Negation** and **Operators**)

Process

Process is an explanation of how to do something or of how something works. Process is sometimes called "how to."

Write a process explanation in exact chronological order. To explain how to do something or give instructions use command (imperative) verb forms. To explain how something works, use the present tense with noun subjects and third-person verbs. (Radio waves *travel* at the speed of light.) Do not mix forms by changing back and forth from one construction to another. Do not mix command verb forms with *you should* or *you must*. (see **Point of view, Commands,** and **Tense, present**)

Using Command Verb Forms

How to Prepare a Wall Surface for Painting

Scrape off any loose paint. *Remove* all nails, brackets, switchplates, and electrical outlet plates from the wall. *Fill* in all holes with plastic wood or spackling compound. Paint according to directions on the paint can.

Using Present Tense, Third Person Verb Forms

How Refrigeration Works

Refrigeration *is* a process of heat transfer. As heat *moves* from warmer bodies to colder ones, the temperature *rises* in the colder body and *falls* in the warmer body. An efficient refrigerating agent *removes* large quantities of heat quickly. In addition to changes in temperature, substances *can change* from gas to liquid to solid, or from solid to liquid to gas. A change from gas to liquid *is called* condensation, but a change from liquid to gas is called vaporization. A change from liquid to solid *is called* freezing, but a change from solid to liquid *is called* melting. Refrigeration systems *use* these changes to operate and to affect the temperature of things that *need* to be kept cold.

Pronouns _____

Most pronouns stand for a noun or a noun phrase. *I, me,* and related pronouns stand for the speaker or writer. The word or words that a pronoun stands for are its *reference* or *antecedent.*
Avoid common problems with pronouns by following these rules:

1. Do not confuse *its* with *it's.* Without an apostrophe, *its* is always the personal possessive form. With an apostrophe, *it's* always means *it is.*

2. Be sure the reference of every pronoun is clear and correct if the pronoun has an antecedent. (Pronouns such as *I, one,* and impersonal *it* do not always have antecedents.) (see **Antecedent, It,** and **Reference of the pronoun**)

3. Do not always use the impersonal *it, you,* and *they* in writing as you would use them in speech. (see below, "Impersonal Pronouns")

4. Do not change pronouns unless you have a reason for the change. (see **Point of view**)

5. Follow the distinction English makes between the personal (people and sometimes higher animals) and nonpersonal (lower animals, inanimate things, events, ideas, and so on). Use forms of *he, she, they,* and *who* to refer to the personal; use forms of *it, they,* and *that* or *which* to refer to the nonpersonal.

6. Learn how to use different kinds of pronouns correctly. You will find them in this section in this order: Personal, Reflexive, Reciprocal, Demonstrative, Indefinite (including Quantity and Numbers), Impersonal, Interrogative, and Relative. (see **Confusing choices,** *amount,* number; *another,* other, others; *any,* some; *any body* and *any one*; *anybody* and *anyone*; *each,* every, everyone, all; *each other,* every other, one another; *few,* only a few; *its,* it is; *little,* only a little, a little; *many,* much; *who,* that, which; *your,* you're)

Personal and Related Pronouns

| | **PERSONAL** | | **POSSESSIVE** | | |
PERSON SINGULAR:	SUBJECT FORM	OBJECT FORM	DETERMINER/ ADJECTIVE	NOUN RE- PLACEMENT	REFLEXIVE/ INTENSIVE
First	I	me	my	mine	myself
Second	you	you	your	yours	yourself
Third					
Masculine	he	him	his	his	himself
Feminine	she	her	her	hers	herself
Neuter	it	it	its	—	itself
PLURAL:					
First	we	us	our	ours	ourselves
Second	you	you	your	yours	yourselves
Third	they	them	their	theirs	themselves

GENDER OF PERSONAL PRONOUNS

In the third person singular, choose the pronoun that agrees with the sex of the person referred to. Animals closely related to people can be referred to by *he, him,* and *his* or *she, her,* and *hers.* Gender distinction in lower animals and other forms of life may sometimes be appropriate.

> The dog is looking for *his/her/its* bone.
> The hen cackled after *she/it* laid *her/its* egg.

Use *it, its* to refer to inanimate objects except ships, which are always referred to as *she.* Sometimes other machinery closely associated with people is referred to as though it were human, usually a woman. Countries are sometimes referred to by *she* or *her.*

Traditionally the *he, him, his,* pronouns have been used for mixed groups or groups in which the sex is unknown. Since many people now object to this use, you can avoid the problem by using plural forms. (see **Gender** and **Women, terms referring to**)

TRADITIONAL:	*Everybody* brought *his* own lunch.
AWKWARD:	*Everybody* brought *his* or *her* own lunch.
ACCEPTABLE:	*All* the students brought *their* own lunches.

OLD FORMS OF PERSONAL PRONOUNS

Old forms for the second person singular pronouns are *thou, thee,* and *thine,* and an old form for the plural is *ye.* You will see these forms in poetry and older literature, but do not use them. Old pronoun forms are often used with old verb forms in *-st,* such as *thou didst, hast,* and so on. Another confusing use of *ye* is to replace *the: Ye* Meeting House. In this phrase it is an article, not a pronoun.

PERSONAL PRONOUNS

SUBJECT:	*I (we, he, they)* went yesterday.
OBJECT:	The storm destroyed the buildings.
	them.
	Jeff brought Nancy some apples.
	her.
	Barry helped George.
	him.

NOTE: If *I, me, my,* or *mine* or *we, us, our,* or *ours* is part of a pair or a series, put it last.

The storm destroyed *his* car and *mine,* too.
Barry helped George with *his* work, and he will help us with *ours* tomorrow.

NOTE: Use the possessive forms, not the article, before parts of the body and personal possessions. Use the article in prepositional phrases and in passive constructions only.

ACTIVE:	Cary blinked *her* eyes constantly. (not *the* eyes)
ACTIVE:	Ted washed *his* face and put on *his* glasses. (not *the* face and *the* glasses)
ACTIVE:	The ball hit *John's* head.
	The ball hit *his* head.
PREPOSITIONAL PHRASE:	The ball hit John on *the* head.
	his
PASSIVE:	John was hit on *the* head by the ball.

POSSESSIVE PRONOUNS THAT REPLACE A NOUN

He put his hand on *mine.* (my hand)
That is Julie's bicycle, but this is *mine.* (my bicycle)
This book is *yours.*
Her family lives in Oregon, but *his* lives in California. (his family)

OWN: Use the intensifier *own* only with possessive forms. You can use it two ways: after a personal possessive as a pronoun (*our own*) or between a possessive and a noun (*our own house*).

> The face that I saw in the mirror was *mine.*
> The face that I saw in the mirror was *my own.*
> The face that I saw in the mirror was *my own face.*

Reflexive Pronouns

Use a reflexive pronoun only as the object of a verb form or preposition to refer to the subject of the sentence.

> The child is able to dress *himself.*
> Albert hit *himself* on the elbow with a bat.
> The hunter accidentally shot *himself* in the foot.
> The boy is old enough to go on the bus *all by himself.*

NOTE: The phrase *by* + *self* means *alone* or *without any help.* An even more emphatic form is *all by* + *self.*

EXCEPTION: In prepositional phrases that show space, the object pronoun is used instead of the reflexive form.

> They put their books on the tables *in front of them.*
> Walter looked up at the light *above him.*
> The little girl hid her hands *behind her.*

INTENSIVE PRONOUNS

The intensive form is the same as the reflexive form. Put an intensive form directly after the word it modifies or at the end of the clause.

> The president *herself* spoke to us. or The president spoke to us *herself.*
> The drivers *themselves* were to blame for the accident. or The drivers were to blame for the accident *themselves.*
> The dean *himself* visited the class. or The dean visited the class *himself.*
> Margaret and I did the work *ourselves.*

If you use a first-person pronoun with a second-person pronoun or with a third-person noun or pronoun, use the first person form pronoun later in the clause to refer to both the other pronouns. If you use a second-person pronoun with a third-person noun or pronoun use a second-person form later in the sentence to refer to both the other pronouns.

> *third   first   first*
> *person   person   person*
> Don and   I   found *ourselves* wandering through the building looking for the right classroom.

> *second   third   second*
> *person   person   person*
> You   and   Paul   lost control of *yourselves* at the party last night.

	third *person*	*first* *person*		*first* *person*

Betty, Helen, and   I   have already told you that these places are *ours*.

Reciprocal Pronouns

Each other and *one another* must be objects of verb forms or objects of prepositions. They mean that each part of the subject did the action and also received the action. Some people prefer to use *each other* for two people or things and *one another* for more than two.

> Martha and Harold gave *each other* gifts on their wedding anniversary.
> The students greeted *each other* after their long summer vacation.
> Members of the class were asked to prepare questions for *one another*.

Demonstrative Pronouns

Use demonstratives alone as pronouns or before nouns as determiners. (see **Determiners**) Demonstratives can show distance or contrast not connected with distance. (see **Adjectives, endings**)

	SINGULAR	PLURAL
NEARER THE SPEAKER or **ON THE ONE HAND:**	this	these
FARTHER FROM THE SPEAKER or **ON THE OTHER HAND:**	that	those

DISTANCE:	One car is parked at the curb; another is in the parking lot. *This* car is parked at the curb; *that* is in the parking lot over there. *This* is mine here; *that* is yours over there.
CONTRAST BUT NOT DISTANCE:	Which of these two cakes would you like, *this* one or *that* one? Two courses of action are possible: on the one hand *this* course seems correct, but on the other hand *that* one seems safer.

Those can be an indefinite pronoun meaning *people* or *ones*.

> *Those* who eat too much gain weight.
> *Those* who are friendly have many friends.
> The supplies for drafting cost more than *those* for art.

That can also be used as an indefinite pronoun. Use it in comparisons to avoid repeating nouns. (see **Adjectives, comparison and contrast,** and **Pronouns**)

> The *lumber industry* of Finland is more important than *that* of Spain. (replaces a singular noun modified by an *of* phrase)
> *Bread* baked this morning tastes fresher than *that* baked yesterday.

Indefinite, Quantity, and Number Pronouns

Use singular verbs with the first eight pronouns if they replace uncountable nouns, but use plural verbs if they replace countable nouns. Compound pronouns—see below—are always singular. (See **Countable and uncountable nouns** and **Agreement of subject and verb;** and **Confusing choices** for difference in usage between *any* and *some*.)

SINGULAR COUNTABLE	SINGULAR UNCOUNTABLE	PLURAL
	all	all
	any	any
	enough	enough
	half	half
	more	more
	most	most
	none	none
	some	some
another	other	others
or		
determiner + other		
each		
either		
neither		
one		ones
		several
	less	few
	much	many
one, first		two, second, three, third and all cardinal and ordinal plural numbers
	a lot (informal)	lots (informal)
	a good/great deal of (informal)	a good/great deal of (informal)

Many single-word indefinite pronouns and words of quantity and number can be determiners before nouns. (see **Determiners**)

Compound Indefinite Pronouns

			none		another
PERSONAL:	anyone	everyone	no one	someone	other ones
	anybody	everybody	nobody	somebody	others
					another
NONPERSONAL:	anything	everything	nothing	something	other ones
		every one	none		others

PRONOUNS THAT CAN ALSO BE ADVERBS:	anywhere	everywhere	nowhere	somewhere

NUMBER

Use singular verbs with compound pronouns and use singular pronouns to refer to them in formal writing. (Plural pronouns are often used to refer to compound pronouns in speech.)

> **FORMAL:** *Anyone* who has lost *his* friend in this crowd will never find *him* again today.
>
> **INFORMAL:** *Everybody* can find *their* own seats in the theater.
>
> **FORMAL:** *Nobody* brought *his* book.
>
> **INFORMAL:** *Nobody* brought *their* books.

(see **Negation** for use of *no-* compounds)

SPELLING

When *every one* does not refer to persons, spell it as two words. Spell *no one, other ones, each one, either one,* and *neither one* as two words.

POSSESSIVE FORMS

Make all the compound pronoun forms possessive by adding -*'s*.

> **POSSESSIVES:** *Somebody's* car was just towed away.
> *Everybody's* business is *nobody's* business.

MODIFYING COMPOUND PRONOUNS

Adjectives follow compound pronouns.

>   *adjective*
> *Someone intelligent* is needed.
> *Nothing sensible* has been done yet.

ELSE: Use *else* after compound pronouns to emphasize the idea of *other* or *more*.

> *Someone else* can try now.
> *No one else* can help us.

Else can be a possessive following a compound pronoun that refers to a person. (see *Else*)

> Someone *else's* friend came too.
> Anyone *else's* ideas are welcome.

Impersonal pronouns

Use *it* in certain constructions of weather and time. (see **It**)

> *It* is rainy and cold today.
> *It* is still early in the evening.

Avoid using *it, you,* or *they* in an indefinite meaning if you can write a clearer sentence. Many constructions that are common in speech should be avoided in writing.

> WEAK: It says almost nothing in our world literature textbook about writers from South America.
>
> IMPROVED: Our world literature textbook says almost nothing about writers from South America.
>
> WEAK: When *you* change a tire, first jack up the car and then *you* take off the hubcap.
>
> IMPROVED: To change a tire, first jack up the car and then remove the hubcap.
>
> WEAK: When I came to register, *they* told me to come back in a week.
>
> IMPROVED: When I came to register, the clerk told me to come back in a week.
>
> **or**
>
> IMPROVED: When I came to register, I was told to come back in a week. (see **Voice**)

Question (Interrogative) Pronouns

Who, whom, whose, which, and *what* can begin questions. Use *who, whom, whose,* and *which* to refer to persons. Use *which* and *what* to refer to things or events. Although *who* is often used in conversation as both a subject and an object form, use *who* for the subject of a clause and *whom* for the object of a preposition or verb in formal writing. (see **Case**, **WH-words**, and **Questions**)

> *subject*   *subject*
> *Who* remembers *what* they did?
>
>   *object*
> The supervisor to *whom* the request was originally made must sign the form.
>
> *subject*   *possessive*
> *Who* knows *whose* voice the people will follow?

Relative Pronouns

Relative pronouns (sometimes called clause markers) introduce dependent clauses (sometimes called relative clauses). They may introduce dependent clauses used as adjectives or nouns. (see **Clauses**)

Relative pronouns used in adjective clauses are *that, who, whom, whose,* and *which.*

That may introduce a relative clause used as an adjective. If *that* could be used but is left out, the clause is called *unmarked.* If two *that* clauses are used in the same sentence, at least one will usually be unmarked. Both may be unmarked.

> The best pie *that* I have eaten lately is the one *that* you made last night. (marked)
> The best pie I have eaten lately is the one you made last night. (unmarked)

That, which, and *whom* are the only relative pronouns you can leave out. Do not put commas around clauses beginning with *that* since *that* should be used only in essential clauses. (see **Essential and nonessential modifiers** and **Punctuation, comma**)

Who, whom, and *whose* can be used in both essential and nonessential clauses. (These words can also begin a question in an independent clause—see **Questions**.)

In informal writing, *whom* is not always used when an object is needed, but in formal writing *whom* must be used. (see **Style**) Decide between *who* and *whom* by asking whether you could use *he* or *him* or *they* or *them.*

> Dale is my friend *who* was in my history class last year.
> > *he* was in my history class—*who* is correct.
> Beth is the girl *who/whom* you saw in the park yesterday.
> > you saw *she/her*—you saw *her* is correct.
> > *whom you saw in the park yesterday* is correct.

Often *that* can replace *whom* in less formal writing, or the clause can be unmarked.

> Some earlier poets *who* influenced Shakespeare can be identified. (subject)
> These are the earlier poets *from whom* Shakespeare drew many of his ideas. (object, formal)
> These are the earlier poets *that* Shakespeare drew his ideas *from.* (less formal)
> These are the earlier poets Shakespeare drew his ideas *from.* (less formal with unmarked clause)
> The earlier poets *whose* ideas Shakespeare used can be identified. (possessive)

Use *which* in nonessential clauses. Separate nonessential clauses from the rest of the sentence by commas.

> Our TV set, *which* has been broken for three weeks, should be ready this afternoon.

NOTE: *Which* is sometimes used instead of *that* in essential clauses, but most writers in the United States prefer *that* in essential clauses.

BE CAREFUL: Do not use *which* to refer to a whole clause, sentence, or paragraph. You should always be able to show a noun or pronoun that the *which* stands for. In the sentence above, *which* stands for *set.* (see **Antecedent**)

> INCORRECT: A good watchdog barks loudly when strangers come on your property, *which* gives you a feeling of security.

In the sentence above, *which* refers to all the ideas in the sentence that go before it, including a verb, *barks*, and the entire clause following *barks*. Improve the sentence by leaving out *which* and changing the following verb to an -*ing* form or by changing the subject.

> CORRECT: A good watchdog barks loudly when strangers come on your property, giving you a feeling of security.
>
> **or**
>
> Knowing your watchdog barks loudly when strangers come on your property gives you a feeling of security.

Use *which* or *whom* after prepositions in formal writing. In less formal writing, the preposition followed by *which* or *whom* may be replaced by *that* or the clause may be unmarked.

> Mr. Johnson is the man *to whom* I sent my application. (*that* I sent my application *to*)
> Ajax Manufacturing is the company *to which* I sent my application. (*that* I sent my application *to*)

Relative pronouns used in noun clauses are *that, what, whatever, whoever, whomever,* and *whichever.*

Use *that* or *what* after *say* and similar verbs in indirect speech. (see **Indirect speech**).

> Mary $\left\{ \begin{array}{l} \text{said} \\ \text{told us} \\ \text{explained} \end{array} \right\}$ $\left\{ \begin{array}{l} \textit{that} \text{ she had lost her schedule.} \\ \textit{what} \text{ she had done.} \end{array} \right.$

Whatever may be used to introduce a clause used as a subject or object.

> *noun clause as subject*
> *Whatever you discover* will be interesting.

>   *noun clause as direct object*
> He will do   *whatever he likes.*

BE CAREFUL: Choose *who/whom/whose* and *whoever/whomever* after looking at how the word is used *in its own clause.* Whether or not the *clause* is a subject or object of the main verb in the sentence does not affect the choice of *who* or *whom.*

The noun clause is the object of *scolded*:

> The teacher scolded *whoever came* late. (*Whoever* is the subject of *came.*)

The noun clause is the object of *scolded*:

> The teacher scolded *whomever* he *disliked.* (*Whoever* is the object of *disliked.*)

Avoid common problems with relative pronouns:
  1. Choose the right form.

> Use *that* in essential clauses instead of *which.*
> Use *who, whom,* and *whose* as you would use *he, him,* and *his* or *they, their,* and *theirs.*
> Use *which* in nonessential clauses or after prepositions.

In formal writing, if both *who* and *that* or both *who* and *which* seem possible, use *who* (*whom, whose*) to refer to people.
  2. Construct your sentence so that a noun or pronoun is the clear antecedent of the relative pronoun.
  3. Do not punctuate a dependent clause as a complete sentence. In a statement (not in a question), a relative pronoun is always followed by a dependent clause. (see **Fragments**)

>   *dependent clause*
> INCORRECT: *Which* I fixed for dinner.
>   *That* you bought in the bookstore.

Fragments can be corrected by adding an independent clause to make **a** complete sentence.

> Your recipe for chicken and rice, which I fixed for dinner last night, **is** delicious.
> The pen that you bought in the bookstore writes well.

  4. Do not use a relative pronoun and a personal pronoun in the same clause to stand for the same antecedent.

	relative		*personal*
	antecedent *pronoun*		*pronoun*

INCORRECT: The book *that* he borrowed *it* is very difficult to understand.

In the sentence above, *that* refers to *book* and *it* refers to *book*; leave out *it*.

antecedent

CORRECT: The *book* *that* he borrowed is very difficult to understand.

Even if the dependent clause is unmarked (*that* is left out), do not use a personal pronoun to refer to the antecedent of the omitted *that*.

personal
antecedent *pronoun*

INCORRECT: The *book* (*that* omitted) he borrowed *it* is very difficult to understand.

CORRECT: The *book* he borrowed is very difficult to understand.

5. Look at the antecedent of *who, that,* or *which* when used as subject to decide whether the verb following should be singular or plural. (see **Agreement of subject and verb**)

The *man who is* coming is my father. (The antecedent of *who* is *man,* singular; so the verb following *who* must be singular.)
The *men who are* coming are from my home town. (The antecedent of *who* is *men,* plural; so the verb following *who* must be plural.)
The *book that is* on the table can be sold now. (The antecedent of *that* is *book,* singular; so the verb following *that* must be singular.)
The *books that are* on the table can be sold now. (The antecedent of *that* is *books,* plural; so the verb following *books* must be plural.)

6. Do not use *that* immediately after a subordinating conjunction at the beginning of an adverb clause.

INCORRECT: Because *that* Janet is my friend, she helps me.

CORRECT: Because Janet is my friend, she helps me.

INCORRECT: Since *that* we have moved here, we have been happy.

CORRECT: Since we have moved here, we have been happy.

Proofreading

Proofreading is reading over a finished paper, finding mistakes, and correcting them. Sometimes you will be required to hand in a perfect copy; this instruction means that you must rewrite and correct every page on which you have found mistakes.

Several methods of finding mistakes in spelling, punctuation, and grammar are helpful. Unless you are writing in class, always allow at least several hours or, better yet, a whole day between the time you finish the paper and the time you must hand it in. Reread your paper after a day, and you will find mistakes you did not see when you first finished it. Another method is to read your sentences in reverse order, beginning at the end of the paper, sentence by sentence. This method will help you find spelling, punctuation, and grammar mistakes. If you skip every second line when you write on lined paper, you will be able to see your mistakes more easily and you will have more space for the corrections.

Punctuation

Apostrophe (')

1. Use an apostrophe to show possession, ownership, or a relation similar to ownership.

a. If a noun ends in a sound other than *s* or *z*, add an apostrophe and an -*s*. These words are usually singular, but not always.

The jackets of the children	The children's jackets
The jacket of the child	The child's jacket
The jacket of Mrs. March	Mrs. March's jacket

b. If a noun already ends in an *s* or *z* sound, put the apostrophe after the *s*.

The jackets of the girls	The girls' jackets
The jacket of Charles	Charles' jacket
The jackets of the students	The students' jackets
The jacket of Mr. Pitts	Mr. Pitts' jacket

NOTE: You will see -*'s* after plural nouns, but current usage does not require it.

c. Never put an apostrophe on a personal pronoun even when it ends in -*s*.

my books, mine	our books, ours
your books, yours	their books, theirs
her books, hers	its (the dog's) bone, *its*
his books, his	NOTE: *It's* always means *it is.*

d. Use an apostrophe and -*s* to make possessive forms of impersonal pronouns.

anyone's books	nobody's books
everyone's books	everybody's books

e. The *-'s* follows the last element of a hyphenated word.

singular	*plural*
My sister-in-law's house	My sisters-in-law's houses
The commander-in-chief's order	

f. Avoid uses of the possessive form that are unclear. *Jane's photograph* may mean

a photograph that Jane owns, or
a photograph that is a picture of Jane, or
a photograph that Jane has taken.

2. The apostrophe and *-s* are used in certain conventional expressions, usually of time. In this construction, *-s* replaces a prepositional phrase beginning with *of*.

a day's, month's, year's *work*	an hour's, a day's, week's,
an hour's, a day's, two-weeks' *wait* or *delay*	month's, year's *wages*
	a month's, year's *salary*

And in other conventional expressions:

at death's door (near death)	to the journey's end (to the end)
a hair's breadth (extremely narrow)	in the mind's eye
to your heart's content (as much as you want)	

3. Use an apostrophe and *-s* to form plurals of words, letters, or symbols being discussed as words, letters, or symbols. (Some styles leave out the apostrophe.)

He always forgets to cross his *t*'s and dot his *i*'s when he writes fast.
Most people in the world cross their 7's, but people in the United States do not.
She often confuses *its* with *it's*.

4. The apostrophe shows that a letter or letters have been left out of a word. (see **Contractions**)

it's	it is or it has
it isn't	it is not
I'd	I had or I would
didn't	did not, and so on

Other common forms:

o'clock	of the clock
ma'am	madam

Forms used in songs and poetry:

e'en	even
e'er	ever
ne'er	never
o'er	over

Asterisk (*)

1. Asterisks are sometimes used to indicate footnotes if there are very few footnotes. Numbers set slightly higher than the line of type are usually used to indicate footnotes. (see **Footnotes**)

2. Asterisks are used in linguistics to show incorrect examples.

*They no know how to do it.   *They do not know how doing it.

Absence of an asterisk in linguistics shows that an example is correct.

They do not know how to do it.

3. Three asterisks *** show an ellipsis. Three periods show an omission ellipsis of parts of sentences or sentences. Three asterisks usually show that a whole paragraph or an even longer passage has been left out. (See "Ellipsis" in this section.)

Brackets ([ ])

Always use brackets in pairs. They show that you have put an explanation of your own into a direct quotation.

Poets sometimes use contractions that are not common in speech : " 'Twas [it was] the night before Christmas . . . . "

Colon (:)

Use a colon to separate a statement from a further explanation or detail. Never put a colon at the beginning of a line.

1. A colon may introduce a list or explanation that is not grammatically necessary to the sentence.

list

Paula bought several items at the bookstore: a notebook, two pens, and some typing paper.

explanation

Sue has difficulty understanding punctuation rules: she thinks the examples are not clear.

Never use a colon immediately after a preposition or a verb.

INCORRECT:	He went to the store for: milk, bread, cheese, and tea.
INCORRECT:	The cities in the United States that I would like to visit are: Miami, San Francisco, and New York.

The sentences must be grammatically complete before the colon.

CORRECT:	He went to the store for several items: milk, bread, cheese, and tea.
CORRECT:	The cities in the United States that I would like to visit are three: Miami, San Francisco, and New York.
CORRECT:	The cities in the United States that I would like to visit are Miami, San Francisco, and New York.

2. A colon introduces a long quotation separated from the rest of the text.

William Wordsworth wrote about nature:

> "My heart leaps up when I behold
> A rainbow in the sky:
> So was it when my life began;
> So is it now I am a man:
> So be it when I shall grow old,
>   Or let me die!"

3. In a book title, a colon separates the title from the subtitle.

Writing Research Papers: A Complete Guide
Women at Work: Case Studies of Working Mothers

4. A colon separates hours and minutes:

2:15 p.m.

A colon also separates minutes and seconds, if necessary:

2:15:03

Comma (,)

Never put a comma at the beginning of a line.

1. Put a comma after each item except the last in a series of three or more words, phrases, or short clauses.

WORDS:	Debbie, Sue, and Janet have all made the team.
PHRASES:	The mayor of the city, the sheriff of the country, and the governor of the state are all elected officials.
	She put down the phone, picked up her purse, and left.
CLAUSES:	The dog growled, then he barked, and finally he began to chase the cat.

2. Put a comma between two independent clauses if they are connected by *and, but, for, or, nor, yet,* or *so.* (see **Coordinating conjunctions**)

> He walked down the street to the bus stop, and he waited for a bus for nearly twenty minutes.
> Nelson is always complaining about not having any friends, but he is not a friendly person himself.

Do not put a comma before or after a coordinating conjunction that joins two verbs in the same clause.

> He went down the street to the bus stop and waited for a bus for nearly twenty minutes.
> Nelson is always complaining about not having any friends but is not a friendly person himself.

3. Put a comma after a person's last name if the last name is written before the first name.

> On the application for a new job, Jane had to write her last name first: Ashford, Jane. She also had to give her father's name: Ashford, William.

4. Put a comma after every item in an address or date if there is more than one item (month and date together count as one item).

ONE ITEM:	On May 15 she will be ten years old.
	Only in New York can you see the Statue of Liberty.
MORE THAN ONE ITEM:	He was born on March 23, 1965, the youngest of four brothers.
	She lived in New Haven, Connecticut, before she moved to Denver, Colorado, with her family.
	They have lived at 291 Redfern Avenue, Dayton, Texas, since September, 1976, in a house that is a hundred years old.

In addresses, use *at* when the street number is given, but use *on* when the street is given without the number. *In* can replace a comma between street and city in a sentence but not in a mailing address.

> They lived *on* Redfern Avenue *in* Dayton, Texas.
> They lived *at* 291 Redfern Avenue.

Do not put a comma between state and zip code numbers in writing a mailing address.

> Miss Susan Jackson
> 291 Redfern Avenue
> Dayton, Texas 76109

5. Put commas after certain words, phrases, and clauses at the beginning of a sentence

a. after a word that does not flow into the rest of the sentence. (To express stronger emotion, use an exclamation mark.)

| | Oh, I wish I could go with you. |
| | Yes, you have the right number. |

| | Well, that was the end of that. |
| STRONGER: | Well! That was the end of that! |

| | No, that is not the right answer. |
| STRONGER: | No! That is not the right answer. |

b. Put a comma after a long participial, infinitive, or prepositional phrase at the beginning of the sentence.

| PARTICIPIAL: | Seeing his father coming down the street, the child shouted and ran to the door. |

Both present and past participles can be used.

PHRASE WITH PRESENT PARTICIPLE:	Tying the manager's hands and feet, the robber warned him not to make any noise.
PHRASE WITH PAST PARTICIPLE:	Tied hand and foot, the manager struggled to reach the burglar alarm.
INFINITIVE PHRASE:	To find the street you are looking for, turn left at the first stop sign.
PREPOSITIONAL PHRASE:	Before making a final decision on a career, you should think about what you dislike as well as what you like.

NOTE: The comma is often left out after a short phrase (usually four words or fewer) at the beginning of a sentence.

c. Put a comma after an introductory dependent clause introduced by a word such as *if, when, after, since, although,* or *because.* (see **Clauses, dependent**)

When he heard that she had already left, he rushed out of the house.

After she had locked the door and shut the curtains, she turned out the light and went to bed.

A NOTE ON WORD ORDER: When infinitive phrases, prepositional phrases, or dependent adverbial clauses come at the *end* of a sentence, do not separate them from the rest of the sentence by a comma.

PHRASE AT BEGINNING:	To find the street you are looking for, turn left at the first stop sign.
PHRASE AT END:	Turn left at the first stop sign to find the street you are looking for.
PHRASE AT BEGINNING:	Before making a final decision on a career, you should think about what you dislike as well as what you like.
PHRASE AT END:	You should think about what you dislike as well as what you like before making a final decision on a career.
CLAUSE AT BEGINNING:	When he heard that she had already left, he rushed out of the house.
CLAUSE AT END:	He rushed out of the house when he heard that she had already left.
CLAUSE AT BEGINNING:	After she had locked the door and shut the curtains, she turned out the light and went to bed.
CLAUSE AT END:	She turned out the light and went to bed after she had locked the door and shut the curtains.

6. Put a comma before a tag question or other contrasting phrase at the end of a sentence.

She is late today, isn't she?
They will not leave early, will they?
He wore his new suit, not his old one.

7. Put a comma in a direct quotation to separate the speaker's exact words (the dialogue guide) from the rest of the sentence. (See **Direct speech** for complete rules and examples.)

"She needs to get her lunch now," he said.
He said, "She needs to get her lunch now."

8. Put a comma between coordinate adjectives which can be separated by *and*. (See **Adjectives, order of** for more rules and examples.)

They were well-trained and intelligent horses.
They were intelligent, well-trained horses.

or

They were well-trained, intelligent horses.

Her rich and famous brother was coming to visit her.
Her rich, famous brother was coming to visit her.

or

Her famous, rich brother was coming to visit her.

Do not use commas instead of *and* to separate coordinate adjectives that follow the verb.

> Her brother was rich and famous.

9. Use *pairs* of commas to separate certain words, phrases, and clauses from the rest of the sentence. When these words, phrases, and clauses come at the beginning or end of the clause, put only one comma.

a. Words and phrases such as *however, nevertheless, furthermore, in addition, of course, consequently, on the other hand, namely, that is, as a result, subsequently,* and *after that.* (see **Interrupters**)

IN THE MIDDLE OF THE CLAUSE:	Most authorities, however, disagree with these conclusions.
AT THE BEGINNING OF THE CLAUSE:	However, most authorities disagree with these conclusions.
AT THE END OF THE CLAUSE:	Most authorities disagree with these conclusions, however.
IN THE MIDDLE OF THE CLAUSE:	The results, therefore, seem to be conclusive.
IN THE MIDDLE OF THE CLAUSE:	A final judgment, of course, must wait for more evidence.

Do not put an interrupter between two independent clauses and leave out the semicolon.

WRONG:	The results of this experiment were very interesting, however, most authorities disagree with the conclusions.
RIGHT:	The results of this experiment were very interesting; however, most authorities disagree with the conclusions.

b. Put pairs of commas to separate the name or title of a person spoken to from the rest of the sentence.

IN THE MIDDLE OF THE CLAUSE:	Please, John, come early tomorrow.
AT THE END OF THE CLAUSE:	Thank you for the help, Mrs. Johnson.
AT THE BEGINNING OF THE CLAUSE:	Mark, bring those notebooks here now.

c. Use pairs of commas to separate words, phrases, and clauses that give additional information or rename a person or thing already identified (see **Essential and nonessential modifiers** and **Appositives**)

WORDS:	My history professor, Dr. Brown, lives near us.
	Dr. Brown, my history professor, lives near us.
	My father, a history professor, lives in Chicago.
CLAUSE:	Dr. Brown, who is my history professor, lives near us.
	My father, who moved to Chicago last year, is a history professor.
INCORRECT:	My father who moved to Chicago last year is a history professor. (This sentence implies that I have more than one father.)

BE CAREFUL: Words and clauses which are *essential* to identification are *not* separated by commas from the rest of the sentence:

| ESSENTIAL: | My former neighbor who moved to Chicago last year is a history professor. |
| ESSENTIAL: | My brother John came yesterday. |

Dash (—)

Avoid using a dash in most formal writing. In informal writing a dash can replace a colon, and a pair of dashes can replace a pair of commas or parentheses.

COLON:	They checked their camping equipment carefully: backpacks, tents, clothing, and food.
DASH:	They checked their camping equipment carefully —backpacks, tents, clothing, and food.
PAIR OF COMMAS:	They checked their camping equipment, especially the backpacks and tent, before leaving for the mountains.
PARENTHESES:	They checked their camping equipment (especially the backpacks and tent) before leaving for the mountains.
DASH:	They checked their camping equipment—especially the backpacks and tent—before leaving for the mountains.

Use a dash or a pair of dashes to set off a long interrupter that already has commas in it.

They checked their camping equipment carefully—backpacks, tent, camping equipment, clothing, and food—before leaving for the mountains.
All of John's family—his father, mother, brother, and sister—will visit him next summer.

Ellipsis (...)

An ellipsis is three dots indicating that part of a direct quotation has been left out. If the words left out are at the end of a sentence, a fourth dot is added for the period.

"So was it when my life began . . . so be it when I shall grow old . . . ."

Exclamation Point (!)

Never put an exclamation point at the beginning of a line. Put an exclamation point after a statement or a word of strong feeling.

Well! When can you come?	They are looking for you!
Watch out!	Run!
Help!	Call the ambulance!

Hyphen (-)

Never put a hyphen at the beginning of a line. Put a hyphen slightly above the line if you are writing by hand on lined paper. Never put a hyphen below the line.

1. Use a hyphen to separate parts of words as conventional spelling indicates.

vice-president	but	vice admiral
mother-in-law	but	stepmother
pre-engineering	but	premature

Look up the word in a dictionary if you are not sure whether or not it needs a hyphen and/or a capital letter.

2. Use a hyphen between all numbers of two words from twenty-one through ninety-nine and in compound numbers that contain them.

thirty-three (33)
one hundred thirty-three (133)

3. Use a hyphen between the parts of fractions when they are written as words but not if an article replaces one.

three-fourths (¾)	one-fourth (¼)
seven-eighths (⅞)	but a/the half

4. Use a hyphen to separate syllables of a word between the end of one line and the beginning of another. *Always* put the hyphen with the *first* part of the word.

He is holding his hands together, making a big fist, rhythmically rub-
bing one thumb against the other.

No simple, general rule can teach you where syllables in English words begin and end. Look the word up in a dictionary if you are not sure.

5. Use a hyphen to join compound adjectives; that is, if two words together modify a following noun they are joined by a hyphen.

> We bought hamburgers at a *fast-food* restaurant.
> Mrs. Patterson paid a *special-delivery* fee for an important letter.
> A hospital must have a *germ-free* environment.

6. A woman who wants to keep her maiden name after she marries uses a hyphen to join her name to her husband's name.

> Martha Arnold will become Martha Arnold-Smith after she marries John Smith.

Period (full stop) (.)

1. Put a period, question mark, or exclamation point at the end of every sentence. (These three marks are sometimes called *end punctuation.*)

> It is raining.
> This is a rainy day!
> Is it raining?

2. A period follows many abbreviations. (see **Abbreviations**)

> etc., a.m./p.m., Mrs., Mr., Dr., Ms.

But not all abbreviations are followed by a period:

> UNESCO (*United Nations Educational, Cultural, and Scientific Organization*), WHO (*World Health Organization*), and other acronyms (abbreviations formed from the first letters of words).

Do not put a period after *Miss* unless the word is the last one in a sentence. As a general rule, avoid abbreviations in formal writing.

3. Use a period as a decimal point in money expressed in a decimal system and in mathematics.

> $4.95 (four dollars and ninety-five cents)
> 9,743.75 (nine thousand, seven hundred forty-three and seventy-five hundredths)

Question Mark (?)

Never put a question mark at the beginning of a line in English.

1. Put a question mark at the end of a direct question.

> Will you be leaving soon? (replacing a period)
> "How many days are left?" he asked. (replacing a comma)

2. Never put a question mark after an indirect question.

They asked whether the storm would be severe.
She wants to know when you will come back.

3. Use a question mark to show uncertainty about facts.

The dates of Socrates are 470?–399 B.C.

4. A question mark is not usually used after a polite request or command put in the form of a question.

Would you please carry these books for me.
(Meaning: Please carry these books for me.)

Would you hold the door open, please.
(Meaning: Please hold the door open.)

Quotation Marks (" " and ' ')

Double marks are usual in American usage; single marks (sometimes called inverted commas) are usual in British usage.

1. Use quotation marks to set off the exact words of a speaker or to show material quoted from writing.

"Come here," the woman said; "I want to look at you." (speaker's exact words)
Lincoln's Gettysburg address begins, "Fourscore and seven years ago." (quoted from a book)

2. Show titles of works that are not published separately by putting quotation marks around them. (See also "underlining" in this section: titles of works published separately are underlined in handwriting and typing.)

A short story:	"The Last Leaf"
A poem:	"The Raven"
A magazine or newspaper article:	"The State Visit of the President"
A chapter in a book:	"The Vertebrates"

These are titles of works by other people. Never put the title of a paper that you are writing in quotation marks on that paper or on the title page for it.

3. If quotation marks are needed inside a passage that is already enclosed in quotation marks, single marks instead of double marks are used. (British usage reverses this order.)

"Now," he said, "I have finished reading 'The Raven'."

4. Quotation marks are always used in pairs. The first *opens* and the second *closes* the quotation. Always put periods and commas inside the close of quotation marks.

"Now," he said, "I have finished the work."

5. Other punctuation marks may be inside or outside the quotation marks, depending on the meaning and structure of the sentence.

What is the theme of "The River"?
He asked, "Have you finished reading 'The Raven'?"
There are only three characters in the story "A Worn Path": Phoenix, a man, and a nurse.

Semicolon (;)

A semicolon is stronger than a comma. Never put a semicolon at the beginning of a line.

1. Two independent clauses may be joined by a semicolon. (see **Comma splice**)

The athletes who were training for the championships were running six miles every day; they were also eating a special diet.

2. Two independent clauses may be joined by a comma and coordinating conjunction. The comma may be replaced by a semicolon, however, if there are other commas in the sentence.

COMMA AND COORDINATING CONJUNCTION
The athletes who were training for the championships were running six miles a day, but I was not.

SEMICOLON AND COORDINATING CONJUNCTION
The athletes who were training for the championships were running six miles a day, lifting weights, swimming every afternoon, and eating a special diet; but I was not.

Slash (also called diagonal or virgule) (/)

Use a slash between two words to show that both or either one of them can give the correct meaning.

Mary and/or Bob must sign the checks in their joint account.
Infinitive/gerund choice is difficult to learn. Some verbs can be followed by only a gerund, other verbs can be followed by only an infinitive, and some can be followed by either gerunds or infinitives.

Underlining (Italics)

Words that are printed in italics are indicated by underling in handwriting or typing.

1. Underline titles of complete publications: books, periodicals, movies, television programs, record albums, and plays, but not the Bible or other sacred writings or their parts. (NOTE: In scientific writing, book and periodical titles are not always underlined.) (see **Style, scientific and technical writing**)

BOOKS:	A Tale of Two Cities
NEWSPAPERS:	The New York Times
MAGAZINES:	The Reader's Digest
SACRED WRITINGS:	the Koran, the Bible, the Gita, Genesis, the Gospels

Do not underline the title of a paper that you are writing, either on that paper or on the title page for that paper.

2. Underline foreign words and phrases.

She did not know he was a Frenchman until he said, *"Bonjour, mademoiselle."*

The abbreviation for the Latin word *confer, cf.,* is often used in scholarly writing. It directs the reader to compare one idea with another.

3. Underline words or numbers used as words or numbers.

He crossed his *t*'s and dotted his *i*'s carefully.
I never know whether to use *it's* or *its*.
Write your *1*'s, *7*'s, and *9*'s so that people will not confuse them.

4. Underline for emphasis, but *very* sparingly.

Do *not* bring that dog in here!

5. Underline the names of ships, trains, and aircraft.

The *Queen Elizabeth II* is sailing today.
The Goodyear blimp *Liberty* is over the stadium.

Puns, see **Spelling**

Quantity

Choose a word of quantity according to the kind of noun it refers to. Different words are used with countable and uncountable nouns. (see **Adjectives, order of, Articles, Countable and uncountable nouns,** and **Determiners**)

Question mark, see **Punctuation, question mark**)

Questions, Direct

Direct questions give the speaker's exact words. In dialogue they are enclosed in quotation marks.

Indirect questions report what was said but do not give the speaker's exact words. (see **Reported speech**)

If you have difficulty with the question forms in English, think of the statement before changing it into a question. Look at the verb. Is it an operator? If it is not an operator, you must use a form of *do*. (see **Operators**)

Yes-No questions expect an answer of agreement or disagreement (see **Negative**), often in a short form without the main verb repeated. The operator comes before the subject in a Yes-No question.

	verb
STATEMENT:	Jane *studied* yesterday.
	verb *verb*
QUESTION:	*Did* Jane *study* yesterday?
ANSWER (SHORT):	(Yes,) she *did*. or (No,) she *didn't*.
ANSWER (LONG):	Yes, she *studied*. or No, she *did* not *study*.

Yes-No questions that are made from sentences that contain the verb *be* (*am, is, are, was, were*) or other auxiliaries or modals (*have* when used as an auxiliary, *shall, should, will, would, can, could, may, might, must*) move these words to the beginning of the sentence to make the question. Do not add any form of *do*. These verbs change position, not form.

STATEMENT:	John *is* studying.
	He *will* study tomorrow.
QUESTION:	*Is* John studying?
	Is John a student?
	Will he study tomorrow?

The short answer is made with the same verb that is moved to make the question (the operator):

ANSWER (SHORT):	Yes, he *is*. or No, he *isn't/is* not.
	Yes, they *are*. or No, they *aren't/are* not.
	Yes, he *will*. or No, he *won't/will* not.
ANSWER (LONG):	Yes, he *is* (he's) studying. or No, he *is* not (isn't) studying.
	Yes, he *is* (he's) a student. or No, he *is* not (he's not, he *isn't*) a student.
	Yes, he *will* (he'll) study tomorrow. or No, he *will* not (won't) study tomorrow.

WH-questions are formed with words that begin with *WH* or *H*: *who, whose, whom, what, which, when, where, how,* and *why.* If *who, what,* or *which* is the *subject* of the sentence, it is followed by the normal word order of a statement.

	subject *verb*
STATEMENT:	*Those students* lost their books.
	subject verb
QUESTION:	*Who* lost their books?
ANSWER:	Those students.
	subject *verb*
STATEMENT:	*Finding the book I need* is difficult.
	subject verb
QUESTION:	*What* is difficult?
ANSWER:	Finding the book I need.
	subject verb
STATEMENT:	*That dog* bothered him yesterday.
	subject verb
QUESTION:	*Which dog* bothered him yesterday?
ANSWER:	That dog.

Other examples:

	subject verb verb
STATEMENT:	John must go now.

	subject verb verb
QUESTION:	Who must go now?
ANSWER:	John.

	subject verb verb
STATEMENT:	Our team will win.

	subject verb verb
QUESTION:	Who will win?
ANSWER:	Our team.

	subject verb
STATEMENT:	Registration is frustrating.

	subject verb
QUESTION:	What is frustrating?
ANSWER:	Registration.

	subject verb
STATEMENT:	My oldest sister is here.

	subject verb
QUESTION:	Which sister is here?
ANSWER:	The oldest one.

Whom (*who* in informal English), *what*, and *which as objects* form questions by putting the WH-words first and *do, does,* or *did* second.

	subject verb object
STATEMENT:	He wanted John.

	object verb subject verb
QUESTION:	Who (whom) did he want?
ANSWER:	John.

	subject verb object
STATEMENT:	Arnold ate an apple this morning.

	object verb subject verb
	What did Arnold eat this morning?
ANSWER:	An apple.

	object
STATEMENT:	Mr. Jones mowed the grass.

	object
QUESTION:	What did Mr. Jones mow? (The information wanted is the direct object.)
ANSWER (SHORT):	The grass.

	object
ANSWER (LONG):	Mr.. Jones mowed the grass.

Notice that when the action of the verb is the information the questioner wants, the *main verb* is not used in the question but is replaced by *do*:

Question asking for *action* in the answer:

	verb
QUESTION:	*What* did Mr. Jones *do?* (The information wanted is the action of the verb.)

	verb
ANSWER (SHORT):	He *mowed.*

	verb
ANSWER (LONG):	He *mowed* the grass.

Notice that the long answer for both of the last two questions is the same: *He mowed the grass.*

STATEMENT:	Sally can fix her own bicycle.
QUESTION:	What *can* Sally *do?* (Asks for action of the verb.)
ANSWER:	(Sally can) fix her own bicycle.

A modal (*can*) cannot be replaced by *do, does* or *did.* The *do* here replaces the main verb, *fix,* because the question is asking for an action.

Which? (The answer will be one of two or one of a limited group.)

STATEMENT:	He did *Part II* first on this examination.
QUESTION:	*Which part* did he do first?
ANSWER:	Part II. He did Part II.

STATEMENT:	She should do *Part II* first.
QUESTION:	*Which part* should she do first?
ANSWER:	Part II. She should do Part II.

When? (The answer will be a time or an occasion.)

STATEMENT:	He is leaving *tomorrow.*
QUESTION:	*When* is he leaving?
ANSWER:	Tomorrow.

STATEMENT:	They will leave *before the party.*
QUESTION:	*When* will they leave?
ANSWER:	Before the party.

Where? (The answer will be a place or a situation.)

STATEMENT:	They went to *New York* yesterday.
QUESTION:	*Where* did they go yesterday?
ANSWER:	To New York. They went to New York.

STATEMENT:	We will be *in trouble* when they find us.
QUESTION:	*Where* will we be when they find us?
ANSWER:	In trouble.

How? (The answer will show manner, means, or degree.)

	verb verb
STATEMENT:	We *are* going by bus. (The verb has a form of *be*.)
	verb verb
QUESTION:	How *are* you going?
ANSWER:	By bus. We are going by bus.
	verb
STATEMENT:	We *went* by bus. (The verb is a form of *go*.)
	verb verb
QUESTION:	How *did* you go?
ANSWER:	By bus.
STATEMENT:	The word *receive* is spelled R-E-C-E-I-V-E.
QUESTION:	*How* is *receive* spelled?
ANSWER:	R-E-C-E-I-V-E. It is spelled R-E-C-E-I-V-E.
STATEMENT:	This family is *very* happy.
QUESTION:	*How* happy do you think this family is?
ANSWER:	Very happy. This family is very happy.

How much? (The answer will be connected with an uncountable [mass] noun.)

STATEMENT:	I need *a lot* of money.
QUESTION:	*How much* money do you need?
ANSWER:	A lot, a great deal.
STATEMENT:	I need *a lot* of rice.
QUESTION:	*How much* rice do you need?
ANSWER:	A lot, a hundred pounds.

How many? (The answer will be connected with a countable noun.)

STATEMENT:	I am taking *four* courses, too many.
QUESTION:	*How many* courses are you taking?
ANSWER:	Four, too many.

How often? (The answer will indicate frequency.)

STATEMENT:	Mary goes to the lab *every day*.
QUESTION:	*How often* does Mary go to the lab?
ANSWER:	Every day.

How come? is an informal spoken form that means *why is it that* . . . ? Avoid using it in writing.

Why? (The answer will be a reason.)

STATEMENT:	John is leaving early *to avoid the heavy traffic*.
QUESTION:	*Why* is John leaving early?
ANSWER:	To avoid the heavy traffic.

STATEMENT:	He had difficulty registering *because the records from his former school were lost.*
QUESTION:	*Why* did he have difficulty registering?
ANSWER:	Because the records from his former school were lost.

Quotations, see Direct speech

Quotation marks, see Punctuation, quotation marks

R

Reference of the Pronoun _____

A pronoun must agree in *number* (singular or plural) and *gender* (masculine, feminine, neuter, or common) with the word it stands for (its antecedent).

1. Use the *subject* or *object* form according to the use of the pronoun in its own clause. (see **Antecedent, Case, Gender,** and **Pronouns**)

                                        singular
                                        masculine
                                        possessive
Uncle Bill gave Diana and Barbara   *his*   cat.

                    singular
                    masculine
                    object form
Uncle Bill asked Diana and Barbara to help   *him.*

                    singular   *plural*
                    masculine   *common*
                    subject form   *object form*
Uncle Bill asked Diana and Barbara if   *he*   could help   *them.*

              singular   *singular*
              feminine   *feminine*
              subject form   *possessive*
Barbara asked Uncle Bill if   *she*   could call   *her*   father.

2. Use a singular pronoun to refer to *each, either, neither, no one, nobody, everybody, everyone, anyone, anybody, someone,* and *somebody.* To avoid using *he, him,* or *his* to refer to an unknown person who may be female, put the sentence in the plural or leave out the pronoun. (see **Women, terms referring to**)

CORRECT:	Someone has left *his* umbrella. (*Their* is often used in speech)
CORRECT:	Someone has left *an* umbrella.
CORRECT:	Everyone wants *his* breakfast now.
CORRECT:	Everyone *wants* breakfast now.

3. Use *which* and *that* for ideas, actions, animals, and things; use *who, whose,* and *whom* for people and sometimes for animals associated with them. *That* is sometimes used for people but *which* never is. *Which* and *who, whose,* and *whom* can introduce nonessential clauses. (see **Essential and nonessential modifiers** and **Pronouns, relative**)

Sally is the one *who* asked.
Mr. and Mrs. Parker are the ones *who* asked.
These books are the ones *that* were lost.
This dog is the one *that* was lost.
My algebra book, *which* was on the table this morning, has disappeared.
Mrs. Allen, *who* signed the receipt for the letter, says that the delivery was made three days ago.

Use *whose* for persons and use *it* or *its* with animals and things. Use *whose* with animals and things if necessary to avoid awkward constructions.

The man *whose* hat blew off chased *it* down the street.
The car *whose* brakes failed finally stopped at the corner.

4. Do not use *this, that, which,* and *it* to refer to an implied idea (especially to an idea in the verb only) or to one of several ideas. Make sure you have one specific noun or pronoun as the antecedent for every pronoun that requires one.

UNCLEAR:	The cook made a mistake and put too much salt in the soup, *which* made it impossible to eat.
IMPROVED:	The cook's mistake, putting too much salt in the soup, made the soup inedible.
IMPROVED:	Too much salt in the soup made eating it impossible.
UNCLEAR:	Agnes cried when the cat died. *This* upset everyone. (Agnes' crying or the cat dying?)
IMPROVED:	Agnes' crying when the cat died upset everyone.
IMPROVED:	The cat's death upset everyone so much that Agnes cried.
IMPROVED:	Agnes cried when the cat died. Her grief upset everyone.

5. Do not use impersonal *they* or *you* without antecedents or in a way that is not clear.

UNCLEAR:	When a clown at the circus wants to make *you* laugh, he falls down.
IMPROVED:	When a clown at the circus wants to make the audience laugh, he falls down.
UNCLEAR:	As soon as *they* open the doors to the theater, *you* can go in.
IMPROVED:	As soon as the ushers open the doors to the theater, we/the audience can go in.

6. Do not use a pronoun to refer to one of several possible antecedents.

UNCLEAR:	The little *boy* asked the *man* selling balloons if *he* could help.
CLEAR:	The little boy asked the man selling balloons for help.
CLEAR:	The little boy offered to help the man selling balloons.

7. A pronoun should follow its antecedent closely. Relative pronouns that introduce adjective clauses usually follow immediately after their antecedents.

INCORRECT: The books can be sold now *that* are on the table.

CORRECT: The books *that* are on the table can be sold now.

INCORRECT: The man is coming *who* is my best friend.

CORRECT: The man *who* is my best friend is coming.

INCORRECT: The car is in the garage *that* was in a wreck.

CORRECT: The car *that* was in a wreck is in the garage.

Other pronouns must follow their antecedents closely. If the antecedent is more than one sentence removed from the pronoun, the reference is unclear.

INCORRECT:	Harriet's mother is coming to visit her. Next week will be a good time for a visit because of the Thanksgiving holidays. *She* is excited because *she* has been away from home for two years now, and *she* has not seen *her* in all that time.

The pronouns in the passage above are unclear for two reasons: *She* and *her* are ambiguous and could refer to either *Harriet* or *her mother,* and they are also too far from their antecedents, the words they stand for.

IMPROVED:	Harriet is excited because she has not seen her mother since leaving home three years ago.

8. The gender of an English personal pronoun must be the same as its antecedent, not the same as the noun it modifies.

FEMININE	FEMININE	FEMININE OR MASCULINE
Harriet (Harriet's)	her	mother, sister, aunt, daughter
	her	father, brother, uncle, son
MASCULINE	MASCULINE	FEMININE OR MASCULINE
George (George's)	his	mother, sister, aunt, daughter
	his	father, brother, uncle, son

9. Never put a second pronoun with the same antecedent as the relative pronoun in the same dependent clause.

	antecedent	*relative pronoun*	*second pronoun with the same antecedent*	
INCORRECT:	The books	*that*	*they*	are on the table can be sold now.

	antecedent	*relative pronoun*	
CORRECT:	The books	*that*	are on the table can be sold now.

	antecedent	*relative pronoun*	*second pronoun with the same antecedent*	
INCORRECT:	The books	*that*	we sold	*them*	are on the table.

	antecedent	*relative pronoun*	
CORRECT:	The books	*that*	we sold are on the table.

	antecedent	*relative pronoun*		*second pronoun with the same antecedent*	
INCORRECT:	The sunset	*that*	we saw	*it*	was beautiful.

	antecedent	*relative pronoun*	
CORRECT:	The sunset	*that*	we saw was beautiful.

You can put a second pronoun in a dependent clause if it has a different antecedent from the relative pronoun.

	antecedent of her	*antecedent of who*	*relative pronoun— refers to friends*	
CORRECT:	Jane's	friends	*who*	were helping

personal pronoun— refers to Jane		
her	went on vacation.	

	antecedent of he	*antecedent of that*	*relative pronoun— refers to book*	*personal pronoun— refers to Ken*	
CORRECT:	Ken's	book	*that*	*he*	lost

has been found.

Relevant Material

Relevant is often used to describe facts, illustrations, and examples that develop a topic sentence or a thesis statement. Relevant material has a clear connection with the idea you are writing about. To be relevant, you must stay on the subject you have stated in your thesis statement or topic sentence. A statement may be true and/or interesting but not relevant to the subject you are writing about. Material that is not relevant is called irrelevant. Do not use irrelevant facts, ideas, or examples in your writing.

Repetition

Repetition is using the same word, structure, or idea more than once for emphasis or for a special effect.

Word

Repeating the same word can give effective emphasis. Too much repetition, however, can be dull. Using synonyms is sometimes better than using the same word again. (see **Synonyms**)

> To everything there is a season, and a time to every purpose under the
> heaven:
> A time to be born, and a time to die; a time to plant and a time to pluck
> up . . .
> A time to kill, and a time to heal; a time to break down, and a time to
> build up;
> A time to weep, and a time to laugh; a time to mourn and a time to
> dance . . .
> A time to love, and a time to speak; a time of war and a time of peace.
> *Ecclesiastes*

Structure

Repeating the same grammatical structure to express different ideas can
give effective emphasis. The structure can be a phrase, a clause, or a
complete sentence. (see **Parallel structure**)

> *Phrase:* . . . that the government *of the people, by the people,* and *for the*
> *people* shall not perish from the earth. (*Abraham Lincoln*)
> *Clause:* Life can only be understood backwards; but it must be lived for-
> words. (*Søren Kierkegaard*)
> *Sentence:* Work consists of whatever a body is *obliged* to do. . . . Play
> consists of whatever a body is *not obliged* to do. (*Mark Twain*)

Idea

Repeating the same idea in different words emphasizes the idea.

> Stolen waters are sweet, and bread eaten in secret is pleasant. (*Proverbs*)
> In much wisdom is much grief, and whoever increases knowledge in-
> creases sorrow. (*Ecclesiastes*)

Reported Speech _____

Reported or indirect speech tells what a person says without writing
the speaker's exact words. In reported speech, the phrase telling who
speaks or writes must come first.

DIRECT SPEECH: "We want to go," the students said.

or

The students said, "We want to go."

REPORTED SPEECH: The student said that they wanted to go.

Reported speech does not use quotation marks and capital letters to show
the beginning of the words that a person actually speaks or writes. Reported speech uses words such as *say, said, say that,* or *said that* to intro-

duce the indirect quotation. Sometimes the word *that* is left out, but if the meaning is not clear without it, use it.

> The students said (that) they wanted to go.

Verbs in Reported Speech

Tell must be followed by a word referring to a person.

The students told $\left\{ \begin{array}{l} us \\ John \\ the\ teacher \end{array} \right\}$ (that) they wanted to go.

or

The students told *us* to go.

Other verbs that give the ideas of reported speech have an infinitive phrase (to + simple verb) after the main verb and do not use *that*.

The students $\begin{array}{l} demanded \\ begged \\ asked \\ wanted \end{array}$ to go.

Some verbs use other forms.

The students asked $\begin{array}{l} insisted\ on\ going. \\ for\ permission\ to\ go. \\ requested\ permission\ to\ go. \end{array}$

Back-shifting of Tense in Reported Speech

Tense in reported speech can be different from tense in direct speech if the main verb is in the past tense. If the main verb is in the present tense, do not change the phrase reporting what was said.

	main verb	*second verb*
	(who is speaking)	(what they say)
DIRECT:	The students say, "We want to go."	
REPORTED:	The students *say* (that) they *want* to go.	

The main verb is in the past tense; the second verb is in the present tense.

DIRECT:	The students said, "We want to go."
REPORTED:	The students *said* (that) they *wanted* to go.

1. *After a main verb in the present tense* in reported speech, the reporting verb stays the same.

> The students say that they *want* to go. ("We *want* to go.")
> The students say that they *will* go. ("We *will* go.")
> The students say that they *went.* ("We *went.*")

2. *After a main verb in the past tense,* the reporting verb changes if it is not already past or past perfect; do not use a present-tense verb after a main verb in the past tense.

The students said that they *wanted* to go. ("We *want* to go.")
The students said that they *would* go. ("We *will* go.")
The students said that they *had gone.* "We *went.*")

A verb in the *present becomes past* if it follows a main verb that is past.

A verb in the *future becomes past* if it follows a main verb that is past.

A verb in the *past becomes past perfect* if it follows a main verb that is past.

EXCEPTIONS

1. The verb *to be* rarely becomes the past perfect.

He said, "I *was* sorry about that."   becomes
He said that he *was* sorry about that.

2. The historical present tense shows ideas that are reported in the past but may still be considered to be true.

He believed that might *makes* right.
They taught that God *is* love.
Didn't you know that I *am* living in California now?

3. The present tense may be used when reporting opinions, statements, and comments from writers and characters in literature, even though they actually happened in the past.

Shakespeare shows us the danger of ambition.
Achilles refuses to fight the Trojans.

Pronouns in Reported Speech

Pronouns in reported speech must be changed if they are first person (I/me, we/us, and so on) or second person (you, your, yours). They must be changed to third person (he/him, she/her, they/them, and so on).

DIRECT:	The students say, "*We* want to go."
REPORTED:	The students say that *they* want to go.
DIRECT:	Mary said, "*I* want to go."
REPORTED:	Mary said that *she* wanted to go.
DIRECT:	John asked Peter, "Do *you* want to go?"
REPORTED:	John asked Peter if *he* wanted to go.

Reported (indirect) questions (see also **Questions, direct**) are not followed by a question mark.

Yes-no questions are introduced in reported speech by *whether* or *if*. *If* is considered informal.

DIRECT:	John asked, "Do you want to go?"
REPORTED:	John asked whether she wanted to go (or not).
	John asked if she wanted to go.

Questions after a WH-word follow the subject-verb word order of a statement. Notice the pronoun and tense changes.

DIRECT:	John asked, "*When will you* go?"
REPORTED:	John asked *when she would* go.
DIRECT:	Amy asked, "*Where are you* going?"
REPORTED:	Amy asked *where he was* going.
DIRECT:	Mrs. Jones asked the boys, "*How can you* finish on time?"
REPORTED:	Mrs. Jones asked the boys *how they could* finish on time.
DIRECT:	Mr. Jones asked the girls, "*What are you* doing?"
REPORTED:	Mr. Jones asked the girls *what they were* doing.
DIRECT:	We asked them, "*Why don't you* come now?"
REPORTED:	We asked them *why they didn't* come now.

Reported (indirect) commands are usually made with *tell* + a word referring to a person + an infinitive phrase.

DIRECT:	The dean said, "Register on March 15."
REPORTED:	The dean told *the students to register* on March 15.
DIRECT:	My uncle always said, "Prepare for the future."
REPORTED:	My uncle always told *us to prepare* for the future.

Adverbs in Reported Speech

Adverbs in reported speech must be changed when the tense of the verb is changed.

DIRECT:	The director said, "Come back *tomorrow*."
REPORTED:	The director told us to come back *the following day*.

DIRECT:	Harry said, "I found my book *yesterday*."
REPORTED:	Harry said that he had found his book *the day before*.
DIRECT:	They said, "We were married *last year*."
REPORTED:	They said that they had been married *a year earlier*.

Rhetoric

In ancient Greece *rhetoric* meant the art of composing speeches to convince an audience. Later rhetoric also came to mean the art of writing effectively. Today the word is usually applied to writing rather than to speech, particularly to prose composition that is consciously organized in special ways. Sometimes rhetoric means language that uses many figures of speech.

Just rhetoric or *empty rhetoric* sometimes means speech or writing that is cleverly organized with showy literary devices but that does not actually say very much.

A *rhetorical question* is a question written or spoken only for emphasis or effect. The writer or speaker does not expect an answer.

Rhyme

Rhyme means the repetition of a certain combination of consonant and vowel sounds: *rain/lane, hint/tint, seem/team,* and *thought/taught,* for example. An accented vowel is followed by the same sounds. Rhyme is often a feature of English poetry, but not always. When poets use rhyme, the rhyming syllable or syllables are usually at the end of the line, but rhyme can be internal, two words in the same line. *Rhyme* is sometimes spelled *rime.*

INTERNAL RHYME
And crown thy *good* with brother*hood* . . .
        Julia Ward Howe

END RHYME
Loveliest of trees, the cherry *now*
Is hung with bloom along the *bough.*
        A. E. Housman

END RHYME
For of all sad words of tongue or *pen*
The saddest are these: "It might have *been!*"
        John Greenleaf Whittier

Rhymes at the end of a line often form a pattern: four lines may rhyme *a b c b*. Here, the first line does not rhyme with the third line, but the second line rhymes with the fourth line. The lines that are needed to complete one pattern are called a *stanza*.

> **STANZA**
> I never saw a *moor,* (*a*)
> I never saw the *sea;* (*b*)
> Yet know I how the heather *looks,* (*c*)
> And what a wave must *be.* (*b*)
> > *Emily Dickinson*

Special kinds of stanzas are named according to the number of lines in them and the pattern of the end rhyme.

Roots, see **Word formation**

Run-on Sentences _____

A run-on sentence is a serious error in sentence construction. It is sometimes called a *fused* sentence. *Never* write two or more independent clauses without any punctuation at all between them. (see **Comma splice**)

independent clause

INCORRECT: Jane is going to Miami on her vacation

no punctuation   *independent clause*
Mary is going to New York.

RUN-ON SENTENCE
independent clause   *no punctuation*

INCORRECT: Jane has already been to New York

independent clause
therefore, she is going to Miami on her vacation.

Connect independent clauses in one of four ways:
1. Put a semicolon between two independent clauses.

independent clause

CORRECT: Jane is going to Miami on her vacation;

independent clause
Mary is going to New York.

independent clause

CORRECT: Jane has already been to New York; therefore,

independent clause
she is going to Miami on her vacation.

2. Put a comma and a coordinating conjunction between independent clauses. The coordinating conjunctions are *and, but, or, nor, for, yet,* and *so.*

independent clause   *, + coordinating conjunction*

CORRECT: Jane is going to Miami on her vacation,   and
                                                              but

independent clause
Mary is going to New York.

Do not be confused by words like *therefore* and *however.* Putting them between the two clauses and putting commas before and after them does not correct the sentence. You then have a comma splice. These words, called interrupters or conjunctive adverbs, cannot join independent clauses unless you also put a semicolon between the clauses. (see **Interrupters**)

In a series of independent clauses, put a coordinating conjunction between the last two clauses.

independent clause
CORRECT: Jane is going to Miami on her vacation,

                          , + coordinating
independent clause   *conjunction*
Mary is going to New York,   *and*

independent clause
Brenda is going to Chicago.

3. Put a period and a capital letter between independent clauses, making them separate sentences.

CORRECT: Jane is going to Miami on her vacation.
                Mary is going to New York.

CORRECT: Jane has already been to New York. Therefore, she
                is going to Miami on her vacation.

4. Make one of the independent clauses into a dependent clause or into another subordinate construction. (see **Subordinating and reducing**)

dependent clause
CORRECT: Because Jane has already been to New York,

independent clause
she is going to Miami on her vacation.

participial phrase
CORRECT: Having already been to New York,

independent clause
Jane is going to Miami on her vacation.

Keep at least one independent clause, or you will have a sentence fragment. (see **Fragments**)

S

Semicolon, see **Punctuation, semicolon**

Sentence _____

A written English sentence is a group of words that says something in a fixed structure of grammar and punctuation. Every written declarative sentence must have a subject and a finite verb. (see **Finite verbs** and **Clauses**).

Avoid common errors in writing sentences:
1. Be sure you begin with a capital letter.
2. Do not write fragments as sentences. (see **Fragments**)
3. Do not make your sentences too long, putting many subordinate structures one after the other and separating them only by commas or by no punctuation at all. (see **Sentence structure, Comma splice,** and **Run-on sentences**)
4. Do not make all your sentences short and simple because you are afraid you will make a mistake if you write longer sentences. Learn how to show relationships between ideas. (see **Subordinating and reducing**)
5. Mix the kinds of sentences you write. (see **Sentence variety**)
6. Be sure to put end punctuation—a period, a question mark, or an exclamation point—at the end of each sentence. (see **Punctuation**)
7. Do not indent from the left-hand margin every time you begin a new sentence, but organize several sentences or more into a paragraph. (see **Paragraph**)
8. Put the main idea of your sentence in an independent clause. (see **Subordinating and reducing**)

Sentence combining, see **Subordinating and reducing** and **Wordiness**

S

Sentence Patterns

Sentence pattern or verb pattern means the different grammatical constructions in a clause that are possible with different kinds of verbs. (see **Verbs, kinds of**)

Patterns with Intransitive Verbs

	SUBJECT	VERB	ADVERB (optional)
S + V:	The man	coughed.	
	The students	laughed.	
S + V + Adv:	The children	walked	down the street.
	Paul	hurried	away from the door.

Patterns with Linking Verbs

	SUBJECT	VERB	PREDICATE NOUN OR ADJECTIVE	ADVERB (required)
S + V + PN or Adj:	The baby	is	fat. (adj.)	
	Maureen	seems	unhappy. (adj.)	
	This building	is	the library. (noun)	
	Jonathan	has become	a student. (noun)	
S + V + Adv:	My house	is		on River Road.
	The groceries	are		in the kitchen.

Patterns with Active Transitive Verbs (see Voice and Passive verbs)

	SUBJECT	VERB	DIRECT OBJECT	ADVERB (required)
S + V + DO:	The baby	likes	bananas.	
	Dogs	chase	cats.	
S + V + DO + Adv:	Jerry	put	the key	in the door.
	Phyllis	treated	the old man	politely.

	SUBJECT	VERB	DIRECT OBJECT	OBJECTIVE COMPLEMENT
S + V + DO + OC:	The child	made	her mother	happy. (adj.)
	The committee	elected	Alan	treasurer. (noun)

	SUBJECT	VERB	INDIRECT OBJECT	DIRECT OBJECT	TO + INDIRECT OBJECT
S + V + IO + DO:	Mother	gave	Charles	ten dollars.	
	Pearl	sent	Tom	a book.	
S + V + DO + to + IO:	Mother	gave		ten dollars	to Charles.
	Pearl	sent		a book	to Tom.

(see also **Indirect object, Objective complement,** and **Predicate complements**)

Sentence patterns can be expanded by modifiers (adjective and adverbs). Many transitive sentences can be changed into passive sentences, and all patterns can be changed into questions and commands. (see **Commands, Modifiers,** and **Verbs, kinds of**)

Inverted word order is used in questions, for emphasis, and with expletives (It is . . . , There is . . . , Here is . . .). (see **Emphasis** and **Expletive**)

Sentence Structure _____

Sentence structure can be *simple, compound, complex,* or *compound-complex* according to the kinds of clauses in the sentence. (see **Clauses**)

A *simple sentence* has one independent or main clause (one subject-main verb combination).

> *We were* sorry.
> The *car stopped.*

A simple sentence can be expanded into a very long sentence, but adding modifiers does not change its basic structure.

> Feeling the disappointment of our friends at our early departure, *we were* sorry to leave before meeting all the guests.

In the sentence above, *feeling, to leave,* and *meeting* are verbals, not finite or main verbs. Although the sentence is long, it still has the structure of a simple sentence: one subject and one main verb or verb phrase. (see **Verbals**)

A simple sentence can have a compound subject (two or more subjects joined by a coordinating conjunction). (see **Coordinating conjunctions**)

> *Francis and Chris* were sorry.
> *Francis, Chris,* and *Joe* were sorry.

A simple sentence can have a compound verb (two or more verb forms joined by a coordinating conjunction).

> Francis *ate* peanuts and *drank* coffee.

A simple sentence can have a compound subject and a compound verb.

> *Francis* and *Chris ate* peanuts and *drank* coffee. (Both parts of the subject performed the action in both parts of the verb.)

The verb in one clause (a simple sentence) can be a verb phrase (more than one word). Verb phrases form most English tenses.

PRESENT TENSE:	*Francis eats* peanuts often.
	verb phrase
FUTURE TENSE:	*Francis will eat* peanuts tomorrow.
PRESENT PERFECT	*verb phrase*
TENSE:	*Francis has been eating* peanuts today.

A *compound sentence* has two or more independent clauses without any dependent or subordinate clauses. Sometimes a compound sentence is called a balanced sentence. (see **Parallel structure**)

> *Francis has been happy* today, and *he will be happier* still tomorrow.

The clauses of a compound sentence may be joined either by a semicolon or by a comma and a coordinating conjunction (*and, but, or, for, nor, yet,* and *so.*) (see **Comma splice** and **Run-on sentences**)

> *independent clause* + *semicolon* +   *independent clause*
> The bus was crowded ; I had to stand all the way.

> *independent clause* +*,*+ *coordinating conjunction* + *independent clause*
> The bus was crowded, *and/so* I had to stand all the way.

> *independent clause* +*,*+ *coordinating conjunction* + *independent clause*
> We had to stand all the way, *but/yet* we were not very tired.

A *complex sentence* has one independent clause and one or more dependent clauses. (see **Clauses, dependent**)

> *independent clause* + *dependent clause*
> *(adverb)*
> *We were* sorry when *we left* early.

> *independent clause* + *dependent clause*
> *(noun)*
> *James said* that *he was* very *pleased.*

A *compound-complex* sentence has two or more independent clauses and at least one dependent clause. A compound sentence becomes a compound-complex sentence when one or more dependent clauses are added to it.

> *independent clause*
> Many *men* and *women* today *are being trained on their jobs,* and

> *independent clause*
> *some* of them later *study* at colleges and technical schools

> *dependent clause*
> where *they improve* their skills.

Sentence Variety

Writing can be correct but dull. To make your writing more interesting, write sentences that are not all the same. Sentences can vary in length, in grammatical structure, and in the placement of their parts.

Length

Your writing will be more interesting if you have some short sentences, some sentences of moderate length, and some long sentences. Do not be afraid of short sentences, as they can be very effective for emphasis, but too many short sentences make your writing seem childish. On the other hand, many very long sentences one after the other may make your ideas hard to follow and make your writing dull. If you have more than four or five clauses in one sentence, your sentence is getting too long and you are likely to have made errors such as subject-verb agreement, incorrect reference of pronouns, and comma splices.

Grammatical Structure

Mix simple sentences, compound sentences, complex sentences, and compound-complex sentences. (see **Sentence structure**)

Placement of Subject and Verb

You can give your sentences variety by sometimes putting a dependent clause, an *-ing* phrase, or a prepositional phrase at the beginning of the sentence. (see **Emphasis** and **Inverted word order**)

A *loose* sentence has the subject and verb at the beginning of the sentence followed by modifiers.

A *periodic* sentence has modifiers (words, phrases, or dependent clauses) at the beginning of the sentence and is not grammatically complete until the end or near the end.

A *balanced* sentence has two or more clauses with the same structures and word order. (see **Parallel structure**)

A clause or sentence in *inverted order* has the verb before the subject. (see **Inverted word order**)

LOOSE:
> *Steve could* not *pass* the written test for his driver's license although he know how to drive well enough to pass the driving test.
> The *beginning* of the war *should* not *have been* surprising when considered in the light of all its causes.

PERIODIC:	Although Steve knew how to drive well enough to pass the driving test, *he could* not *pass* the written test.
	When considered in the light of all the causes, the *beginning* of the war *should* not *have been* surprising.
BALANCED:	*Steve knew* how to drive well enough to pass the driving test, but *he did* not *know* the traffic laws well enough to pass the written test.
	The *beginning* of the war *should* not *have been* surprising; its *causes should have* already *been* well known.
INVERTED (PERIODIC):	*Had he* (if he had) *known* the traffic laws well enough, *Steve would have passed* the written test.
	Had we (if we had) *considered* all the causes, the *beginning* of the war *would* not *have surprised* us.

Sentences, Kinds of _____

Sentences can be classified in several different ways.

1. *Simple, compound, complex,* and *compound-complex* sentences are classifications according to the kinds of clauses in them. (see **Sentence structure**)

2. *Loose, balanced,* and *periodic* sentences are classifications according to the position of the subject and verb. (see **Sentence variety**)

3. An *embedded sentence* is a grammatical structure that must be attached to an independent clause. (see **Subordinating and reducing**)

4. *Declarative, interrogative, imperative,* and *exclamatory* sentences are classifications according to the way the sentence communicates an idea.

a. A declarative sentence makes a statement and ends with a period. Most sentences that explain or persuade are declarative.

They are coming.

b. An interrogative sentence asks a question and ends with a question mark. (see **Questions, direct**)

Are they coming?

c. An imperative sentence is a command and ends with a period. (see **Commands**)

Come here.

The subject is not expressed, but it is understood to be *you*.

d. An exclamatory sentence expresses strong feeling and ends with an exclamation mark.

They must come now!

An exclamatory sentence has the same grammatical structure as a declarative sentence. Use exclamatory sentences very rarely if at all in formal writing.

If you write dialogue, you will try to reproduce what someone really said or what you imagine someone said. Then you will write interrogative, imperative, and exclamatory sentences. (see **Direct speech**) In almost all academic and business writing, however, you will write declarative sentences most of the time.

Simile

A simile is a comparison that shows similarities in things that are basically different. A simile uses *like* or *as* in the comparison. Similes are often used in both poetry and prose.

And *like* music on the waters
Is thy sweet voice to me.
　George Gordon, Lord Byron

The wild tulip, at the end of its tube, blows
　out its great red bell
Like a thin clear bubble of blood.
　　Robert Browning

They [the old men] had hands *like* claws, and
　their knees
Were twisted *like* the old thorn trees.
　　William Butler Yeats

My heart is *like* a singing bird
　Whose nest is in a watered shoot;
My heart is *like* an apple tree
　Whose boughs are bent with thickest fruit.
　　Christina Rossetti

The ship . . . went on lonely and swift *like* a small planet.
　　Joseph Conrad

He was *like* a cock who thought the sun had risen to hear him crow.
　　George Eliot

My life is *like* a stroll upon the beach,
As near the ocean's edge as I can go.
　　Henry David Thoreau

Slang

Slang is a label for words that are usually not acceptable in formal writing because they are imprecise, have changing meanings, or are understood by only a few people or special groups. Slang words sometimes become so widely used and understood that they are considered informal usage instead of slang, and a few slang words become completely acceptable. When you are not sure whether a word is slang or not, look it up in a dictionary. (see **Jargon**)

Pad is slang when it means a place to live.

> John's *pad* is near the university.

Guy, meaning a man or fellow, was once considered slang, but many authorities now accept it as informal usage (conversation). Do not use *guy* in formal writing.

> We said that David seems to be a nice *guy*.

Square, meaning unsophisticated or too conservative, is considered slang in some dictionaries and informal in others.

> Julia is *square* (or a *square*).

So

So has several different uses with different meanings.
So + an adjective or adverb + *that* means *in a way or degree* to bring a certain result.

> *adjective*
> The concert was *so   good   that* we stayed to the end.

> *adverb*
> The band played *so   well   that* we stayed to the end.

So can introduce a clause that shows result.

CAUSE	RESULT
The concert was good,	*so* we stayed to the end.
The party lasted a long time,	*so* we left before it was over.

So long as can mean *if* and introduce a conditional clause.

> We will go to the concert *so long as* (if) you buy the tickets.

So often replaces the first *as* in *as . . . as* in negative statements.

> The nights are nearly *as* long *as* the days this time of the year.
> The nights are not *so* long *as* the days in summer in the arctic.

So + an operator can introduce a shortened clause. (see **Operators**)

> Julia can learn to drive a truck, and *so* can Martha.
> If Julia can learn to drive a truck, *so* can Martha.

So can replace a noun clause beginning with *that* after verbs such as *believe, expect, fear, gather* (in the sense of understand), *hope, imagine, say, suppose,* and *think.*

$$\text{Do you} \begin{Bmatrix} \text{believe} \\ \text{expect} \\ \text{hope} \\ \text{suppose} \\ \text{think} \end{Bmatrix} \text{that it will rain today?}$$

$$\text{I (don't)} \begin{Bmatrix} \text{believe} \\ \text{expect} \\ \text{hope} \\ \text{suppose} \\ \text{think} \end{Bmatrix} so.$$

$$\text{I} \begin{Bmatrix} \text{believe} \\ \text{expect} \\ \text{hope} \\ \text{suppose} \\ \text{think} \end{Bmatrix} \text{not}$$

So far (time) means *up to now* or *up to a certain time.*

> *So far* Paul has had enough money.
> Linda has made good grades *so far.*

Spatial Order

Spatial order is the arrangement of objects and people in space (note the spelling of spa*t*ial). It is particularly important in writing description.

> *In front of* the library, *north of* the walk *leading to* the main door, stands a large oak tree with a bed of dark red flowers *around* its base.

(see **Prepositions, space and movement**)

Speech, direct, see **Direct speech**

Speech, indirect, see **Reported speech**

Spelling

English spelling is difficult and irregular, but some rules work almost all the time.

Adding Endings

Look at the last letter or letters in the base word before adding *-s* to make a noun plural or a simple verb into the third person singular, present tense. Add *-es* if the base word ends in

1. an *s* sound: *-ch, -s, -sh, -tch,* or *-x.*

chur*ch*, chur*ches*	ma*tch*, ma*tches*
lun*ch*, lun*ches*	hi*tch*, hi*tches*
bu*s*, bu*ses*	bo*x*, bo*xes*
fus*s*, fus*ses*	thora*x*, thora*xes* (also thoraces)
ga*s*, ga*ses*	so*x* is an alternate plural for sock, socks
ma*sh*, ma*shes*	
ru*sh*, ru*shes*	

NOTE: Many scientific words have several plural forms: *apex, apexes, apices.* (see **Nouns, foreign words**)

Most words ending in *-z* already have a double *z* at the end of the base word or double the *z* before adding *-es: fuzz, fuzzes; whiz, whizzes; quiz, quizzes*

2. *-o:* For words ending in *-o* add *-s* or *-es.* Most add *-s,* some are correct with either ending, and a few must have *-es.* Most dictionaries agree that the following words end in *-es.*

do, does	go, goes	potato, potatoes
echo, echoes	hero, heroes	tomato, tomatoes
embargo, embargoes	Negro, Negroes	torpedo, torpedoes
		veto, vetoes

NOTE: Words relating to music (*alto, piano, solo, trio*) and words in which a vowel comes before the *-o* (bamboo, patio, stereo, zoo) never add *-es.*

3. *-y:* when a consonant comes before a final *y,* change the *y* to *i* and add *-es.*

CONSONANT BEFORE *-y*		VOWEL BEFORE *-y*
berr*y*, berr*ies*	tr*y*, tr*ies*	pa*y*, pa*ys*
bur*y*, bur*ies*	satisf*y*, satisf*ies*	bu*y*, bu*ys*

NOTE: This rule applies to other endings except those beginning in *-i* and to proper names. Drop the *y* before *-ize.*

-ize

bury, buries,
   buried, burying
study, studies,
   studied, studying
try, tries, tried,
   trying

beauty, beautiful
friendly, friendlier,
   friendliest,
   friendliness
happy, happier,
   happiest,
   happiness
lucky, luckily

agony, agonize
harmony, harmonize
sympathy,
   sympathize

PROPER NAMES
Kelly, Kellys
Murphy, Murphys
Bundy, Bundys

SOME IRREGULAR FORMS

pay, paid, paying
say, said, saying
shy, shyly, shyer or shier
lady, ladyship, ladylike

day, days, daily
dry, drier, dryness
wry, wryness
busyness (state of being busy)

Doubling the Final Consonant

When the last letter of a word is a consonant, *double* it if you are adding
-ed, -er, -est, -ing, and *-ish* and if (1) it is a single consonant, (2) it has
a single vowel before it, (3) it is the last letter of the word, (4) and the
word has one syllable or is accented on the last syllable.

ONE-SYLLABLE WORD	ACCENT ON LAST SYLLABLE OF BASE WORD
big, bigger, biggest	begín, begínner, begínning
hot, hotter, hottest	omít, omítted, omítting
pit, pitted, pitting	occúr, occúrred, occúrring
win, winner, winning	refér, reférred, but réference (accent changes to first syllable) and referée (accent on last syllable)

fit, fitted, fitting, but bénefit, bénefited (accent on first syllable)

smart, smarter, smartest (two consonants together at end of words—do
   not double either consonant)

fast, faster, fastest

clean, cleaner, cleanest (two vowels come before the final consonant—do
   not double the consonant)

soon, sooner, soonest

man, mannish, but manly (ending is *-ly*—do not double final consonant)

Words Ending in One Final -e

Drop a single, final *-e* before endings beginning with a vowel. (Final *-e*
usually shows that the vowel sound in the last syllable is "long"—that is,
the vowel "sounds its name" in English. No final *-e* usually means that
the vowel sound in the last syllable is not the sound of the name of the
letter in English. Note the differences in pronunciation of the words listed
below.)

WORDS WITHOUT FINAL -*e*—DOUBLE FINAL CONSONANT	WORDS WITH FINAL -*e*—DROP -*e* BEFORE ADDING ENDING
ho*p*, hop*ped*, hop*ping*	ho*pe*, hop*ed*, hop*ing*
wi*n*, win*ner*, win*ning*	wi*ne*, win*ed*, win*ing*
si*t*, sit*ter*, sit*ting*	si*te*, sit*ed*, sit*ing*
fa*t*, fat*ter*, fat*test*	fa*te*, fat*ed*
ma*t*, mat*ted*, mat*ting*	ma*te*, mat*ed*, mat*ing*

NOTE: *mow, mower,* mow*ing* and who*le,* who*lly. Changeable* and *singeing* keep the final -*e* because of pronunciation, but in the United States the *e* is dropped in *acknowledg*ment and *judg*ment. Words in -*ye* keep the -*e* before -*ing:* d*ye,* dy*eing;* e*ye,* ey*eing.*

Learn this rhyme to decide whether to use *ie* or *ei:*

	EXAMPLES
I before *e*	achi*e*ve, beli*e*ve, vi*e*w, fri*e*nd, fi*e*ld, reli*e*f, si*e*ge, thi*e*f
Except after *c*	c*ei*ling, conc*ei*t, dec*ei*ve, perc*ei*ve, rec*ei*ve, rec*ei*pt
Or when sounded as *a*	*ei*ght, fr*ei*ght, r*ei*n, r*ei*gn, sl*ei*gh, v*ei*l, v*ei*n
As in n*ei*ghbor and w*ei*gh.	
	ADDITIONAL EXCEPTIONS
	caff*ei*ne, cod*ei*ne, consci*e*nce, count*er*f*ei*t, forf*ei*t, for*ei*gn, h*ei*fer, h*ei*r, pro-
*Ei*ther, n*ei*ther, l*ei*sure, s*ei*ze	t*ei*n, sover*ei*gn, w*ei*rd
Are exceptions; watch for these.	

NOTE: The rhyming rule does not apply to most words that end in -*r* or to words that have been formed by changing *y* to *i* before adding an ending:

cashi*er*, cavali*er*, fronti*er*, pi*er*, merri*er*, pretti*er*, and so on.

(See **Confusing choices** for words that are often confused and misspelled; **Nouns** for irregular plurals in -*ves*, old plural forms, singular forms with plural meanings, and foreign plurals; **Punctuation, apostrophe** for spelling of possessives; and see also **Contractions, Syllable division,** and **Word formation**)

Homonyms are words that sound alike but are spelled differently and have different meanings. The English language has many homonyms. Using the same-sounding word in different meanings to make a joke or to get attention is common in English. A joke or riddle that depends on words that sound the same is called a *pun.*

Puns

What is black and white and red (read) all over? A newspaper.
What ingredients do newlyweds like in salads? Lettuce alone. (Let us alone.)

Some of the words in the following list are not pronounced exactly alike by native speakers of English, but they are close enough in pronunciation to confuse you. Sometimes it is difficult to tell whether you are hearing one word or two words. In rapid speech most people pronounce pairs such as *meter* and *meet her* very nearly the same. Contractions also often sound very much like other words.

let's and *lets*   *he'll* and *heel*
it's and *its*   *he'd* and *heed*
I'll and *isle* or *aisle*   *we'd* and *weed*

Some Homonyms and Near Homonyms

accept, except
a choir, acquire
a rest, arrest
ate, eight
a way, away, aweigh

bail, bale
bare, bear
be, bee
beat, beet
blew, blue
bough, bow

cede, seed
choir, quire
chorale, corral
cite, sight, site
clothes, close
council, counsel

eyes, *i*'s

fair, fare
faze, phase
feat, feet
flea, flee
for, four
foreward, forward
freeze, frieze
friar, fryer

grate, great
guise, guys

hail, hale
hair, hare
hear, here
higher, hire
hole, whole
hue, hew

knead, need
knew, new
knight, night
knot, not
know, no

ladder, latter
lead, led
load, lode
loan, lone
lo, low

made, maid
mail, male
meat, meet, mete
medal, metal, meddle
might, mite

one, won
our, hour

pail, pale
pair, pare, pear
pause, paws
peace, piece

peak, peek
pedal, petal, peddle
pleas, please

rain, reign, rein
read, red
read, reed
real, reel
right, rite, write
ring, wring
road, rode
roe, row

sail, sale
scene, seen
seam, seem
seas, sees, seize
sew, so
sighs, size
steal, steel
suite, sweet

tail, tale
there, there, they're
threw, through
to, too, two
toe, tow

wait, weight
way, weigh
who's, whose
wood, would

Statement _____

A statement is a declarative sentence. It is not a question, command, or exclamation. A *positive statement* is made without negatives such as *no, not, never,* and *none*. A *negative statement* has negative words in it that show denial, disagreement, differences, or opposition. (see **Negation**)

Stative Verbs _____

Some verbs are not usually used in the continuous/progressive forms in certain meanings, especially when these verbs have a meaning of knowledge, of sense perception, or of emotion. When these verbs show a state or condition rather than an activity or an event they can be called *stative*.

Knowledge and Mental Activity

When you use verbs that show knowledge, they are often followed by a noun clause beginning with *that*.

believe (that)	guess (that)	remember to,
doubt (that)	imagine (that)	remember (that)
feel (that)	know (how to)	think (that)
forget to,	recognize (that)	understand (that)
forget (that)		want to

Do not use stative verbs in the continuous/progressive forms except in special meanings.

> Dr. Hanson *believes* (that) his diagnosis is correct. (not *is believing*)
> Paul *imagines* (that) she will be a great actress someday. (not *is imagining*)
> Paula *imagines* herself to be more beautiful than she is. (not *is imagining*)
> John *wants* a cup of coffee. (not *is wanting*)
> Sometimes Dan *forgets* (that) he has to put gas in his car. (not *is forgetting*)
> Martha *understands* my problems. (not *is understanding*)
> Pat *feels* the cold air blowing on him. (not *is feeling*)
> > **but**
> Pat had a cold last week, but he *is feeling* better now. (change in physical condition)
> I *doubt* the truth of that statement. (not *am doubting*)
> I *know* how to drive. (not *am knowing*)
> Ed *knows* tennis. (not *is knowing*)
> We *know* (are acquainted with) our neighbors. (not *are knowing*)
> Our dog *knows* when she has disobeyed. (not *is knowing*)

Sometimes these verbs are used with *always* in the continuous/progressive forms in an unfavorable meaning: "You do this all the time, but especially now, and it is a bad thing to do."

> Paula *is always imagining* herself to be more beautiful than she is.
> Dan *is always forgetting* to put gas in his car.
> They *are always doubting* that their team will win.

NOTE: *Remember* and *forget* can be followed by either the infinitive or *-ing* form, but the meaning of the forms is different. (see **Infinitive/-ing choice**)

An *-ing* form after *forget* or *remember* shows an action or situation happening *before* the action of the main verb.

> Martha *remembers* faint*ing*.
> I had *forgotten* asking you to come to the office today. (that I asked you)

An infinitive form after *forget* means that the action did not happen.

> I *forgot to ask* you to come today.
> We *forgot to bring* our books.
> Dan often *forgets to put* gas in the car.

An infinitive form after *remember* means that the action of the infinitive takes place *after* the action of the main verb.

> I *will remember to come* today.
> Martha *remembers to be* more careful now.
> Please *remember to bring* your books.
> Dan *will remember to put* gas in the car tomorrow.
> Penny *remembered to buy* bread yesterday.

Sense Perception

Verbs of the senses are not usually used in the continuous/progressive forms except for special emphasis on the duration of the activity.

hear	see	sound
notice	smell	taste

> Tom is deaf; he does not *hear* well.
> An eagle *sees* small animals from far above the ground.
> The rotten meat *smells* bad.
> Your plans *sound* interesting.
> My music teacher *notices* every mistake.

> **but**

> The coach *was noticing* how the swimmers were making their turns during practice this afternoon.

Condition Rather Than Event

Some other verbs are not used in the continuous progressive forms when they mean that the subject is in a state or condition instead of showing that an activity is taking place during a limited time. The following list gives examples of verbs that can be used in stative meanings.

appear (meaning *seem*)	equal	need
	fit	owe
be	have (meaning	own
belong to	*possess*)	please
cast	include	possess
consist of	involve	resemble
contain	lack	seem
depend on	matter	tend
deserve		

STATIVE USES

The brothers *resemble* each other.
New shoes *please* small children.
My cousin *owes* me twenty dollars.
The Parkers *own* a house in the city.
We do not always get what we *deserve*.
Wilma *has* many friends.
This experiment *seems* easy.
Our lives *are* not always what they *appear* to be.
Two and two *equals* four.

VERB	STATE OR CONDITION	ACTIVITY OF LIMITED DURATION
be	Tom *is* tall.	Tom *is being* difficult.
involve	The problem *involves* three steps.	Our present difficulties *are involving* several people.
fit	The coat *fits* well.	The tailor is *fitting the coat.*
depend on	Our plans *depend on* the weather.	I *am depending on* your help to finish the project.

Past and Perfect Tenses

The examples above are all in the present tense. Verbs in stative meanings can be used in the past and perfect tenses.

We *believed* what they told us. (not *were believing*)
John *wanted* a cup of coffee. (not *was wanting*)
I *doubted* the truth of his statement. (not *was doubting*)
Charles *needed* to buy a new coat. (not *was needing*)
My brother *has owed* me twenty dollars for a month. (not *has been owing*)
Dorothy *lacked* the money to buy a new car. (not *was lacking*)

Stems, see **Word formation, roots**

Style _____

Style means the overall effect of your writing. The effect depends on your choice of words and grammatical structures since several ways to say the same thing are always possible. Look up words in a dictionary to see whether or not they are standard English. Dictionaries written for students who are studying English as a second language give more exact labels for words than dictionaries for native English speakers give. (see **Usage labels**)

Most academic writing is in a style called standard English or standard edited English. *Edited* shows that the style is for writing, not for speaking. Standard edited English is closely related to spoken English, but it is different in some important ways.

Follow the rules of written English. Do not try to imitate speech exactly in compositions, reports, and business letters.

1. Do not use contractions unless you are reporting dialogue. (see **Contractions** and **Dialogue**)

2. Do not use most abbreviations or short forms of words. Use *examination* instead of *exam*, for example. Some abbreviations are acceptable: a.m., p.m., and o'clock. (see **Abbreviations**)

3. Use the pronoun form that is grammatically correct in formal writing. Use the pronouns *whom, me, him, her,* and *them* in every place that grammar requires an object form even though the subject form is often used in speech. (see **Pronouns** and **Case**)

INFORMAL:	Mrs. Castleberry is a teacher *who* we all respect.
FORMAL:	Mrs. Castleberry is a teacher *whom* we all respect.

direct
object

INCORRECT:	My landlord invited Tom and *I* to go with him to the mountains.
CORRECT:	My landlord invited Tom and *me* to go with him to the mountains.
INCORRECT:	If you leave now, it will be too early for Susan

object of
preposition

and   *I*   to go with you.

CORRECT:	If you leave now, it will be too early for Susan and *me* to go with you.

Use the pronouns *who, I, he, she,* and *they* in every place that grammar requires a subject form.

	<div align="center">*after* *than*</div>
INFORMAL:	Paul's brother is older than *him.*
FORMAL:	Paul's brother is older than *he* (is).
	<div align="center">*predicate* *nominative*</div>
INFORMAL:	Who is it? It's *him.*
FORMAL:	Who is it? It's Arthur. (Many people think that *it's I, she, he,* or *they* sounds pompous and avoid using them.)
	<div align="center">*subject*</div>
INCORRECT:	Ray and *me* are leaving tomorrow.
CORRECT:	Ray and *I* are leaving tomorrow.

4. Choose words that are precise. Use a single verb with one precise meaning instead of a two-word verb that can have several different meanings.

blow up	can mean	explode
		cause to explode or destroy
		inflate
		cause to inflate
		enlarge (a photograph, an investigation)
		show anger
		come (a storm)

In some of its meanings, *blow up* is more vivid than any other way to say the same thing.

The bridge was *blown up.* (*Blown up* is more direct and vivid than *destroyed by an explosion.*)

A storm *blew up.* (*Blew up* gives a more vivid idea of the wind than *came up* does.)

The old man *blew up* when his neighbor's chickens got into his garden. (*Showed great anger* would be less vivid.)

In some meanings of *blow up,* a more precise word can be used.

The dynamite *exploded.*
When Sharon saw that her tires were low, she *inflated* them.

show up	can mean	appear or cause to appear
		arrive
		make visible or clear

Use a more precise word in place of *show up* if possible.

> The guests *arrived* (showed up) late for the party.
>
> When the rash *appeared* (showed up), the doctor knew the baby had measles.
>
> Bright light *showed up* the difference in the color of paint on the two walls. (*Made visible* would be longer than *showed up* and would be awkward if separated with *visible* at the end of the sentence.)

In formal writing, use a one-word verb of Latin origin instead of a two-word verb if you want to avoid an informal tone. Too many words that come from Latin may make your writing overblown and pompous, however. Choosing the best word from among several possibilities that seem to have the same meaning is difficult even for experienced writers. The more you read and write and notice the connotation of words, the easier choosing suitable words will become. (see **Connotation** and **Two-word verbs**)

TWO-WORD VERBS	ONE-WORD VERBS
carry on	continue
find out	discover
keep on	persevere
put up (with)	endure
take back	accept as a return
	return
	recant
	withdraw
	reinstate (in a position)

5. Condense or reduce some long sentence structures into shorter ones. Be careful not to put so much content into one sentence, however, that you write run-on sentences with comma splices. (If you need a second semicolon, your sentence is probably too complicated.) (see **Sentence structure** and **Wordiness**)

6. Write sentences of different lengths and structures (see **Sentence variety**)

7. Use the subjunctive form of the verb where it is needed. (see **Subjunctive**, **Conditional sentences**, and **Contrary-to-fact statements**)

Except for fiction writers and dramatists, who try to reproduce speech, nearly all serious writers follow the rules given above. After following these rules, however, academic, scientific and technical, and business writers follow somewhat different styles.

Academic Writing (Humanities)

1. Avoid using the first person (I, me, my, and mine) unless you are told to use it. (see **Point of view**)

2. Avoid using the passive voice of the verb if you can. For acceptable uses, see **Passive verbs**.

Scientific and Technical Writing

1. Use the passive voice in an impersonal style when the discovery, experiment, or result is more important than the person involved.

In a biography of Madame Curie, make the *Curies* the subject.

> After the Curies extracted radium from pitchblende, several years passed before they became concerned about its effects on the people who were using it.

In a scientific paper, put the emphasis on the experiment.

> Radium had been used in science, industry, and medicine for some years before its dangers began to be understood.

Today some editors of scientific and technical journals prefer a style that avoids the passive and uses the personal *I* or *we* to report the results of experiments.

PASSIVE:	After several weeks the rabbits were observed to be losing their fur.
ACTIVE:	After several weeks *I* (*we* if more than one researcher is involved) observed loss of fur in the rabbits.

2. Use *will* + verb or the present tense to state a natural law or usual result.

> Ice *will* form from water at 0°C.
> Ice *forms* from water at 0°C.
> When you stand in front of the car and open the hood, you *will see* the radiator at the front end, in front of the engine.

3. Use the command (imperative) form and the present tense in mathematics.

To change a common fraction to a decimal fraction, *divide* the numerator by the denominator. For example, ¾ *is* 0.75 (3 ÷ 4) expressed as a decimal fraction.

NOTE: Stated problems are problems told as a story and can use other tenses.

4. Write instructions using commands (imperative verbs). Keep all verbs in the form of commands if possible. Do not mix commands and statements unless you have a clear reason to do so. (see **Process**)

To Apply This Paint

Unpainted Surfaces: Apply primer. Then *apply* one or two coats by brush or roller.

Old Surfaces: Prepare by scraping off loose paint, tearing off or pasting down loose wallpaper, and filling nailholes. *Prime* patched areas. *Sand* unpainted woodwork. *Sand* or *wash* painted woodwork with a strong cleanser and rinse before applying this paint.

Do not paint in temperatures below 50°F. *Thin* with water if necessary. *Clean up* with soap and hot water if necessary.

Business Writing

Business writing is done for a customer, someone outside the company in government or business, or someone else in the same company. The letter, proposal, report, or memo must please the person who gets it. Letters to customers are more personal than academic writing, but reports and proposals are similar in tone to academic and scientific writing.

Business Letters

1. Use personal pronouns, especially *I, we,* and *you,* when suitable. If you use *I,* you show your personal opinion. If you use *we,* you speak for the company.

2. Use familiar and short words rather than difficult ones if their meaning is exact. Avoid foreign phrases.

Use *eat* instead of *ingest.*
Use *pay* instead of *remuneration.*
Use *plan* instead of *intention.*
Use *genuine* instead of *bona fide.*

3. Although you should use short and familiar words, use specific words instead of general ones.

Use *receive* for *get.*
Use *pour* for *put in.*
Use *forecast* or *report* for *tell about.*

4. Avoid the passive voice unless you have a reason to use it. (For acceptable uses, see **Passive verbs.**)

5. Follow the format your company uses for business letters. Most companies today follow a block letter format (you do not indent anywhere in the letter).

Full Block Format

(Put return address here if you are not using letterhead stationery.)
September 24, 198–

2 spaces

Mr. James Pierce
691 Allentown Drive
Atlanta, Georgia 30307

2 spaces

Dear Mr. Pierce:

2 spaces

XXXXXXXXXXXXXXXXXXXXXXXXXXXXXXXXXXXXXXX
XXXXXXXXXXXXXXXXXXXXXXXXXXXXXXXXXXXXXXX
XXXXXXXXXXXXXXX.

2 spaces

XXXXXXXXXXXXXXXXXXXXXXXXXXXXXXXXXXXXXXX
XXXXXXXXXXXXXXXXXXXXXXXXXXXXXXXXXXXX
XXXXXXXXXXXXXXXXXXXXXXXXXXXXXX
XXXXXXXXXXXXXXXXXXXXXXXXXXXXXXXXXXXXXXX
XXXXXXXXXXX.

2 spaces

Sincerely,

4 spaces

Susan C. Liles

2 spaces

SCL/gwp (if necessary)

2 spaces

Enclosures (2) (if necessary)

2 spaces

c: Anna Padmore (if necessary)

SCL/gwp shows the initials of the writer and the initials of the typist. Use your own initials to identify yourself when you type a letter for someone else.

Enclosures means that something besides the letter is included and should be in the same envelope. The number shows how many different documents are enclosed.

c or *cc:* means that a copy or copies of this letter are being sent to another person or persons who are named.

In a *modified block* format, indent at the beginning of each paragraph. If the letter is not written on letterhead stationery (paper on which the name of the company or organization is already printed), you must also put the return address of your own organization or company. Put the return address before the date, and do not double-space between the return address and the date. In block style, put the return address and date at the left-hand margin as shown in the letter above; in a modified block style, sometimes the return address and date are put to the right of center of the page.

Subject, Grammatical _____

The grammatical subject of a clause is the noun or pronoun that is most closely associated with the meaning of the verb. Clauses can be divided into two parts: one is the noun (with all its modifiers) or the pronoun that is the subject; the other part is the predicate, made up of the main (finite) verb, complements, if there are any, and adverb modifiers, if there are any. (see **Sentence patterns**)

A command (imperative) does not state a subject. We understand that the subject of a command is *you.*

(You) Shut the door now, please.
(You) Put the books on the table.

Subject of a Composition _____

The subject of a composition is what you are writing about. Usually you have to *limit* your subject so that you can discuss one part of it fully. You cannot write well about a subject that is too *broad* (general). Sometimes *topic* is used to mean *subject.* (see **Abstract and concrete, Generalization, Thesis statement,** and **Topic, meanings of**)

Subjunctive _____

The subjunctive is rarely used in spoken English except in a few set phrases such as *if I were you* and *as it were*. Most of the meanings that are shown in other languages by the subjunctive are shown in English by the modals, by *should* (especially by British speakers), and by other constructions shown in the table. Subjunctive forms express *nonfact*: actions or states that *can, may, might, should,* but not necessarily *do* happen or *have* happened. (see **Modals**) Subjunctive forms also express actions or contrary-to-fact or impossible states. (See **Conditional sentences** for forms after *if.*)

Use the simple verb form (bare infinitive) after verbs that suggest or request or use one of the other constructions given in the table below.

subjunctive

It is *recommended that* our chairman   *be*   given a vote of thanks.

subjunctive

Robert's employer *suggested that* he   *transfer*   to another division.

or with a modal

modal

Robert's employer *suggested that* he *should transfer* to another division.

or

noun

Robert's employer *suggested* a *transfer* for him.

subjunctive

The report *urged that* the company   *hire*   another accountant.

or, less formal

infinitive

The report urged the company   *to hire*   another accountant.

Use the past subjunctive (the same form as the plural past tense) after *wish.*

I *wish* I *had* more help. (I wish I *could have* more help.)
The children *wish* they *visited* the zoo every day.

Use the past perfect form of the verb to show actual past time after *wish.*

The children *wish* they *had visited* the zoo last week.
Joan *wishes* she *had had* more time to clean her apartment yesterday.

Style

The subjunctive is often very formal. It is used in legal documents, parliamentary proceedings, and bureaucratic communications. Use a simpler construction if you can. (Some writers use this construction with the present indicative—he/she/it come*s*.)

Common Verbs That Can Be Followed by the Subjunctive

VERB	WITH SUBJUNCTIVE	WITH ANOTHER CONSTRUCTION
advise	advise that she come	advise her to come her coming
ask (only in the sense of *request*)	ask that she come	her to come
demand	demand that he come	
desire	desire that he come	desire him to come his coming
forbid	forbid that he come	forbid him to come his coming
insist	insist that she come	insist on her coming
prefer	prefer that she come	prefer her to come her coming (to her going)
plan	plan that she come	plan for her to come her coming
propose	propose that he come	propose his coming
recommend	recommend that he come	recommend him to come his coming
request	request that he come	request him to come his coming
require	require that he come	require him to come his coming
suggest	suggest that she come	suggest her to come her coming
urge	urge that she come	urge her to come her coming

It is + past participles of the verbs above + *that* clause requires the subjunctive.

It is $\begin{matrix} \text{required} \\ \text{suggested} \end{matrix}$ that he come.

It is $\begin{matrix} \text{recommended} \\ \text{necessary} \end{matrix}$ that she come.

In the "other constructions" listed above, the emphasis may be different from the emphasis when the subjunctive is used. The personal object is emphasized before an infinitive phrase.

We recommend that Joan come.

We $\begin{matrix} \text{recommend} \\ \text{suggest} \end{matrix}$ Joan to come. (emphasis on *Joan* instead of someone else)

Subordinating and Reducing _____

Subordination means putting less important ideas in less important grammatical structures. Put the most important idea in a sentence in the subject and verb of the main clause. Put less important ideas in single-word modifiers, in modifying phrases, and in dependent clauses. (see **Clauses** and **Modifiers**)

Embedded clauses are ideas that could be put in separate clauses, but that are put in subordinate grammatical structures. Sometimes putting several ideas together into one sentence is called *sentence combining* or *reducing*. (see **Wordiness**)

> Cynthia won the hundred-yard dash.
> Cynthia was almost late for the start of the race.

Which idea is more important? Put that idea in the independent clause.

> *dependent clause*
> Although Cynthia was almost late for the start of the race,
>
> *independent clause*
> she won the hundred-yard dash.

The sentence above can be reduced even more.

> *dependent participial phrase*   *independent clause*
> Although almost late for the start, Cynthia won the hundred-yard dash.

By choosing which idea is most important and leaving out all unnecessary words, you will write effective, focused sentences.

> The security guard who was watching the parking lot saw a thief who was breaking into my car.
> The security guard caught the thief.

Which idea is more important? How can the number of words be reduced?

> The security guard watching the parking lot caught the thief breaking into my car.

Reduce an independent clause to a dependent clause, to a phrase or to a single word, if possible.

> *independent clause*
> Frank was studying for a history examination.
>
> *independent clause*   *dependent clause*
> His roommate was annoying him because he was making so much noise.

1. Replace the dependent clause with one word: *noisy*.
2. Subordinate one of the independent clauses.

dependent clause
While Frank was studying for a history examination,

independent clause
his noisy roommate annoyed him.

or

participial phrase
Studying for a history examination,

independent clause
Frank found his roommate's noise very annoying.

Reduce a dependent adjective clause to a phrase or to a single word. (see **Clauses, adjective**)

dependent adjective clause
Frank's book *that was found in the student center yesterday* had been lost for two weeks.

participial phrase
Frank's book *found in the student center yesterday* had been lost for two weeks.

If the past participle is commonly used as an adjective and if it has no modifiers, you can put it before the noun. You cannot put *found* in the sentence above before *book* because it is not used as an adjective and it has modifiers that cannot move. A past participle like *tired* can come before a noun. (see **Participles used as adjectives**)

The children who were *tired* sat on the grass waiting for the bus.
The *tired* children sat on the grass waiting for the bus.

Sometimes both a participle and modifiers can move to a place before the subject of the clause.

dependent adjective clause
The drivers *who were waiting behind the accident* grew impatient.

The dependent clause can become a prepositional phrase and an adjective:

prepositional phrase   adjective
Behind the accident the *waiting* drivers grew impatient.

The dependent clause can become a participial phrase:

participial phrase
Waiting behind the accident, the drivers grew impatient.

Sometimes a single-word synonym can replace a clause or a phrase.

dependent adjective clause
The children *who were watching carefully* crossed the street safely.

adjective
The *alert* children crossed the street safely.

dependent adverb clause

The children crossed the street safely *because they were careful.*

adjective

The *careful* children crossed the street safely.

(Although *careful* is not explicitly stated as the *cause* of safe crossing in the second sentence, it is a reasonable implication that carefulness results in safety.)

Reduce by leaving out a repeated verb or by replacing it with an operator. (see **Operators**) Leave out a repeated verb after an operator that follows another verb.

Gerald has written as much as he *can write* tonight. (Leave out *write.*)
Gerald has written as much as he *can* tonight.

Charles is not working as hard as Bill *is working.* (Leave out the second *working.*)
Charles is not working as hard as Bill *is.*

Penny will do all the work that she *must do* before tomorrow. (Leave out the second *do.*)
Penny will do all the work that she *must* before tomorrow.

Reduce a predicate by replacing it with an operator after *so* and *as.* **Do not repeat complements after the main verb.** (see **Adjectives, comparison of**)

Penny works three hours every night, and *so does* Marcia. (Do not repeat *three hours every night.*)

The conduct of the election continues to puzzle experts as much as its results *do.* (*Do* replaces *continues* and *to puzzle experts* is not repeated.)

The results appear to be as indefinite as the last results *were.* (Put *were* in place of *appears to be* and leave out *indefinite.* Do not leave out *were; were* shows the change in tense.)

Leave out a repetition of the verb and complements in a second clause when they can be easily remembered from the first part of the sentence.

The traffic began to move as soon as the policeman signaled. (Do not repeat *to move* after *signaled.*)

Sometimes *do so* replaces part of the sentence, especially in formal writing.

The crowd began to leave as soon as the dean asked them to *do so.* (leave)
The children got ready to board the bus as soon as their teacher asked them to *do so.* (get ready to board the bus)
Fill out these forms. As soon as you *do so,* we can process your application. (*Do so* replaces a repetition of *fill out these forms.*)

Use the correct form of *do* as a substitute for the main verb in *do so* constructions.

> Marcia finish*ed* her work early, and *so did* Penny. (past tense replacing *finished*)
>
> Pat refused when John asked her to go to the game with him last night. If she had not *done so,* she could not have gone to meet her father at the airport. (if she had not *refused*—past participle)
>
> My mother has never learned *to play* the piano, but she hopes to *do so* soon. (infinitive replacing *to play the piano*)

Following *maybe* or *perhaps, so* by itself can mean agreement, and *not* by itself can mean disagreement.

> Perhaps   perhaps
> Will we be able to go to the lake this weekend? Maybe *so,* maybe *not.*

Substantiation

Substantiation is proof; it is the facts, illustrations, evidence, and examples to support a generalization. In writing, substantiation supports a thesis statement or a topic sentence. In an outline, substantiation is given by the points that support the main divisions and subdivisions. *Supporting detail* is another term for substantiation. (see **Generalization, Thesis statement,** and **Topic sentence**)

Substantiation is often introduced by a phrase such as *for example, to illustrate,* or *for instance.* Be sure to punctuate correctly. (see **Interrupters**)

Unless you are writing about absolute scientific evidence, use words such as *usually, rarely, seldom, hardly ever,* and *often.* Do not use *always* and *never* unless you can prove that your generalization is absolute (true in all instances).

Substitutions

Pronouns can take the place of nouns, other pronouns, and sometimes phrases and clauses. (see **Pronouns**)

Some adverbs can replace other expressions of time, place, and manner.

Then or *that* for time:

> Mary came *at ten o'clock* and Tom came *then,* too.
> *That* (time) was sooner than we had expected.

Here or *there* for place:

> Mary is visiting her home and her sister is *there* too.
> Mary has just come in the house and her sister is *here* too.

This way, the way, or *that way* for manner:

> Marie always looks carefully for bargains when she shops. That is *the way* to save money.

So and *thus* for manner in formal writing (see *So*):

> Walt Whitman wrote poetry filled with images, both literal and figurative. By writing *thus,* / By *so* doing, he appealed to romantic readers of the nineteenth century. (*Thus* and *so* replace *poetry filled with images, both literal and figurative.*)

Operators can take the place of other verbs in questions, in negative statements, in tag questions, and in shortened clauses after *so* and *as*. (see **Operators**)

Do so can replace parts of a sentence. (see **Subordinating and reducing**)

Suffixes, see **Word formation, suffixes**

Summary _____

A summary gives the main points of a speech, article, section, chapter, or book without giving the details. A summary does not attempt to keep the same style or tone as the original. The verb is *summarize*.

Names for other shortened versions of longer works are

> *Abridgement*—a shorter version of speech or writing, usually with some detail included.
> *Abstract*—the main points of a scholarly paper, a book, a speech, or of legal proceedings.
> *Condensation*—a shorter version of a piece of writing, an abridgement.
> *Plot summary*—a brief statement of the action in a short story, novel, play, or opera.
> *Précis*—the main points without supporting detail, keeping the tone and style of the original as much as possible.

Syllable Division _____

In writing, single words can be divided at the right-hand end of a line in order to make the lines even at the right-hand margin. Always divide words between syllables. Syllable division is based on pronunciation, but pronunciation does not always show where the division should be in writing. If you need to divide a word in two parts, put the hyphen after the first part of the word. Do not put a hyphen at the beginning of the following line. (see **Punctuation, hyphen**)

Look the word up in a dictionary to find out if it can be divided and, if so, where it can be divided. Most dictionaries use dots between syllables instead of hyphens. Dictionaries show hyphens only in words that must always have hyphens in them.

1. Never divide a word of one syllable.

five	bought	helped
sewed	strength	plague

2. Never divide a word of more than one syllable so that one letter stands alone on either line. In handwriting do not separate just two letters, especially *-er* and *-ed*.

bury	open	bony
awake	opal	army

3. Divide compound words between their parts.

down - stairs	house - keeper	hair - dresser
come - back	drum - beat	money - bag

4. Divide most words that contain consonants or consonant combinations that represent different sounds between the two consonants.

hol - low	cancel - lation	tac - tics
mid - dle	cab - bage	crys - tal

EXCEPTION: Never divide two different letters that stand for one sound.

nor*th* - ern	sym - *phony*	gra*ph* - ics
psy - *ch*ology	syn - *th*etic	ba*ch* - elor

5. Separate most prefixes and suffixes of three letters or more from the root of the word. (see **Word formation**)

dis - honest	comfort - *able*	confine - *ment*
sui - cide	number - *less*	thank - *ful*

EXCEPTION: When prefixes or suffixes result in a doubled consonant, the word is often divided between the doubled consonants following rule 4.

swim - ming	ad-mit - tance

Use rules 4 and 5 as guidelines when you do not have a dictionary at hand. Look up all doubtful words, as there are many exceptions and conflicting rules.

Synonyms _____

Synonyms are words with the same meaning. Not many exact synonyms exist, but many words have similar meanings. Be careful in using synonyms, because they may have different connotations even though they seem to have the same meaning according to a dictionary. Usage notes in dictionaries and grammar books can help you avoid mistakes. (see **Connotation** and **Usage labels**)

A *thesaurus* is a book of synonyms. Use a word from it only if you are sure you know the connotation and usage of the word you find.

T

Tag Questions

Tag questions are questions asking for agreement or disagreement at the end of a statement. Tag questions are negative after a positive statement, but they are positive after a negative statement. Tag questions are used in speech much more than they are used in writing. (see **Negation**)

POSITIVE	NEGATIVE
The mail has come today,	hasn't it?
It's raining,	isn't it?

NEGATIVE	POSITIVE
The mail hasn't come today,	has it?
It isn't raining,	is it?

Make tag questions with the operator if there is one in the first clause. Use *do, does,* or *did* if there is no operator. (see **Operators**)

Tense

Tense is the term used to show relationship between time and other conditions and the form of the verb. Not all changes in the verb form are directly related to time. The way the action is understood to take place also affects verb forms. In addition to showing time, different forms show conditions such as certainty, definiteness, possibility, and whether or not the action is completed. *Mood* and *aspect* are grammatical terms that show how the verb expresses ideas that go beyond yesterday/today/tomorrow divisions. (see **Mood** and **Aspect**) You do not need to know

333

all the grammatical terms to express yourself clearly, but you must learn the exact verb forms to use to express your ideas if you want your readers to understand your writing.

Most of the conjugations in this section are with *walk*, an intransitive verb that does not need a complement. Sometimes another verb must be used to illustrate differences in meaning. For a complete conjugation of *to be*, see **Be**. See **Voice** for examples of transitive verbs in active and passive forms. Passive forms are not shown in this section.

Although contractions are common in speech, avoid them in formal writing. See **Contractions** for contracted forms if you need to use them in direct quotations.

The Present Tense

Add -*s* to make the third person singular. Remembering to add -*s* in the present tense is very important in academic and technical writing, since a large part of it is done in the present tense.

Walk

SINGULAR	PLURAL
I walk	we walk
you walk	you walk
he, she, it walk*s*	they walk

The present tense can be used in several ways. It does not always show what is happening *now*, as you would think from its name. (The present continuous/progressive tense more often shows what is actually happening now; see below.)

1. Use the present tense to show present state or condition, particularly with stative verbs. (see **Stative verbs**)

ADVERBS:	
now	Ben *is* hungry.
at this time/moment	I *believe* (that) you are right.
today	That cake *smells* good.
tonight	Do you *realize* what you are saying?
this minute/morning	Harold *lives* in Rome now.
noon/evening	Caroline *attends* college in Canada.

2. Use the present tense to show an eternal truth or natural law.

ADVERBS:	
always/never	The moon *affects* the tides.
inevitably	Man *proposes* but God *disposes*.
without fail	Parallel lines never *meet*.
at all times	Hydrogen and oxygen *combine* to make water.
invariably	Subjects and verbs *agree* in number.
	Hot air *rises*.

3. Use the present tense to show habitual action—repetition or non-repetition of the same act.

ADVERBS:

always/never	Beverly *drinks* coffee every morning.
usually/seldom	We always *celebrate* my birthday with a family party.
sometimes	
rarely	The Browns *do* not *wash* their windows every week.
not ever	
occasionally	The Andersons *plant* tomatoes every year.
often/not often	Sometimes we *go* to a soccer game on Sunday afternoon.
every	
each	

4. Use the present tense to show the historical present in criticism to discuss writing, drama, music, and art, and in research that quotes or paraphrases what other people have said or written in the past.

ADVERBS OF VALUE JUDGMENT RATHER THAN TIME—A FEW OF MANY POSSIBILITIES
skillfully, cleverly
(in)correctly
clumsily, brilliantly
well, poorly,
(in)adequately,
properly, rightly,
wrongly

In the short story "The Lottery," Shirley Jackson *writes* an allegory of the injustices of life.
Darwin *presents* evidence for the development of life from lower to higher forms.
Looking at all the evidence, one agrees with the critic who *calls* the play a success.
The author of this textbook *explains* the problems clearly.

5. Use the present tense for definitions and explanations.

ADVERBS:
always/never
then
next
after that

Gross National Product *means* the total value of all goods produced and services performed in one country in one year.
The screw *is* inserted in the lower right-hand corner of the frame.
Plate B *replaces* Plate A in the old model, as shown in Diagram 2.

6. Use the present tense to show future possibility in conditional and time clauses (see below under "sequence of Tenses").

Uncle Robert will give you fifty dollars *if* he *likes* your work. (condition)
Uncle Robert will give you fifty dollars *when* he *sees* you. (time)

7. Use the present tense to show future events that are considered certain to happen.

The plane *leaves* at 9:25 tonight.
The term *is* over on December 16.

The Present Perfect Tense

Make the present perfect tense from *have* (*has* in the third person singular) + past participle (*-ed* form) of the main verb. (See **Verbs, irregular** for irregular past participles.)

Walk

SINGULAR	PLURAL
I have walked	we have walked
you have walked	you have walked
he, she, it has walked	they have walked

The present perfect tense usually shows an action that began in the past and goes on to the present or to an indefinite time closely related to the present.

1. Use the present perfect tense to show an action that began in the past and is still going on.

Do not use *ago* with any meanings.

ADVERBS:
for + period of time
since + specific date or time
in or during the last or past hour, day, week, month, year, decade, century
yet, so far
up to now

Shirley *has lived* in Chicago for six years. (still living in Chicago)

They *have waited* since ten o'clock. (still waiting)

During the last century, many people *have moved* from rural to urban areas. (the movement continues)

I *have* not *finished* that problem yet. (still unfinished)

2. Use the present perfect tense to show an action that began in the past and was finished at an indefinite time but is closely related to the present and/or future.

ADVERBS:
already, not yet
early, late, just
this minute, today
this month/year
recently, lately

I *have* already *finished* those exercises.

You *have been* absent a great deal lately. (I expect that you will be absent again.)

The players *have come* early.

The players *have* just *arrived*.

Paul *has rebuilt* the engine of his car. (Although the project is finished, he is capable of doing the work again.)

They *have* recently *announced* their engagement. (They are still engaged.)

The Present Continuous/Progressive Tense

Make the present continuous from the present tense of *to be* and the *-ing* form of the main verb (present participle). (see *Be*)

Walk

SINGULAR	PLURAL
I am walking	we are walking
you are walking	you are walking
he, she, it is walking	they are walking

NOTE: Many verbs do not occur in the continuous forms in their usual meanings. (see **Stative verbs**)

A meaning similar to that of the continuous/progressive tense can be made with *keep on* or *go on* + *-ing* form.

He *keeps on* walking.   He *goes on* walking.
She *keeps on* talking.   She *goes on* talking.

The present continuous/progressive tense shows action as a process that is incomplete now but will end. With an adverb of frequency the continuous can show habitual action and in certain situations it can show future action.

1. Use the present continuous/progressive tense to show action as a process that is going on now.

ADVERBS:	
now, today	Our dog *is chasing* your cat.
this minute, this	The children *are playing* outside.
month, this year	It *is raining/snowing/sleeting*.
at the moment	This winter we *are seeing* a weather pattern that is different from last year's pattern.

2. Use the present continuous/progressive tense to show habitual action, often with the idea of showing dislike or disapproval.

ADVERBS:	
always, usually	The dog *is* usually *chasing* the cat.
most of the time	They *are* always *asking* for special favors.
more often than not	That little girl *is* always *biting* her fingernails.
	Tracy *is* always *eating* too much.

3. Use the present continuous/progressive tense to show future action that you are looking forward to now.

ADVERBS:	
Use an adverb of the	My father and mother *are arriving* from New
future appropriate to	York at 2:15 tomorrow afternoon.
the time the event will	A storm *is coming* tonight.
take place, such as this	They *are going* to a concert tomorrow night.
afternoon, tonight,	We *are repeating* the experiment next month.
tomorrow, next week,	
soon, next month.	

The Present Perfect Continuous Tense

Make the present perfect continuous from the present tense of *have* + *been* + *-ing* (present participle) form of the main verb.

Walk

SINGULAR	PLURAL
I have been walking	we have been walking
you have been walking	you have been walking
he, she, it has been walking	they have been walking

Be sure to keep subject-verb agreement correct by using *has* in the third person singular.

The present perfect continuous shows incompleteness or indefiniteness very close to the present time, often contrasted with *now*. *Just* shows that the activity is very recent.

ADVERBS:
just
just now
recently

He *has been washing* his car, but he isn't now.
She *has been feeling* ill, but she feels better now.
Our car *has been giving* us trouble recently, but it is running better now.
He *has been looking* everywhere for you, and he still is.
She *has* just *been asking* about you.

The Past Tense (sometimes called the simple past)

Make the past tense in regular verbs by adding *-ed* to the simple present. (See *Be* and **Verbs, irregular** for their past forms.)

I, you, he, she, it, we, they walked.

1. Use the past tense for events that happened at a specific time in the past. Use the past tense for a single event or for events that took place over a period of time if that period is finished. Phrases with *ago* (*two weeks ago, ten years ago, two thousand years ago*) can be used with all the past tenses. Do not use *already* with past tenses.

ADVERBS:
a minute, hour, day,
week, year, century
ago
for + period of time
at + specific time
in + specific year
on + day of week or
date, yesterday, in
the morning/evening
last week/month/year/
century
when . . .

Gerald *was* in Australia twenty years ago.
They *came* at 2:30 this afternoon.
Jean *started* kindergarten two weeks ago.
Winifred *came* here yesterday.
Tom and I *worked* in the same office for two years.
Last year the number of children in school in this city *increased* two percent.
When we *heard* about the eclipse, we *wanted* to see it.

Use the past tense as above to tell a story or to discuss history. (see **Chronological order** and **Narration**)

2. Use the past tense when changing from direct to reported speech if the verb in the dialogue guide is in the past (see **Reported speech** and "Sequences of Tenses" at the end of this section)

DIRECT QUOTATION:

present   *past*
"*Is*   Joyce at home?" Susan *asked*.

past   *present*
Francis *said*, "I *understand* this problem now."

REPORTED SPEECH:

past   *past*
Susan *asked* if Joyce *was* at home.
Francis *said* that she *understood* this problem.

3. Use the past tense after *if* to write about events that are not true or that are not likely to happen. Use *would* in the independent clause. (see **Conditional sentences**)

If Michael *ran* a red light, he *would* be to blame for the accident.
If Arthur *wore* a blue tie with that jacket, it *would* look better.
Unless a miracle *happened*, I *would* never make the honor roll.
If you *loved* me, you *would* not leave now.

The implication is that these events are not likely to happen.

NOTE: Using the past instead of the present makes a statement very tentative and polite. "I *wanted* to tell you about the problem" can mean "I *want* to . . . ."

The Past Perfect Tense

Make the past perfect tense with *had* + past participle of the main verb. (See **Verbs, irregular** for irregular past participles.)

I, you, he, she, it, we, they had walked.

The past perfect tense shows action in the past that happened before some other action in the past shown by a past tense verb.

ADVERBS:
already and all
adverbs that can be
used with the
past tense

past   *past perfect*
Before Karen *came* here, she *had studied* in Paris for two years.

past perfect   *past*
After Philip *had failed* twice, he finally *passed* his test for his driver's liecnse.

past   *past perfect*
When Philip *found* out that he *had failed* again,
past
he *gave* up.

If the meaning of "past before past" is clear from an adverb in the sentence, such as *before* and *after* in the sentences above or from the context, the past tense is often used for both verbs.

past   *past*
Before Karen *came* here, she *studied* in Paris for two years.

past   *past*
After Philip *failed* twice, he finally *passed* his test for his driver's license.

The Past Continuous Tense

Make the past continuous tense with the past tense of *be* (*was/were*) + *-ing* form (present participle) of the main verb.

Walk

SINGULAR	PLURAL
I was walking	we were walking
you were walking	you were walking
he, she, it was walking	they were walking

Use the past continuous tense to show the temporary duration or incompletion of an action in the past, particularly in contrast to a specific act shown in the past tense.

1. Use the past continuous tense to show duration, with emphasis on the length of time, of an act that is no longer going on.

ADVERBS: Betsy *was training* her horse *for five years.*
the same as for the   They *were waiting* to buy a house *for three years.*
past tense   We *were waiting* for my mother's plane to arrive *for six hours.*

2. Use the past continuous tense for an action in the past that was not completed in the time period mentioned.

I *was trying* to clean house last week. (I did not complete the cleaning.)
They *were looking* for an apartment yesterday. (They did not find one.)
We *were doing* a difficult experiment in the lab this morning. (We did not finish it.)

3. Use the past continuous tense for an action that was going on at a time in the past when something else happened.

James and I *were watching* television when lightning *struck* the house.

or

While James and I *were watching* television, lightning *struck* the house.

While means *during the time*. *While* often introduces the clause showing duration. *When* means *at that time*. *When* often introduces the clause showing the intervening action. Do not use both *while* and *when* in the same sentence. *After* or *before* can replace *when*.

> The driver of the car *was* not *paying* attention when he *ran* off the road.
> The cook *was* not *watching* the pot when the sauce *boiled* over.

The Past Perfect Continuous Tense

Use the past perfect continuous tense to show that an action in the remote past was temporary or that the time it lasted was important or that an action was going on when something else happened.

Walk

I, you, he, she, it, they had been walking.
No one knew that Mr. Allen had a wig because he *had been wearing* it secretly.
John *had been trying* to meet Mary for three months before he finally succeeded.
Jane *had been looking* for a new roommate for six weeks before she finally found one.
Women *had been demanding* the right to vote for many years before they finally got it.
The Chinese *had been using* gunpowder for centuries before its use was known in Europe.

The Future Tense

Make the future tense by using *will* or *shall* + the infinitive (simple present) form of the main verb.

Walk

I, you, he, she, it, we, they will walk

In the United States, *will* is commonly used in all forms of the future. In England, *shall* is used with *I* and *we*, but the usage is reversed in an emphatic statement. (I, we *will* and he, she, it, they, you *shall* are emphatic in this usage.) For other meanings of *will* and *shall* besides showing the future, see **Modals**.

Avoid the contracted *'ll* and *won't* form in formal writing. (see **Contractions**)

Other verb forms can also show the future.

Is Going to *as Future*

Use the present tense of *Be + going + to + base infinitive* (simple present) of the main verb to show the future.

> I *am going to walk* two miles every day.
> You (we, they) *are going to walk* two miles every day.
> He (she, it) *is going to walk* two miles every day.

The *is going to* future is more informal and wordy than the *will* future. Do not overuse it. Both the *will* and *is going to* futures can be used with both personal and inanimate subjects.

> The art class *will* visit the museum tomorrow.
> The art class *is going to* visit the museum tomorrow.
> The weather report predicts that *it will rain* tonight.
> The weather report predicts that it *is going to rain* tonight.

Three additional verb constructions can be used to show future events. Use these three constructions mainly with events, states, or statements that are subject to human control.

Present of Be + *Infinitive as Future*

(See *Be* for conjugation.)

> New students *are to register* at two o'clock this afternoon.
> Our dog *is to get* a rabies shot next week.

This construction shows obligation or regulation. It is similar in meaning to *have to.*

Present Tense as Future

You can use the present tense to show future events that are fixed or certain, whether personal or impersonal, after *if, unless,* and *whether* and after relative adverbs of time.

> If the price *is* reasonable, Steve will buy a new car.
> The sun *sets* at 6:05 this evening.
> Our train *leaves* at 9:07 a.m. tomorrow.
> The cost of first-class mail *increases* after January 1.
> When you *find* the answer to that problem, you can go.

The Present Continuous Tense as Future

The present continuous tense can show action that will happen in the future. (See the section above, "Present Tenses," for conjugation)

We *are having* dinner at seven this evening.
My parents *are coming* to visit me next month.
Our soccer team *is not playing* in the regional championship games this year.

The Future Perfect Tense

Make future perfect forms with *will* + *have* + past participle (*-ed* form) of the main verb. (See **Verbs, irregular** for irregular past participles.) English speakers in the United States use *will* in all persons. (See above, "Future Tense," for more about the *shall/will* distinction.)

Walk
I, you, he, she, it, we, they will have walked.

Use the future perfect to show an action that will be completed in the future.

ADVERBS:	This obedience school *will have trained* fifty dogs by the end of the year.
by phrase	
at that time	By the end of the winter season, more tourists *will have visited* the island than ever before.
(by) tomorrow	
(by) this afternoon	I left several letters unfinished on my desk, but I *will have finished* them before noon tomorrow.
(by) tonight	
(by) next week, month, year, specific time or date in the future, before . . .	

The Future Continuous Tense

Make the future with *will* + *be* + *-ing* form. (See "Future Tense" above for more about the *shall/will* distinction.)

Walk
I, you, he, she, it, we, they will be walking.

Use the future continuous to show duration, intention, or a temporary condition in the future.

I will mail that package for you since I *will be walking* by the post office this afternoon.
As long as we live next to you, our dog *will be chasing* your cat.
Sometimes I think I *will be studying* English the rest of my life.
Our salesman *will be calling* you soon to confirm your order.

The Future Perfect Continuous Tense

Make the future perfect continuous with *will* + *have* + *been* + past participle (*-ed* form) + *-ing* form. (See **Verbs, irregular** for irregular past participles and see "Future Tense" above for more about the *shall/will* distinction.)

Walk

I, you, he, she, it, we, they will have been walking.

Use the future perfect to combine the ideas of completeness and duration of time in the future.

> By the end of this year, the Anderson family *will have been living* in the same house for a hundred years.
> Soon he *will have been studying* here six months.
> He started out hiking at sunrise this morning; by eight o'clock he *will have been walking* for three hours.

The Future Time in the Past

Several constructions can be used to show future time as viewed from a point in the past.

would + INFINITIVE

       past
Finally the time *came* to leave; later he *would remember* how everyone stood waving goodbye.

   past
Sam *bought* new tires so that his car *would pass* the safety inspection.

was/were going to + INFINITIVE

   past   *past*
We *hurried* because we *knew* that we *were going to be* late.

   past
Jane *was* happy because she thought she *was going to pass* the examination.

The Past Continuous Tense

See **Reported speech** for back-shift after reporting verbs in the past tense.

> They knew that we *were having* a party the next day.
> Carl said that he *was* never *climbing* that mountain again.

The Past Tense of Be + Infinitive to Show Expectation

The president *was to open* the new building the next day.
The winner *was to receive* a trophy at the banquet later that night.

Sequence of Tenses

Do not make unnecessary shifts in tense in your writing. Often you can choose to use a framework in the present or you can use a framework in the past, but be consistent and do not change back and forth without a reason for the change.

IN REPORTED SPEECH

You must change from the present to the past tense when you change direct speech to reported speech if the reporting verb is in the past. (See **Reported speech** for illustrations and expectations.)

STATEMENT: "Literature courses *are* difficult for me," Henry said.
                   Henry *said* that literature courses *were* difficult for him.

QUESTION: "Why *do* you want to work while you *are* in school?" the interviewer asked Sue.
                   The interviewer *asked* Sue why she *wanted* to work while she *was* in school.

IN TIME CLAUSES

In a sentence that has a dependent clause beginning with

when(ever)	before	the day (that)
as soon as	until, till	the week (that)
after	the moment (that)	the year (that)

if you use the future tense in the independent clause, use the present tense in the dependent clause.

                              after
Mr. Johnson *will read* your report   when   he *comes* in.
                         as soon as

I *will look* for your book whenever I *have* time.
                            as soon as

The doctor *will* not *examine* patients before they *fill* out these forms.

(see also **Conditional sentences** and **Subjunctive**)

Thesis, Meanings of _____

The word *thesis* can mean several different things in composition.

A thesis is sometimes the main idea of an argument.

> The mayor's thesis was that money should be spent on public housing rather than on public transportation.

A thesis is sometimes a long written presentation of research required in many academic programs that award a master's degree—an M.A. or an M.S.

> Charlotte's course in public health required her to write a thesis, but Janet's course did not.

Sometimes seniors in an undergraduate college or university course must write a thesis related to their major subject.

> A thesis is different from a *dissertation.* A dissertation is required in most academic fields for a doctor's degree. A dissertation is longer than a thesis and is based on more research. A *thesis statement* is a short statement at the beginning of a formal composition that gives the idea you will write about. (see **Thesis statement**)

NOTE: The plural of *thesis* is *theses,* but before a noun, always use the singular form: *thesis statements.*

Thesis Statement _____

A thesis statement is short, usually only one sentence. It tells what you will write in a formal composition of several paragraphs or longer. Anyone who reads your thesis statement knows what your paper will be about. Only the idea in your thesis statement and other ideas, facts, and illustrations related to the idea in your thesis statement should be in your composition.

If a fact, interpretation, or illustration is related to your thesis statement, write about it.

If a fact, interpretation, or illustration is not related to your thesis statement, do not write about it. (see **Relevant material**)

A thesis statement is different from a topic sentence. A thesis statement tells what an entire composition is about. A composition may have several paragraphs, or it may be many thousand words long and have hundreds of paragraphs. A topic sentence tells what one paragraph is about. (see **Paragraph**)

The thesis statement for a composition is often written separately from the composition. It should also be written explicitly in the first paragraph as part of the introduction. It is often paraphrased in the last paragraph as part of the conclusion.

1. Write your thesis statements as statements, not as questions.

UNACCEPTABLE
THESIS: Should wearing seatbelts in cars be required by law?

In your thesis statement, you should show the reader what your opinion or development is going to be. A question cannot show your choice of possible answers to the problems that you have raised.

2. Write positive statements, not negative statements. If you disagree with a subject, rewrite the statement so that your disagreement is a positive statement.

POSITIVE: Wearing seatbelts in cars should be required by law.

NEGATIVE
(poor thesis):   Wearing seatbelts in cars should not be required by law.

POSITIVE: Wearing seatbelts in cars should be voluntary.

The last two sentences mean the same thing. The last sentence is better because it avoids using a negative such as *not* or *never*.

3. Write a simple or a complex sentence as a thesis statement. Since a compound sentence gives two ideas equal importance, it cannot be a good expression of a *single idea*. (see **Sentence structure**) If your thesis statement needs a semicolon in it, it is almost surely a bad thesis statement.

4. Limit the ideas in your thesis statement according to the length of the composition you are writing. A good thesis statement related to education for a five hundred-word theme must be much more limited and specific than a good thesis for a ten thousand-word term paper will be.

For a five hundred-word theme you need to be able to develop your thesis statement fully in only a few paragraphs. You must limit *education* to some very specific part of education: *My first math class in high school*, for example. What will you say about it?

I nearly failed my first math class in high school because I waited until the end of the term to begin to study.

You may want to write a thesis statement that is not personal.

Students in my country must study two foreign languages because our neighbors all speak different languages from ours.

For a long paper of several thousand words or more, you can write a thesis statement that will need discussion of more than one specific part of education.

> Secondary education in my country must change more radically than it has in the past twenty years if it is going to prepare our citizens for the next twenty years.

This thesis statement covers more material than a thesis statement for a five hundred-word theme does, but it is still limited. You must stick to your subject. You can discuss

> secondary education in your country at this time
> changes that have taken place in the last twenty years
> changes needed during the next twenty years
> reasons that changes are needed

In developing the thesis statement above, you must *not* discuss things such as

> an experience your grandfather had
> your own problems in the third grade
> why your school was given its name

You can discuss certain subjects only if you show how they are relevant to your thesis statement. If you discuss school architecture, you must show how it is relevant to changes in education. If you discuss medical education, you must show its relation to secondary education and how changes in secondary education affect it. **You must show a clear relationship between everything you write in your composition and your thesis statement.**

Time, words for, see **Chronological order** .

Titles

Books, Magazines, and Newspapers

Capitalize words in titles of books, magazines, and newspapers, according to conventional usage. (see **Capitalization**) Underline titles in handwriting and typing to show that these titles would be printed in italics. (see **Punctuation, underlining**)

> *A Tale of Two Cities* (book)
> *Treasure Island* (book)
> *Science for Today* (book)
> *Newsweek* (magazine)
> *Reader's Digest* (magazine)
> *The New York Times* (newspaper)
> *The Wall Street Journal* (newspaper)

Capitalize but do not underline titles of books that are sacred to a religion.

The Bible	The Gita	Revelations
The Koran	The New Testament	The Torah

Put quotation marks around titles of articles in magazines, newspapers, and journals and capitalize them. (see **Punctuation, quotation marks**)

"New Crisis in California" (article in a newspaper)
"The Future of Metals" (article in a magazine)
"New Developments in Solar Cells" (article in a journal)

Put quotation marks around chapters of books, short stories, and poems unless a single poem is published as a separate book.

"The Unicorn in the Garden" (short story)
"Patterns" (poem)
"The Expository Paragraph" (chapter in a book)
"A Rose for Emily" (short story)

People

Capitalize but do not underline or put quotation marks around titles of people.

the President
Professor Susan C. Thompson
Doctor Albert Jones
Miss Pamela Rockston

Write titles out in full in formal writing. In business letters and addresses, however, use the abbreviations Mr., Mrs., and Ms. Professional titles are often written out in full in business correspondence. (Miss is not an abbreviation.)

Ms. Gladys Beckman
Mr. Peter Smith
Doctor Edward Prentiss
Professor Thomas Carlson

Some married women prefer Mrs. to Ms. They may use their own first name for business affairs and their husband's name for social affairs.

Mrs. Elizabeth Jones (business)
Mrs. Arthur Jones (social)

Compositions

Do not underline or put quotation marks around titles on the pages of your own compositions.

Tone _____

Tone shows an emotion or attitude such as anger, happiness, impatience, sarcasm, gratitude, or objectivity. An impersonal or objective tone is particularly important in scientific and technical writing.

Tone is much more difficult to express in writing than in speech because intonation and stress in the voice easily indicate emotions without using specific words. In writing, careful choice of words (see **Connotation**) and constructions (see **Style**) indicates tone. Sometimes words are printed in italics underlined in writing) to indicate stress of the voice, but you should avoid this device in formal writing.

OBJECTIVE:	That book is due at the library at 8:00 tomorrow morning.
ANGRY:	You had better get that book back to the library by 8:00 tomorrow morning!
POLITE:	Please bring the book back early tomorrow morning, by 8:00 at the latest.
IMPATIENT:	I can't understand why you haven't brought that book back yet. Other students will need it first thing in the morning.
PATIENT:	I can understand why you haven't brought that book back yet, but please bring it back tomorrow morning because someone else really needs it.

Some scientific and technical writings avoid personal pronouns as much as possible in order to have an impersonal style. (see **Style, scientific writing**)

Point of view is sometimes used for the idea of emotion or attitude the writer takes, but more often it means the pronoun framework of a composition. (see **Point of view**)

Topic, Meanings of _____

The word *topic* has several different meanings connected with writing and composition.

The *topic of a composition* means the subject that you are writing about. Most assigned topics are general and need to be limited in order to be suitable for a paragraph or the length of theme that you are writing. Education, for example, is much too broad a subject. You could limit it to secondary education, then to secondary education in your country, then to your secondary school, and finally to an experience that taught you how to study for examination. (see **Abstract and concrete**)

A *topic outline* is an outline in which no part is a complete sentence. In a topic outline, each number and letter must be followed by a noun, a noun phrase, an infinitive, or an *-ing* form. (see **Outlining**)

A *topic sentence* expresses the main idea that will be developed in a paragraph. (see **Generalization** and **Paragraph**)

A *topical subject* is a subject that is current and up to date, connected with recent news or interests.

Topic Sentence

A topic sentence is a generalization to which every statement in a body paragraph (paragraph of development) should be related. (see **Generalization**) Sometimes the topic sentence is called the *controlling idea* of the paragraph.

A good topic sentence makes writing a paragraph much easier.

1. Use key words that you can develop.
2. Write a simple or complex sentence, not a compound one.
3. Make a positive rather than a negative statement.
4. Choose an idea limited enough to develop fully in 75 to 125 words.

Place your topic sentence at or near the beginning of the paragraph unless there is a clear reason for putting it in the middle or at the end. Do not try to write a paragraph with an implied topic sentence (one that is not stated).

Often you are given a subject that you must limit and make more specific before you can write a topic sentence. You might start with the subject of food. You could first limit food to American food, then to fast food, and then to hamburgers.

TOO BROAD	MORE LIMITED
Some American food is good.	Just thinking about hamburgers makes my mouth water.
I like fruit.	The flavor of tropical fruits fades when they are shipped long distances.

If you want to take a negative position, try to think of a way to state your ideas in a positive statement. Writing about food for instance, instead of saying, "I do not like hamburgers," you could say, "I dislike hamburgers." Even better, you could say, "I prefer the food of my country (name a specific dish) to hamburgers." Then you could develop the topic sentence by telling *why:* "I prefer the food of my country to hamburgers because . . . ."

If you have been told not to write in the first person (using *I, me, my,* or *mine*), instead of "I prefer" you can say, "The food of my country is better than hamburgers because . . . ."

While you are deciding how to state your topic sentence, think about the different kinds of order that you can use to develop it. Spatial order, chronological order, and the different kinds of logical order follow from different key words and different ways of stating your topic sentence.

TOPIC SENTENCE	DEVELOPMENT
The food of my country is better than hamburgers.	Logical: Comparison and contrast
Just thinking about hamburgers makes my mouth water.	Logical: Cause and effect
Fast food has changed the eating habits of many Americans.	Logical: Cause and effect
The fast food industry has developed rapidly in recent years.	Chronological order
MacDonald's means run, eat, and run.	Definition
From King to hut, some kind of fast food pleases every taste.	Logical: Classification
Anyone can learn to make a hamburger.	Process: "how to"
Fast food customers know what to expect from the time they sight the sign to the time they leave the parking lot.	Spatial order or chronological order or both combined

Transitions _____

Transitions are words and phrases that show relationships between ideas and between grammatical structures. Use WH-words and other subordinating conjunctions between independent and dependent clauses. Use coordinating conjunctions and interrupters between independent clauses and between sentences. Use personal pronouns and determiners carefully and correctly. Be sure that all personal pronouns have clear antecedents. (see **Clauses, Conjunctions, Determiners, Interrupters, Pronouns,** and **Reference of the pronoun**)

Repeat nouns and verbs as much as you need to and use synonyms to make ideas clear as you write. Clearly connect clause to clause, sentence to sentence, and paragraph to paragraph. (see **Substitutions** and **Synonyms**)

Transitions Within A Sentence

Use adverbs, conjunctions, and prepositions to show the relationships between ideas. (see **Coordinating conjunctions** and **Subordinating and reducing**)

Transitions Between Sentences

Use adverbs and conjunctions to show the relationship between ideas in separate sentences. Use a personal pronoun only when its antecedent is no farther away than the sentence before the one you are writing.

Transitions Between Paragraphs

Use adverbs and conjunctions to show the relationship between ideas in one paragraph and the next paragraph. Do not use a personal pronoun if its antecedent is in another paragraph, but repeat the noun it stands for.

Good transitions give writing coherence or unity. Transitions are the glue that holds a composition together. (see **Coherence**)

Transitive verbs, see **Verbs, kinds of,** and **Voice**

Trite Words and Expressions _____

A trite word or expression is a word that has been used so much that it has very little meaning, interest, or freshness. The noun that means nearly the same thing is *cliché. Nice,* for example, is almost meaningless. *Nice* dog, *nice* house, *nice* sunset, *nice* person, *nice* meal, *nice* car, *nice* friend—what do all these things have in common that can be described by the same word? *Nice* means something pleasing in a very indefinite sense. Trite words are often vague as well as stale. Look for a more vivid and concrete adjective, such as a *friendly* dog, a *spacious* house, a *brilliant* sunset, a *helpful* person, a *nourishing* meal, a *luxurious* car, or a *steadfast* friend.

A *cliché* is a descriptive phrase that has been overused.

solid as the rock of Gibraltar (dependable)
strong as an ox (very strong)
a babe in the woods (an innocent or inexperienced person)
a lamb among wolves (in great danger; defenseless)

Two-Word Verbs _____

Two-word verbs are formed from a verb and a preposition or an adverb (sometimes called a particle). These verbs are sometimes called phrasal verbs or idioms. Two-word verbs are used more often in speech and informal writing than in formal writing, but they may be used in formal writing also.

Meaning

A two-word verb often has a one-word synonym, a single word which has the same meaning. The one-word form is generally more formal. (see **Style**)

call up	telephone/summon
catch on	understand
cry out	exclaim
give in/up	surrender
go/come along	accompany/agree
keep on	continue
leave out	omit
pay back	repay
pick out	choose
put off	postpone
turn off	appear/find

The meanings of many two-word verbs are idiomatic; that is, you cannot easily figure out their meanings from the meanings of the separate parts. Many slang expressions that are vulgar or taboo are two-word verbs. United States and British meanings of two-word verbs are not always the same. *Call on,* for example, means *ask for help* in both usages. People in the United States also use *call on* in the sense of *visit,* but the British do not. In the United States people *call* others *up* on the telephone, but the British *ring* them *up.* Look in dictionaries and books of idioms for the meanings of two-word verbs. Many of the two-word combinations have more than one meaning, and some fit in more than one of the constructions explained below. *The Longman Dictionary of Contemporary English* lists two-word verbs as separate entries. *The Oxford Advanced Learner's Dictionary* and some dictionaries written for native English speakers list two-word verbs in the listing for the first word.

Inseparable Two-Word Verbs

Do not separate the parts of inseparable two-word verbs. If there is a direct object, it follows the second word.

(These two-word verbs are sometimes called *prepositional verbs.*)

	direct object
You must *account for* the	money.
You must *account for*	it.
Shirley *got over*	her *cold.*
She *got over*	it.
Look after	your *brother.*
Look after	him.

Some Inseparable Two-Word Verbs and Idiomatic Phrases

The nouns in parentheses are possible objects for the verbs listed. If no noun follows the verb, the verb is intransitive (is not followed by an object). Other meanings are possible for some of the combinations given.

account for (the money)
ask for (help)
bear up
boil over
break in
    into (the house)
    out
call for (a decision)
    on (friends)
care for (a person)
carry on
clean up (with a direct object, *clean up* is separable; see below)
clear up (with a direct object, *clear up* is separable; see below)
come away
come into (the house)
    out
get over (the illness)—*get it over* means *be finished with*

give in
    out
go ahead
    back
    up
grow up
hold off
    up
look after (my family)
    ahead
    away
    for (help)
pull up
run over (a nail)
see through (the curtain)
send for (a friend)
show off (her ability)
stand by (a friend)
stand for (something)
stay up
talk back
turn up
wear away

Separable Two-Word Verbs

Like inseparable two-word verbs, these verbs have idiomatic meanings. The object, however, is movable. A pronoun object comes between the first and second part of a separable two-word verb. A short noun object can come between the two parts, or can follow the second part. Separable two-word verbs are transitive (they have an object). Separable two-word verbs are sometimes called *phrasal verbs*.

             object
Margaret *turned on* the *light.*

          object
Margaret *turned* the *light on.*

        object
Margaret *turned* *it* *on.*

If the direct object is long, especially if it is modified by a phrase or a clause, put it after the second part of the two-word verb.

> *object*
> Margaret *turned on* the *light* by the door.

> *object*
> Margaret *turned on* the *light* that had just been fixed.

Some two-word verbs can be either separable or inseparable according to their meanings in a certain context.

> She *passed out*. (fainted)
> She *passed out* the tickets. (distributed)

> The car *broke down*. (stopped operating)
> The police *broke down* the door. (opened by force)

> He *showed up* late. (arrived)
> George *showed* him *up* as a fool. (exposed)

Right as an adverb meaning *immediately* or *completely* may come between the two parts of both separable and inseparable two-word verbs. With separable two-word verbs, *right* comes just before the second part of the verb. *Right* is informal; do not use it in very formal writing.

> The new buildings are going *right* up.
> Margaret turned the light *right* on.
> Margaret turned it *right* on.

Some Separable Two-Word Verbs

Use a pronoun or a noun object. Never use both. Many other nouns are possible; these are given as examples.

back	(it)	up	(the car)
blow	(it)	out	(the candle)
	(it)	up	(the balloon)
break	(them)	down	(the statistics)
	(them)	off	(the negotiations)
bring	(it)	about	(change)
	(it)	up	(the subject)
burn	(it)	down	(the building)
	(them)	up	(the papers)
clear	(them)	away	(the dishes)
	(it)	up	(the misunderstanding)
close	(it)	down	(the business)
draw	(it)	up	(an agreement)
fill	(it)	in/out	(a form)
	(it)	up	(the cup)
find	(it)	out	(the answer)

give	(it)	away	(this old coat)
	(it)	up	(eating candy)
	(it)	out	(the news)
hand	(it)	in/out	(the news, the work)
keep	(them)	down	(expenses)
	(it)	on	(the radio)
leave	(it)	out	(the question)
let	(them)	in/out	(our friends)
lock	(them)	up	(the prisoners)
look	(them)	up	(our friends in Detroit)
make	(it)	out	(the handwriting)
	(it)	up	(a story)

NOTE: *Make it up to* someone, if there is no antecedent for *it*, means *repay*.

mix	(it)	up	(a story, food being prepared)
	(them)	up	(people—confuse them or make them acquainted with each other)
pass	(it)	on	(the responsibility)
pay	(it)	back	(the money)
	(them)	back	(my enemies)
pick	(it)	out	(a new coat)
point	(it)	out	(the problem)
put	(it)	across	(an idea)
	(it)	away	(the laundry)
	(it)	off	(the work)
	(them)	out	(the cats)
round	(them)	off	(the numbers)
	(them)	up	(the cattle)
set	(it)	up	(the appointment)
take	(them)	in	(people)
	(it)	up	(a project)
talk	(it)	over	(the problem)
think	(it)	over	(the offer)
throw	(it)	away	(the trash)
try	(it)	on	(the coat)
turn	(them)	away	(the demonstrators)
	(it)	down	(the radio)
	(it)	off	(the light)
	(it)	over	(the mattress)
	(it)	up	(the volume)
wear	(them)	out	(the shoes)
wind	(it)	up	(the clock, the business)
wipe	(it)	out	(the dirt)
work	(it)	out	(the problem)

Many nouns are formed from two-word verbs: *breakup, cleanup,* and *showoff,* for example. (see **Word formation**)

Three-Word Verbs

A verb that must be followed by two words, an adverb and a preposition, is sometimes called a three-word verb. These verbs are common in speech, but avoid using them if possible in formal writing, especially if one of the particles comes at the end of the sentence. Do not put any other words between the parts of a three-word verb.

INFORMAL: Some discomfort has to be *put up with.* (endured)

I won't *put up with* that. (endure)

That's what he's *holding out for.* (demanding, refusing to compromise)

The old lady's daughter *looks in on* her every day. (visits)

When you cross the street, $\begin{smallmatrix} watch \\ look \end{smallmatrix}$ *out for* cars. (watch for, be careful of)

Some Three-Word Verbs

break in on	get down to	put up with
catch up on	go back on	stand up for
catch up with	go through with	stand up to
check up on	live up to	try out for
come down with	look in on	tune in to
cut down on	look out for	turn out for
do away with	look up to	walk off with
face up to	make up for	walk out on

U

Uncountable nouns, see Countable and uncountable nouns

Usage Labels

In all languages people speak in different ways to different kinds of people on different occasions. You do not, for example, speak to your best friend in exactly the same way you speak to your grandmother. You choose language that is suitable for the person you are speaking to. Written and spoken English are similar but not exactly the same. In dictionaries, grammar books, and textbooks, you can find *usage labels* that tell the connotations of words. Usage labels also tell when words are polite or impolite. Each dictionary has a key to the labels it uses and their abbreviations. All dictionaries show the difference between formal or standard usage for writing, and informal or colloquial usage for speech. (see **Connotation**)

Geographical labels such as *American, British, Canadian,* and *Australian* are labels for words and structures that may be considered standard in those areas but are not used over the world.

archaic—once common but now rare
colloquial—language of familiar speech not used in formal writing
dialect—language of a limited region or class
formal—standard English or sometimes ceremonial English, as in a court or church
informal—speech of educated people; often a substitute for *colloquial*
literary—used mainly in literature
modern—shows a change in meaning from an earlier time
obscene—connected with functions of the body such as sex or the bowels; generally vulgar or taboo

obsolete—disappeared from current use but found in older writings

old use—sometimes obsolete; sometimes words that have nearly disappeared from current use

poetic—used mainly in poetry

profanity—irreverence or contempt for God, religious beliefs, or religious objects; includes blasphemy, cursing, and swearing

regional—used in a limited geographical area

slang—language of a special group that uses words in unusual meanings (see **Slang**)

standard English and standard edited English—language used in writing, particularly in academic, business, and scientific writing

taboo—never used in polite society; profane or obscene

vulgar—rarely used in polite society; sometimes means obscene

Special *registers* show acceptable uses of special groups such as those working in engineering, music, medicine, and sports. Words from a special register that are not understood by the general public are sometimes called *jargon*. (see **Jargon**)

A *euphemism* is a word that replaces another word of similar but stronger meaning. Words that are obscene and profane often have milder forms. *Shoot* can replace *shit, darn* can replace *damn,* and *gosh* can replace *God.* Sometimes words with unpleasant associations are replaced by other words or expressions, such as *powder room, bathroom, ladies'/men's room,* or *rest room* for *toilet.* People who do not like to use *die* use *pass on* instead.

Verb patterns, see **Sentence patterns**

Verb Phrase _____

A *verb phrase* is the word or words used to show dictionary meaning (head word), tense, aspect, mood, and voice in a finite verb; or the word or words that show dictionary meaning, aspect, and voice in a nonfinite verb. (see **Aspect, Finite verbs, Infinitive, Mood, Participles, Tense,** and **Voice**)

NONFINITE

After *looking* everywhere,

Without *standing* on a stool,
Never *having had* biology before,

Having been caught earlier,

FINITE
   found
Peter *has found* his geography book.

El*l*en *can reach* the top shelf.
Al *is finding*   it difficult.
   has been finding

the burglar *escaped.*
       was taken to jail.

Help me.
I *would help* you if I *could.*

Verbals _____

Verbals are verb forms that are used as nouns or modifiers in a clause rather than as the main verb or as part of a verb phrase that is the main verb. (see **Infinitives, Gerunds,** and **Participles**)

Infinitive phrases are made of *to* + the infinitive form of the verb.

Gerunds are *-ing* forms of the verb used as nouns.

Present participles are *-ing* forms of the verb used as adjectives and in verb phrases in forming the continuous/progressive tenses.

Past participles are *-ed* forms of regular verbs. (See **Verbs, irregular** for past participles with other endings.) Past participles are used as adjectives and in verb phrases in forming the perfect tenses.

Verbs

Many sections of this book deal with verbs. These sections are listed alphabetically here and in the book.

Agreement of subject and verb	Infinitive	Reported speech
Aspect	Infinitive/-*ing* choice	Sentence structure
Auxiliary verbs	Modals	Stative verbs
Be	Negation	Subjunctive
Clauses	Numbers, singular and plural	Substitutions
Complements	Operators	Tag questions
Direct object	Participles	Tense
Do	Predicate	Two-word verbs
Finite verbs	Principal parts of verbs	Verb phrase
Gerunds	Questions, direct	Verbs, irregular
Have		Verbs, kinds of
Indirect object		Voice
		Word formation

If you are having difficulty with *subject-verb agreement,* look up

Agreement of subject and verb	Operators
Auxiliary verbs	Number, singular and plural
Finite verbs (main verb in the sentence)	Questions, direct

If you are having difficulty with the verb *to be,* look up

Be	Voice
Mood	Tense
Operators	

If you are having difficulty using the right *verb form,* look up

Agreement of subject and verb	Negation
Finite verb	Principal parts of verbs
Infinitive/-*ing* choice	Subjunctive operators
Irregular verbs	Tense
Modals	Verb phrase

If you are having difficulty using the right *tense,* look up

Conditional sentences   Reported speech
Modals   Tense

If you are having difficulty with the *word order* of verb forms, look up

Finite verbs   Questions, direct
Operators   Reported speech

Classifications of Verbs

Aspect
   Simple
   Perfect
   Continuous/Progressive

Mood
   Indicative
   Interrogative
   Imperative
   Subjunctive

Number
   Singular
   Plural

Person (see Point of View)
   First
   Second
   Third

Voice (transitive verbs only)
   Active
   Passive

Tense
   Present
   Past
   Future
   Present perfect
   Past perfect
   Future perfect and
   Continuous/progressive aspects
      of these tenses

Complementation (words that follow verbs)

Linking (predicate nominative)
Intransitive (no noun or adjective complement)
Transitive
   Active (direct object required, indirect object and objective comple-
      ment possible)
   Passive (no complement required)

Verbs, Irregular _____

Many of the most common verbs in English are irregular; that is,
their past and past participle forms are not made by adding *-ed* to the
present form. Most irregular verb forms were regular forms hundreds of
years ago. They represent ways of making tenses that we do not use any-

more. This list *does not include* (1) modals (see **Modals**); (2) irregular verbs that you see in reading but that you are not likely to use in writing —look them up in a dictionary when necessary (lists of all irregular verbs in alphabetical order are in the *Oxford Advanced Learner's Dictionary* and in the *Longman Dictionary of Contemporary English*); (3) irregular verbs that have a regular form that means the same thing (*proved, proven* and *sowed, sown,* for example)—you will always be correct if you use the regular form; and (4) *-ing* forms, since they are regular in all verbs (see **Spelling, some alternate irregular forms**).

Examples of Use of the Principal Parts (see also **Principal parts of Verbs**)

PRESENT:	We *eat* breakfast every day.
PAST:	We *ate* breakfast yesterday.
PAST PARTICIPLE:	We *have* already *eaten* breakfast today.
-ing FORM (SIMPLE PRESENT + *-ing*):	We *are* not *eating* breakfast now.

GROUP I: SPELLING

Irregular verbs in which the past participle ends in *-n* or *-ne* usually have different forms for the past and the past participle. (Exceptions in this list are *shine, spin,* and *win.*) Most of the *-ne* verbs have a spelling change in the vowel from the past to the past participle, also. Verbs in this list that do not have this change in spelling are marked (1).

SIMPLE PRESENT	PAST	PAST PARTICIPLE
be	was/were	been
bear	bore	born (1)
bear (forbear)	bore	borne (1)
beat	beat	beaten (1)
begin	began	begun
bite	bit	bitten (1)
blow	blew	blown
break	broke	broken (1)
choose	chose	chosen (1)
do	did	done
draw	drew	drawn
drive	drove	driven
fall	fell	fallen
fly	flew	flown
forget	forgot	forgot, forgotten (1)
forgive	forgave	forgiven

SIMPLE PRESENT	PAST	PAST PARTICIPLE
freeze	froze	frozen (1)
get	got	got, gotten (1)
give	gave	given
go	went	gone
grow	grew	grown
hide	hid	hidden (1)
know	knew	known
lie (2)	lay	lain
ride	rode	ridden
rise	rose	risen
run	ran	run
see	saw	seen
shake	shook	shaken
shine (2)	shone	shone (1)
speak	spoke	spoken (1)
spin	spun	spun (1)
steal	stole	stolen (1)
strike	struck	stricken (3)
swear	swore	sworn (1)
take	took	taken
tear	tore	torn (1)
throw	threw	thrown
wear	wore	worn (1)
weave	wove	woven
win	won	won (1)
write	wrote	written

(1) The vowel(s) is (are) the same in the past and past participle.
(2) A regular verb with the same simple present has a different meaning. (see **Confusing choices**)
(3) Another irregular past participle with the same simple present has a different meaning. (see **Confusing choices**)

GROUP II

Irregular verbs in which the past participle ends in -*t* have the same forms for the past and the part participle.

SIMPLE PRESENT	PAST	PAST PARTICIPLE
bend	bent	bent
bring	brought	brought
build	built	built
buy	bought	bought
catch	caught	caught
deal	dealt	dealt
feel	felt	felt

SIMPLE PRESENT	PAST	PAST PARTICIPLE
fight	fought	fought
keep	kept	kept
kneel	knelt	knelt
leave	left	left
lend	lent	lent
lose	lost	lost
mean	meant	meant
meet	met	met
seek	sought	sought
send	sent	sent
sit	sat	sat
shoot	shot	shot
sleep	slept	slept
spend	spent	spent
sweep	swept	swept
teach	taught	taught
think	thought	thought

GROUP III

Irregular verbs in which the past participle ends in *-d* have the same form for the past and the past participle.

SIMPLE PRESENT	PAST	PAST PARTICIPLE
bind	bound	bound
bleed	bled	bled
breed	bred	bred
feed	fed	fed
find	found	found
grind	ground	ground
have	had	had
hear	heard	heard
hold	held	held
lay	laid	laid
lead	led	led
make	made	made
pay	paid	paid
say	said	said
sell	sold	sold
slide	slid	slid
stand	stood	stood
tell	told	told
understand	understood	understood
wind (1)	wound	wound

(1) A regular verb with the same spelling in the simple present has a different meaning.

GROUP IV

Irregular verbs in this group have a vowel change from the simple present to the past and past participle, which are usually the same form. This vowel change is clear in both pronunciation and spelling.

	SIMPLE PRESENT	PAST	PAST PARTICIPLE
	cling	clung	clung
	come	came	come
NOTE:	*welcome* is regular	*welcomed*	*welcomed*
	dig	dug	dug
	fling	flung	flung
	hang (1)	hung	hung
	ring	rang	rung
	shrink	shrunk (2)	shrunk
	sing	sang	sung
	spring	sprung (2)	sprung
	stick	stuck	stuck
	sting	stung	stung
	stink	stunk (2)	stunk
	strike (3)	struck	struck
	string	strung	strung
	swim	swam	swum
	swing	swung	swung
	wake	woke, waked	woke, waked

(1) A regular verb with the same simple present spelling has a different meaning.

(2) An alternate form with *a* is sometimes used in the past only; *shrank, sprang,* and *stank.*

(3) Another irregular verb with the same simple present has a different meaning and a past participle. (see **Confusing choices**)

GROUP V

These irregular verbs have only one form for the present, the past, and the past participle. Notice that all of them end in *-d* or *-t*.

bet	cut	put	shed	spread
bid (1)	fit	quit	shut	thrust
burst	hit	read (2)	slit	wet (3)
cast	hurt	rid	spit	
cost	let	set	split	

(1) Another irregular verb with the same simple present has a different meaning.

(2) All three forms are spelled the same, but the past and past participle are pronounced differently (rhymes with *lead, led, led*).

(3) Regular forms are sometimes used.

Verbs, Kinds of _____

Verbs can be classified according to whether or not they require a complement and, if they do need a complement, according to what kind must be used. (For a table of verbs and their complements, see **Sentence patterns.**)

Very _____

As an adverb *very* usually means *extremely* or *to a high degree*. It can be used before adjectives or adverbs, but only before gradable ones. (If you can use *more* before a modifier or if the modifier has an *-er* form, it is gradable).

> Virginia is *very* sick. (adjective)
> Clara is *very* intelligent. (adjective)
> The problem was solved *very* quickly. (adverb)
> The car in the accident had been going *very* fast. (adverb)
> The *very* tall man must be a basketball player. (adjective)

The + *very* can be used before the superlative form of an adjective (*-est* form) but not before the comparative form (*-er* form).

> This coffee is the *very* best.
> The *very* best coffee I ever drank was at Jane's.
> Dale's clothes are always the *very* finest.
> We must find the *very* earliest flight.

NOTE: *Very* sometimes weakens the force of the sentence, especially in writing. The examples above—*very* best, *very* finest, and *very* earliest— would be as strong or stronger without *very*.

Very can be used before *many, much, few,* and *little*.

> The mountains had *very many* storms.
> Jim was *very much* opposed to the plan.
> *Very few* people came to the baseball game.
> The child had *very little* fear of dogs.

As an adjective *very* usually means *exactly* or *same*.

> She is the *very* girl I was talking about.
> This is the *very* book Steve was looking for.

As an adjective before *own, very* makes the idea of ownership stronger.

> At last Douglas had a car of his *own*.
> At last Douglas had his *very* own car.

Do not use *very* before words that cannot be compared or measured.

really	only	perfect
truly	all	unique
exactly	whole	superb

Do not use *very* before adverbs that show definite time.

then	hourly	twice
now	daily	three times
once	monthly	
always	yearly	
already		

but

very often, *very* frequently, *very* seldom

Do not use *very* before most adverbs that refer to place.

right/left (*extreme* right/left)
north/south/east/west (*due* or *far* north/south/east/west)
here (*right* here)
below (*very much* below)

Some adverbs that refer to place can be used with *very* meaning *extreme*. Do not modify these adverbs in formal writing.

The *very* beginning.
       end
       top
       bottom
       middle
       center

Do not use *very* directly before a noun except when it means *exactly* or *same*.

INCORRECT:	Martha is my *very* friend.
CORRECT:	Martha is my *very best* friend.
IMPROVED:	Martha is my best friend. (The meaning is stronger without *very*.)

Voice

Transitive verbs—verbs that take direct objects—can usually be used in two ways: as active verbs and as passive verbs. (see also **Indirect object** and **Passive verbs**) Whether you are using an active verb or a passive verb, some of the information in the sentence is the same. The difference is in the way you present the facts and how many facts you give. Understand both forms in order to choose the one that gives the emphasis you want.

Advantages of the Active Voice

1. An active clause can give more information in fewer words. (see **Wordiness**)

2. An active verb makes your writing livelier and more vivid.

3. In an active clause the subject is in a strong position, but in the passive construction you may leave out some information in the active subject or put it in a weak position after *by*.

4. If the indirect object is important information, it is stronger in the active sentence.

Advantages of the Passive Voice

1. A passive construction emphasizes the result in an impersonal style. This use is sometimes desirable in scientific and technical writing. Today, however, many editors of scientific and technical journals prefer a style that avoids the passive.

> Water was produced by mixing two parts of hydrogen and one part of oxygen.
> The effects of confinement in a small space were repeatedly observed in the experimental animals.

2. A passive verb emphasizes a victim or the result of a disaster.

> ACTIVE: The *motorcycle* injured the child.
> PASSIVE: The *child* was injured.

When the injury of the child is more important than the motorcycle, the passive sentence is better. Usually in accidents and disasters the result is more important than the cause.

> ACTIVE: The *tornado* blew the roof off Mr. Halwell's house.
> PASSIVE: Mr. Halwell's *roof* was blown off (by the tornado).

3. Use a passive verb when the agent or actor is so unimportant or obvious that you do not need to mention it.

> The *school auditorium* was built in 1912. (Who did the construction is unimportant.)
> The *thief* was arrested. (Unless several law enforcement agencies are working on the same case, you can assume that the agent is the local police.)

4. Use a passive verb if you want to hide the name of the person who is responsible for an unpleasant decision or result. Bureaucrats and administrators write in the passive so that no specific person can be blamed for unpopular decisions and rulings.

> The proposal to raise taxes was approved. (no agent)
> An increase in tuition fees was proposed. (no agent)

Who is responsible? These sentences do not tell us.

Formation of Active and Passive Forms

The active form takes a direct object. See *Passive verbs* for formation of passives and for other forms you might confuse with them.

Active to Passive and Passive to Active

As shown in the examples below, active sentences must have a subject, verb, and direct object. But the passive must have only a subject and verb. Additional information is optional in the passive.

	subject	active verb	optional indirect object	direct object	optional indirect object
ACTIVE:	Shirley	paid	(him) (the waiter)	the bill	(to him). (to the waiter).

	subject	passive verb	optional indirect object	optional agent
PASSIVE:	The bill	was paid	(to the waiter)	(by Shirley).
ACTIVE:	Shirley	paid	(the waiter) (him)	the bill (to him).
PASSIVE:	The bill	was paid	(to the waiter)	(by Shirley).

See **Indirect object** for more on position of the indirect object for verbs which must have *to* or *for* before the indirect object, and for constructions in which the active direct object becomes the passive object.

Not all active clauses can be changed to passive ones, nor can all passive clauses be changed to active ones. Some active constructions do not occur in the passive at all:

have when it means *possess, eat,* or *drink:*

> ACTIVE: My parents *have* a new car.
>
> ACTIVE: He has already *had* his breakfast.

constructions in which a pronoun referring to the subject is part of the direct object:

> ACTIVE: They helped *each other.* (reciprocal pronoun)
>
> ACTIVE: He hit *himself* on the head with his bat. (reflexive pronoun)

clauses in which a possessive pronoun modifies the direct object:

ACTIVE: Tom drove *his car* to the concert. (*His* refers to subject.)

clauses in which the direct object is made from the same root as the verb:

ACTIVE: Sarah *dreamed* an unusual *dream* last night.

Some additional verbs do not naturally occur in the passive in the meanings in these sentences (they may occur in the passive in other meanings).

ACTIVE: My brother *got* a new job.

ACTIVE: Susan *wanted* many friends.

ACTIVE: John *resembles* his brother.

ACTIVE: The stadium *seats* (*holds*) 50,000 people.

ACTIVE: Chris *lacks* enough money to pay her bills.

ACTIVE: Peter *likes* ice cream.

ACTIVE: Charles *hates* spinach.

Some constructions cannot change directly from passive to active with certain verbs.

PASSIVE: John *was said* to be in Chicago.

INCORRECT: His friends *said* John to be in Chicago.

ACTIVE: John's friends *said* that he was in Chicago.

Vowels _____

Vowels in spelling are *a, e, i, o, u,* and sometimes *y* when it has the sound of an *i* or u: m*y*th, m*y*, m*y*rtle. A *diphthong* is a combination of vowel sounds pronounced one after the other in one syllable: m*oi*st, b*ai*t, b*oy*, for example. A syllable spelled with two or more vowels together is not always pronounced as a diphthong, nor is a diphthong in sound always spelled with two vowels. *Through,* for example, is spelled with more than one vowel, but is not pronounced as a diphthong. *By* is spelled with only one vowel, but it is pronounced as a diphthong as are *bye* and *buy.* (see **Spelling** and **Syllables**)

W

WH-questions, see **Questions**

WH-Words

WH-words form a group of words that take special positions in the clause. Most of them begin with WH-.

who, whose, whom, and whoever, whomever
what, whatever
which, whichever
when, whenever
where, wherever
how, however
why, whyever
whether
if (when it means *whether*)

All the WH-words except *whether* and *if* can introduce a direct question. (see **Questions, direct**)
All the WH-words can introduce an indirect question in reported speech. (see **Reported speech**)
When a WH-word in a question is not the subject of its own clause, it must be followed by an operator. (see **Operators** and **Questions, direct**)
WH-words can introduce noun clauses. (see **Clauses, noun**)

Wishes, see **Contrary-to-fact statements**

W

Women, Terms Referring to _____

Speech and writing that make unnecessary distinctions based on sex are called *sexist language*. Many people today object to some features of English usage that do not treat men and women in the same way.

Ms. does not show whether or not a woman is married. The traditional terms *Mrs.* for a married woman and *Miss* for a single woman make this distinction. Since *Mr.* does not show whether or not a man is married, many people feel that women need a title that does not give this information.

He, him, and *his* have often been used to refer to a male or a female or to some whose sex is not known.

> The child has thrown *his* ball. (*Child* can refer to a male or female.)
> A student lost *his* book. (*Student* can refer to a female or male.)

To avoid the problem of using a masculine pronoun for someone who may be feminine, you can often use an article or determiner in place of the pronoun.

> The child has thrown *the* ball.
> A student lost *this* book.

Sometimes *his/her, she/he* or *(s)he* is used.

> Every student must have paid *his/her* fees by Wednesday.

Avoid the awkward *his/her* by putting the sentence into the plural.

> All students must have paid *their* fees by Wednesday.

or avoid the problem by rewriting the sentence without pronouns.

> All student fees must be paid by Wednesday.

Some people object to occupational terms that show the sex of the person who is doing the work.

TRADITIONAL	NONSEXIST
stewardess	flight attendant
postman	postal worker
chairman	chairperson or chair
saleslady	salesperson or salesclerk

Avoid using *man* or *mankind* to refer to people of both sexes.

TRADITIONAL	NONSEXIST
mankind	human beings
man and wife	man and woman or husband and wife (Do not identify one person by sex and the other by marital status: Use the same categories for both.)
all men everywhere	all people everywhere

lady, woman, female—Lady has traditionally meant a woman of high station and breeding and *woman* has been a more general term that means an adult female. Some people today dislike *lady* because of its connection with class distinctions. Some people like it because it has a connotation of good manners. *Female* means a person, plant, or animal of the sex that bears young.

Word Formation

Many English words are formed by adding to the *base word* or *root*. A base word is a form that exists as a word in English; a root or stem is a form that is not used by itself but joins with other word parts. Sometimes the addition comes at the beginning of the base word or root and sometimes it comes at the end. These additions can be called *affixes*. An affix at the beginning of the word is a *prefix*. An affix at the end of a word is a *suffix* or an *ending*. Prefixes change or add to the *meaning* of the base word or root, but most suffixes change the *part of speech* of the word; sometimes they change the meaning also.

Compound Words

Compound words are two words put together. Knowing when to use a hyphen and when to spell them as one word is difficult. British and U.S. usage do not always agree, and different dictionaries published in the same country do not always agree. In U.S. usage, fewer hyphens are used than in British usage. Many more compound words are written as one word today than were written that way in the past. Compound adjectives are two separate words that together modify a noun. They are usually written with a hyphen if they come before the word they modify, but sometimes usage changes and they become one word. (see **Punctuation, hyphen**)

WRITTEN AS ONE WORD	WRITTEN WITH A HYPHEN	WRITTEN AS TWO SEPARATE WORDS
firsthand	first-degree (adjective)	first aid
landholder	land-poor (adjective)	land office
steamboat		steam engine
postgraduate	post-Victorian post-mortem	post meridiem (p.m)

NOTE: After prefixes such as *post*, a hyphen is usually used if the word that follows is a proper name or a Latin form.

Some Examples of Prefixes and Suffixes

BASE WORD:	beauty (n)	self (n)	harmony (n)	hand (n and v)
SUFFIX				
noun to adjective	beauti*ful* beaut*eous*	self*ish*	harmoni*ous* harmon*ic*	hand*y* hand*ed* (verb to adjective)
adjective to noun		selfish*ness*	harmonious*ness*	handi*ness*
adjective or noun to adverb	beautiful*ly*	selfish*ly*	harmonious*ly*	handi*ly*
noun or adjective to verb	beauti*fy*		harmon*ize*	
verb to verb				two-word verbs: ha hand *over*, hand *do* and so on.
verb to noun	beautifi*cation* beautifi*er*		harmoni*zation* harmoni*zer*	hand*ful*
noun to noun	beauti*cian*	self*hood*		compound nouns: hand*book*, handgu*r* hand*out*, and so on.
negation (without)		self*less* (adj) self*less*ly (adv) self*less*ness (n)		hand*less* (adj)
PREFIX				
negation *un*		*un*selfish (adj) *un*selfishly (adv) *un*selfishness (n)		*un*hand (v)
dis			*dis*harmony	
in			*in*harmonious (adj) *in*harmoniously (adv) *in*harmoniousness (n)	
self	*self*-beautifi- cation			

NOTE: *Self* as a prefix is always followed by a hyphen except in *selfhood.*

Blends

Some words are made by combining two words, but using only parts of them in the new word. Advertisers and journalists form many words in this way. Some of them are forgotten almost at once, but a few of them become part of the general vocabulary.

agriculture + business	becomes	agribusiness
electro + execution	becomes	electrocution
helicopter + airport	becomes	heliport
motor + hotel	becomes	motel
news + broadcast	becomes	newscast
smoke + fog	becomes	smog
stagnation + inflation	becomes	stagflation
television + marathon	becomes	telethon
transfer + resistor	becomes	transistor

Acronyms

Acronyms are made from the first letters of a group of words. They are often written in capital letters without periods between them and pronounced as words instead of initials. A few acronyms have become common nouns, particularly some words connected with science.

laser	comes from	*l*ightwave *a*mplification by *s*imulated *e*mission of *r*adiation
loran	comes from	*lo*ng *ra*nging *n*avigation
radar	comes from	*ra*dio *d*etection *a*nd *r*anging
sonar	comes from	*so*und *n*avigation *r*anging

Two-Word Verbs

Many two-word verbs become nouns. Some of these nouns are written as one word with no hyphen, and others are written with a hyphen between the two words. Many of these nouns are slang. (see **Slang**)

NOUN FORMED FROM A TWO-WORD VERB	MEANING
a blowout	bursting of a tire
	uncontrolled activity of an oil or gas well
a blow-up	a photographic enlargement
	an explosion
	sudden anger
a buildup	an increase
a callup	an order to report for military service
a cutback	a reduction
a cutoff	an endpoint
a cutout	something cut out, usually from paper or wood

NOUN FORMED FROM A TWO-WORD VERB	MEANING
a payoff	a payment
a rip-off (slang)	a theft or an overcharge
a runaway	a person who leaves for another place without permission
a run-down	a summary
a run-in	a quarrel
a run-off	an overflow
	a competition to decide the winner of heats or to break a tie
a run-through	a rapid review
a show-off	a person who tries to get attention
a slowdown	a decrease in speed, especially in work

A few nouns have the verb last: *input, intake, outbreak, outcome, outlet, output, outreach, upbringing,* and *upkeep,* for example.

A few verbs are formed with the verb last and written as one word: *overdo, overlook, overturn,* and *uphold,* for example.

Prefixes

Prefixes are one- or two-syllable additions at the beginning of a word that change its meaning but do not change its part of speech. In this list nouns are indicated by an article in front of them, *a* or *an* for a countable noun and *the* for an uncountable noun. Verbs are indicated by *to.* All other words in the list are adjectives.

Today most prefixes are not followed by a hyphen, but always look in a dictionary if you are not sure whether to use one or not.

Notice the large number of prefixes that are negative: *a-, counter-, dis-, in-, non-,* and *un-.* Different negative forms on the same base word can have different connotations and meanings. (see **Connotation, Countable and uncountable nouns, Negation,** and **Style**)

PREFIX	MEANING	EXAMPLE
a-	not	*a*moral
		an *a*theist
ante-	before	to *ante*date
anti-	against	an *anti*body
		the *anti*freeze
arch-	highest	an *arch*bishop
auto-	self	an *auto*biography
bi-	two	a *bi*cycle
		to *bi*sect
		a *bi*centennial
co-	with	to *co*ordinate
		a *co*pilot

PREFIX	MEANING	EXAMPLE
counter-	against, opposite to	*counter*clockwise a *counter*revolution
de-	reverse action	to *de*frost
dis-	not reverse action	*dis*loyal to *dis*connect
ex-	former out of	an *ex*-president an *ex*patriate
exo-	outside	an *exo*-skeleton
fore-	before	to *fore*tell
hyper-	too much	*hyper*sensitive
in- (il-, im-, ir-)	not	*in*sensitive *il*logical *im*moral *ir*religious
inter-	between, among	*inter*national
mal-	bad, badly	*mal*formed
maxi-	most, large	a *maxi*skirt
mini-	least, small	a *mini*skirt
mis-	wrong, wrongly	a *mis*print to *mis*print
mono-	one	a *mono*rail
multi-	many	*multi*racial
neo-	new, revived	*neo*colonialism
non-	not, without	*non*stop
out-	to do something to a greater degree	to *out*do
	away from	an *out*patient
over-	too much	to *over*eat
	above	an *over*pass
para-	alongside, resembling	a *para*phrase
post-	after	*post*war
pre-	before	*pre*war
pro-	on the side of, in favor of	*pro*-communist
proto-	first, original	a *proto*type
pseudo-	false, imitation	*pseudo*-classic
quad-	four	a *quad*rangle
re-	again, renew	to *re*start
semi-	half, partly	*semi*private a *semi*circle
sub-	beneath, less, lower than	a *sub*way *sub*normal
trans-	from one place to another, across	to *trans*port *trans*atlantic
tri-	three	a *tri*cycle

PREFIX	MEANING	EXAMPLE
ultra-	extremely, beyond	*ultra*nationalism
		*ultra*sonic
un-	reverse action	to *un*cover
	not	*un*broken
under-	too little	to *under*expose
uni-	one	(a) *uni*form
vice-	deputy, one who acts in place of	a *vice*-president

NOTE: A few prefixes change their spelling before roots beginning with certain consonants. An example of a prefix that does this in the table above is *in*, which becomes *il*- before a root beginning with *l*, *im*- before a root beginning with *m*, and *ir*- before a root beginning with *r*.

Suffixes

A suffix is an ending added to a word, which usually changes the part of speech of the word and may also change the meaning of the word. Look up forms that are new to you in a dictionary, as not all suffixes can be added to all words. In some cases, more than one suffix can be added to the same word: nation, nation*al*, nation*ality*, nation*alism*.

The endings -*s* and -*ed* on regular verbs and -*s* and -*es* on nouns do not change the part of speech. (see **Nouns, Spelling,** and **Tense**)

ADJECTIVES
The following suffixes change other words into adjectives.

SUFFIX	MEANING	EXAMPLE
-able, -ible	able to be, having the quality of	teach, teach*able*
		reduce, reduc*ible*
-al	having the quality of, related to	nation, nation*al*
		person, person*al*
-ant	having the quality to	tolerate, toler*ant*
		dominate, domin*ant*
-arian	having the quality of	authority, authorit*arian*
-ative	connected with	argument, argument*ative*
-ed	adjective form of nouns and verbs (see **Participles**)	wall, wall*ed*
		please, pleas*ed*
-ese	showing national origin	Lebanon, Leban*ese*
		China, Chin*ese*
-esque	in the style of	picture, pictur*esque*
		Roman, Roman*esque*

SUFFIX	MEANING	EXAMPLE
-ful	having, full of	meaning, meaning*ful* thank, thank*ful*
-ic	having the quality of	democracy, democrat*ic*
-ical	having the quality of	theory, theoret*ical*
-ish	belonging to (national origin)	Swede, Swed*ish* Ireland, Ir*ish*
-ish	somewhat, approximately	red, redd*ish* young, young*ish*
-ive	having the quality of	explode, explos*ive* collect, collect*ive*
-less	without, lacking in	child, child*less*
-like	having the quality of	child, child*like*
-ous, -eous, -ious	having the quality of	virtue, virtu*ous* courtesy, courte*ous* ambition, ambit*ious*
-some	full of	burden, burden*some* bother, bother*some*
-worthy	deserving	praise, praise*worthy*
-y	full of, covered with, having the quality of	hair, hair*y* sand, sand*y* brain, brain*y*

(See **Adjectives, comparison of,** for *-er* and *-est* endings on gradable adjectives.)

NOUNS

The following suffixes change other words into nouns.

Nouns Referring to People

SUFFIX	MEANING	EXAMPLE
-an	member of, belonging to, favoring	Atlanta, Atlant*an* republic, republic*an*
-ant, -ent	agent, a person who does, makes	inhabit, inhabit*ant* correspond, correspond*ent*
-arian	belonging to a group, favoring	vegetables, veget*arian* authority, authorit*arian*
-crat	a person connected with	democracy, demo*crat* bureaucracy, bureau*crat*

SUFFIX	MEANING	EXAMPLE
-ee	variation of -er, a person	absent, absent*ee* employ, employ*ee*
-eer	a person who does, makes, operates	auction, auction*eer* engine, engin*eer*
-er	a person who does, makes	bake, bak*er* dream, dream*er*
-ese	national origin	Portugal, Portugu*ese* China, Chin*ese*
-ess	feminine form	waiter, waitr*ess*
-ette	feminine form	usher, usher*ette*
-ian	connected with	Paris, Paris*ian*
-ite	member of a group	social, social*ite*
-let	small, unimportant	star, star*let*
-ling	unimportant (derogatory)	weak, weak*ling*
-or	variation of -er, a person who . . .	survive, surviv*or*
-ster	a person making or doing something, a member of	trick, trick*ster* gang, gang*ster*
-y	familiar form (usually used in family, with children)	dad, dadd*y* Bill, Bill*y*

Impersonal Nouns

SUFFIX	MEANING	EXAMPLE
-age	extent, amount	drain, drain*age* sink, sink*age*
-ant	agent, personal or impersonal: the thing that . . . the person who . . .	lubricate, lubric*ant* inform, inform*ant*
-ation, -ition	institution, condition of being done	organize, organiz*ation* educate, educ*ation* nourish, nutr*ition* note, not*ation*
-er	agent, the thing that . . . , something having	silence, silenc*er* two wheels, two-wheel*er*
-ery	place of activity	refine, refin*ery* surgeon, surg*ery*
-ery	collective, uncountable	machine, machin*ery* baskets, basket*ry*

SUFFIX	MEANING	EXAMPLE
-ette	small, compact	kitchen, kitchen*ette*
		room, room*ette*
	imitation	leather, leather*ette*
-ful	the amount contained	mouth, mouth*ful*
		cup, cup*ful*
-ing	turns countable nouns into uncountable nouns indicating material	pipe, pip*ing*
		wire, wir*ing*
		panel, panell*ing*
	activity from action of the verb (see **Gerunds**)	walk, walk*ing*
-let	small, unimportant	pig, pig*let*
-or	thing that . . .	conduct, conduct*or*
-y (sometimes -ie)	familiar	nightgown, night*ie*
		dog, dog*gy*
		bird, bird*ie*

Abstract Nouns

SUFFIX	MEANING	EXAMPLE
-age	act of, extent	marry, marri*age*
		cover, cover*age*
		shrink, shrink*age*
-ance, -ence	activity, condition	guide, guid*ance*
		attend, attend*ance*
		independent, independ*ence*
-ancy, -ency	activity, condition of being	constant, const*ancy*
-ation	state of doing something	dominate, domin*ation*
		communicate, communic*ation*
-ery	domain, condition	brave, brav*ery*
		slave, slav*ery*
-hood	status	false, false*hood*
		mother, mother*hood*
-ion	act of doing something	confess, confess*ion*
-ism	doctrine, belief, condition	commun*ism*, absentee*ism*
-ity	state, quality	complex, complex*ity*
		curious, curios*ity*
		sane, san*ity*

ROOT	MEANING	ENGLISH WORDS
-ment	state, action	arrange, arrange*ment* govern, govern*ment*
-ness	state, condition	ill, ill*ness* selfish, selfish*ness*
-ocracy	system of government organization	democrat, dem*ocracy* autocrat, auto*cracy*
-ship	status, condition	friend, friend*ship* hard, hard*ship*

ADVERBS

SUFFIX	MEANING	EXAMPLE
-ly (*-ally* after *-ic* and *-ment*)	in the manner of	strange, strange*ly* happy, happi*ly* comic, comical*ly* basic, basical*ly* fundamental*ly*
-ward	manner, direction of movement	home, home*ward* on, on*ward* after, after*ward*(s) back, back*ward*(s)
-wise	in the manner of	clock, clock*wise*

VERBS

The following suffixes change adjectives and nouns into verbs.

SUFFIX	MEANING	EXAMPLE
-ate	cause to become	regular, regul*ate*
-en	cause to become	active, activ*ate* tight, tight*en* deaf, deaf*en*
-ify	cause to become	beauty, beaut*ify* simple, simpl*ify*
-ize	cause to become	popular, popular*ize* hospital, hospital*ize* regular, regular*ize*

Roots

You can improve your vocabulary by learning Latin and Greek roots. Over half of all English words come from them. The roots in this list are common and easy to see in English words. They are marked (L) if they come from Latin and (G) if they come from Greek, but you do not need to learn this to use them. Most scientific terms are made from Greek roots, and many literary words are made from Latin roots. A few of these roots are English words without prefixes or suffixes added to them.

ROOT	MEANING	ENGLISH WORDS
alien (L)	another, foreign	*alien*ate, in*alien*able, *alien*ation
am (L)	love	*am*iable, *am*ity, *am*icable
anim (L)	mind, life	*anim*al, *anim*ate, *anim*ism
ann (L)	year	*ann*als, *ann*ual, *ann*uity
anthrop (G)	human being	*anthrop*ology, *anthrop*omorphic, mis*anthrope*
arch (G)	rule, chief	an*arch*y, mon*arch*y, *arch*itect
aud (L)	hear	*aud*io, *aud*itorium, *aud*ible
auto (G)	self	*auto*mobile, *auto*matic, *auto*biography
bene (L)	good, well	*bene*ficial, *bene*factor, *bene*volent
bio (G)	life	*bio*logy, *bio*sphere, *bio*graphy
caust (L)	burn	*caust*ic, *caut*erize, holo*caust*
cent (L)	hundred	*cent*ury, *cent*ipede, *cent*igrade
chron (G)	time	*chron*ic, *chron*ology, ana*chron*ism
cide (L)	kill	sui*cide*, insecti*cide*, geno*cide*
cosm (G)	order, world	*cosm*ic, *cosm*etic, *cosm*opolitan
cred (L)	believe	*cred*it, *cred*, dis*cred*it
crit (L)	judge	*crit*ic, *crit*erion, *crit*icism
dem (G)	people	*dem*ocracy, epi*dem*ic, en*dem*ic
derm (G)	skin	*derm*atitis, *derm*atology, epi*derm*is
domin (L)	master, lord	*domin*ion, *domin*ate, pre*domin*ate
dynam (G)	power, force	*dynam*ic, *dynam*o, *dynam*ite
fac (L)	make	*fac*tory, manu*fac*ture, *fac*simile
fin (L)	end, limit	*fin*ish, *fin*ite, de*fin*e
fort (L)	strong	*fort*ress, *fort*ify, ef*fort*
frat (L)	brother	*frat*ernity, *frat*ernal, *frat*ernize
geo (G)	earth	*geo*graphy, *geo*logy, *geo*de
graph (G)	write	*graph*ic, mono*graph*, demo*graph*y
hydra (G)	water	*hydra*nt, *hydra*ulic, de*hydra*te
litera (L)	letter	*litera*ture, il*litera*te, *litera*l
log (G)	word, science of	bio*log*y, astro*log*y, physio*log*y
magn (L)	great	*magn*ify, *magn*ate, *magn*animous
manu (L)	hand	*manu*al, *manu*script, *manu*ipulate
mater (L)	mother	*mater*on, *mater*nal, *mater*nity
meter (L)	measure	kilo*meter*, thermo*meter*, *metr*ic
micro (G)	small	*micro*scope, *micro*be, *micro*cosm
multi (L)	much, many	*multi*ply, *multi*tude, *multi*form
mon (G)	alone	*mon*opoly, *mon*otone, *mon*otonous
mut (L)	change	*mut*ant, com*mut*e, im*mut*able
neo (G)	new	*neo*natal, *neo*classical, *neo*colonialism
nom (G)	law	astro*nom*y, agro*nom*y, eco*nom*y

ROOT	MEANING	ENGLISH WORDS
nomin, nomen (L)	name	*nomin*ate, *nomin*al, misno*mer*
nym (G)	name	anon*ymous*, pseud*onym*, syn*onym*
op, oper (L)	work	*op*erate, co*op*erate, in*oper*able
pan (G)	all, whole	*pan*orama, *pan*acea, *pan*theism
pater, patr (L)	father	*pater*nal, *pater*nity, *patr*iotic
path (G)	feeling	a*path*y, *path*etic, *path*os
ped (G)	child	*ped*iatrics, *ped*ant, *ped*agogy
ped (L)	foot	*ped*al, *ped*estrian, bi*ped*
phil (G)	love	*phil*osophy, *phil*anthropy, *phil*harmonic
phys (G)	body, nature	*phys*ical, *phys*ician, *phys*ics
phon (G)	sound, voice	tele*phon*e, *phon*etic, *phon*ograph
phos, phot (G)	light	*phot*ograph, *phot*ocopier, *phos*phorescent
plen (L)	full	*plen*ty, *plen*ary, re*plen*ish
poli (G)	city	*poli*tics, cosmo*poli*tan, metro*polis*
port (L)	carry	*port*able, ex*port*, im*port*
prim (L)	first, original	*prim*e, *prim*itive, *prim*er
psych (G)	soul	*psych*ology, *psych*otic, *psych*ic
rupt (L)	break	*rupt*ure, inter*rupt*, bank*rupt*
scop (G)	book at	*scop*e, micro*scop*e, tele*scop*e
scrib, script (L)	write	*script*, de*scrib*e, in*script*ion
sect (L)	cut	*sect*ion, dis*sect*, bi*sect*
simil (L)	like	*simil*ar, *simil*e, *simul*ate
soph (G)	wisdom	philo*soph*y, *soph*istry, *soph*isticated
tele (G)	far away	*tele*vision, *tele*graph, *tele*phone
tempor (L)	time	*tempor*ary, *tempor*al, con*tempor*ary
theo (G)	God	*theo*logy, *theo*cracy, a*theist*
therm (G)	heat	*therm*al, *therm*ometer, *therm*odynamics
uni (L)	one	*uni*t, *uni*on, *uni*te
vac (L)	empty	*vac*uum, *vac*ant, e*vac*uation
verb (L)	word	*verb*al, *verb*ose, ad*verb*
vol (L)	wish, willing	*vol*unteer, *vol*ition, bene*vol*ent
volv (L)	roll	e*volv*e, *volv*ume, in*volv*e

Word Order _____

Normal word order is the subject before the verb with most adverbs following the verb. *Inverted* word order is the verb before the subject. Since English words do not usually change their forms when their grammatical use changes, word order is very important in English. Special problems of word order are found in the following sections.

Absolutes	*Else*	Participles as
Adverbs, order of	Emphasis	adjectives
Adjectives, order of	*Enough*	Questions, direct
Agreement of sub-	Expletive	Reported speech
ject and verb	Indirect object	Sentence variety
Appositives	Interrupters	*So*
Complements	Modifiers	Two-word verbs
Determiners	Operators	Voice
Direct Speech	Parallel Structure	

Wordiness

Wordiness (adjective *wordy*) means using more words than you need. *Redundancy* (adjective *redundant*) means the same as wordiness. *Conciseness* means being brief and to the point, or the opposite of wordiness. Getting rid of wordiness is sometimes called *reduction* or *reducing wordiness*.

1. Avoid unnecessary repetition of the same idea in different words. Avoid common expressions with modifiers that do not add meaning. The words in parentheses are unnecessary.

return (back)	combine (together)
repeat (again)	(personal) friend
(past) history	(mistaken) error
each (and every) one	(final) outcome
many (in number)	(necessary) essentials
large (in size)	(optional) choice
early (in time)	(end) result

2. Avoid unnecessary prepositional phrases, especially phrdases beginning with *of*.

	WORDY		IMPROVED
Reduce	the house of the Johnsons	to	the Johnsons' house
	one of the purposes		one purpose
	one of the results		one result
	two of the reasons		two reasons
	several of the students		several students
	height of five feet		five feet high
	weight of ten pounds		ten pounds
	the potatoes are ten pounds in weight		the potatoes weigh ten pounds
	with the exception of		except
	in this day and age		today, now

WORDY	IMPROVED
at the present time	today, now
at this point in time	today, now
at that point in time	then
in regard to	about
by the time (that)	when
subsequent to	after
before long	soon
during the time (that)	while

3. Use the shorter form when an idea can be expressed by a single word or by a phrase.

WORDY	IMPROVED
as a result of	because of
in the event (that)	if
on condition (that)	if
provided, providing (that)	if
due to the fact (that)	since
inasmuch as	since
in view of the fact (that)	since
prior to	before

4. Avoid using expletives, especially *there*. (see **Expletives**)

WORDY: There are four books that Bill needs from the library.

IMPROVED: Bill needs four books from the library.

WORDY: There are several buses that are waiting in the parking lot.

IMPROVED: Several buses are waiting in the parking lot.

5. Reduce the number of words by changing grammatical structure. Reduce two or more sentences into one. (see **Subordinating and reducing** and **Substitutions**)

WORDY: Will is a basketball player. He is the captain of his team. He is the best player, too.

IMPROVED: Will, the captain, plays basketball better than anyone else on his team.

or

IMPROVED: Will, the captain of his basketball team, is its best player.

WORDY: Diane plays tennis every day. She hopes that she will be able to play in the tournament for the whole state. It will take place next summer.

IMPROVED: Playing tennis every day, Diane is training for the state tournament next summer.

Reduce a compound sentence to a complex or a simple sentence.

WORDY:	Robert has been studying agriculture for three-and-a-half years, and he will soon graduate.
IMPROVED (simple sentence):	After studying Having studied agriculture for three-and-a-half years, Robert will soon graduate.
WORDY:	Eleanor's car has been giving her a great deal of trouble by breaking down recently, so she thinks perhaps she should buy a new one.
IMPROVED (complex):	Eleanor is considering buying a new car since her old one has often been breaking down.

Reduce a complex sentence to a simple sentence by reducing clauses to phrases.

WORDY:	The windstorm blew down the trees *that line the road* along the lake.
IMPROVED:	The windstorm blow down the trees *lining the road* along the lake.
WORDY:	Very cold weather killed the flowers *that bloom early in the spring* weather.
IMPROVED:	Very cold weather killed the *early-blooming spring* flowers.

Reduce clauses and phrases to single words.

WORDY:	The brown haze *that was polluting the air* could be seen from the freeway.
IMPROVED:	The *polluting* brown haze could be seen from the freeway.
WORDY:	The birds *that were migrating* settled in the trees of the orchard.
IMPROVED:	The *migrating* birds settled in the orchard.
WORDY:	In the distance we were looking at an island in the tropics. The mountains that rose inland behind the port city were green from the color of the palm trees growing on their slopes.

Reduction into one complex sentence:

In the distance we were looking at an island in the tropics, the mountains of which, rising inland behind the port city, were green from the color of palm trees.

Reduction of phrases to words:

IMPROVED: We saw a distant, tropical island, its palm-topped mountains rising behind the port.

6. Avoid using the passive voice except in special circumstances. (see **Voice**)

WORDY WITH
INCORRECT
EMPHASIS: The bone that had been buried by the dog was dug up later by him.

IMPROVED: The dog buried his bone and later dug it up.

Use the passive voice in writing about an accident or a disaster when the result is more important than the cause.

ACCEPTABLE: The boy riding his bicycle was struck by a car. (Major interest is in the boy.)

ACCEPTABLE: Seven horses were killed when the barn burned. (Major interest is in the horses.)

Use the passive voice in an impersonal, scientific style when the result of an experiment is more important than the person who did it and when this style is required.

After ten days it could be observed that . . .
As the reaction took place, it could be seen that . . .
As the dissection continued, the muscles could be observed to be . . .

INDEX